Isaiah

John Goldingay

BakerBooks

a division of Baker Publishing Group
Grand Rapids, Michigan

© 2001 by John Goldingay

Published by Baker Books
a division of Baker Publishing Group
P.O. Box 6287, Grand Rapids, MI 49516-6287
www.bakerbooks.com

Previously published jointly in 2001, in the United States by Hendrickson Publishers, and in the United Kingdom by the Paternoster Press.

Baker Books edition published 2012
ISBN 978-0-8010-4638-4

Printed in the United States of America

The Library of Congress has cataloged the original edition as follows:
Goldingay, John.
    Isaiah / John E. Goldingay.
    (Old Testament series New International biblical commentary; 13)
        p.   cm.
    "Based on the New International Version"
    Includes bibliographical references and indexes.
    ISBN 978-1-56563-223-3 (pbk.)
    1. Bible. O.T. Isaiah—Commentaries. I. Title. II. Series.
BS1515.3.G65   2001
224'.1077—dc21   2001039055

12 13 14 15 16 17 18   7 6 5 4 3 2 1

In keeping with biblical principles of creation stewardship, Baker Publishing Group advocates the responsible use of our natural resources. As a member of the Green Press Initiative, our company uses recycled paper when possible. The text paper of this book is composed in part of post-consumer waste.

Isaiah

UNDERSTANDING THE BIBLE
COMMENTARY SERIES

GENERAL EDITORS

W. Ward Gasque

Robert L. Hubbard Jr.

Robert K. Johnston

Table of Contents

Foreword

As an ancient document, the Old Testament often seems something quite foreign to modern men and women. Opening its pages may feel, to the modern reader, like traversing a kind of literary time warp into a whole other world. In that world sisters and brothers marry, long hair mysteriously makes men super-human, and temple altars daily smell of savory burning flesh and sweet incense. There, desert bushes burn but leave no ashes, water gushes from rocks, and cities fall because people march around them. A different world, indeed!

Even God, the Old Testament's main character, seems a stranger compared to his more familiar New Testament counter-part. Sometimes the divine is portrayed as a loving father and faithful friend, someone who rescues people from their greatest dangers or generously rewards them for heroic deeds. At other times, however, God resembles more a cruel despot, one furious at human failures, raving against enemies, and bloodthirsty for re-venge. Thus, skittish about the Old Testament's diverse portrayal of God, some readers carefully select which portions of the text to study, or they avoid the Old Testament altogether.

The purpose of this commentary series is to help readers navigate this strange and sometimes forbidding literary and spiritual terrain. Its goal is to break down the barriers between the ancient and modern worlds so that the power and meaning of these biblical texts become transparent to contemporary readers. How is this to be done? And what sets this series apart from others currently on the market?

This commentary series will bypass several popular ap-proaches to biblical interpretation. It will not follow a *precritical* approach that interprets the text without reference to recent scholarly conversations. Such a commentary contents itself with offering little more than a paraphrase of the text with occasional supplements from archaeology, word studies, and classical theol-ogy. It mistakenly believes that there have been few insights into the Bible since Calvin or Luther. Nor will this series pursue an *anticritical* approach whose preoccupation is to defend the Bible against its detractors, especially scholarly ones. Such a commentary has little space left to move beyond showing why the Bible's critics are wrong to explaining what the biblical text means. The result is a paucity of vibrant biblical theology. Again, this series finds inadequate a *critical* approach that seeks to understand the text apart from belief in the meaning it conveys. Though modern readers have been taught to be discerning, they do not want to live in the "desert of criticism" either.

Instead, as its editors, we have sought to align this series with what has been labeled *believing criticism.* This approach marries probing, reflective interpretation of the text to loyal biblical devotion and warm Christian affection. Our contributors tackle the task of interpretation using the full range of critical methodologies and practices. Yet they do so as people of faith who hold the text in the highest regard. The commentators in this series use criticism to bring the message of the biblical texts vividly to life so the minds of modern readers may be illumined and their faith deepened.

The authors in this series combine a firm commitment to modern scholarship with a similar commitment to the Bible's full authority for Christians. They bring to the task the highest technical skills, warm theological commitment, and rich insight from their various communities. In so doing, they hope to enrich the life of the academy as well as the life of the church.

Part of the richness of this commentary series derives from its authors' breadth of experience and ecclesial background. As editors, we have consciously brought together a diverse group of scholars in terms of age, gender, denominational affiliation, and race. We make no claim that they represent the full expression of the people of God, but they do bring fresh, broad perspectives to the interpretive task. But though this series has sought out diversity among its contributors, they also reflect a commitment to a common center. These commentators write as "believing critics"—scholars who desire to speak for church and academy, for academy and church. As editors, we offer this series in devotion to God and for the enrichment of God's people.

ROBERT L. HUBBARD JR.
ROBERT K. JOHNSTON
Editors

Abbreviations

ANET	J. B. Pritchard (ed.), *Ancient Near Eastern Texts Relating to the Old Testament.* Princeton: Princeton University Press, 1950; 3d ed., 1969
BDB	F. Brown, S. R. Driver, and C. A. Briggs, *A Hebrew and English Lexicon of the Old Testament.* New York: Oxford University Press, 1907; corrected ed., 1953
ch(s).	chapter(s)
esp.	especially
GK	*Gesenius' Hebrew Grammar,* edited and enlarged by E. Kautsch, revised by A. E. Cowley. English translation New York: Oxford University Press, 2d ed., 1910; corrected ed., 1966
GNB	Good News Bible
JB	Jerusalem Bible
JSOT	*Journal for the Study of the OT*
JSOTSup	Journal for the Study of the Old Testament: Supplement Series
KJV	King James Version (=Authorized Version)
LXX	Septuagint (Greek) translation of the OT
lit.	literally
mg.	marginal (alternative) reading or explanation
MT	Masoretic Text (traditional Hebrew text of the OT)
NEB	New English Bible
NIV	New International Version
NJB	New Jerusalem Bible
NRSV	New Revised Standard Version
NT	New Testament
OT	Old Testament
RSV	Revised Standard Version

v(v).	verse(s)
VT	*Vetus Testamentum*
VTSup	Vetus Testamentum Supplements

Full information on the works to which I have referred in the commentary appear in the section "For Further Reading" beginning on page 375. Where I give no page number in connection with commentaries and similar works, the reference is to the work's discussion of the passage in question.

I am grateful to my research assistant Curtis McNeil for his careful reading of the manuscript of this book and for pointing out mistakes and obscurities, to the staff at Hendrickson for finding more, and to Justin Winger and Deepak Babu for preparing the indices.

Introduction

Yahweh's Vision, Yahweh's Word

The opening verse of the book called Isaiah proclaims it to be a vision. Elsewhere the OT implicitly rejoices in the creativity of the human imagination that tells stories and composes prayers and paints word pictures and knows that these human productions can open eyes to God's truth and can have God's creativity behind them. But this is not how it presents the work of a prophet. A prophet is one who has seen something, and has seen something because Yahweh has made the seeing possible. It is as if God opened a window in heaven. Indeed Isaiah speaks in almost these terms in chapter 6 in telling us how he came to be "sent" to the people by Yahweh. He saw the Lord seated on a throne in heaven. With horror he realized that he had seen the King, Almighty Yahweh. And often the vision he was given to share was horrific rather than pretty (see 21:2). Yes, a prophet saw visions. The passage from Isaiah that has most influenced Christian faith is a description of a vision (see 52:13–53:12).

Yet the book presents us not with a set of paintings of such scenes but with a collection of words. Within three lines the book has moved from talking in terms of vision to saying "Yahweh has spoken," "listen to Yahweh's word," "Yahweh says," "for Yahweh's mouth has spoken," "oracle of the Sovereign, Almighty Yahweh" (1:2, 10, 11, 18, 20, 24). Yahweh communicates the message in words. In that vision of Yahweh in chapter 6 Isaiah actually hears Yahweh's voice, though the words might have been audible to him alone. It led to his volunteering to become Yahweh's gofer (6:8–9), and a gofer's task is to act and speak on the sovereign's behalf with the sovereign's authority. Speaking on the sovereign's behalf is the gofer's way of acting on the sovereign's behalf to implement the sovereign's purpose. It puts that purpose into effect (6:10–13). By speaking, a prophet acts.

When a prophet introduces a message with the common opening words "the Sovereign Yahweh has said this . . . ," these are indeed the words of a sovereign's representative. Such a formula may be heard in its ordinary human context in 36:4; see also 36:13 for another form of the summons to listen to the (so-called) great king's words. The presupposition of a prophet's taking up this way of speaking is that a prophet, too, has heard a sovereign's words and now passes them on. A sovereign leaves the representative to frame the detail of the words, of course, but they still have the sovereign's authority. Presumably the same is true of Yahweh and the prophet. Yahweh gives the gist of the message; the prophet frames the actual words, though these then have all Yahweh's authority (and this process explains, in part, why Isaiah's words differ from—say—Jeremiah's).

The book called Isaiah presents us with a vision from Yahweh and with words from Yahweh. The book interweaves the language of sight and speech. It opens with a chapter of words that it calls a vision; it closes that chapter by describing it as the *word* that Isaiah *saw* (see 2:1 and the comment). It also interweaves the language of sight and speech in another way. In 20:2 Yahweh *speaks* "by the hand of Isaiah," "by means of Isaiah." Again the image parallels one used of human gofers (37:24), but in 20:2–3 it seems that Yahweh speaks via Isaiah through the actions that the people see rather than the words that they hear. When we read accounts of a prophet's experiences (e.g., 49:1–6; 50:4–9; 61:1–3) these are designed to communicate with us in a way that involves ear and visual imagination. The book called Isaiah, then, includes stories of what the prophets did and what happened to them as part of their ministry, as well as reports of what God gave them to say and enabled them to see. All of this constitutes Yahweh's vision and Yahweh's word.

The Four Human Voices

The traditional assumption has been that the prophet Isaiah ben Amoz, who is mentioned in its title, wrote the whole of this book. In English the book is often called "the Book of Isaiah," a designation that implies that Isaiah authored it, but NIV correctly renders the Hebrew title simply "Isaiah." This is a more open title that implies that the whole book links with Isaiah in some way but need not suggest a position about the book's authorship (any more than is the case when a book is called "Joshua" or "Ruth"). A read of the book suggests that Yahweh's revelation comes through at least four human voices (or pens).

Ambassador   We must of course begin with the voice of that ambassador of Yahweh who was actually called Isaiah. In chapter 6 he tells us of that vision that led him to volunteer to serve Yahweh. His voice speaks again in chapter 8. Here he tells of naming a son in such a way that he will embody his father's message, of receiving Yahweh's warning that he should distance himself from his people's paralyzing fear that is causing them to walk the wrong way, and of his duly turning his back on the people. But the voice of Isaiah is much more pervasive than reference to one or two autobiographical stories would imply. Because he volunteers to be the person Yahweh sends and consequently often speaks as one "sent," like the ambassador of a human sovereign, it is through Isaiah's voice that we hear Yahweh's voice. It is Isaiah the ambassador's words that introduce Yahweh's own words, "this is what Yahweh says." If the parallel with a human ambassador works, then Isaiah contributed significantly to the formulating of the words.

Disciple   Isaiah's is not the only human voice that speaks in this book. Indeed, the book begins with someone speaking about Isaiah in the third person in order to introduce him (1:1). This person also speaks *about* "Isaiah the prophet" in passages such as 37:2; 38:1. Evidently someone other than Isaiah introduces him. Isaiah in due course commissions the preserving of his teaching among his "disciples" (8:16), so we will infer that it is such a disciple or disciples who tell us stories about Isaiah such as those in chapters 7, 21, and 36–39 (though those chapters also appear in 2 Kgs.; we do not know whether the disciples borrowed them from there or whether the authors of 2 Kgs. were themselves the borrowers). So the second voice in the book belongs to this disciple or disciples. It is they who structure the book with other introductions such as the one in 13:1; we will think of them as the people who put the book together. Recognizing the words of Yahweh in those of Isaiah, they sought to preserve those words so they could also address future generations. They likely sought to show *how* these words addressed later generations, adapting and adding to Isaiah's own words. In the modern world we would want to distinguish clearly between the work of a teacher and that of a disciple, but in the ancient world a disciple would more likely have felt a desire to

honor a teacher by speaking in his name. A currently popular
scholarly theory is that some parts of chapters 1–39 represent
the way Isaiah's own words were expounded thus a century after
Isaiah's day in the time of King Josiah,[1] and we may think of this
exposition as the work of one of Isaiah's later disciples. As a very
rough guide, within chapters 1–39 we may assume that the poetic
oracles are Isaiah's own, while the passages in prose are his disciples' sermons on his "texts." Chapters 24–27 comprise the main
collection of poetic material that is usually reckoned to come from
a prophet much later than Isaiah himself, and who arguably deserves to be thought of as a fifth voice.

Poet   "Isaiah the prophet" appears for the last time in 39:3.
In chapter 40 we hear a third voice. It has heard a command to
"cry out" (40:6). This voice will in due course also be identified
as belonging to a disciple (50:4; see comment). But it is distinctive
for the fact that it speaks more poetically or more lyrically than
any of the other voices. The time to which this voice speaks is 150
years after Isaiah's own day, when the leaders of the Judean community have been deported to Babylon. Indeed, they and their
descendants have been there for half a century. This poet wonders what to cry out in the circumstances, but becomes the one
who, like Isaiah, acts as Yahweh's representative, declares "this is
what Yahweh says," and is sent by the sovereign Yahweh with the
spirit of Yahweh (48:16). Like Isaiah, too, the poet meets with little
success and is tempted to conclude "I have labored to no purpose," but stays convinced of Yahweh's support and vindication
(49:4; 50:7).

Preacher   In the last part of the book (chs. 56–66) we hear
yet another voice, that of one anointed to be a preacher, a bringer
of good news, a binder up of the broken-hearted (61:1). That had
already been the task of the poet, but this preacher's ministry
takes place in Palestine a few decades later and addresses a community with needs and temptations that are different from those
of the community that dwelled in Babylon. Or, rather, this community combines the needs of the Judeans in Babylon (they have
still not recovered from the disasters brought about by the inva-
sions of Judah at the beginning of the sixth century) and the temptations of the community that Isaiah addressed (they are still
addicted to the forms of traditional religion from which prophets

could not wean Israel or Judah). So a new preacher takes up the task of being Yahweh's ambassador.

The Ambassador, the Poet, and the Preacher have been known for a century as First, Second, and Third Isaiah. Their voices appear within chapters 1–39, 40–55, and 56–66, arranged and orchestrated by the Disciple(s). Indeed, we can think of the Poet as in part a disciple of the Ambassador: that is, Second Isaiah sometimes preached on texts from First Isaiah and perhaps produced the first edition of the material that now appears in chapters 1–55.[2] And/or we can think of the Preacher as in effect a disciple of the Poet (and the Ambassador): that is, Third Isaiah sometimes preached on texts from Second and First Isaiah and perhaps produced a new edition of their words. Further, as there will have been more than one Disciple who contributed to the book, so there may have been more than one Poet: that is, more than one person may have contributed to chapters 40–55. More certainly, there was probably more than one Preacher: that is, chapters 56–66 may contain more than one prophet's words.[3]

Theories of this kind regarding the origin of the material in the book are popular in the scholarly world, but they change with fashion.[4] The evidence within the book is insufficient for us to achieve anything like certainty regarding the process whereby the actual book called Isaiah came into being. The theories involve trying to work out the history lying behind the book as we have it, and there is no way of checking them. But at least these four voices speak from the book as we have it, and we can see the book as mediated by them. Isaiah is a many-voiced book, throughout which the voice of Yahweh comes to us.

In being a book of many voices, Isaiah parallels other OT books. In Exodus to Deuteronomy, Moses has a place analogous to that of Isaiah ben Amoz in Isaiah; the different collections of *torah* in Exodus, Leviticus, Numbers, and Deuteronomy represent voices that mediate Yahweh's authoritative teaching from a number of different periods and backgrounds. David is the name we associate with the Psalms, but the Psalter as a whole is a book of the prayers and praises of many voices. Proverbs begins by telling us that it is Solomon's book, but it later makes clear that it includes voices from other times and places (see 25:1; 30:1; 31:1). Ecclesiastes brings together the voice of orthodox faith and the voice of questioning. Jeremiah combines oracles from the prophet himself with sermons and stories that were told about Jeremiah.

The One Book

In what sense, then, is this one book? Various features characterize the book of Isaiah as a whole.

It Has a Structure   The book divides into half after chapter 33; the most complete manuscript of Isaiah from Qumran (see on "Text" below) leaves a space there. Chapters 1 and 33 form a bracket round the material that emerges from the ministry of the Ambassador, summarizing its concerns prospectively and then reviewing it retrospectively. Chapters 34–35 then introduce the second half of the book and constitute an anticipatory summary of it, and chapters 65–66 round off this second half. They also round off the book as a whole; they have their own links with chapter 1, in the "rebellion" expressed in the religious practices that are condemned, which people "choose" and "delight in" and which will be burned in unquenchable fire.[5]

It Presupposes the Vitality of God's Word   The book relates back to Isaiah in a number of different ways. For the material that presupposes an audience later than Isaiah's day, Isaiah is key to its inspiration, in a different sense from that in which the whole was of course inspired by God as a God-given vision or revelation. The second half of the book continues Isaiah's ministry and needs to be read in the light of his being its major fountainhead, though other influences contributed to it (especially Jeremiah). Its message is thus in part inspired by Isaiah, when not authored by Isaiah (see for instance 42:18–25). Texts from the first half of the book are preached in chapters 40–55 (e.g., 2:2–4 in 42:1–9), and texts from chapters 40–55 in chapters 56–66 (e.g., the promises of Zion's restoration in chapter 60). Accounts of the call and ministry of a prophet are in part inspired by Isaiah when they are relating the later experience of Yahweh's servants (see 40:1–11; 49:1–6; 50:4–9; 61:1–11).

So the book reflects the activity of individuals or groups who had in common two convictions about the material that we now know within the book called Isaiah, in the form in which it existed in their day. One was that these words of God from the past were significant for their own day. The other was that people in their own day needed to be shown how they were significant. So by God's inspiration they collected, arranged, and reworked this material to let it speak to their day. There are many guesses regarding the process whereby this happened, and we will never have grounds for confidence regarding its nature, but the untellable story of this ongoing process among people who had a common commitment to the preserving and preaching of this strand of prophecy lies behind the book as we have it and constitutes another facet of its unity.

It Concerns "Judah and Jerusalem" The first sentence tells us that "Judah and Jerusalem" is the distinctive subject of chapter 1, and since chapter 1 is the introduction to the work as a whole, we are not surprised to find that this is also the subject of the whole book. The focus is on Judah rather than northern Israel, Ephraim. In 11:13 there is a prophecy of the restoration of the whole people, and the story about Ahaz in chapter 7 inevitably refers to Ephraim, as do the prophecies in 9:8–21; 17:3; 28:1–4, but Ephraim is mentioned as background to what is going on between Yahweh and Judah. The reason Isaiah gives extensive attention to Ephraim and to far-off nations such as Assyria, Babylon, Arabia, Elam, and Media, and nearer ones such as Philistia, Moab, Edom, Aram (Syria), Egypt, and Cush usually lies in their importance to Judah as allies or threats. While Yahweh's sovereignty and care for such peoples does come into focus, the primary reason for talking about them lies in their significance for Judah. The book focuses on the life, the shortcomings, the fate, and the destiny of the city of Jerusalem, in a fashion unequaled in Scripture. Chapter 1 as a whole sets the book's agenda with its portrait of Jerusalem stained, attacked, purged, and restored. The ministry of the Poet opens with a concern to "speak tenderly to Jerusalem" and so emphasizes the city's restoration (vital for people in Babylon as for people in Judah). The Preacher also ministers "for Zion's sake" (62:1) and all but closes off the book with a vision of people flocking to Jerusalem from all over the world (66:20).

It Presents Yahweh as "The Holy One of Israel" This description of God is a distinctive feature of the book. It is hardly coincidence that in his vision in chapter 6 Isaiah himself had heard the seraphim proclaiming "Holy, holy, holy is Almighty Yahweh." The whole book works out the implications of that vision. In chapters 1–27, and then again in chapters 28–66, the message of this vision spreads in ever widening circles. Each section leads to the next, but each also relates to that key awareness that Yahweh is the

Holy One of Israel (see the references in square brackets below—
in one or two there are slight variants on the title).

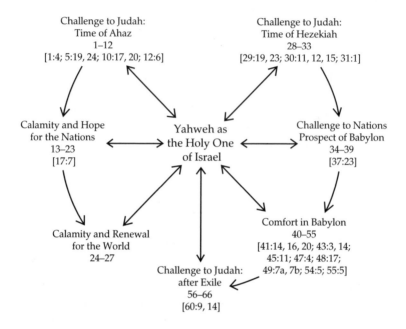

It Has the Unity of a Drama   A dialogue between different
voices constitutes this one book. W. Brueggemann characterizes
the voices as follows.[6] Isaiah 1–39 articulates a radical sustained
critique of the dominant ideology of its culture, on the basis of the
conviction that all social transformation begins in social criticism.
It presupposes that there is a normative reality (Yahweh's purpose), that the present world is a contrived world not a given
world, and that it is contrived in the interests of its contrivers. Isaiah
40–55 is then the voice of a pastoral poet who acknowledges the
pain and grief of a community that has lived through the social
criticism of Isaiah and has now acknowledged (as we learn from
Lamentations) that the contrived world that has collapsed did not
link with reality. Critique of ideology thus permits embrace of pain
and brings about new contact with memories that can generate
life. In Isaiah 56–66 this public embrace of pain releases social

imagination. It is social in the sense of being this-worldly, but imaginative rather than a matter of the formulation of policy (that is, the business of people such as scribes and law-makers). It gives the community freedom, energy, and courage to envision the world arranged in a different way. The book has the unity of a drama or a narrative. Isaiah 1–39 could have been the end; there was no necessity that generated Isaiah 40–55 (except, perhaps, the necessity of Yahweh's gracious purposefulness). Nor could Isaiah 1–39 have led straight into Isaiah 56–66, for the embrace of pain is necessary before creative imagination can be released.

It Concerns What Is "Right"   R. Rendtorff in a paper on Isaiah 56:1 as a key to the formation of Isaiah points to another way of seeing the "plot" of this "story."[7] Isaiah 56–66 opens with the exhortation "maintain justice and do what is right." It thereby raises an eyebrow after Isaiah 40–55, for there justice and right were Yahweh's business. On the other hand, justice and right are Israel's business in Isaiah 1–39. But the exhortation in 56:1 goes on, "for my salvation is close at hand and my righteousness [the same word as that translated "what is right"] will soon be revealed." That is exactly the message of chapters 40–55. It is as if 56:1 puts the combined message of chapters 1–55 into a nutshell. And that is exactly the point. The distinguishing feature of chapters 56–66 is to hold together the messages of the first two parts of the book, interwoven in the chiasm described later in this Introduction. The release of creative imagination (to use Brueggemann's term) requires both a commitment to taking seriously the challenges of the Ambassador and a trust in the promises of the Poet. Either one on its own will not work. The book handles the tension between election and obedience and declares that God's people are challenged to do right in the light of the right that God intends to do for them.[8]

The Spoken Word

The Ambassador, the Disciple, the Poet, and the Preacher usually delivered their messages by means of the spoken word. In doing so they took up ways of speech that were familiar to their audiences and adapted them so that the forms themselves helped to communicate the message.

In our own world we regularly use set forms of speech in different contexts, though we do so partly unconsciously. Church worship has forms of speech that follow familiar patterns, such as the sermon, the announcements, and the prayers. Television has conventional forms, such as those of the news, the talk show, or the advertisement. The academy has its forms, such as the lecture, the seminar, or the faculty meeting. The special occasions of everyday life have them, such as the speeches of various participants in a wedding. In each case one can analyze the regular structure, language, and conventions of the forms of speech used in these different social contexts, which carry a significant part of the burden of communication. The fact that they do so means that people from outside the culture in which they operate have to become familiar with their conventions in order to understand what is said. The importance of this will vary. In cases such as the wedding and television advertisements it is crucial; without it, the bulk of the message will probably be misunderstood. In much other communication, conventions are so general that someone outside the culture may miss very little.

The contributors to the book of Isaiah use the forms of speech that were familiar in their culture. Often they address their audiences in a generally exhortatory way, and knowledge of the conventions of such exhortation may then help little, but on many other occasions they use forms of speech that readers from another culture need to recognize if we are to understand what is being said and how it has its impact.

In Isaiah, forms of speech from three social contexts are especially prominent: the palace, the law, and the temple. We have noted the characteristic introduction "this is what Yahweh says," the words of an ambassador. The metaphor pictures a prophet as a king's representative. The story of Sennacherib and Hezekiah in chapters 36–37 illustrates this way of speaking used in its original context (see 36:4, 14, 16) and then taken into the speech of a prophet (see 37:6, 21, 33). The metaphor of the royal court also lies behind the "Fear not" oracles that characterize the ministry of both Ambassador and Poet (e.g., 7:4–9; 41:8–13; 43:1–7; 44:1–5) and lies behind the announcement of and promises to a king in passages such as 11:1–9; 32:1–8; 42:1–9; 44:24–45:7. To appreciate these forms of speech we need to imagine ourselves immersed in Middle Eastern politics, aware of the frightening authority of the king and the king's servants, aware of the life-enhancing and death-dealing power of the king and his crucial significance for the destiny of the nation—and aware therefore of the pressures on him.

The book actually begins in a metaphorical law court (1:2–3; see also 3:12–15), and legal forms of speech are prominent throughout. Yahweh speaks like someone making an accusation in the presence of the witnesses who constitute a Middle Eastern community court, or like the king acting as judge in Jerusalem. Behind the issuing of that accusation is the challenge to begin a legal proceeding: see 1:18–20. Following it is the more systematic legal indictment and announcement of judgment: see 1:21–26 (cf. 3:16–17; 5:8–30; 8:5–8; 10:12–19; 17:9–11; 57:3–6; 65:8–16). In such passages Yahweh speaks as both plaintiff and judge. In passages such as 41:1–7, 21–29; 43:8–15; 44:6–8 Yahweh presupposes a community gathering that can come to a decision on the case against the other nations and their so-called gods—though in reality there is no case to answer. In 42:18–25 and 43:22–28 Yahweh speaks as a spirited defendant in a case brought by Israel, and aggressively turns the accusation round on Israel. Implicit in these forms of speech is the message "Do you see? It is as if you were being taken to court by someone who had a cast-iron case against you; you are bound to be found guilty and to have to pay a terrible penalty," or "Do you see? It is as if you were trying to put Yahweh on trial, but you are bound to lose and (to say the least) to experience terrible humiliation before the whole community."

From the context of the temple and other places of worship, the book takes up forms of worship such as a hymn (e.g., 42:10–17), a lament (26:7–21; 37:16–20; 63:7–64:12), a call to lament (23:1–14; 32:9–14), a prophetic response to a lament (41:17–20), and a thanksgiving (9:2–7; 12:1–6; 25:1–5; 38:9–20; 44:23; 49:13). The exhortation to listen to Yahweh's word or *torah* in 1:10 introduces a challenge that adapts the form of a sermon such as a priest might preach. Isaiah also has a close relationship with the teachers of Israel whose work and resources appear in Proverbs, and this affects his "preaching" style. He takes up their ways of speaking in passages such as 2:22; 3:10–11; 32:20. This (rather than the law court) may also be the background to the argumentative speech that often characterizes the four voices, whereby they may (for instance) state an opponent's conviction, set against it their own, and argue for the latter (see, e.g., 40:12–31; 45:9–13).

Beyond these longer forms of speech, the four voices use a number of shorter conventional expressions such as an oath (e.g., 5:9; 14:24–25; 22:14) with the formula "as I live" (see 49:18), the oracle formula "Yahweh's word" (e.g., 1:24; 41:14; 59:20), and the "Oh" introduction (NIV "Woe") which can lead into teaching or a dirge or a threat and is thus used in various ways to catch an audience's attention.

For rhetorical effect we ourselves sometimes consciously use a conventional form of speech in a novel way, or we take a form and utilize it in a different context for different effect: so a sermon may take the format of a talk show or a television comedian may pretend to be preaching a sermon. It is of the essence of the prophets' use of conventional ways of speech that they combine the familiar with the revolutionary. This begins with the very fact that the speaker is turning the literal court into a metaphorical one. But the speaker will commonly find that the message bursts the boundaries of the way of speaking, and the listeners dare not take the risk of assuming that they know what is coming. In 1:21–26, for instance, the announcement of judgment turns into an announcement of purification and restoration. In 5:1–7 the Ambassador composes a very strange love song. In 6:1–13 his version of someone's call to Yahweh's service comes to a very strange conclusion. In 10:24–27 and 41:8–16 the "Fear not" oracle that belongs in an address to a king is addressed to the community as a whole. In 14:4b–23 a funeral dirge is sung over a king who is still very much alive; chapters 15–16 similarly lament an invasion that has not yet happened. In 40:27 and 49:14 the Poet quotes very strange forms of lament that are not actually addressed to God, so depressed has the community become. In 52:13–53:12 a very strange coronation oracle is declared for a king.

The Written Word

We have been considering communication by means of the spoken word, but these spoken words eventually became writing. Indeed, the Disciples perhaps did most of their work by writing. The Poet, too, may well have composed the material in chapters 40–55 in writing (though it will have been proclaimed orally) and will have used the Ambassador's words. The Preacher in turn evidently had access to written material from both the Ambassador and the Poet.

We owe to the Disciples an arrangement of the material into a book with a clear structure. We have noted that chapter 1 opens and chapter 33 closes the first half. Chapters 2–12 and 28–32 transmit the Ambassador's addresses to Judah in the reigns of Ahaz and Hezekiah. Chapters 13–23 and 24–27, while also addressed to Judah, focus more directly on the nations of Judah's world and on the world as a whole, respectively. So the first half of the book works as follows:

Introduction (ch. 1)
    Challenge to Judah: time of Ahaz (chs. 2–12)
    The destiny of the nations (chs. 13–23)
    The destiny of the world (chs. 24–27)
    Challenge to Judah: time of Hezekiah (chs. 28–32)
Summary (ch. 33)

The introductory summary in chapter 1 takes material from several periods of the Ambassador's ministry and reworks them into a comprehensive vision of the story of Jerusalem—chastised for its rebellion, challenged to turn from a life of worship without justice, and painfully purged. The retrospective summary in chapter 33 takes a different form that testifies more clearly to its written nature. Line by line, even word by word, it takes up phrases and words from the immediately preceding chapters (chs. 28–32), from that opening introductory chapter, and from other intervening chapters. It thereby pulls the whole together like a net pulling together all the fish caught in it.

Within the chapters caught by this net there are many further instances of cross-reference whereby themes and words occur and then are picked up and reaffirmed or restated later. The motif of the people's inability to see or hear is an example (see 6:9–10; 29:18; 30:20; 32:3). It is quite possible to imagine such links resulting from cross-reference within the Ambassador's oral ministry (preachers do repeat themselves), but it is the written form of the book that enables us to perceive them.

The second half of the book begins with a linking collection of prophecies and stories that form the most concentrated contribution of the Disciple, and then follows that with the work of the Poet and the work of the Preacher:

The Disciple: looking forward to disaster and renewal
    (chs. 34–39)
The Poet: a message for Judeans in Babylon (?)
    (chs. 40–55)
The Preacher: challenge to Judah after the exile
    (chs. 56–66)

In chapters 40–55, the Poet has arranged material that may have begun its life as fairly short individual spoken prophecies into a carefully structured whole. In 41:1–42:17, for instance, there appear at least six units that may once have stood on their own, but in the written text they form two balancing threefold sequences. Motifs within the Poet's opening words in 40:1–11 take up elements from that anticipatory summary in chapter 35, and themselves announce themes that will be taken up nearer the other end of this section, in 52:7–10 and 55:10–11. In addition, these chapters take up themes from the Ambassador such as Israel's blindness and deafness (see 35:5; 42:7, 16, 18, 19; 43:8; 44:18).

In chapter 56, the Preacher begins with two lines that sum up the material from the Ambassador and the Poet and subsequently incorporates motifs from both. Like chapters 1–33, chapters 56–66 as a whole are arranged as a chiasm, in which the second half mirrors the first half:

> A Preface: The inclusion of the excluded (56:1–8)
>   B Challenges about the people's life (56:9–59:8)
>   C Prayer for forgiveness and restoration (59:9–15a)
>   D Vision of Yahweh acting in wrath (59:15b–20)
>   E Visions of Jerusalem restored (59:21–62:12)
>   D' Vision of Yahweh acting in wrath (63:1–6)
>   C' Prayer for forgiveness and restoration
>   (63:7–64:12)
>   B' Challenges about the people's life (65:1–66:16)
> A' Conclusion: The inclusion of the excluded (66:17–24)

The interplay between the promises at the center, the major sections of challenge, and the prayers in between, is integral to the dynamic of chapters 56–66.

We have noted that it will usually be the case that the material in this book began life as the oral proclamation of individual prophecies, and it is possible to seek to get behind the arrangement of the book as we have it to the original form of these individual prophecies or to intermediate stages in the development of the book, but this is another hypothetical matter that we will not systematically consider.

Yahweh in Isaiah: The Holy One

The book of Isaiah presents us with a visionary (sometimes a nightmarish) portrayal of the God of Israel and the people of Yahweh. The fundamental description of Yahweh is as "the Holy

One of Israel." Describing Yahweh as the Holy One is as close as the Bible can get to a literal statement about God, for the phrase describes God in God's otherness. To add "of Israel" is to say something that risks undoing the expression "Holy One"; the title as a whole threatens to deconstruct. It puts the Holy One into a relationship with a non-holy entity, a relationship from which Yahweh apparently now has no exit. It radically compromises the notion of holiness. The separate one becomes the attached one. Conversely, the fundamental description of Israel is that it has been grasped by the Holy One. It has been won into relationship but has been therefore cut off from independence. And it has been drawn into Yahweh's separateness and thereby cut off from other peoples. In the first half of the book its being in relationship with the Holy One is the fact that threatens its well-being when it looks secure. In the second half of the book this relationship is the fact that promises its well-being when it looks as if Israel has no future.

The following three attributes of the Holy One come into distinctive focus in Isaiah.

Yahweh's Majesty and Authority In his vision of the Holy One, the Ambassador sees Yahweh as exalted king, but he has already presupposed an emphasis on this majesty in the warning of calamity in 2:6–22, which fulminates against all who dare to exalt themselves over against Yahweh who alone is exalted. That warning applies to Judah, but it also applies to foreign nations who simply by virtue of achieving power in the world may seem to compromise Yahweh's authority. The warning applies more specifically to rulers in Judah or elsewhere, for the same reason (see the warning to the king of Babylon in 14:4–21). It also applies to other supernatural powers, who are supposed to reflect and support Yahweh's majesty, but may subvert it and need to be put down (e.g., 24:21–23). We might wonder whether it is a rather unimpressive deity who needs to go to such lengths to protect his (sic: patriarchy rules here) authority. But Isaiah declares that it is in the exercise of just judgment that Almighty Yahweh is exalted (5:16), reminding us that the authority and majesty of Yahweh are the protection of the powerless. Similarly, the fact that Yahweh is sovereign over the world as creator and king is fundamental to the good news for the Judean community in the exilic period in chapters 40–55, and to the vision of new creation in chapters 56–66.

Yahweh's Passion   On the one hand, Yahweh is passionate in anger. The book uses a whole dictionary of terms for anger, fury, and wrath. It implies that anger is a normal personal emotion that is therefore as natural and right to Yahweh as a person as it is to a human being as a person, so long as it is rightly directed (see the comment on 5:25–30). The book perhaps also assumes that anger is part of relationships. It is the people with whom we are in relationship with whom we most get angry, partly because they have most scope for letting us down, partly because the fact of the relationship gives the security to express the anger. Yahweh keeps enough cool to be fair and just, and is capable of controlling anger, saying in effect in 1:24 "I have been doing that for a long time, but now the time has come and I intend to hold it in no longer." Thus Israel may lament Yahweh's inactivity and Yahweh may in due course respond, "Yes, I have not been expressing my anger, it is time to do so" (42:13–16; cf. 64:12).

Yet raging is Yahweh's shadow side (28:21). Yahweh is also passionate in compassion. Like Yahweh's concern with authority and majesty, Yahweh's anger is a threat to the powerful but a protection for the powerless. Yahweh's compassion is more directly good news for the powerless. It is first promised in 14:1 but then becomes an important motif in the Poet's ministry, especially in chapters 49–55; it reappears in chapters 60–63. The word for compassion is related to that for a woman's womb, and the use of this word is thus one of the aspects of chapters 40–55 that may suggest that a woman's voice can be heard in the words of the Poet.[9] Whereas Ms Babylon fails in this womanly instinct (ch. 47), Yahweh promises to have the compassion of a mother for Jerusalem and her children.

Yahweh's Insight and Capacity to Formulate a Plan and Put It into Effect   The book has an ambivalent relationship with insight and planning. It attacks human wisdom as something upon which people rely as an alternative to relying on Yahweh (e.g., 5:21; 8:10; 29:14–15; 30:1) or as a means of frustrating Yahweh's purpose (e.g., 19:3, 11; 44:25; 47:10, 13). The book also uses the imagery of wisdom and planning to describe Yahweh, who is the person of supreme insight and capacity to make and implement plans in history (e.g., 9:6; 14:24–27; 19:12, 17; 23:8–9; 25:1; 28:23–29; 31:2; 40:13–14; 44:26; 46:10–11), as well as to describe what Yahweh will in due course give to Israel (11:2; 33:6). Admittedly this tactic can backfire; people can question or even ridicule Yahweh as strategist (5:19). One assumption of this imagery is that Yahweh is capable of determining what should happen in political events and then seeing that this does in fact happen. Another assumption is that the way Yahweh goes about making it happen frequently contrasts with what human insight would have imagined (see 55:8–9).

Israel in Isaiah

Five ways of thinking about the people of God especially characterize the book. With regard to each we may ask about the vision, the reality, the calamity, and the promise.

The People of God Is a Family[10]   Yahweh is the parent who begot Israel or bore it and then brought up these children. Yahweh then had the experience of the parent of teenage or grown-up children who rebel against the authority of their parents and refuse to shape their lives by their parents' values (1:2). Yahweh can then chastise these children, but cannot cast them off and cannot avoid maintaining a commitment to them; parenthood is like that. So the people can appeal to Yahweh to behave like a father, especially when their earthly fathers seem to have cast them off (63:15; 64:8). To put it another way, Yahweh is committed to being the people's "redeemer," its next of kin or guardian, the close member of their family who has a moral obligation to provide and support and defend when they need that. Even when they seem to have given up their side of the family obligation, Yahweh has not given up on the correlative commitment (e.g., 41:14).

The People of God Is a Society   It is a nation as well as a people. Yahweh expects that they implement certain standards in their life as a society. Specifically, Yahweh intends that it be an egalitarian and fair society in which (for instance) the powerful do not use their power to the disadvantage of the powerless. Yahweh also makes a commitment to supporting this nation as it seeks to hold its own in the international world. In fact the society has become as stratified as any other and the nation prefers to exercise responsibility for its own destiny rather than to leave this to Yahweh. Both developments issue in calamity in its corporate life which reduces the society to a remnant of what it once was and eventually deprives it of its leadership and skilled classes, who are deported to Babylon. The book's vision is that the society should be reestablished in Judah—or rather, that it should be established for the first time. As a society, Yahweh promises it the leadership that will reflect Yahweh's own nature (e.g., 11:1–5; 32:1–8).

The People of God Is a Church   It is a worshiping church in the sense of being a worshiping community. Initially Yahweh dismisses this aspect of its life and implicitly this model for understanding it (see 1:10–15) and terminates this activity in bringing down the state and allowing the temple to be destroyed (43:23–24). But when Yahweh restores the people, worship will be one right response (12:1–6). It will indeed be the final object of this restoration (27:12–13). Zion will be able to become festival city (33:20). And this church will be able to resume the normal life of Yahweh's people, calling on Yahweh in need and knowing Yahweh responds (30:19).

The People of God Is a City   We have described Jerusalem as *the* subject or theme of the book, which is thus "the great urban document of the Bible."[11] Many of the prophecies concern Ms Zion or address Ms Zion: the community is seen as the city that is its focus and home and is then personified as a woman. As a city it is under threat from enemies drawn against it by Yahweh, but its ultimate destiny is guaranteed. At least that means that the enemies are defeated at the last minute as Yahweh becomes protector rather than attacker (29:1–8; 31:1–5), but if necessary Yahweh will let the city fall—but then reestablish it and gloriously rebuild it. Thus when it feels abandoned and forgotten, Yahweh promises that it will never be forgotten and will be restored, and Yahweh promises to return to it. At the beginning, the book announces that it is a message to Judah and Jerusalem; near the close, it is a message about a renewed Jerusalem (65:17–25; see also the promises in chs. 60–62). Ms Zion was designed to be Righteous City, slipped into being Faithless City, was reduced to Desolate City, but was destined to become Purified City (1:2–31).

The People of God Is a Magnet   The vision in 2:2–4 takes Zion much further than purification, to being a city set on a high mountain and a light that draws the whole world (cf. 26:1–6). From Zion Yahweh can thus resolve the world's conflicts and bring its disputing to an end. Other peoples seek help from Jerusalem (16:1–5) and bring gifts to Yahweh there (18:7). As Yahweh's servant, Israel *is* a covenant to such people (see 42:1–9). In other words, it models and promises what their relationship with Yahweh could be. It also is a witness to them of Yahweh's acts (55:1–5). Zion's festivals and offerings will not be for Judah alone, but will be for people from all over the world whom Judah will go and fetch (66:18–21).

The World in Isaiah

While the bulk of Isaiah focuses on the affairs of Judah and Jerusalem, like the rest of the OT it presupposes and from time to time explicitly recalls that the one powerful God, Yahweh, is in a position to mastermind the affairs of the whole world and has responsibility for its destiny. Yahweh's involvement with Israel and with the nations then interweaves.

The Nations Are Yahweh's Agents in Bringing Disaster to Judah This is the connection in which the nations first appear as they have devastated Judah because it turned its back on Yahweh. The first of the great Middle Eastern empires, Assyria, is the means of disaster that stops one step short of bringing the state down. The second, Babylon, takes the one extra step. The extent of Yahweh's sovereignty is underlined by the fact that it can also influence the way the nations can bring disaster to each other at points that do not directly involve Judah (e.g., 19:1). Some vivid images express its reality (5:26; 7:18; 10:5). The Assyrian emperor does indeed claim to be working for Yahweh (36:10), though the point is made with some irony and/or for rhetorical effect and contrasts with his later claim to be greater than any of these nations' gods (36:18–20). In truth he is involved in creating an empire for his own sake (10:5–19).

The Nations Are Yahweh's Agents in Delivering and Restoring Judah The self-aggrandizement that characterizes Assyria means that Yahweh must put down this agent in due course (10:5–34). Because Yahweh is the ultimate sovereign in history, Israel has nothing to fear from the nations (40:12–24). While Yahweh can see to them without human help (37:36), more characteristically human agency is involved (37:38), and this will be so when Assyria actually falls to Babylon. Then in due course Babylon will fall to Persia when the Day of Yahweh comes for it (13:1–14:23; 47:1–15). In both cases these empires fall because they have played God, but also because they have unwittingly stood in the way of Yahweh's ultimate purpose to bless Israel as well as furthering that interim purpose to chastise Israel: their downfall is for Israel's sake (14:1–3,

24–25). The Persian emperor is then Yahweh's anointed agent in restoring Judah (45:1). So the nations who were the means of scattering the people will be the means of gathering them again (11:10–16).

The Nations Are to Experience Yahweh's Comfort and Join in Yahweh's Worship   The news of what Yahweh has done for Judah is to be proclaimed to the world (12:4–5), and the world will come to bow the knee to Yahweh (45:18–25) and see Yahweh's glory (66:18). This is not just for Yahweh and Judah's glory, though it is that. We have noted that Jerusalem is to be the magnet that draws them to the one who can effect some conflict resolution in their affairs. Aliens will join in the worship of Jerusalem (56:1–8). Yahweh will be worshiped in Egypt, Egypt and Assyria will be called Yahweh's people and Yahweh's handiwork, and Egyptians and Assyrians will worship together (19:19–25). They will join in a banquet on Mount Zion and know the relief of their mourning and the end of their shame (25:6–9).

Spirituality in Isaiah

Yahweh looks for five priorities in the people.

Trust and Hope Rather Than Fear and Anxiety   "I will trust and not be afraid," declares the song of praise that closes chapters 1–12. It sums up a distinctive strand in the spirituality that Isaiah presses for. Ahaz and Hezekiah were inclined to assume that the survival of their city depended on their defensive measures or diplomatic activity. Isaiah reminds them of Yahweh's promise to David and reminds them that Yahweh is the only one worth calling refuge and protection. A major concern of the prophecies about the nations (chs. 13–23) is the declaration that these nations deserve neither fear nor reliance. In the vision of world calamity that begins in chapter 24, trust is the key to peace (26:3). Chapters 40–48 emphasize how Yahweh's commitment and power are also the reason that the community in the time of the exile can be urged to trust and not be afraid—of their neighbors or of the embattled Babylonian government or of the coming Persian conquerors. These chapters invite them to prove that those who wait on Yahweh renew their strength. The people of God can afford to relax. When Yahweh's promises seem only half-fulfilled, the right response is to determine to keep trusting and hoping (see chs. 60–62).

Justice and Not Merely Worship   Apparently the community of Isaiah's day was enthusiastic about prayer, praise, and giving, but Yahweh felt more ambivalent about it (1:10–20). People came to worship with blood on their hands, because of their involvement in legal procedures that led to people's being deprived of their land and their livelihood and because of their declining to be involved in procedures and practices that would protect the needy and vulnerable (cf. 59:1–8). They were able to indulge themselves in worship and festivity, in banqueting and finery, because they had their way of making a profit from ordinary people. Much later, the community was disciplined in its observance of fasting as it sought Yahweh's restoration of the city, but Yahweh was again not impressed, because of the way people treated their workers (58:1–9a). All these emphases clearly relate especially to people in power and confront the misuse of power. They warn about the temptations of power. These themes may thus be linked with the book's stress on putting down people in exalted positions and the reminder that Yahweh dwells with the humiliated (57:15).

Faithfulness Rather Than Worship by Means of Images   Throughout the centuries covered by the book of Isaiah, the community was inclined to indulge in the practices of traditional religion that paralleled those of the indigenous peoples of Canaan. Some of those practices are also similar to those of our own world. For example, they worshiped a number of gods, used images in worshiping Yahweh, sought to maintain contact with the dead, and used this and other means to gain supernatural guidance for their lives. Throughout the book these inclinations are confronted (e.g., 2:6–21; 8:19; 31:6–7; 44:6–20; 46:1–7; 57:3–13; 66:17). The book challenges people to recognize that Yahweh alone is God, that an image can only be a misleading representation of Yahweh, and that Yahweh is all the guide they need. One day a remnant will turn (10:21).

Awe Rather Than Confidence   One of the difficulties with images is that they domesticate God. They cut God down to size. Perhaps one of the problems with the language of the family for relationships with God, which traditional religion uses, is that it does the same. The book of Isaiah emphasizes the awesome greatness of Yahweh. When the people are defeated, they cannot simply decide to pick themselves up, dust themselves off, and start all over again (9:10). How stupid to think that you could build a house for the God who has the earth itself as a footstool (66:1). Paradoxically, it is when you have been humiliated and cut down to size that you may find God reaching out to you (66:2). The publican, not the Pharisee, goes home right with God.

Insight Rather Than Stupidity, Self-Deception, or Blindness   Yahweh's people decline to recognize what their God is doing, and so they will go into exile for lack of understanding (5:12–13). The irony is that they think they are being distinctively wise. In due course they will have to be taught in words of one syllable (28:11–14). The covenant they have made is actually a covenant with death (28:18). Their sources of insight will be removed (29:9–12). Even then, they resist learning Yahweh's lesson. The threat that they will be made deaf and blind is only too chillingly fulfilled (6:9–10; 22:8–14; 42:18–25). It is again the leadership that is especially the problem here (56:10–11). But one day God will grant the people leadership that knows what real insight is (11:2–5). They will learn to learn (29:24).

The Text

The starting point for our access to this book is the Hebrew "Masoretic Text." The Masoretes were Jewish scholars who made a series of contributions to the preservation and understanding of the Bible. Over the period between the immediate pre-Christian period and the end of the first millennium A.D. they made it their business to survey the manuscripts of the Hebrew Scriptures in order to ensure that the Jewish community possessed an authentic version of them. They divided the text into chapters and verses. They put into the manuscripts the system of dots and dashes that indicate vowel sounds (written Semitic languages otherwise comprise only the consonants of words, on the assumption that readers can provide the vowels). They also added a further system of dots, dashes, and other signs that indicate the way the words relate to each other and thus clarify aspects of the text's exegesis.

The Masoretes' text became the standard text of the Hebrew Bible, and it is represented in the oldest manuscripts of the complete (or nearly complete) Hebrew Bible now in existence, which date from the tenth century A.D. It is this text that provides the foundation for the NIV's translation, as well as for other translations. Clearly it might be a matter of concern that our knowledge of Isaiah is dependent on manuscripts that are in date substantially nearer to us than they are to any of the four voices. Monumental changes in the text might have come about over the millennia. It was therefore very significant when archaeologists discovered in 1947, among scrolls in caves at Qumran, by the Dead Sea, a complete manuscript of Isaiah from about a century before Christ. It was twice as old as the Masoretic manuscripts. Its text turned out to be in substance virtually identical with that of the Masoretes. This was the more noteworthy given the fact that the spelling of the text had been significantly updated.

Admittedly there are a number of points where this manuscript (and other more fragmentary Qumran manuscripts) differ from those of the Masoretes. Sometimes it was apparent that the Qumran manuscripts' reading represented a slip of the pen, sometimes that it represented an updating application of the text to the community, but sometimes it potentially offered a witness to a different, older, Hebrew text. In this way it complemented the resources offered by translations of Isaiah into Greek, Latin, Syriac, and Aramaic (the Septuagint, the Vulgate, the Peshitta, and the Targum) and other languages. These were older than the Masoretic Text and thus offered the possibility of trying to translate them back into Hebrew and recovering the Hebrew text that they had used. Admittedly they sometimes translated loosely, misunderstood the text, or were also involved in updating its application for their communities, but when allowance has been made for this fact, they too might enable us to discover an older Hebrew text tradition than that of the Masoretes.

The NIV is more inclined to stay with the Masoretic Text than are other recent translations, but it does occasionally follow another tradition (see 5:17; 21:8; 23:10; 33:8; 37:20, 25; 45:2; 49:12, 24; 51:19; 52:5; 53:11). The NIV does not draw attention to the most interesting of these choices, at 40:6, where "and I said" presupposes a change in the vowels of the word from the Masoretic Hebrew. It has "and he said," but the change is supported by that complete Qumran manuscript "a," by the Septuagint, and by the Vulgate. At a number of other points NIV keeps the Masoretic Text but notes in the margin an alternative suggested by these others (see 6:9–10; 7:14; 10:27; 11:6; 23:2–3; 29:13; 40:3, 52:15; 61:1). In a number of these examples NIV seems to make the point because the Septuagint has a translation that corresponds to the NT quotation of the text.

It is when the Masoretic text does not seem to make sense that translators have been particularly interested in evidence from other Hebrew traditions. Admittedly such difficulties may reflect our not having enough knowledge of the Hebrew of Isaiah's day, but they may indicate that an intelligible text has been accidentally changed into an unintelligible one. There are a number of places in Isaiah where the NIV notes in the margin that the Hebrew is difficult but does not change the text (see 25:11; 26:16; 28:25; 54:11; 66:18), and sometimes the translators have followed the Septuagint's understanding without changing the text (see 27:8). In circumstances where the Hebrew is very difficult, translations such as NRSV will attempt to work out what might have been the original text even if the other traditions offer no help. In 41:27a, for instance, the Hebrew literally reads "First to Zion—behold, behold them." To make sense of the line NIV paraphrases, while NRSV alters one of the words to make the line read "I first have declared it to Zion."

The Masoretes' verse divisions have generally been maintained, but their chapter divisions were later replaced by the chapter system that appears in English Bibles. These are sometimes odd (e.g., 4:1, where the Masoretic division more naturally comes at 4:2; 32:1, where chapter 32 continues chapter 31 and a new chapter has been introduced to highlight the "messianic" prophecy in chapter 32; 42:1, where the same consideration has split up the section 41:21–42:17—indeed we will see that many of the chapter divisions in chapters 40–53 are odd). Further, the version of the later chapter divisions that appears in printed Hebrew Bibles differs from that in English Bibles at 9:1 (which is 8:23 in the printed Hebrew Bible): this reflects a difficulty in making the right division, and it is noticeable that the Masoretes made 8:19–9:6 one chapter. Similarly the Masoretes rightly treated 63:7–64:11 as a chapter, while the later division could not make up its mind where to start a new chapter, so that 64:1a is 63:19b in the printed Hebrew Bible.

The Language

The language of the book is "classical Hebrew" (cf. the idea of "classical Greek"). It is the language of the literary heyday of the Jewish people, the period to which subsequent times look back.

This does not mean that the language itself is inherently high-flown. The Disciple presumably wrote in something like the ordinary prose of the day.

The poetry in the book, like that in any language, is written in what almost amounts to a different language from that of prose. It is tighter and it omits the little words that facilitate everyday communication, and it uses more unusual words and more imagery. Like the omitting of little words, this makes for denseness. Poetry has to be read more slowly than prose. All that also makes for greater difficulty in understanding the poetry when we live in another culture two or three millennia later. A comparison of the way two translations render Isaiah will reveal many more differences of substance in the poetry than in the prose.

On the other hand, Hebrew poetry resembles some modern poetry in English in being blank verse (there is no rhyme) and in keeping no rules about length of lines. Generally the first formal characteristic of a piece of poetry in Hebrew is that it can be divided into self-contained sentences or semi-self-contained phrases with about six words in them (there are usually one or two of these per "verse" of our translations). Hebrew is a highly inflected language and words tend to be longer than English words, so six words make for a sentence with more content than would be the case with a six-word sentence in English. In this calculation, little words such as "for" or "not" can be ignored, or they and other words can be linked to the next word, so that the sentence still has about six stresses.

The second formal characteristic is that such a sentence will usually divide naturally into two in such a way that the second half complements or extends or completes the first half. This feature was analyzed by the first great modern commentator on Isaiah, Robert Lowth, who called it parallelism.

A look at the first verse of Isaiah makes it immediately apparent that it has the features of prose and not those of poetry. It is prosaic and down-to-earth in its content and language, and it comprises one sixteen-word sentence. The opening section of the Ambassador's own words in verses 2–3 contrasts with that. It works with three metaphors, from the royal court, from the family, and from farming, which gives it great depth and denseness, and it divides into four grammatically separate six-word sentences. In the various examples that follow, I have hyphenated words in English so as to make clear where several English words are needed to translate one Hebrew word.

> Hear, heavens, and-listen earth, for Yahweh has-spoken.
> I-reared children and-brought-them-up, but-they rebelled
> against-me.

> Ox recognizes its-master and-donkey its-owner's manger.
> Israel does-not recognize; my-people does-not understand.

The example illustrates the regularity and the irregularity of the conventions just mentioned. In the first line the word "for" has to be ignored if we are to view this as a six-word line, and the line divides 2–2–2. In the second and fourth lines, some little words have to be taken into account if we are to view them as six-word lines. On these matters the printed Hebrew Bible tells us the way the Masoretes linked the words. We may sometimes speculate that the verse points to another arrangement. In 1:4 the MT's (Masoretic Text's) arrangement is 3–3, 2–2, 2–3–2:

> Ah, sinful nation, people loaded with-guilt,
> brood of-evildoers, children acting-corruptly.
> They-have-forsaken Yahweh, they-have-spurned Israel's Holy-
>   One, turned away.

A more plausible arrangement might be 3–3, 2–2–2, 3–2, because it produces more even lines.

> Ah, sinful nation, people loaded with-guilt.
> Brood of-evildoers, children acting-corruptly, they-have-
>   forsaken Yahweh.
> They-have-spurned Israel's Holy-One, turned away.

These verses 2b–4 also illustrate the parallelism whereby each time the second half of the line builds on the first, not merely repeating it but pushing it further in some way.

Some writers on Isaiah over the past hundred years have assumed that all the lines must originally have worked with strict conventions over line length, and these writers have rewritten the book accordingly. It seems more appropriate to allow that the conventions were much looser than that. Often we can see the poetic effect of variation. The fact that verse 4b has three half-lines (to be nonsensical: cola is an alternative term) marks it as the end of a subsection within verses 2–9, while verses 2–9 close with another long line (v. 9a; 3–4):

> Unless Yahweh Almighty   had-left us some survivors

followed by a short line of two two-word halves

> we-would-have-become like-Sodom,   been-like Gomorrah

The distinctive form serves to mark the end of the poem and make it close with a thump that is difficult to reproduce in English.

It may be apparent from the NIV that the five lines in verses 5–6 are shorter lines than the ones in verses 2–4. As the Masoretes understand them, they have only two words or two stresses in the second half of each line: "persist in-rebellion," "your-whole-heart afflicted," "there-is-no soundness," "and-open sores," "nor-soothed with-oil" (actually MT fails to make the link between "nor" and "soothed" in this last half-line). While six stresses in a line is the nearest to a norm in Hebrew poetry, more lyrical poetry does use lines with only two words (or two stresses) in the second half. These keep bringing us up short and conveying a sense of incompleteness; which is appropriate to the kind of statement that appears in verses 5–6.

The short half-lines reappear in verse 8, but in the meantime verse 7 is much more straightforward and prosaic in its form of expression, which matches its content. That points to the fact that the line between verse and prose cannot be drawn too sharply. The two belong to a continuum; there is clear verse and clear prose, but also poetic prose and prosaic verse. A prophet may not have been aware of moving between one and the other, and translators sometimes vary over which way to view particular sections: for instance, NRSV lays out 8:6–8, 12–17; 10:20–27a as prose instead of poetry.

We have noted above that chapters 56–66 as a whole unfold as a chiasm. Sometimes individual sections within this prophecy are chiastic in form. An example is 60:1–3:

> A Arise, shine
>   B for your light has come
>   C and the glory of the LORD rises upon you
>   D see darkness covers the earth
>   D′ and thick darkness is over the peoples
>   C′ but the LORD rises upon you and his glory
>   appears over you
>   B′ nations will come to your light
> A′ and kings to the brightness of your dawn

Each of the outward lines (ABCD) is taken further in some way by the corresponding return line (D′C′B′A′).

The Context

The book of Isaiah refers to a number of Middle Eastern emperors and Judean rulers. In the historical outline that follows, the dates are approximate; all ancient Middle Eastern dating is a matter of controversy. The overlapping in Judean dates reflects the custom whereby a king's designated successor shared rule with him for the latter part of his reign.

Assyria		Judah	
Tiglath-Pileser III	745–727 B.C.	Uzziah	787–736 B.C.
Shalmanezer V	727–722 B.C.	Jotham	756–741 B.C.
Sargon II	722–705 B.C.	Ahaz	741–725 B.C.
Sennacherib	705–681 B.C.	Hezekiah	725–697 B.C.

While 1:1 tells us that Isaiah himself prophesied during the reigns of Uzziah, Jotham, Ahaz, and Hezekiah, chapters 1–39 specifically relate his activity to five moments in Judah in the late eighth century.

The first of these was the death of King Uzziah about 739 B.C., the year in which Isaiah had the vision of Yahweh as king that appears in chapter 6. Uzziah reigned for more than fifty years; for some of these he was co-regent with his father. To judge from 2 Kings 14–15 there are no grounds for seeing his reign as particularly outstanding, and in his last years he had already been effectively succeeded by his son Jotham, and perhaps even by Ahaz (Jotham may well have died before his father). But Uzziah's death might nevertheless appear to be a significant moment, particularly given the efforts of the Assyrian emperor Tiglath-Pileser III to reassert and extend Assyrian sovereignty in the Middle East in this period.

The second significant moment occurred when a coalition comprising Aram and Ephraim put pressure upon Judah to join them in reasserting independence from Assyria, between about 736 and 733 B.C. By now Jotham's son Ahaz was king. The coalition's response to Ahaz's resistance was to seek to replace him on the Judean throne with a man who would work with their plan, Tabeel (7:6). According to 2 Kings 16:7–9, Ahaz reacted by getting help from Assyria itself. Part of the cost was some assimilation of Judean religious practice to that of Assyria (2 Kgs. 16:10–19), which Assyria will have required as a means of developing unity in its empire.

The third and fourth were similar independence movements on the part of Philistia. The death of King Ahaz and his succession by Hezekiah (about 725 B.C.) apparently took place about the same time as an Assyrian emperor's death (see 14:28–29)—perhaps that of Tiglath-Pileser III. That led to the arrival of another embassy in Jerusalem, once again apparently seeking to lean on Judah to join in this movement (14:28–32). Tiglath's successor Shalmanezer V put Philistia in its place. The northern Israelite state, Ephraim, did join in the independence movement, and also shared in paying the cost. Shalmanezer laid siege to its capital at Samaria, which fell in 721 B.C., and made Ephraim a province of the empire. In 711 B.C. Philistia was again put in its place by Shalmanezer's successor Sargon II, the specific victim being Ashdod (see 20:1–6).

Under his successor, Sennacherib, in 703–701 B.C. Judah finally gave in to the idea of throwing off its vassal status and paid the price like the other peoples—the fifth and final moment to which Isaiah's ministry specifically relates. Sennacherib conducted a successful campaign down the Mediterranean coast, but Judah escaped the conquest of its capital and the deportation of its people.

The stories in chapters 36–39 relate to these events. So in all likelihood does the critique of alliance with Egypt in chapters 28–31, though these chapters contain no dates and may connect with the events in 713–711 B.C. Other chapters may connect with one or other of these crises. For instance, 17:1–6 may relate to the events of 733 B.C. Other chapters may relate to other events of which we have no separate knowledge. But in general the unspecificity of the words prevents us from locating a number of chapters with certainty.

Beyond the Ambassador's lifetime, the event that may have led to the initial significant contribution of the first great Disciple(s) was the decline of Assyria late in the seventh century. Another coalition, of Media to Assyria's north and Babylon to its south, reached beyond seeking mere independence from Assyria and aimed at taking over its imperial position. In due course they conquered and destroyed the Assyrian capital, Nineveh, in 612 B.C. The period of Assyrian decline is a period of expansion and religious reform in Judah under King Josiah (640–609 B.C.). The currently popular scholarly view sees the Disciple(s) as declaring that Isaiah's own promise that Assyria would be put down is now about to be fulfilled. Judah need no longer fear Assyria.[12]

This theory offers an attractive and plausible picture of the work of the Disciple(s) in expounding and applying Isaiah's message a century after his own day, but it may be founded on a fallacy. Prophets often declare that events are imminent when in chronological time they are some years away, and Isaiah's declaration that Judah need not fear may have had more of a religious than a political basis. The mere fact that a number of passages speak in these terms looks insufficient to link them chronologically with the event that might have constituted their fulfillment. The sermons are insufficiently specific about their background for us to know whether they come from the Ambassador himself or from Disciples in a much later century.

The situation is different with the work of the Poet, who gives more concrete indication of working in the 540s B.C. Chapter 40 begins by addressing people who have been under God's chastisement for a long period, and chapter 41 indicates that their deliverer has begun to carve out a new empire. Chapters 44–45 make explicit that the Persian king Cyrus is about to take Babylon and set going the process whereby Jerusalem can be restored after its destruction by Babylon in 587 B.C. Cyrus duly captured Babylon in 539 B.C. and soon freed the Judean community to return to the home that most of them had never seen (see Ezra 1–6).

The Preacher again makes no concrete reference to a specific time, but the logic of the book's arrangement points toward the situation back in Jerusalem during the period covered by the books of Ezra and Nehemiah. The circumstances are similar to those described there and alluded to in Haggai, Zechariah, and Malachi. Again, there has been scholarly discussion over whether different chapters link more with the early decades of the Second Temple period (covered by Ezra 1–6) or with the situation in the next century (the time of Ezra and Nehemiah themselves). The texts lack specific historical references.

Conclusion

The New Testament offers us a number of lenses through which to read Isaiah. One of them is the "Jesus" lens: it was from Isaiah that the first Christians gained vital insight on who Jesus was and on the significance of his ministry, death, and resurrection. It is this lens that Christians most readily adopt. But the New Testament also looks at Isaiah through other lenses. There is the "church" lens. From Isaiah we can discover what the church is and what it is called to be. The vision of a suffering servant in Isaiah 53, which Christians see as quintessentially about Jesus, also offers the New Testament writers insight about the church (see, e.g., Phil. 2:5–11; 1 Peter 2:21–24). There is the "ministry and mission" lens. It was the servant testimony in Isaiah 49:1–6 that helped Paul understand the nature of his own mission and ministry (see Acts 13:47; Gal. 1:15). There is the "spiritual life" lens. When Jesus composed his Blessings (Matt. 5:3–11), most were based on the Psalms and Isaiah. There is the "Israel" lens. It was from Isaiah that Jesus could remind Israel of aspects of its own significance and calling and from Isaiah that Paul came to understand these (e.g., Mark 12:1–12; Rom. 9:27–33). There is the "world" lens. As John looks at the nations and their destiny in Revelation, there is hardly a verse that would survive if we removed the allusions to books such as Isaiah. Together, the book called Isaiah and the New Testament invite us to an open-eyed engagement with a many-faceted work.

Notes

1. See R. E. Clements, *Isaiah 1–39* (New Century Bible Commentary; Grand Rapids: Eerdmans, 1980), pp. 6–8.
2. This is the thesis expounded in H. G. M. Williamson, *The Book Called Isaiah: Deutero-Isaiah's Role in Composition and Redaction* (Oxford: Clarendon Press; Oxford/New York: Oxford University Press, 1994).
3. See, e.g., P. A. Smith, *Rhetoric and Redaction in Trito-Isaiah: The Structure, Growth and Authorship of Isaiah 56–66* (VTSup 62; Leiden: Brill, 1995), pp. 22–49.
4. For examples up to 1993, see M. A. Sweeney, "The Book of Isaiah in Recent Research," in *Currents in Research: Biblical Studies* 1 (1993), pp. 141–62.
5. See, e.g., A. J. Tomasino, "Isaiah 1.1–2.4 and 63–66, and the Composition of the Isaianic Corpus," *JSOT* 57 (1993), pp. 81–98; repr. in P. R. Davies, ed., *The Prophets* (Sheffield: Sheffield Academic Press, 1996), pp. 147–63), and D. Carr, "Reading Isaiah from Beginning (Isaiah 1) to End (Isaiah 65–66)" in *New Visions of Isaiah* (ed. R. F. Melugin and M. A. Sweeney; JSOTSup; Sheffield: Sheffield Academic Press, 1996), pp. 188–218. See also D. Carr, "Reaching for Unity in Isaiah," *JSOT* 57 (1993), pp. 61–80; repr. in P. R. Davies, ed., *The Prophets* (Sheffield: Sheffield Academic Press, 1996), pp. 164–83, for a warning about claiming too much for a structure. We consider the structure of the book in more detail below.

6. W. Brueggemann, "Unity and Dynamic in the Isaiah Tradition," *JSOT* 29 (1984), pp. 89–107. Reprinted in W. Brueggemann, *Old Testament Theology,* pp. 252–69. Minneapolis: Fortress, 1992.

7. R. Rendtorff, *Canon and Theology* (Minneapolis: Fortress, 1993), pp. 181–89.

8. J. N. Oswalt, "Righteousness in Isaiah," in *Writing and Reading the Scroll of Isaiah* (2 vols.; eds. C. C. Broyles and C. A. Evans; VTSup 70; Leiden: Brill, 1997), vol. 1, pp. 177–91.

9. See B. W. Stone, "Second Isaiah: Prophet to Patriarchy," *JSOT* 56 (1992), pp. 85–99; repr. in P. R. Davies, ed., *The Prophets* (Sheffield: Sheffield Academic Press, 1996), pp. 219–32.

10. For more on this concept see K. P. Darr, *Isaiah's Vision and the Family of God* (Louisville: Westminster John Knox, 1994).

11. W. Brueggemann, *Using God's Resources Wisely: Isaiah and Urban Possibility* (Louisville: Westminster John Knox, 1993), p. 3.

12. See, e.g., 10:24–27; and Clements, *Isaiah 1–39,* pp. 5–6.

§1 Introduction: Jerusalem Judged and Restored (Isa. 1:1–2:1)

Chapter 1 introduces both the message of Isaiah ben Amoz over three decades and the book as a whole. The people have paid the penalty for abandoning their relationship with Yahweh (vv. 2–9) and need to own the fact that they have perverted their life with Yahweh by practicing religion but not justice (vv. 10–20); judgment can then be a creative purging that restores justice as well as the relationship (vv. 21–31).

1:1 / The fact that the word **vision** always denotes a particular revelation suggests that verse 1 is the introduction to chapter 1 and not the whole book, as the first verse of Ezekiel introduces Ezekiel 1–3. Visions may portend evil or promise good. In this one we move from a focus on the first to a focus on the second before we get to the end of the chapter.

In the OT, the phrase **Judah and Jerusalem** usually refers to the small community living in Judah, with their focus on Jerusalem, after the temple had been rebuilt in the period of Haggai and Zechariah. They were a tiny community, but they understood themselves as the true people of God. The phrase thus invites this small Second Temple community (and by extension other subsequent readers such as ourselves) to read the chapter—and what it in turn introduces—as addressing themselves, not as confined in its application to Isaiah's own day. Reduced to a remnant and consoling itself by focusing on its life of worship, this community too is urged to look to its secular community life, to beware of Yahweh's judgment, but to look for Yahweh's rebuilding.

The vision comes to a particular prophet, **Isaiah son of Amoz**. Isaiah himself is part of his very message and ministry. His name, "Yahweh is salvation," declares Yahweh's promise. His wife and children share in the same involvement (see especially 7:1–8:18). His message relates in the first instance to the time of Judah's four kings **Uzziah, Jotham, Ahaz and Hezekiah** (see 6:1; 7:1,

3, 10, 12; 14:28; 36:1–39:8), from about 740 to 700 B.C. (see Introduction). It was the end of a period of prosperity and achievement and associated social inequality, the beginning of a period of foreign domination, and a time that saw both religious apostasy and religious reform (see 2 Kgs. 15–20; 2 Chron. 26–32; as well as Isaiah and Micah).

1:2–4 / Isaiah's unsurprising introductory **Listen** turns out to be addressed not to Judah (except indirectly), but rather to the **heavens** and the **earth**. Perhaps the picture is of Yahweh standing in court, appealing to the witnesses to the covenant between Yahweh and Israel (cf. Mic. 6:1–2).

Yahweh is in the position of the parent of a rebellious child, expected to bring the child before the community court (see Deut. 21:18–21). **Rebelled** is a relational word, the opposite of being loyal, committed, and faithful. **Forsaken** and **spurned** also describe the actions of a child abandoning its parents and their teaching. Those who have **turned their backs** are people who behave like strangers to their family; the related word for stranger/foreigner comes twice in verse 7. Isaiah expresses the indignation and hurt of Yahweh as the father or mother who has been rejected and despised by his or her children (see Hos. 11).

The one they have spurned is **the Holy One of Israel:** this is the book's distinctive title for God. It was a title that Isaiah especially took up, presumably as a result of the experience that will be described in chapter 6. In the OT, "holy" is not so much a moral term as a metaphysical one. It denotes deity in its awesome differentness and transcendence. So "Holy One of Israel" expresses the paradox whereby the awesome, mighty, sovereign creator enters into a relationship with a specific, ordinary, created, human people. That paradox hints at the trouble that will result if this people resists the holy one (an underlying theme of chs. 1–33), but it also alludes to the security this relationship brings to that people, and thus to its deliverance when they are in need (an underlying theme of chs. 34–66).

Knowing (v. 3) is a matter of recognition and acknowledgment, of will as well as mind; **does not know** thus has similar implications to **rebelled.** Yahweh is Israel's parent and thus teacher. The people of Israel are Yahweh's children, expected to learn from their teacher in the way presupposed in Proverbs as well as Deuteronomy (e.g., Prov. 1:8–9; 4:1–4; Deut. 6:6–7; 11:19–21). But they are willfully lacking in moral and spiritual insight. That is so despite the fact that they are **my people:** the phrase regularly conveys a poignancy as it characteristically occurs in contexts that suggest suffering, calamity, danger, and fear—or, in contrast, deliverance, restoration, and provision (e.g., 3:12, 15; 5:13; 10:2, 24). Here too, it recalls the nature of the relationship between Israel and Yahweh. The trouble is, the arrangement does not work. Even the family animals do better than the children in this respect.

Instead of behaving like Israel, they are a **sinful nation;** instead of behaving like "my people," they are **a people loaded with guilt** (see on 5:18). Judah is both nation (a political entity) and people (a family writ large). They are also **a brood of evildoers,** "offspring who do evil" (NRSV), despite being "holy offspring" by their association with Yahweh (6:13). Although they belong to Yahweh's family, they are **children given to corruption** instead of children with the family likeness. The nature of this evil and corruption remains to be indicated.

1:5–7 / Now direct address to the people describes the pain resulting from their sin. Once more their **rebellion** is spoken of, with its consequences, though strangely (or not) it is spoken of in poignant and grieving terms rather than merely confrontationally and aggressively. The people are bruised and battered like a child who has been beaten by its parents or an adult who has been mugged. Why do they insist on more such punishment? We will learn more in chapter 36 of the invasion described in verse 7, which took place in 701 B.C. toward the end of Isaiah's ministry. Sennacherib's own records tell of his conquering forty-six of Judah's towns, citadels, and villages and driving out more than 200,000 people. In laying siege to Jerusalem he turned Hezekiah into a prisoner there "like a bird in a cage"—though he did not actually take the city.

1:8–9 / **Daughter of Zion** sounds as if it implies that the people is the daughter of the actual city, but more likely it parallels phrases such as "State of Israel" or "City of Jerusalem." Zion does not have a daughter; she is personified as a daughter. The phrase suggests that she should be a woman deserving of respect (not necessarily a young woman), but she has become an isolated, abandoned one. "Zion" refers to the same place as "Jerusalem" but draws more explicit attention to the city's religious significance; "Jerusalem" has more of the resonances of an earthly physical city.

The consequences of invasion for Mademoiselle Zion are expressed in similes. She has become like one of those isolated and primitive structures where lookouts kept watch or the family slept during harvest to protect their crop, or **like a city under siege—** which is exactly what she has been. **Is left/had left us some survivors** announces a major theme in Isaiah, the remnant or remains that are all that is left after decimation (see on 4:2). But at least that is something; they might have been destroyed as comprehensively as **Sodom** and **Gomorrah** (Gen. 19:24–29). On the title **the LORD Almighty**, see on verse 24.

1:10–15a / Yahweh feels a distaste for the people's enthusiastic worship because it is not accompanied by a commitment to justice. The challenge in verses 10–20 evidently belongs to an earlier period, when disaster might still be avoided. **Hear . . . listen** again has the resonances of a court scene. **The law of our God** often refers to the contents of Exodus to Deuteronomy, but the word *torah* can also denote a parent's, sage's, priest's, or prophet's "teaching" (NRSV), and the broader meaning is appropriate in Isaiah.

Judah is now addressed directly, but by means of a metaphor. Zion has played into Yahweh's hands by comparing its fate to Sodom and Gomorrah's. Yahweh wishes to compare Zion's thinking and behavior to theirs, the oppression that caused an outcry (Gen. 18:20–21; 19:13; Ezek. 16:49); see verses 15–17 (and 5:7). While the OT and NT both make clear that the worship of God's people is important to them and to God, they also make clear that this worship easily gains an undue importance. Here Isaiah comprehensively dismisses the people's worship in its various aspects. Yahweh is force-fed unwanted food, and unwanted guests repeatedly invade Yahweh's home. Sacrifice's pleasant accompaniments are **detestable,** the technical term for loathsome religious practices or moral acts, and people's visits for regular worship events are a burdensome nuisance. Lest Christian readers congratulate themselves on not being involved in the kind of worship that so offends Yahweh, Isaiah tells us that this offensiveness extends to prayer, to which Yahweh shuts both eyes and ears. Why?

1:15b–20 / Yahweh thus sets out conditions for hearing prayer. Yahweh's reason for rejecting Judah's worship is not that in their hearts people did not mean what they said and what their sacrifices imply. As far as we can tell, they meant every hallelujah and every amen. The problem was that their sincerely meant worship was not accompanied by a commitment to Yahweh in life in society. The hands raised in prayer **are full of blood,** the blood of people victimized in the community. Zion is supposed to defend the weak (v. 17), but the needs of the weak in society have been ignored, so they fail to get enough to eat, or they lose their land and thus their livelihood, and in due course their lives. As in modern societies, the well-off lived better than the less well-off, and statistics regarding health and life-expectancy reflected this. **Cause** and **case** suggest additional reference to the administration of justice. When someone without family or resources got into debt, creditors could easily and legally get the court to foreclose on the debt and take away the person's land.

The community is therefore bidden to **wash and make yourselves clean** (v. 16a). It is responsible for getting the blood off its own hands by giving up the **evil deeds** that stand scandalously before Yahweh's eyes and make it impossible for Yahweh to look at people when they pray (v. 16a).

Positively, they are to **learn to do right** and **seek justice** (v. 17; and see on v. 21). A paradox appears here, or rather a different understanding of justice. The key principle of justice is not that everyone should be treated the same and in accordance with the law of the land, but that the needy should be protected. It would not count as justice for decisions to be technically legal but to work for the benefit of the powerful and the loss of the weak. To be judged therefore need not be bad news. It can be good news, if it means having the legal system applied to you as a weak person. The community has an obligation to see that this happens, and it has blood on its hands if it neglects this duty.

Verses 18–20 repeat the point. **Reason together** is rather mild; "argue it out" (NRSV) reminds us that all this takes place in the context of a metaphorical court case between Yahweh and Judah. Again Yahweh declares that their hands are **scarlet . . . red . . . crimson,** covered in blood. **They shall be as white as snow . . . like wool** is not an invitation to seek Yahweh's cleansing and forgiveness, which would be to offer cheap grace and to collude with what the people believed already. The **shall** is a "shall" of demand, like that of the Ten Commandments. They must cleanse the blood off their hands and be **obedient** if they want Yahweh to answer their prayers for the harvest (vv. 18–20). The closing line (v. 20b) underlines the certainty of the warning in verses 19–20a.

1:21–23 / Isaiah starts again, sharpening the charge in a way that will lead into an announcement of judgment in verses

24–31. **See how** is the exclamation that introduces a lament or a death dirge. The issue is the same as in verses 2–4, but the husband-wife metaphor has replaced the parent-children metaphor. **Justice** comes from the verb "judge" (see on v. 17); the book of Judges shows how judging involves taking decisive action. It is a power word. **Righteousness** denotes what accords with the norm of rightness embodied in Yahweh (see on 5:16, where a sister word comes). Together, then, justice and righteousness are a key pair suggesting the exercise of authority in accordance with right, or a commitment to right that can be expressed in the exercise of power.

The accusation against the community's **rulers** (v. 23) gives precision to the charge. The term for rulers is a general one, but what follows suggests a reference to people responsible for justice. This fits with verses 11–20 and indicates that their failure issued from seeking wrongful gain (see 5:23). The issue is once again the leadership's responsibility for the administration of justice in a way that exercises positive discrimination on behalf of the weak. Failure here, along with an inclination to use the legal system in a way that might have been legal but was designed to benefit people in power, is what turns leaders into **murderers.**

1:24–25a / After an accusation and implicit declaration of guilt comes a sentencing, introduced by a prophet's characteristic thumping **therefore.** The declaration begins literally "oracle of the Lord . . . ," a common solemn introduction or conclusion to a saying that a prophet thereby emphasizes is God's and not merely the prophet's. The string of titles for God that follows: **the Lord, the LORD Almighty, the Mighty One of Israel . . .** underlines the power of this opening. "The Lord" designates God as sovereign king. The title "the LORD Almighty" suggests that Yahweh (lit., "Yahweh armies") controls mighty resources and is thus able to implement a purpose in the world, while "Mighty One" applies to Yahweh an expression that suggests power like that of a bull (see Additional Notes). Each of these titles adds to the sense that what we are about to hear comes from a mightily powerful God—a comfort no doubt to friends, but a threat to enemies. These names would have been familiar to Isaiah's hearers. Here they are being turned against them.

Get relief and **avenge myself** sound very like each other in Hebrew and combine subjective feelings and objective justice. Yahweh will now get the relief of giving expression to a strongly-felt inner desire to express anger. "Avenge myself" adds the notion of fair punishment; it is a less emotional expression than the English one. **I will turn my hand against you** adds the idea of direct, careful, personal involvement. The hand that was designed to work for them and against their enemies is turned the other way.

1:25b–26 / Now a surprising transition comes about. The act of judgment with wholly negative intent becomes an act of purging with creative, positive intent. The grieved and angered father wants to recreate and not just destroy. Sometimes these events come sequentially—first judgment, then renewal (e.g., 8:21–9:7). Sometimes the one transmogrifies into the other—judgment seems to be happening but it turns into deliverance (e.g., ch. 31). Here the same event is both an act of judgment and an act of restoration, reversing the effects seen in verses 21–23. It is by attacking the dross that God restores the city to what it should be.

Verse 25b is more compressed, more concrete, and more uncomfortable than the translation implies: "I will smelt your dross [by heating to very high temperatures] like potash [used as a flux in the smelting process]." What Yahweh will literally do is **restore your judges/counselors.** They will then be in a position to see that community affairs are conducted in the proper way, whether at the level of the courts or at the level of forming and implementing political policies. Thus Zion will once again be **the City of Righteousness,** "Justice City," and once again **Faithful City.** The ideal is restored.

1:27–31 / The double-sided point about punishment and restoration is now put in a different way. This redeeming of the city is an act of payment expected of the city itself. It has responsibility for the reshaping of its life in accordance with just judgment. The point is the same as in verses 15b–20. There is a redeeming that Yahweh alone can do, but there is also one for which the people themselves are responsible. To put it another way, it is necessary for Zion's people to be **penitent.** Literally they need to be "turners," changing their direction and their ways. "Turn/return/repent" is another key prophetic term that makes its first appearance here. On the other hand, **rebels** (see v. 2) **and sinners** (see v. 4) **will both be broken** together. "Breaking" can be an image for military defeat or emotional distress or bodily crippling. Here it points not merely to loss of life but to loss of power, and in part provides the precondition of the restoration of just judgment. "Both . . . together" introduces yet another of the book's important terms. It implies suddenness, simultaneity, and thus an extraordinariness that hints at the visible activity of God.

Those who forsake the LORD will perish leads into a coda in verses 29–31 which develops a subordinate theme in the chapter. Judah's rebellion has generated a broken and unfair society whose structures the powerful could use to crush the weak (vv. 15b–23), but it has also despised, ignored, and broken a family relationship (vv. 2–4). Further, the people have not merely turned from Yahweh but have turned to another direction completely. The "faithful city" has become a "harlot" (v. 21a).

In Isaiah, sometimes Judah's rebelliousness and faithlessness are expressed in its looking to other human resources of strength (see esp. chs. 30–31). Here, as more often in the prophets, they are expressed in its looking to the resources of another religion. This is the traditional folk religion of Canaan that sought to identify directly with the forces of creation, to be built up by those forces, and to encourage them in their own fruitfulness. The punishment will fit the crime (vv. 29–31). Exposing the folly of their false trust will mean people are **ashamed** and **disgraced** (v. 29). The two words suggest the inner and factual exposure of inadequacy which devastates the person who sees the error that has been committed, as well as the person's public humiliation and shame before others.

2:1 / In 1:1, the word "vision" drew attention to the revelatory content of what Isaiah was to say about the future. In this companion tailpiece (lit. "the word that Isaiah son of Amoz saw . . . "), "word" draws attention to its verbal form, issuing from Yahweh's speaking like a judge (1:2, 10, 18, 20), and to the certainty of its effectively implementing what it announces.

Additional Notes §1

1:2–9 / On some of the poetic features of these verses, see the Introduction above.

1:3 / Elsewhere "Israel" is set over against "Judah" as a political term for the northern kingdom (e.g., 7:1), otherwise known as Ephraim, its dominant tribe. Of course the Judeans whom Isaiah addresses are part of the theological Israel. He can even speak of Judah *as* Israel, and sometimes this can be a pointed usage—Judah is the true Israel (see v. 1). We have to judge from contexts which usage applies.

The parallelism between **Israel** and **my people** (v. 3b) shows that here the name "Israel" is used theologically for Yahweh's people as a whole, as is the name Jacob (e.g., 2:5).

1:24 / **The LORD Almighty** is common in the Prophets, but puzzling. The armies might be those of human nations (see 34:2), but they are more likely heavenly forces (see 13:13; 24:21; 34:4; 40:26; 45:12). The rendering "LORD" avoids the name Yahweh, a foreign-sounding name, but thereby abandons the name God graciously revealed. "Almighty" conveys the idea of "armies," if in a rather abstract way. In the unique phrase "the Mighty One of Israel," mighty is a spelling variant for the word that commonly applies to the power of a bull. The variant is doubtless intended to safeguard any misunderstanding when the word is applied to God.

1:25 / **Thoroughly** apparently takes *bor* as the abstract word "cleanness." It more often means "lye/potash." It used to be thought that lye/potash was not used for smelting; but see H. Wildberger, *Isaiah 1–12. ET* (Minneapolis: Fortress, 1991), p. 60.

1:29–30 / Both verses begin with the Hb. word *ki*, which commonly means "for" (as in vv. 2, 20). NIV assumes that in contexts such as this it simply adds emphasis and draws attention to what follows rather than making a link with what precedes. NIV thus also does not translate the word at the beginning of 2:3b, 6 (also in the second line), 12, 22b, 3:1 (and many other passages). The reader might like to look at these verses and see whether "for" makes sense there, as NRSV assumes.

2:1 / The chapter division implies that 2:1 is the preface to what then follows, but there are no further such prefaces and it makes better sense as the tailpiece to chapter 1, pairing with 1:1.

§2 The Last Days and the Day of Yahweh for Jerusalem (Isa. 2:2–4:6)

With two visions of Zion/Jerusalem's restoration (1:1–2:1 and 5:1–30) bracketing substantial declarations of coming calamity for Zion/Jerusalem/Judah, chapters 1–5 as a whole have a trouble-promise-trouble-promise-trouble arrangement. Worrisomely, trouble enfolds the community even though blessing is its background destiny. Or, encouragingly, blessing does lie enfolded even if trouble dominates the community's immediate prospects. We do not know the date of any of the material or of the composition of the whole.

2:2–5 / The promise of the exaltation of Zion in verses 2–4 appears in a variant form in Micah 4:1–3. We do not know its actual origin. In both contexts it serves to promise that Yahweh's threat of judgment (Isa. 1; Mic. 1–3) is not the final word.

In the last days is literally "at the close of the days." While the phrase always refers to a special moment when Yahweh's promises come true, it does not have to refer to *the* end. When the "days" are depends on the context. The term generally denotes a period that is one step removed from speaker and audience. Here the first event the prophet announces is Zion's judgment. "At the close of the days [of this judgment]" comes Zion's new exaltation. The transformation that 2:2–5 promises is a further expression and development of that in 1:25b–27.

"In the last days" thus does not specify whether the events it introduces will take weeks, years, or centuries to come. It shares in a pattern that appears throughout Scripture. Zion itself saw some fulfillment of this vision in OT times. It saw further fulfillment through the coming of Jesus and specifically through Pentecost. It still awaits complete fulfillment, as hinted by Romans 11:12.

The original Jerusalem-Zion stood below the height of the country around. While relatively secure, standing on a spur of rock, it was not an impressive sight like (say) Tyre, or even Samaria. Its physical location belied its theological significance as a place that pointed to, reflected, and mediated heaven (Ps. 48:2; 78:69). Even after it expanded to the north and west, it stood below the height of the Mount of Olives to the east. Even northern Israel was physically more significant than Judah and Jerusalem, as was many a Canaanite shrine. Its physical unimpressiveness provides a figure for its lack of international significance or reputation.

The promise that this insignificant spur **will be established as chief among the mountains** (cf. Ezek. 40:2) presumably does not predict a geophysical transformation of the Judean mountain ridge. But that is what happens in this vision, which envisages a time when nations will **stream to it** (v. 2). It does not specify what will draw them. Theologically, the vision restates and applies to Zion the promise that Abram will be so blessed that all peoples will receive the same blessing (Gen. 12:1–3). Reasserting this worldwide vision near the beginning of Isaiah (it will recur at the end, in ch. 66) reminds readers of the context in which Judah lives its life of privilege and responsibility and in which all of prophecy operates, including declarations of calamity for individual nations and for the nations as a whole (chs. 10; 13–27). Judah thus recognizes the universality of Yahweh's concern. The nations recognize the particularity of Yahweh's involvement in the world as they speak of **the God of Jacob.**

These peoples **will come** to Yahweh's mountain, **go up** to it, the technical term for pilgrimage. As would often be the case with Israelite pilgrims, they come to seek guidance from Yahweh, so that **he will teach us his ways, so that we may walk in his paths.** The result (rather than the cause?) of the people's being drawn to **Zion/Jerusalem** is that *torah*/**the word of the LORD** (see 1:10) will go out from there. Verse 4 suggests it takes the form not of general teaching but of rulings on specific questions that people ask. Yahweh **will settle disputes for many peoples.** Yahweh as king deals with disputes in the manner of the king in 1 Kings 3:16–28.

Paying heed will mean a peace dividend. They will beat their weapons of war into farming implements. Yahweh's act of destruction (Ps. 46:9) becomes an act of recycling undertaken by the warriors themselves. The finality of such action is underlined: **nation will not take up sword against nation, nor will they train for war any more** (v. 4b). Between them, this passage and Joel 3:10 reflect the fact that there is a time for war and a time for peace

(Eccl. 3:8), but that the time of fulfillment is a time of peace rather than of war.

When compared with Micah 4:1–3, the most distinctive feature of Isaiah's version of this prophecy is the "application" in verse 5. The **house of Jacob** (see on 1:10) is challenged to **walk in the light of the LORD.** If Yahweh is committed to achieving a purpose whereby the nations let their lives be shaped by Yahweh's teaching, the least Israel can do is let that teaching shape their own lives now. Perhaps they may then be in a position to avoid the trouble that 1:2–31 and 2:6–4:1 otherwise envisage. Or perhaps their letting their lives be thus shaped contributes to the achieving of Yahweh's purpose. It becomes part of what draws the nations. The image of light can denote truth as opposed to falsehood, but in the OT *Yahweh's* light suggests not Yahweh's revelation but Yahweh's provision or deliverance or Yahweh's face. The averting of Yahweh's eyes means loss (1:15), but when Yahweh's face shines, deliverance blossoms (Ps. 44:3). Walking in Yahweh's light (v. 5) suggests living by Yahweh's blessing.

2:6–9 / The address to God in verses 6a ("You have abandoned them") and 9b ("do not forgive them") forms a bracket round the description of the community in the rest of verses 6–9, so that throughout these verses the people overhear Isaiah speaking to God about them. The words in verse 6a would have sounded like part of a prayer for Yahweh to return to the people, but this is the first of a number of occasions when the prophet beguiles the people by sounding as if he is speaking in one way in order eventually to say something very different. The two prayers in verses 6a and 9b are a chilling combination. It is up to the people to respond in such a way as to negate the closing request.

One might assume that verse 6a describes and verses 6b–9a indicate the reasons for Yahweh's abandonment of the people, but the order (first the abandonment, then the wrongdoing) implies the opposite. A comparison with Psalm 94 also suggests that the wrongdoing is actually the result of that abandonment (cf. the argument of Rom. 1). The psalm pictures a community characterized by corruption, oppression, and folly, but it expresses a confidence that Yahweh will take action with regard to this, "for Yahweh will not reject his people" (Ps. 94:14; cf. 1 Sam. 12:22). In contrast Isaiah declares, "for you have rejected your people" (cf. Ps. 27:9; Jer. 12:7). God has given up on them (Wildberger, *Isaiah*

1–12, p. 105). We do not know which historical context provoked this judgment.

The evidence of Yahweh's abandonment includes disapproved religious observances (divination, image-making) and the accumulation of financial and military resources. These are presumably related: all are ways of attempting to safeguard the future by means other than trusting in Yahweh (see 30:16; 31:1, 3; 39:1–8).

2:10–22 / The words about humbling (v. 9a) reappear (vv. 11, 17), as does the talk about silver and gold and images (vv. 7–8, 20). The chiastic arrangement emphasizes both the action commended at either end and the basis for it all at the center.

> A The action Isaiah commends (v. 10a)
> > B The dread of Yahweh and the splendor of
> > > Yahweh's majesty (v. 10b)
> > > C People to be brought low, Yahweh to be exalted
> > > > (v. 11)
> > > > D Yahweh has a day against . . . (vv. 12–16)
> > > C' People to be brought low, Yahweh to be
> > > > exalted (vv. 17–18)
> > B' The dread of Yahweh and the splendor of
> > > Yahweh's majesty (vv. 19–21)
> A' The action Isaiah commends (v. 22)

Again the section opens and closes with address, but this address is directed to the people. The commands give them little room to maneuver. They are to **hide** from Yahweh (see further vv. 19–21) and to **stop trusting in** human beings with their feebleness (see v. 22). If they are to avoid God and humanity, who is left? As in his prayer in verses 6–9, Isaiah seeks to drive people into a corner. Of course he wants actually not to make them hide from Yahweh but to make them seek Yahweh. Prophets cannot always (usually?) be taken at face value.

The **dread of the Lord and the splendor of his majesty** (v. 10b) recurs at the beginning and end of verses 19–21, and the motif is also developed in between. The dread is not a feeling but an objective dreadfulness, a terrifying awesomeness, parallel to Yahweh's majestic splendor. Both the dread and the splendor are implicit in Yahweh's holiness, Isaiah's key motif. In being put in touch with Yahweh, Judah is in contact with power that has the

capacity to electrocute if mishandled. The dread is a reason to
hide or **flee,** and also a reason that images in their triviality are
destined to be discarded (vv. 18, 20). The majesty and the **exalted-
ness** are a reason that what is humanly **lofty** and **exalted** must be
put down. By its nature humanity has a tendency to be arrogant
and proud (v. 17), though the words Isaiah uses need not imply
that this is so. The words for loftiness simply denote exalted
height. The mere fact that things are so impressive means that
they may seem to rival Yahweh, win excessive regard and trust,
and need to be cut down. That applies to human beings and to
natural resources (v. 13), impressive religious and urban sites
(v. 14), fortifications (v. 15), and humanly-made assets (v. 16)—to
all that impresses from Lebanon to the Red Sea.

The words used of Yahweh are words for royal majesty and
for secure exalted-ness that imply the capacity to be a defensive
refuge (25:12; 26:5; 33:5, 16). Human impressiveness compromises
the one, human strength the other. The cutting down will be a
feature of Yahweh's **day** (v. 11, 12, 17, 20), the day when Yahweh's
ultimate purpose will be fulfilled. It is designed to be a time of
glory, light, blessing, deliverance, safety, and renewal, and believers looked forward to it like Christians anticipating the second
coming of Christ. But resistance to Yahweh means it becomes a
time of humbling, darkness, calamity, defeat, insecurity, and loss,
as Christ's coming will be for Christians who have resisted Christ.

3:1–7 / Another solemn designation of God (see 1:24)
marks the beginning and end of verses 1–15, and this whole section focuses on the community's leadership and the collapsing
structures of the community. A chiasm describes Yahweh's punishment in verses 1–7:

> A Yahweh's power will destroy human confidence and
>   power (v. 1a)
>   B (Supplies will run out [v. 1b])
>   C The consequences (vv. 2–6)
>   B' (Supplies have run out [v. 7a])
> A' Human beings lack the confidence to take power
>   (v. 7b)

The designation of God explains and guarantees punishment beyond that found in 2:10–22, making more down-to-
earth the warning about the removal of humanly impressive

leadership—military, legal, religious, moral, practical, and political. There is no suggestion that the leaders have misled the people (as in ch. 1), except by looking like a resource of impressiveness and strength and thereby encouraging the people not to lean on **the Lord, the LORD Almighty** as their **supply and support** (words used elsewhere only of Yahweh, Ps. 18:18). The result will be that the people will be governed by children (v. 4), or by no one at all so that society collapses into disorder (v. 5), or by no one because even the incompetent are unwilling (vv. 6–7). The resourcelessness that verse 7 acknowledges testifies to the vindication of statements in chapter 2 (and the only qualification he needed was a cloak!) and underlines that, in a crisis, the test of leadership is a down-to-earth one.

3:8–12 / In the description of the deeds of the wicked and the reward of the righteous, what seem at first disjointed sayings form another chiasm:

> A Judah, Jerusalem and their deeds *(ma'alelehem)* (v. 8)
>> B Alas for those who have earned disaster *(ra',*
>> *gamal)* (v. 9)
>>> C Good news for the righteous given their deeds
>>> *(ma'alelehem)* (v. 10)
>> B′ Alas for those whose earning is disaster *(ra',*
>> *gemul)* (v. 11)
> A′ My people, my people and what is done to them
> *(me'olel)* (v. 12)

Verses 8–9 and 11–12 suggest a horror on the part of the prophet both at the visionary **Jerusalem/Judah** and at the actual city and country. Calamity has been happening before Isaiah's eyes. **Staggers** involves collapsing in ruins (the same word as v. 6), but both this and **is falling** suggest a drunk, perhaps someone who has drunk a glass of Yahweh's anger. The verbs are past tense, like **they have brought disaster on themselves,** as if they describe events that have already taken place, though in verse 11 a more literal future tense appears. Isaiah also sees the people as they literally are now, in word and deed blatantly **defying** (the word translated **rebel** in 1:20) God's **glorious presence** (literally "eyes"), and with their own **faces** looking brazen **like Sodom** (see 1:10).

Yet it is not true, or need not be true, of all of the people. At the heart of the section, in between the woes, Isaiah declares that

the righteous will have their just reward (v. 10). Their **deeds** are very different from the deeds of the community as a whole (v. 8). He does not use "remnant" language, but he presupposes what would become another way of thinking about a remnant (see on 10:20–21). The remnant is a small minority accepting a call to faithfulness when most fall from it. This is the first indication that there is such a group within the community.

At the end we might expect the prophet to return to the visionary Jerusalem, and **youths oppress my people, women rule over them** (v. 12a) could at first be read that way (cf. v. 4). As usual, nothing can be taken for granted—and verse 12b reveals that it comprises a dismissive assessment of the people's actual present leadership, its **guides** who **lead astray** and **turn from the path.** In this way the section comes to a scathing climax that gives it its concrete link with the theme of leadership that holds together the three sections of verses 1–15. The people need to recognize their leaders for what they are. They also need to be prepared either to turn as a community from the attitudes expressed by verses 8–9 or to stand out individually in the way verse 10 envisages, if they are to evade imminent disaster. There is no mention of God's activity here. Wrongdoing and righteousness bring their "natural" fruit in disaster and blessing, though of course God is behind this (v. 1; also 9:18–21).

3:13–15 / Yahweh now declares judgment. Christian theology uses "judgment" as a default model for God's bringing trouble in response to wrongdoing. In the OT, the image of people as guilty and being judged is less common than that of people as (say) a disobedient child being chastised or a resistant student being punished or a faithless spouse being attacked or divorced. But here, in the strict sense Yahweh indeed **enters into judgment,** though this is no routine figure of speech. As usual the prophet keeps his hearers on their toes. He pictures Yahweh standing up to declare judgment on "peoples" (v. 13, NRSV), which might seem good news to Judah if it meant judgment on its enemies, or even judgment *for* them in the sense envisaged by 2:2–4. But suddenly the spotlight returns to **his people** and its **elders** and **leaders** (v. 14), and Isaiah announces a motif that will be developed in chapter 5, Yahweh's **vineyard.** So on one side are "peoples" and Judah's elders/leaders, who are brought into association as objects of Yahweh's judgment, perhaps even identified with each other. On the other side are his people/my vineyard/**my people**

and **the poor** or powerless or afflicted or bowed down (*'ani*;
vv. 14b, 15) who are also brought into association, perhaps even
identified with each other. In 14:32 Yahweh's people as a whole
are designated the "poor" (NIV afflicted) over against the nations,
finding refuge in Zion. Here Judah is divided between the leadership that is associated with the nations, and the powerless to
whom the title "his people" is confined. Revolutionarily, the identity of his people is thus redefined. It is a question not of where
you are born but of your place in the power structure. Yahweh divides the leaders and people according to the way the former
treated the latter. The leaders treated the people as if they did not
belong. As a result, the leaders have lost their own belonging. The
leaders have **ruined**, better "devoured" (NRSV), so that the **plunder is in your houses** (v. 14). To that end they have been **crushing**
and **grinding** (v. 15) as if the poor were themselves grain. Once
again the solemnity of **the Lord, the LORD Almighty** undergirds
Yahweh's oracle, drawing verses 13–15 to a close, as well as concluding the larger section (vv. 1–15).

3:16–4:1 / The women of Jerusalem will also experience
their fall from exaltation to shame. In a patriarchal society, men
have to be leaders and women have to look nice. Feminine beauty
is an alternative way of being exalted (**haughty** is a variant on
words translated "lofty" in 2:15 and "arrogant /arrogance" in 2:11,
17; see also 5:15–16). So the women of Zion have to be taken from
majesty to humiliation, like the community in general (but perhaps the men in particular) in 2:10–22. The beginning and end of
3:16–4:1 mark the two extremes of this journey. There are two facets to the women's fall. Most of the comment centers on the loss of
their fine looks, jewelry, fine clothes, make-up, and accessories.
Haute couture gives way to the appearance of a victim or a prisoner of war.
    The other facet to their fall is the disappearance of the men
upon whom patriarchy requires them to depend. The city itself
will mourn their disappearance (vv. 25–26). Even if they can provide their own livelihood (cf. the earlier reference to the men's inability to provide food and clothing in v. 7), they have no place in
society unless they are attached to a man (4:1).

4:2–6 / **In that day** has been a worrying phrase in 3:7, 18;
4:1, but this time it heralds the promise that calamity is not Yahweh's last word. At point after point, these verses take up the

motifs of 2:6–4:1 and promise reversal. Zion's beauty and security will be restored.

Talk of **the Branch of the LORD** recalls the picture of a tree that has been felled (2:13) or of Yahweh's people as a vineyard that has been devoured (3:14; see later 5:1–7; 6:13). The tree will flourish and produce its fruit again. In other words, the people will flourish once more (see 37:31–32). Thus **the survivors in Israel** will receive replacements for the splendor, exaltedness, and attractiveness that they are destined to lose (2:10–22; 3:16–24). "Survivors," literally "a people who escaped," is another term for the remnant (1:8–9; cf. 10:20; 37:31–32). The notion of a remnant of cloth or carpet left over when the main pieces have been sold gives just the right impression for the idea of **those who are left.** The same applies to **who remain** (translated "left" in 1:8–9; see comment).

The splendor of the leftovers is that they **will be called holy** (cf. 6:13). The holiness that attaches to Yahweh by nature (see on 1:4) attaches to Israel by association (only here is the adjective so used in Isaiah). They are **recorded among the living in Jerusalem.** They do more than merely survive to appear in a political citizen-list. They appear in the book of life or the book of the living, God's book (see Exod. 32:32; Ps. 69:28). They are invited to see God's sovereignty in their survival, another building block for the notion of a remnant.

The **women of Zion** will also be restored, for Yahweh **will wash away** the dirt of their humiliation (v. 4; cf. 3:17, 24) and/or the dirt of their own sin. Yahweh's sovereignty is involved in this washing, too, and the promise that Yahweh will also **cleanse the bloodstains from Jerusalem** contrasts with the earlier demand for human action in 1:15–18. Yet this is no reversion to cheap grace. Renewal involves a white-hot purging **by a spirit of judgment** (see on 1:21) and of **fire** (see 1:25, 31). This first occurrence of **spirit** in Isaiah well illustrates the Hebrew word's capacity to move between spirit, wind, and breath, to bring disaster as well as renewal (see 30:28; 40:7).

In seeking to stand on high as Yahweh does (2:10–22), people evade any need for other security. This security is therefore removed and they have to seek some other hiding place (not least from Yahweh). In assembling for worship people avoid righting their lives in society, so that assembling is resented (1:12). Now Yahweh provides Zion and its assembled worshipers with a comprehensive security and hiding place: **cloud of smoke** and

glow of flaming fire as at the exodus, and **canopy** to be both um-
brella and parasol (vv. 5–6). People who can find no refuge from
oppression or from disaster find it here.

Additional Notes §2

2:6 / **They are full of superstitions from the East:** "of superstitions" is an addition by NIV. In MT, vv. 7–9a will reveal the two sides to
what the people are full of (accumulation of resources and disapproved
religious practices). V. 6 goes on "and soothsayers like the Philistines, and
with the children of foreigners they slap [hands]." These might be the
first announcements of the themes of disapproved religious practices
and accumulation of resources, if that last clause had a commercial significance (as in Prov. 6:1), but that is guesswork. The hand gesture might
as easily be a religious act, to ward off something.

2:9 / **So people will be brought low and** everyone **humbled.**
The verbs are past tense. Prophecies can be put in the past tense because
they are "as good as fulfilled," but these past verbs follow a string of "genuine" past verbs describing the consequences of Yahweh's abandonment, and they more likely continue that description. Cf. NRSV: "So
people are humbled, and everyone is brought low." V. 9a then continues
v. 8, and vv. 7 and 8–9a balance each other in content and length. The
human humiliation lies in bowing to things they have created.
   Forgive and **raise** (NIV mg.) are both possible meanings of *nasa'.*
The latter fits the context better (see v. 12b), but one would expect a different verb form (the piel) to convey this meaning.

2:11 / **The eyes of the arrogant:** lit. "the eyes of exaltedness of a
human being," perhaps "exalted human appearances/opinions/presence."
The word for "eyes" is rendered **presence** in 3:8.

3:9 / **Look** (*hakkarah*) occurs only here. What the look signifies
is unclear; RSV guesses "partiality," but brazenness fits the context.

3:16 / **Flirting** is an interpretation; the word simply means
"looking about."

4:2 / Elsewhere **the Branch of the LORD** could be a future
Davidic king (see 11:1), but the context here offers no hint in this direction. Elsewhere **the fruit of the land** would simply denote what the land
makes grow, but the "Branch of the LORD" is hardly a way of simply referring to "what Yahweh makes grow," and 37:31–32 speaks in similar terms
of the regrowing people as fruit.

4:3 / **Those who are left** is from the same root as the eventual
technical term for the remnant. For the noun, cf. 7:3 (see NIV mg.); 10:19–22;
11:11, 16, and for the verb, 11:11, 16; 37:31.

§3 Judgment Missed and Demonstrated (Isa. 5:1–30)

In length and theme chapter 5 pairs with chapter 1 and closes a bracket around 2:2–4:6. Chapter 5 comprises a mock love song; a series of woes that will be completed in 10:1–4; and a warning about Yahweh's outstretched hand that will continue in chapter 9. In contrast to 1:1–2:1 and 2:2–4:6, no positive note is struck at the beginning or the end. Chapters 1–5 come to a close as bleak as their opening. Rebellion and darkness ultimately bracket them.

5:1–7 / The chapter opens with a lament for a disappointing vineyard. The readers of this book can easily work out what this vineyard stands for (see 3:14; also Ps. 80). For the original audience of Isaiah's song, matters were more complicated. Cultivating a vineyard can be an image for courting someone (see Song 2:15; 7:8–9, 12; 8:11–12). Isaiah appears before his audience as a minstrel singing a love song on behalf of his best friend, perhaps as his best man. It appears at first to be a touching song about the man's efforts to cultivate a fruitful relationship or a fruitful marriage, yet worryingly its lines have the short second half characteristic of the limping lament form, which suggests that it will turn out to be a sad song.

The effort involved in cultivation is considerable, to judge from the analogy. There are many stones on the average Palestinian hillside, and the farmer has no mechanized equipment. Turning these into a wall to keep animals out, and into a permanent watchtower (see 1:8) requires much effort. Constructing a winepress, which is two linked vats of stone, wood, or clay, one for pressing the juice out of the grapes, the lower one for letting the juice settle, involves further labor. Then the farmer must wait two years for the first grapes.

At the end of verse 2 the love song turns overtly into a blues. The grapes are small and sour instead of large and full of juice.

The beloved has turned against Isaiah's friend. The poetic intensity increases as the lines of verse become longer through verses 4–6, mirroring the overflowing indignation of poet and lover. If one may see the lament meter itself as blues-like, in this sense verses 4–6 are less like a blues. As Isaiah (or rather the suitor/ vinedresser himself) asks what should happen now, a modern audience, at least, begins to feel uneasy and embarrassed. Is the woman not free to resist this man's pressing advances? What is the wife's side of the story? And is there more to this song than meets the ear? Or does the average man who has been disappointed in love identify closely with the instinct for violent vengeance expressed in the declarations of excessive intent in verses 5–6? Who can issue commands to the rain clouds? What is going on?

All becomes clear in verse 7. The song was one about the relationship between Yahweh and Israel/Judah. To the metaphorical lament in verses 1–6 is added a double paronomasia: **He looked for justice** *(mishpat)*, **but saw bloodshed** *(mishpakh)*; **for righteousness** *(tsedaqah)*, **but heard cries of distress** *(tse'aqah;* see 1:21 on the pairing of justice and righteousness). The proximity of the words and the similarity of sounds belie the distance between what they refer to and the distance between hope and reality. The men who identified with the man's desire for vengeance have signed the warrant for vengeance on themselves, like David in his judgment in 2 Samuel 12 (Oswalt, *Isaiah 1–39*, p. 151). The technique is one Jesus takes up in his parables, as is the vineyard theme. Jesus' parables will also imitate Isaiah's technique whereby the prophet then leaves the hearers to work out the implications for themselves.

5:8–24 / In the context, these six **woes** (number seven comes in 10:1–4) and their two *therefores* interpret the bad grapes and the wasting of the vineyard.

In the first woe, accumulated property and land will become desolate and fruitless (vv. 8–10). The objection here is neither to the immoral means of the acquisition nor to the contravention of the principle that land cannot be bought because it belongs to Yahweh and/or to the family to whom it is allocated (Lev. 25:23; 1 Kgs. 21). Rather, the problem is the self-indulgence involved in the acquisition, as people (stupidly) create for themselves lonely estates around lonely property instead of gladly sharing with others.

The second woe declares that for nobles and for ordinary people, drinking and entertainment will become starvation, thirst, and exile (which will presumably also be the means of bringing the desolation of vv. 9–10 as the owners are cast out of the land they have monopolized). They will suffer starvation and thirst (vv. 11–13). The objection here is to the way these preoccupations divert people from paying attention to what God is doing (see 1:3). While Isaiah might imply that the masses pay the penalty for the indulgence of the rich, it is more natural to read verses 13–14 as implying that the masses share in the indulgence and in the calamity. Drink is, in any case, commonly a recourse of the poor as well as of the rich.

A more extensive warning **(therefore)** sets these two woes in a broader context (vv. 14–17). In theme, verse 14 links with the second woe and warns not merely about the fact of death but about the nature of it. **Sheol** (NIV mg.) is the home of dead people in general. It is an underground home for people's personalities that is equivalent to the one the grave provides for their bodies, and, like the grave, it is a corporate one. Sometimes in Middle Eastern thinking Death was an individual deity. Here it is simply personified as a person whose appetite matches the revellers' but exceeds it in danger. In turn, verse 17 links with the first woe and pictures animals able to enjoy the fruits of the land's desolation.

In between (vv. 15–16), the theme reverts to one that dominated chapters 2–3, but adds a crucial new statement. God's holiness is God's majestic, extraordinary, supernatural almightiness, so the parallel of **holy** with **exalted** is intelligible enough. Here Isaiah tells us how **holy** becomes an ethical term and not merely a metaphysical one. He associates it with the key word-pair from the climax of the vineyard song. By nature Yahweh is a just God. It is in manifesting **righteousness** (*tsedaqah*) that Yahweh's deity or holiness reveals itself as deity or holiness. This is another way of saying that Yahweh Almighty is exalted in **justice** (*mishpat*). To put the two sayings together, it is in just judgment that the Almighty, holy Yahweh is revealed and exalted as the holy one.

The second sequence of woes works differently. They simply describe the wrongdoers—implicitly the people's leadership. In the third woe, the people pull punishment along as they scornfully invite God to hurry along the plan that the holy one is allegedly pursuing. Their comment on God's **work** takes up and justifies Isaiah's earlier observation about their disregard for it (v. 12), and their chilling taunt about **the Holy One of Israel** resonates with Isaiah's subsequent comment on who this God is (v. 16). One need not suppose that people literally said the words in verse 19 (and suppose that this lets readers off the hook if they can claim not to do so). Isaiah is inclined to put on people's lips the implications of their words (see 28:15).

This scorn involves denying the reality of the crisis that confronts the community, saying things are going well when they are on the way to disaster (v. 20). Even in English, **bitter/sweet** sounds like a reference to suffering/blessing rather than to wrong/right. In Hebrew this is also the natural way to understand **evil/good** and **darkness/light** (cf. v. 30).

This delusion in turn involves living by their own definitions of insight (v. 21). Isaiah offers the first of many critiques of the so-called wisdom that effectively excludes God, though formally it will not have done so. Paradoxically (or not), the woes' concerns parallel those of Proverbs. Far from being against learning, Isaiah includes it, but with God as part of the picture (e.g., 28:23–29; see, e.g., Whedbee, *Isaiah and Wisdom*, pp. 105–7).

Behind all this (see vv. 11–13) is their combining self-indulgence with perversion of justice (vv. 22–23). "Here are pictured the great men of the nation, who are only great behind a bar" (Oswalt, *Isaiah 1–39*, p. 165).

Their judgment comes in another **Therefore**. Again it combines vivid pictures (v. 24a) with a powerful statement about **the Lord Almighty . . . the Holy One** (v. 24b). The fact that people have **rejected/spurned** God's *torah*/**word** (again *torah* will include prophetic teaching) means they are bound to be called to account.

Both series of woes refer to God's **work** or **plan,** which Isaiah later calls "his work, his strange work . . . his task, his alien task" (28:21). Yahweh's work/task is to bring destruction on Judah (see 10:12). While this task is clearly alien to Yahweh's ultimate nature and purpose, it will be done if necessary as a means to that purpose's fulfillment. It is not just wanton destructiveness or fickleness. It is all part of a sensible plan (28:29, NIV "counsel"). Yahweh's positive plan for Israel stands (46:10, NIV "purpose"). Thus Yahweh does not need anyone to offer advice on planning (40:13, NIV "counselor"), and is even able to use foreign generals in this connection (46:11, NIV "purpose"). After being the means of Yahweh's completing his strange work, Assyria is destined by Yahweh's plan to be crushed (14:26; cf. 19:17), but in that ultimate purpose Assyria is itself Yahweh's work (19:25), destined for Yahweh's blessing, as much as Israel is (29:23; 60:21; 64:8). In general, *purpose* is a better translation than *plan*. The latter can give the impression that everything happens as an outworking of a detailed plan of action devised by God centuries beforehand. The OT gives the impression that through (or despite) human actions God always achieves the final purpose determined from before creation. The details of how Israel and the world in general work out that purpose is, however, determined more by human will than by God's plan.

5:25–30 / **Therefore** in verse 25 is a different word from that in verses 13, 14, and 24. It introduces a different theme, that of Yahweh's **anger.** In the context, this anger expressed in destructiveness further interprets the farmer/lover's reaction to his fruitless vineyard/courtship. The anger is expressed via an unnamed army whom Yahweh summons like a general or whistles for like a bee-keeper (see 7:18). Verses 26–30 vividly describe its advance. In the historical context, this is the invading Assyrians (see 10:5–19; 36:1–37:38). Although they do not know it, they are Yahweh's handiwork and agents of Yahweh's purpose (see comments on vv. 8–24). As 5:8–24 will be completed in 10:1–4, so 5:25–30 will be continued in 9:8–10:4. But one of the effects of separating verses 25–30 from what comes later is to make it easy to generalize. This army stands for the armies of all the distant nations that are from time to time summoned to Yahweh's angry purpose.

Anger (*'af*) is the word for nose (cf. our "snorting with anger"). This is thus a fiery and felt wrath, not a cool and unemotional one. Yahweh's anger is relentless (here), violent (10:5), destructive (10:25), fierce (13:9), burning (13:13), aggressive (14:6), raging (30:30), and bloody (63:3), but not unlimited (12:1) or predetermined (48:9). It is sometimes paired with *za'am* (10:5, 25; 30:27) which suggests indignant cursing, with *khemah* (42:25; 63:3; 66:15) which indicates burning rage, and with *'ebrah* (13:9; 14:6) which implies an overflowing outburst. Anger is an aspect of the passion of Yahweh, who is a real person with all the feelings that a human being has—from yearning love (vv. 1–4) to fierce wrath. To put it another way, believing that human beings are made in the image of deity, Middle Eastern peoples do not hesitate to attribute all the facets of human personality to deity. Unlike human passion and the passion of some Middle Eastern deities, however, Yahweh's passion is one with justice and is harnessed to the implementation of justice.

Additional Notes §3

5:8–24 / The translation **woe** may give the wrong impression; *hoy* is a cry or exclamation (NRSV "Ah") that expresses a reaction to appalling wrong or suffering (see 1:4). Whereas the first woe is expressed as an oath by Yahweh about the future, the second is mostly expressed in further already-as-good-as-here past tenses, lit. "they have gone into exile. . . . Sheol has enlarged its appetite. . . . People have been brought low. . . . Yahweh Almighty has been exalted. . . ." This might even signify that the events have taken place and that these prophecies give an explanation of them. Certainly these texts would function to give such account once the events they describe had taken place.

5:16 / **His justice . . . his righteousness:** there is no "his" on either word in the Hb. Justice and righteousness are here seen as realities or absolutes in their own right that Yahweh makes a point of embodying. They are realities to which Yahweh accepts responsibility: cf. Abraham's challenge to Yahweh in Gen. 18.

5:18 / Hb. *'awon* covers iniquity (53:5, 6, 11; 57:17 [KJV]; 59:2, 12), the guilt that follows (1:4; 6:7; 27:9; 59:3), and also the consequent punishment (e.g., Gen. 4:13; Lam. 4:6, 22). Etymologically, *'awon* perhaps suggests wandering out of the right way (see BDB), with a hint of perversity, but we do not know whether prophet and audience were aware of this. Hb. *khatta'ah* and related words cover **sin** (e.g., 1:18; 3:9; 6:7; and see on 1:28), the guilt that follows (e.g., Deut. 15:9; 24:15), and the consequent punishment (e.g., Zech. 14:19; Lam. 3:39). It can also refer to the sin offering (e.g., Ps. 40:6). "Pulling *'awon/khatta'ah* along" might in isolation imply multiplying and encouraging iniquity/sin, perhaps with the implication that it is nevertheless a burden, but v. 19 suggests that the idea is rather of multiplying *guilt* and *punishment*. **Cords of deceit** are making people unaware that they are doing this, that in scornfully hurrying Yahweh (v. 19) they are fatally building up their own guilt and hurrying their own punishment.

5:25–30 / Again, past tense verbs in vv. 25, 28 (see NRSV) interweave with "imperfect" verbs that point more to literal future. The combination suggests both the fact of futureness and the vividness of something as good as actual. Isa. 9:8–21 will link in theme and structure with 5:25–30 (and 10:1–4 with 5:8–24). This encourages us to read these two passages in association with those later ones. But the actual arrangement in the book does encourage us to associate 5:8–24 with 5:25–30, and this puts the "Therefore" in v. 24 *(laken)* and the different "Therefore" in v. 25 *('al-ken)* next to each other. NIV encourages this association by leaving no space between vv. 24 and 25. The rejection in v. 24 becomes the reason for the anger in v. 25.

§4 Isaiah's Commission: To Stop People Hearing (Isa. 6:1–13)

The fact that this testimony comes here rather than as chapter 1 further reflects the fact that the book called Isaiah is arranged logically rather than chronologically. Chapter 6 takes up many of the motifs in chapters 1–5. It also opens a section of the book in which narrative is more dominant (6:1–9:7) and that stands at the center of chapters 1–12 as a whole. Yahweh's holiness and the implications of that holiness are of key importance to the chapter.

6:1–4 / Uzziah/Azariah died between 742 and 735 B.C. after an outstanding, prosperous 52-year reign and a period of coregency with his son Jotham (2 Kgs. 15:5) but leaving Assyrian storm clouds on the horizon. Here Isaiah sees the *real* **Lord seated on a throne, high and exalted,** king and sovereign of the whole of heaven and earth, the King, the LORD Almighty (v. 5). Three times Isaiah calls Yahweh "Lord," Sovereign. The contrast between the limitlessness of Yahweh's reign and the limitations of the earthly king's reign might serve as reassurance at a time of transition. It will transpire that the message is less comforting. Isaiah is apparently in the temple, perhaps having gone there to seek God, or present for a "routine" occasion of worship, or for a great festival when Judah celebrated the kingship of the holy God over its own life and over the whole world, and recommitted itself to being Yahweh's subjects (see, e.g., Ps. 98; 99). In the temple, the symbolism of worship with the incense swirling becomes a vision of the reality the symbolism pointed to.

Yahweh is the human king writ large, sitting in his palace (the secular meaning of the word **temple**), exalted on his throne above the level of mere subjects, arrayed in robes of state, flanked by adulatory attendants (we know nothing of the seraphim's appearance), and possessing the power and authority to make his kingship more than the mere constitutional monarchy of a modern European democracy. The entire forces of the cosmos are at this real King's disposal. Regardless of what is happening to the human monarchy, it is this monarch who counts. Isaiah sees Yahweh awesome in royal honor and splendor (see, e.g., Ps. 97). That **glory** is the outward manifestation of Yahweh's being **holy** (see on 1:4). While the threefold **holy** compares with the threefold acknowledgment of God's holiness in worship in Psalm 99:3, 5, 9, three occurrences of "holy" compare with the twofold repetition elsewhere in Isaiah (e.g., 40:1; and see on 26:3). Only here in Isaiah is a word repeated three times, such is the emphasis it needs (but see Jer. 7:4; 22:29). It is presumably the vision of Yahweh's triple holiness and exaltedness that generates Isaiah's adoption of "the Holy One of Israel" (see on 1:4) as his distinctive title for God, as well as his emphasis on the exaltedness of this holy one (e.g., 2:6–22; 5:15–16).

6:5 / Holiness also means purity. Yahweh's holiness could make a mere creature simply draw back. But because of who Yahweh is, holiness comes to have moral connotations (see on 5:16). Isaiah draws back from God's holiness not just because of God's awesome splendor and his own creatureliness. He also draws back because God is just and righteous and he and his people are polluted *(tame')*, like the king who died that year (2 Kgs. 15:5). They do not fulfill the demands of Psalm 24. The fact that his lips were the part of his person especially involved in serving God as a prophet may lie behind his linking pollution with his lips. But he links his pollutedness with his people's, suggesting that he is identifying the pollution of his lips with Judah's. He has already referred to a number of the wrongs of their lips (e.g., 1:15, 23; 2:6; 3:8; 5:19, 20, 24). In the context of worship, the first of these (1:15) would have been especially relevant. Whichever it is, Isaiah finds that a vision of the holy God shuts the mouth.

6:6–7 / Isaiah's instinct to infer that holiness will be the end of him turns out to be mistaken. He also learns that holiness can mean forgiveness. In keeping with his stress on fire as a means of judging/purging (1:25; 4:4), a coal from the incense altar touches the part of Isaiah's body that he recognized to be the place of pollution (cf. Num. 16:46–47). The high and lofty One (the same phrase as in v. 1) dwells in a high and holy place, but also with those who are crushed and lowly in spirit (57:15). Merciful grace belongs as much to the essence of God's holiness as justice and purity. Once more, a return to Yahweh is not the only requirement for a restored relationship with Yahweh, as chapter 1 might have seemed to imply (**guilt/sin** recur from 1:4). People who do nothing and presume on God's forgiveness indeed fail to experience it; those who acknowledge the justice of God's judgment and turn from the ways that earned it can escape it.

The sign of cleansing that Isaiah receives is absurdly inadequate. How could being touched with a coal effect this sort of purification? The insufficiency of the sign highlights the fact that the cleansing originates within the person of the holy God. Sacramental rites such as this are the means by which Yahweh incarnates grace to humankind.

6:8–10 / It now becomes clear that holiness does mean judgment. Even if no specific pollution attached to Isaiah's lips, if he is to function as a prophet there is a special appropriateness about his having his lips cleansed so that he can use them in God's service. The image of Yahweh sending someone as messenger presupposes the model of Yahweh as the King surrounded by his court or cabinet. Usually it is permanent members of this cabinet that Yahweh sends to announce or execute the cabinet's decisions (e.g., 1 Kgs. 22:19–23), and there is no presumption that Yahweh's question in verse 8 expects a response from a mere human would-be aide. Whereas the accounts of Moses' and Jeremiah's commissioning stress their hesitation, Isaiah (like Ezekiel) is at the other extreme. He volunteers. A prophet is a human person who is admitted to Yahweh's cabinet and thus becomes another means of executing heaven's decisions on earth and a transmitter of messages between earth and heaven. This works both ways, for the prophet intercedes in the cabinet, speaking on earth's behalf there, as well as bringing announcements of heaven's decisions to earth.

It is a somber commission Yahweh then gives to Isaiah. Isaiah 6:1–8 is commonly read independently of what follows, simply as an instructive account of God's call. This ignores where verses 1–8 lead. Like the story of Elijah hearing the gentle whisper (1 Kgs. 19:12), the chapter is about the way God implements judgment. Indeed, every account of a prophet's call has this focus. Perhaps God hardly has need to call someone in this way for an ordinary, more pastoral ministry. Chapter 6 introduces 6:1–9:7, which functions as an explanation why people should take God's word seriously. This is so with other accounts of the call of prophets, such as those of Jeremiah and Ezekiel, though it is especially clear in the account of Amos's call (Amos 7:10–17). The content of the message of these prophets meant that it was not welcome, and people would be inclined not to believe that it came from God. The prophet therefore told of his call as one way of trying to get people to listen to his word. Thus the experience of a call is not something that other people would expect to have in common with a prophet. It is what makes a prophet different. The account of a call invites readers to see themselves not as prophets, called the way God called Isaiah, but rather as the audience of prophecy.

What then happens to them when they read on is frightening. Yahweh sends Isaiah to tell people that God is closing their minds (vv. 9–10). They have reached the point when God's judgment must fall, and the closing of their minds is the form this judgment will take. After all, they are willfully closing their own minds, actively or indirectly (e.g., 1:4; 5:12–13, 19–21). As a judgment Yahweh wills that the natural result should follow. They are closing their minds, and God will let that have its natural effect. They will become unable to realize what God is doing with them. Nevertheless, the words in verses 9 and 10 may be ironic. They constitute a warning of where the people will find themselves unless they respond and turn. Isaiah says **Be ever hearing, but never understanding** (v. 9), but he does not mean it. His preaching of judgment resembles Jonah's in Nineveh. It is designed to bring people to their senses, to repentance, and to forgiveness, even though it does not explicitly urge them to repentance and indicate that there is any way out. Isaiah will urge them to turn and will not merely repeat what 6:9–10 literally says, but he will meet a response that supports its truth (see ch. 7).

6:11–13 / Even if judgment is inevitable, that is not the end of the story, for holiness also means faithfulness. **For how long** is the question that often appears in the Psalms, not as a request for information, but as a plea for mercy. Initially Isaiah receives only a somber reiteration of how devastating the judgment must be. This reaffirms earlier declarations (e.g., 1:7–9, 29–31; 2:12–13; 5:5–6, 9, 13, 17) and provides part of the justification for his delivering his subsequent tough message (e.g., 7:17–25). Soon, in 721 B.C., the capital of the northern kingdom, Samaria, will fall to the Assyrians. The decimation of Yahweh's people as a whole when that happens could make Judah feel self-congratulatory. Even that is not the end (v. 13a). But this is not all Isaiah receives. Like the prophet, the people will find that God's holiness has room for mercy, which they will experience after the most horrifying devastation if not before it. Even the felled tree can grow again. They were once a brood (*zera'*, lit. "seed") of evildoers (1:4). Now they are (literally) "a seed of holiness," who are promised that they **will be the stump in the land** that can become a tree again (v. 13b; cf. 62:12). Despite the nightmare prospect set up by 5:1–7, their once-for-all association with Yahweh means (as a particular sign of Yahweh's mercy) that the word holy indeed applies to them, too (cf. 4:3). This tree will not be finally uprooted. Yahweh's promise will be taken further in 11:1–12:6.

Additional Notes §4

6:2 / They covered their **faces** so that they would not look at God (despite the sense in which Isaiah himself did) and covered their **feet** for modesty (if this is a euphemism for genitals).

6:8 / **For us:** presumably the heavenly court (see 1 Kgs. 22).

6:9–10 / NIV mg. notes that the LXX renders this as a prediction rather than a statement of the intention of Isaiah's ministry (when Jesus repeats these words, Mark 4 gives a version like the Hb., while Matt. 13 gives one like LXX). This becomes in effect God's intention insofar as God still sends Isaiah. It has thus been suggested that Isaiah wrote the account of his call in light of how things turned out, and that in reality it was only after the event that he saw that this was what he had been called to. It has also been suggested that God indeed revealed that this was what Isaiah was being called to, so that when it turned out thus, Isaiah would not be overwhelmed by his failure. Such theories reflect the sense of scandal interpreters feel at Isaiah's words, but they start from a problem Isaiah evidently did not sense himself.

6:13 / **So the holy seed will be the stump in the land:** lit., "the holy seed [is] its stump" or "its stump [is] the holy seed," interprets the word **stump** (actually singular) in the previous line. "So" and "in the land" are NIV interpretations.

§5 Coping with the Pressure from Syria and Ephraim (Isa. 7:1–8:10)

The heart of 6:1–9:7 is story and prophecy focusing on a crisis in Jerusalem about 733 B.C., soon after Isaiah's commission. Ahaz is now king. Jotham may have died before his father and only ever been co-regent. Northern **Israel** (see Additional Notes on 1:3) and **Aram** (Syria) had been forced to become part of the Assyrian empire, and they had now combined forces to try to compel Judah to join them in their efforts to gain independence from Assyria. They failed to do so and both capitals were sacked. The first verse of chapter 7 summarizes the context in which the events in 7:1–8:10 take place, but we have to live through them with Ahaz, not knowing their outcome.

7:1–9 / The theological issue raised by the allies' pressure lay in God's promises to Jerusalem and to David (see 2 Sam. 7): hence Ahaz is called **the house of David** (v. 2). The question is whether Ahaz will live by those promises. In Isaiah's conviction, they mean that Ahaz need not panic. Isaiah can see what Aram and Ephraim will look like when Yahweh has finished with them (vv. 4–9a). They are no bigger than their kings, for whom Isaiah evidently has little regard—again no doubt more for theological than for political reasons.

Indeed, those promises mean Ahaz *must not* panic. His city's security depends not on the security of the water supply which Ahaz is out investigating (v. 3), but on the security of his trust in Israel's God. He needs a different kind of being **careful**. As well as, or instead of, this politician's apparently responsible activity, he needs to **keep calm**, "be quiet" (NRSV), which may imply relaxing even while thus acting responsibly, or may imply doing nothing (see 18:4; 57:20; 62:1). Certainly it would exclude having recourse to defensive alliance with Assyria itself (see 30:15; 32:17), which is what Ahaz actually sought (2 Kgs. 16). **Don't be afraid** is a Middle Eastern deity's standard invitation/challenge to a devotee, especially a king. **Do not lose heart** suggests "be tough-minded" (lit. "your mind must not be tender"). It is soft to be activist, in the mistaken conviction that you are responsible for your people's destiny.

Key to Isaiah's challenge is the name of the son he brings with him, **Shear-Jashub,** "a remnant will return," though this name conveys an ambiguous message (see on 1:8–9; 3:10; 4:2–3). Only a remnant of the Assyrians will return to their land if Ahaz trusts in Yahweh; only a remnant of Judah will survive if he does not. If deportation comes on Judah, the name will suggest that at least a remnant will return to the land. Given that the people as a whole have turned away from Yahweh, the name promises that at least a remnant will turn back; it is at the same time a challenge, that at least a remnant should return to Yahweh.

The first ambiguity is re-worked in another paronomasia in verse 9, **if you do not stand firm in faith, you will not stand firm at all.** Different forms of the verb *'amen* denote being firm in faith, reliable, committed, and trustworthy (see 28:16; also 1:21), and also thus being established and secure. Such trust in the promises of Yahweh as the one who guarantees the people's future is a key emphasis in Isaiah's message.

7:10–17 / Yahweh now offers Ahaz any testing **sign** he likes, not only to prove that Yahweh **your God** (note the change of pronoun when Isaiah speaks of **my God** in v. 13) is trustworthy, but also to implement Yahweh's purpose. The offer functions to expose Ahaz as a man who did not want to trust in God even if he had the evidence, in keeping with 6:9–10. Admittedly he is also a man good at *argumentum ad hominem* who knows how to sound scriptural (Deut. 6:16) when it suits (v. 12). "It is really the king himself who is being tested" (Oswalt, *Isaiah 1–39*, p. 203). Despite his refusal, they are all still given the **sign,** but told it will do them no good.

The virgin will be with child and will give birth to a son, and will call him Immanuel. Isaiah need not have a particular woman in mind; she could be any woman who will soon marry and conceive in the ordinary way. When her baby is born, it will be a time of deliverance from Aram and Ephraim. By the time he can choose between good and bad food, he will have good food to enjoy and the allies will themselves be devastated (vv. 15–16). So they were. Thus his mother will call him **God** [is] **with us** out of gratitude for God's amazing faithfulness. But because of his stance, this will not do Ahaz any good (v. 17).

7:18–25 / Sometimes **in that day** suggests a somewhat distant event, even one associated with *the* end, but here it evidently refers to an imminent calamity. Four pictures of calamity supplement Isaiah's warning to Ahaz. Two describe Yahweh's initiative in relation to Assyria, two the consequences for people and land. Assyria is for the first time identified as Yahweh's agent, despite its not acknowledging Yahweh, a concept with "a revolutionary flavor" (Oswalt, *Isaiah 1–39*, p. 263).

In the first such picture (vv. 18–19), Egypt and Assyria are like **flies** and **bees** invading every corner of the land. Egypt appears as the traditional rather than the present enemy, and/or as one of the two current superpowers. In verse 20, Assyria is like a barber shaving from top to toe, a synecdoche for the grief and humiliation of defeat and exile (see 3:17; 2 Sam. 10:4–5; 2 Kgs. 2:23; Jer. 41:5). Ahaz hired his own demon barber in allying with Assyria. The next picture is of the few people left (or **who remain,** v. 22, again the same verb as in 1:8–9) who will be reduced to subsistence farming. But they at least will be able to keep themselves alive with abundance of **milk, curds, and honey** (vv. 21–22). The fourth and final picture of calamity describes the best vineyards and hill terraces given over to **briers and thorns,** to wild animals, and to casual grazing (cf. 5:1–7). As in chapter 5, the sequence closes with deepest gloom such as might drive the people to turn. There is no gleam of hope for the sake of survivors, as we saw in chapters 1; 2–4, and 6.

8:1–10 / Chapter 8 begins with a further series of warnings. Their context is the same, and themes and structure from chapter 7 recur. Once again:

A commission from Yahweh (7:3; 8:1) is executed and then followed up by a word from Yahweh (7:10; 8:5).

Isaiah embodies Yahweh's message in the name of a son (8:1, 3) that expresses Yahweh's intention, to drive people to reflect on what Yahweh is doing.

A promise of deliverance, even when fulfilled, will be good news only if it meets the response of trust.

The son's name signifies that Assyria will defeat the allies before he is a year or two old.

The king of Assyria is twice mentioned as Yahweh's agent (7:17, 20; 8:4, 7).

Yahweh warns of the disaster that will issue from failing to trust.

The warning is qualified by hints of hope beyond disaster.

God [is] **with us** recurs (8:8, 10).

As happens with poetic parallelism, the second unit (ch. 8) goes beyond the first (ch. 7).

Isaiah speaks rather than being spoken of.

It involves two signs (8:18, referring to 8:1–2 and 3–4) rather than one offered and one imposed (7:11, 14).

To naming is added putting into writing, which puts Yahweh's intention into effect and attracts attention by the use of a **large scroll** (8:1).

Witnessing is also added (v. 2), so that people who refuse to believe cannot evade the fact that Yahweh and Isaiah said what they did at this moment, particularly given the high-powered nature of the witnesses (2 Kgs. 16:10–16; 18:2).

The signs are presented to the whole people, not just the king.

To a birth that leads to a phrase that comes into being before an actual birth.

To the promise regarding conceiving and bearing a son is added the actual event of conceiving and bearing a son.

To an unnamed mother is added a mother who is herself a prophet, presumably a member of the temple staff like the later prophet Huldah.

The child's name speaks unambiguously of coming defeat, taking up the sarcastic challenge of 5:19 as the words **quick/swift** (NIV mg.) are related to **hurry/hasten** there.

To language that might have implied calamity in a decade's time or so (7:16) is added language establishing that calamity will come sooner (8:4).

The literal precious water supply in 7:3 becomes a two-edged symbol of destruction in 8:6–8 (**Shiloah** was the channel that carried the water from the spring along the side of the city).

The people's refusal (8:5; cf. 5:24: Yahweh's word, not least the prophetic word of promise and challenge) is explicit rather than only hinted at alongside the king's (7:2, 14, 17).

They have moved seamlessly from shaking over the allies to re-joicing (over their downfall, expected to issue from Ahaz's ap-proach to the Assyrians?).

Small-scale survival beyond disaster with a close that reverts to devastating calamity (7:21–25) is followed by the unexpected shattering of foes instead of their victory, and the ringing declara-tion **God is with us** (8:9–10).

Talk of two allies and two superpowers (7:18) gives way to an ap-peal to nations in general (8:9; cf. 5:26–30).

The nations' plans as well as the allies' plans **will not stand** (8:10, the same expression as 7:7). The nations' **strategy/plan** in opposi-tion to Yahweh and Israel (cf. Ps. 2; 48) will fail, because it conflicts with Yahweh's. **Strategy** is **plan** in 5:19, **plan** is **word** in 2:3.

Additional Notes §5

7:6 / We do not know who **the son of Tabeel** was, though it is striking that there was a contemporary king of Tyre called Tubail, so this might imply that the plan involved the imposition of a Tyrian king (Irvine, *Isaiah*, pp. 154–55).

7:8 / **Within sixty-five years:** this is the event referred to in Ezra 4:2, 10.

7:14 / **The virgin:** NIV usually renders *'almah* **young woman,** which fits the contexts and its meaning in related languages (see BDB); *betulah* is the word NIV renders **virgin** (e.g., 37:22). "Young woman" also fits here (see NRSV). The precise difference in meaning between the two Hb. words is uncertain. If the word means "young woman" it would probably imply someone who was not yet married, but it might refer to Isaiah's own wife's having another baby. The other children mentioned in chs. 7–8 are theirs. Or it might refer to the king's own wife. The child can hardly be the heir to the Davidic promises and calling, Hezekiah, who was apparently born some years before, but it might be some other royal child whose birth will again prove to the house of David that **God** [is] **with us** (see 9:1–7). Understood to mean **virgin,** these words will eventually turn out to be much more telling in another connection than Isaiah dreamed. This application of the prophecy to Jesus as one born without a human father compares with other reapplications in Matt. 1–2. These do not depend on a link with the actual meaning of the passages in question. They are inspired *re*applications of the inspired words. This particular reapplication may have been encouraged by the fact that the Greek translation of the OT, which Matthew likely knew, translated *'almah* by Greek *parthenos,* which means "virgin."

7:15 / **Curds** (or butter or cream) **and honey** are simple but good, even self-indulgent, food (v. 22). **When he knows enough to reject the wrong and choose the right** suggests "when he grows up." Fulfillment would then be the fall of Ephraim in 721 B.C. But *ra'* and *tob* mean "bad" and "good," even "nasty" and "nice," and suggest the much earlier moment when a child has opinions about food, which fits better.

8:1 / The name **Maher-Shalal-Hash-Baz** lacks prepositions, hence NRSV "The spoil speeds, the prey hastens."

8:6 / **Rejoices over:** NRSV "melt in fear before" understands *meśos* as an alternative for *mesos* (see 10:18, waste away). The difference would have been difficult to discern aurally and might have made the audience think about the dual implications.

8:8 / Whoever **Immanuel** is, how can he be addressed here? More likely "God [is] with us" is a statement, as at the end of 8:10; the two occurrences form a bracket round vv. 8–10.

§6 Isaiah's Significance, and the Fall of Darkness (Isa. 8:11–9:7)

We come to the close of the material that focuses on the crisis presented by the pressure of the northern allies (6:1–9:7). Isaiah speaks further about his ministry and its significance for Judah (8:11–22) and Yahweh offers a vision of light dawning the other side of the coming darkness (9:1–7).

8:11–15 / After the twin passages 7:1–25 and 8:1–10 comes a passage twinning with 6:1–13. Isaiah again tells us of Yahweh's word to him personally and here describes the traps set before him and the people. In 6:1–13 Yahweh overwhelmed him visually. Here Yahweh overwhelms him physically and verbally. Isaiah stands between deity and people, called to represent each to the other. Being identified with the people could mean being wrongly influenced by them (cf. 6:5). They are too concerned about the allies' **conspiracy,** or too inclined to make a treaty with them or with Assyria out of fear. What needs to be feared and dreaded instead is the disaster Yahweh is bringing and the awesomeness of Yahweh's own person (7:25; 2:19, 21). People need to recognize Almighty Yahweh's awesome holiness and thus find Yahweh as a holy place (and thus a sanctuary/refuge?). Judah does not know where to direct its fear (7:4). Thus the likelihood is that Yahweh will become their downfall.

8:16–18 / Isaiah has put his esteem on the line in the names of his children which make them **signs and symbols from the LORD.** Isaiah does what he calls Judah to do, living by commitment to what he says will happen, by trust in Yahweh. He speaks as if he is convinced that he will never meet with a response from Judah—of course this may be designed to provoke a response (see on 6:9–10). He adds to his self-commitment by arranging secure sealing of his **testimony** or teaching (NIV **law**) against the time when Yahweh acts and it is proved true. This may denote

entrusting the contents of his message to his disciples, or perhaps
actually putting it into writing and literally sealing it. That might
be the beginning of the origin of the book called Isaiah. The exhortations in verses 12–13 are plural; Isaiah's **disciples** (v. 16) are included in them.

8:19–22 / This teaching/**testimony** ought to be the people's
recourse when they want to know how to look to the future. Instead, in their anxiety about the future their recourse is to other
forms of traditional religion (see on 1:29–31). But their last state
will be worse than their first (vv. 20b–22).

9:1–7 / To close 6:1–9:7, **light** replaces **darkness** (v. 2), **joy**
replaces **death** (v. 3), and deliverance replaces oppression (v. 4).
An earlier vision pictured weapons destroyed (2:4); this vision
pictures battle-clothing burnt (v. 5). Both houses of Israel were
bringing trouble on themselves (8:14), but the people of the north
most directly experienced the darkness of Assyria's invasion.
They will share in the renewal that will come to Jerusalem (e.g.,
4:2–6). Indeed, where darkness first fell, there will light dawn.

The vision describes events as if they have already taken
place or at least begun (including the whole of v. 6, despite NIV). It
resembles a song of thanksgiving for what Yahweh has already
done (cf. Isa. 12), until the promise in verse 7b makes explicit that
in real time the whole lies in the future. Its reference to Yahweh's
zeal further illustrates the importance of Yahweh's passion to Israel's reaching its destiny (see on 5:25–30). The birth of another
son, explicitly David's rather than Isaiah's, is the key to the move
from death to life. The words in verse 6a are the words used to announce a child's birth (cf. Jer. 20:15; Ruth 4:17). Does this imply
two or three decades' delay while this child grows up? Verses 6–7
resemble promises to a king at his accession, and promises to his
people, to whom such words are indeed good news. Perhaps,
then, this son's "birth" is his accession, when God makes him a
son (Ps. 2:7).

In one sense the promises simply picture what any king
should be, an executor of **justice and righteousness** (see on 1:21)
and a bringer of **peace** (see on v. 6b below), one who will bring a
fulfillment of the vision underlying chapters 1–8 as a whole. Yet
that also means that the promises go far beyond anything that any
king ever achieved, or even sought. They are "messianic." The
basis for conviction that the vision will be fulfilled lies in the son's
name (v. 6b). Hebrew names of the kind that we have already met

in Isaiah, such as Isaiah, Uzziah, Hezekiah, Shear-Jashub, Maher-Shalal-Hash-Baz, and Uriah generally have significant meanings. In all these cases, and most others, their significance does not lie in describing the person to whom the name belongs, but rather in something else to which they point. We have reckoned that this is also so with Immanuel ("God is with us"). It would thus be quite natural for this fourfold name in verse 6, too, to be a statement about God—and not a statement about this son. And this fits the meaning of the name.

Wonderful Counselor (lit. "wonder-planner," i.e., "wonder-working planner") immediately recalls Isaiah's emphasis on Yahweh as one who effectively designs and implements a purpose (see on 5:19b, 26). It more specifically anticipates the description of Yahweh as wonderful in counsel (28:29; see also 25:1; 29:14). **Mighty God** recurs as a description of Yahweh in 10:21, but we have already seen the word for God (*'el*) in the name Immanuel, while 42:13 uses the word for mighty in describing Yahweh going out to battle like a champion. **Everlasting Father** recalls the book's opening description of God as one who brought up children and had to watch them run away. In this son's name it would also more pointedly recall Yahweh's commitment to David's line as father . . . for ever (Ps. 89:26, 29—the same words as here).

In the phrase **Prince of Peace**, the first word suggests an army commander (cf. Gen. 21:22; describing God, Dan. 8:11, 25). It thus links well with Mighty, and with Isaiah's emphasis on Israel's God being "Yahweh Armies," as well as confronting by anticipation the boast of Assyria in 10:8. Unlike that of the Assyrians, this commander's warmaking is destined to bring *shalom*. That suggests both an end to warmaking (cf. v. 5) and the broader well-being in all aspects of life suggested by the word—growth, blessing, joy, and fairness (see vv. 3, 7).

The son's name asserts that these four phrases indeed express key truths about Yahweh, who is committed to working with him and through him so that his reign will bring peace and justice (v. 7). The book gives no indication who this son is. It gives no hint about a fulfillment in some contemporary figure. We may call it a messianic vision, but we need to remember that the OT does not use the word messiah for a future redeemer, nor does the promise give the impression of a figure not due to come for centuries. While the beginning of Jesus' ministry recalls verses 1–2 (Matt. 4:13–16), the NT does not refer verses 6–7 to Jesus, and a

reign of *shalom* and justice does not seem yet to have been implemented in the world—any more than it was in the time of Isaiah.
      Christians will see what God did in Jesus as guaranteeing
the vision's fulfillment. In Jesus we see the evidence that the
Mighty God really will bring to effect a wonderful purpose and
that the Everlasting Father will act effectively as a commander, for
the sake of people's spiritual and physical well-being. But this is a
judgment and a statement of hope based on what we know of
Jesus rather than an exegetical judgment about the meaning of
this passage. The passage is a vision of what God is committed to
achieving through David's line. It receives partial fulfillments in
the achievements of kings such as Hezekiah and Josiah, and
then a fulfillment in Jesus that is potentially final even if its potential remains unrealized. It thus still indicates the agenda to which
God has made a commitment and gives human beings grounds
for hope.

Additional Notes §6

      8:12 / **Conspiracy:** this refers perhaps to the allies' rebellion
against Assyria, or perhaps to a conspiracy in Jerusalem (to collaborate
with the plan in 7:6b?).

      9:1 / **Zebulun and Napthali** occupied the Galilean mountains,
north of the plain of Jezreel and west of Lake Galilee. The **way of the sea**
suggests the area further west, on the Mediterranean. **Along** (or "beyond") **the Jordan** suggests the area further east, north of and/or beyond
Lake Galilee. **Galilee of the Gentiles** may be explained by 2 Kgs. 15:29, in
the period that 6:1–9:7 addresses (see also 1 Kgs. 9:11).

      9:4 / **The day of Midian's defeat:** see Judg. 6–8.

      9:6 / It is usually assumed that the name in v. 6b comprises a
series of asyndetic phrases (so NIV) and describes the person named. The
son then *is* the **Wonderful Counselor.** Christian claims that Jesus fulfills
the vision of v. 6b can do justice to the designation **Mighty God,** but the
difficulty comes with **Everlasting Father,** which hardly applies to Jesus.
Conversely, a reading in the light of eighth-century B.C. Middle Eastern
thinking can perhaps do justice to **Everlasting Father** as an extravagant
OT description of a king's relationship with his people, but **Mighty God** is
unparalleled in the OT in such designations. Wildberger (*Isaiah 1–12,*
p. 405) suggests it is based on Egyptian ways of speaking of the king, but
even these hardly parallel such an extravagant description. It is difficult
to know what the original hearers would have made of the words if this

is how Isaiah meant them. It is significant that the Jewish exegetical tradition assumed that at least the first three phrases referred to God, though it took them as describing God as namer rather than as part of the name.

The Hb. of the first two phrases reads literally "Wonder planner, God warrior." NIV **wonderful counselor** apparently takes the first phrase to mean "wonder of a planner." If that is a natural rendering of the first phrase, the natural way for the prophet to expect people to understand the second is to take it to suggest "God of a warrior," "God-like warrior" (rather than "warrior-like God," presupposed by NIV). The plural of the phrase rendered **Mighty God** indeed appears in Ezek. 32:21 to mean "mighty leaders." In isolation, the four terms would then be quite intelligible as descriptions of a hoped-for king.

But the recurrence of the phrase rendered "Mighty God" (*'el gibbor*) in 10:21 with definite reference to Yahweh makes it harder to accept that here the phrase means "God-like warrior" or that it refers to the promised king. Indeed, to say that someone is a "wonder of a planner" is to call him God-like (see on 5:8–24), and Wildberger (*Isaiah 1–12*, p. 403) argues strongly that the phrase must mean "Wonder-planner." The basis for translating the second phrase "God-like warrior" then disappears. Even Father, let alone Everlasting Father, is not otherwise instanced as a title for a king.

There is a further point. Other names such as Isaiah, Shear-Jashub, and Immanuel comprise statements rather than merely strings of epithets. They mean "Yahweh [is] salvation," "A remnant will return," "God [is] with us." It is natural also to assume that the designation of Yahweh in v. 6b is one or two statements. How to construe the statements is then open to discussion, as is the case with Maher-shalal-hash-baz (see Additional Note on 8:1). As the middle two phrases are the ones that apply most distinctively to God, we might take the four as a characteristic prophetic chiasm: "A Wonderful Counselor is the Mighty God; the Everlasting Father is a Prince of Peace."

§7 Yahweh's Unsated Anger with Israel
(Isa. 9:8–10:4)

After 6:1–9:7 comes to an end, 9:8–10:4 pairs with the preceding section, chapter 5. The section as a whole takes further the earlier talk of Yahweh's raised hand (5:25–30). The six woes (5:8–24) also come to a conclusion in 10:1–4. The fact that speaks of disaster for northern Israel might suggest that it is the background for the disaster for northern Israel presupposed by 9:1, but this material also confronts Isaiah's own audience in Judah with the prospect of their invasion by Assyria.

As Yahweh's anger still burns and Yahweh's hand is still raised, "past" and "future" verbs interweave throughout the rest of chapter 9, as they do in 5:25–30. This juxtaposition of tenses suggests events that have begun, at least within Yahweh's purpose, if they have not yet reached full fruition. This would fit with other indications of a date between the allies' failed revolt against Assyria and Samaria's fall in 721 B.C. Three warnings of Yahweh's anger portray external national disaster, internal political collapse, and social anarchy within the community and between the "two households" of Israel (see J. A. Motyer, *The Prophecy of Isaiah: An Introduction and Commentary* [Downers Grove, Ill.: InterVarsity, 1993], p. 106). No matter how terrible the events narrated, the even more terrible refrain is that Yahweh's anger is still not sated.

9:8–12 / In 5:25–30 the context suggested that Yahweh's hand was raised in anger against Judah. The same might be true here when the object of Yahweh's attack is initially termed **Israel/ Jacob**, but what follows rather identifies **the people** as **Ephraim and the inhabitants of Samaria**. Once more Judah overhears Yahweh speaking of someone else, but the message is meant for Judah itself. Again Judah is advised not to tie its future to Ephraim. Ephraim shares Judah's **pride** (v. 9; 2:12), which is confronted by Yahweh's majesty (2:10, 19, 21: related words each time). Its people are tough-minded (NIV **arrogance of heart**) rather than soft-minded (v. 9; 7:2, 4). A reversal has strengthened rather than destroyed their determination.

Yahweh has fired a devastating missile, and they are vulnerable to it (v. 8). When Yahweh speaks (**message** is lit. "word"), that sets a process under way (see 55:10–11). Eventually people will have to acknowledge it (v. 9a), as they did not in 1:3. They will have to acknowledge what Yahweh has put down (v. 10), though their words pointedly avoid acknowledging that it was Yahweh who was responsible for the falling/felling. They will have to acknowledge what Yahweh has raised (the more literal meaning of **strengthened** in v. 11: see on 2:11). Aram is in danger from Assyria (v. 11) and is also a danger to Israel (v. 12). Philistia has been a danger, too, even if it is not a present threat. But like Aram it is also well-enough known as a threat from the past to make a mention here rhetorically effective. Verses 11–12 thus illustrate the way in which international politics involves dog eating dog, the same people being at one moment aggressor, at another victim. And the talk of Yahweh's anger not being sated (v. 12b) implicitly invites Judah to wonder whether it will be sated until it engulfs Judah as well as bringing Ephraim down (J. F. A. Sawyer, *Isaiah* [2 vols.; The Daily Study Bible Series; Philadelphia: Westminster, 1984], vol. 1, pp. 102–4).

9:13–17 / Presumably the **people** continues to refer to Ephraim. Once more its failures and its danger parallel those of Judah (e.g., 6:10 turn, 5:25 strikes, 8:19 inquire of, 1:5–6; 7:20 head to foot, and so on), including the fact that ordinary people are implicated as much as the leadership (cf. 5:13–14). All that also means that this critique, too, cannot leave Judah merely feeling superior and secure. Indeed, the people's unnamed-ness could enable Judah to see itself in this portrait of Ephraim, and to make the appropriate response (v. 13).

9:18–21 / This third indictment powerfully states the OT conviction that right and wrong bring their own results by an immanent process. This declaration sits alongside the repeated strong statement of Yahweh's personal involvement in bringing disaster to the wicked. There are thus two ways of viewing the same processes. To put it one way, **wickedness** sets the world on fire. To put it the other way, Yahweh's **wrath** sets the world on fire, passionate in its **anger** and active in the exercise of Yahweh's powerful **hand**. By implication, both models of understanding causation in the world are necessary to grasp how things happen.

Events are both logical and "natural" and also personal and felt (see further on 24:5–6). Verses 19b–21 implicitly add another model, for they speak of human activity in a way that presupposes that we retain responsibility for our acts. Our acts reflect inbuilt and divinely-willed processes, but those do not make us mere victims of personal or impersonal forces outside ourselves. Verse 21 finally declares grim further implications of all this for Judah itself; the two great northern tribes (named after two sons of Joseph) do not stop at devouring each other. For the internal political chaos that engulfed Ephraim in its last decades, see 2 Kings 15.

10:1–4 / A final reminder of Yahweh's undiverted anger and still-upraised hand concludes 9:8–10:4, but verses 1–4a themselves take the form of a "woe" resembling the ones in 5:8–24. The pattern in 9:8–10:4 corresponds to the one in chapter 5, where the first of the refrains about Yahweh's upraised hand (5:25) served to link those first six woes with the first announcement of Yahweh's angry summoning of the nations (5:26–30). In the present context, this **Woe** for people who make the legal system work in a way that favors the "haves" rather than the "have-nots" again works as an indictment of Ephraim as well as of Judah (see on 1:15b–23), at least initially. One need not assume that people in power consciously ran the legal system for their own benefit; people in power do not usually admit that—even to themselves.

The day of reckoning (v. 3) is the day when Yahweh "visits" people or comes to inspect them, an uncomfortable visit like those of the mafia or of a tough inspection team ("punish" in v. 12 is the related verb). The Hebrew word for **disaster** is *sho'ah*, the word for total desolation that modern Judaism took as its term for the Nazi attempt to annihilate the Jewish people. The related verb, "[lie] ruined," occurs twice in 6:11; this warning repeats that one. And it is addressed to **you**, implying that Isaiah has moved seamlessly from speaking to Judah indirectly to doing so directly, as also happens at the end of 5:1–7. The refrain in verse 4b therefore has new force, for it explicitly confronts Judah, not just Ephraim (Sawyer, *Isaiah*, vol. 1, pp. 106–7).

Riches (v. 3b) is the word "glory," the outward splendor that reveals inner worth—at least in theory. Here the word takes a place in a suggestive sequence. Real splendor belongs to Yahweh alone and can sometimes be seen as such (6:3), but Judah has attempted to defy that splendor (3:8). Yahweh has promised Judah its own splendor (4:2; 11:10; and note 17:3) and the protection of it (4:5). But in the meantime it will lose that which belongs to itself, or at least to its leadership (those of high rank, 5:13; cf. 17:4; 22:18). Judah will be the victim of the splendor possessed by Assyria (8:7). Assyria will, of course, lose that in due course (10:16, 18; cf. 16:14; 21:16), or will retain it only in paradoxical and useless form (14:18—NIV "lie in state").

Additional Notes §7

9:8–21 / Some of the verbs translated as future in NIV are actually past tense in vv. 14 **(will cut off)**, 19 **(will be scorched, will be fuel)**, and 20 **(will devour, be hungry, will eat, not be satisfied)**.

9:10 / Ordinary houses were built of mud-**brick**, their framework and roofs utilizing beams of a commonplace wood such as that of the **fig tree**. Impressive houses were built of hewn **stone** and **cedar**. See e.g., Gen. 11:3; 1 Kgs.10:27; Jer. 22:14; Song 1:17.

9:15 / **The prophets:** interestingly, Isaiah gives no indication that he sees himself as a prophet or approves of prophets, though he is designated by this word in chs. 37–39. Like Micah, he uses the word pejoratively in 28:7; 29:10; more neutrally in 3:2. He does refer to his wife as **prophetess** (8:3), which might indicate that for him **prophets** and **prophetesses** were temple ministers, with the temptations that come from identification with the religious institution—the reason for his ambivalence about them. If so, it was later that the word "prophets" came to refer more generally to people who spoke in God's name, whether they were temple ministers or not.

§8 The Felling of Assyria and the Growth of a Branch (Isa. 10:5–11:16)

As 7:1–8:10 comprised two parallel sequences, so does 10:5–11:16. The immediately preceding section has come to a worrying end, but there now follows an unexpectedly encouraging reversal. Yahweh has been using Assyria to punish Judah, but Assyria's own woe, or moment of punishment, is coming—as is Judah's moment of restoration, the restoring of a remnant.

We have been told that Yahweh's anger is still unsated, but then we discover that it is being redirected. Yahweh's horror and offendedness now apply to Assyria (10:5–15). Assyria is now the forest of trees to be destroyed (10:16–19). Judah's remnant will find its way back to Yahweh, though this promise leaves us in some uncertainty because of the way it ends (10:20–23).

The section 10:24–11:16 then parallels 10:5–23. Again the audience is encouraged that Yahweh has finished using Assyria to punish Judah (10:24–27), again a triumphant Assyrian advance will turn into the felling of its forest (10:28–34), and again Israel's contrasting stump/remnant will grow (11:1–16). Once more, this second sequence takes matters further. The description of Assyria's fall is vivid but brief, while 11:1–16 much more than makes up for the strangely half-hearted account of the remnant's transformation in 10:20–23 which brought 10:5–23 to semi-closure.

10:5–15 / So yet another woe follows, but at last this one comes as genuine relief to Isaiah's audience. There is no sting in its tail. Instead of a familiar form of speech being turned against the audience, it is being turned the other way—or turned back to its earlier significance. A declaration of judgment on Judah's enemies is exactly that. Once again a woe expresses Yahweh's intention to "visit" someone (see on v. 3), out of distaste for their tough-mindedness (see on 9:9) and exalted impressiveness of look (see 2:11, 17; 3:18). But the recipient of this visit is Assyria, not Judah (v. 12). Assyria was the one through whom Yahweh expressed that snorting wrath (v. 4: see on 5:25). Assyria's was the hand that Yahweh sent to wield the truncheon or club against the twin peoples with whom Yahweh was so angry because of their godless impiety, their disregard of God, their failure to revere Yahweh as holy (8:13).

In that strength of feeling Yahweh is quite happy for the Assyrians to loot and pillage, without at first seeming to worry too much about atrocities, war crimes, or the ethics of just war, in the manner of Amos 1–2 (v. 6: the language recalls 5:5, Assyria being the means of that trampling). Then comes the critique that retrospectively establishes the irony in Yahweh's using a godless, anger-provoking agent to bring trouble to godless, anger-provoking Judah (Oswalt, *Isaiah 1–39*, p. 263). It draws attention to the way in which being used by God is never an index of closeness to God (see Matt. 7:22–23). It also draws out the implication that the purpose of the rod is to save the child, not kill it (Prov. 23:13–14; Sawyer, *Isaiah*, vol. 1, p. 109).

> Assyria indulges in war because of its own warlike spirit, its love of killing and destruction, and its appetite to construct an empire out of lands formerly occupied by independent peoples, in the manner of European powers creating their empires or of settlers in America (v. 7).
>
> It is proud of its own military might and confident of its ability to conquer anyone (vv. 8–9).
>
> It is unwilling to recognize that the two houses of Israel have a special significance, and ironically assimilates their religion to its own (cf. 37:10–13). On the other hand, it is to be noted that (as in Amos 1–2) disaster does not come to the foreign power merely because of its ill-treatment of Yahweh's people (vv. 10–11).
>
> It assumes that its achievements stem from its own strength and wisdom rather than from something God-given, as if human hands, wisdom, and understanding could produce anything that could stand before Yahweh: contrast 3:3, 11; 5:21 (v. 13a).
>
> It behaves as if it is a law unto itself in its control of the destinies of other peoples and in its destructiveness, seeing itself as **like a mighty one**—a spelling variant on the term for God in 1:24 (vv. 13b–14).
>
> It thus has a higher opinion of itself than it has of God (v. 15).

Isaiah's critique of Assyria provides insight on the difficulty modern Christians feel about Israel's own warmaking. The acts for which Assyria is faulted are the acts of Joshua's people. The verbs in verse 7b are the verbs used of Israel's acts in Deuteronomy and

Joshua. On its own account, there Israel acts as executor of Yahweh's anger at the behavior of Canaanite peoples. The execution of Yahweh's anger in punishing the wicked is also a theme in the NT. The only difference there is that God no longer uses a human agent. But in the OT the human agent is called to act as divine executor, not to act because the agent personally wants to destroy and kill. This does not resolve the difficulty of the fact that violence seems invariably to beget violence, even when its vision is to terminate it, and even when the violence is Yahweh's (52:13–53:12 will take that issue as far as it can be taken). But this distinction does take the edge off one aspect of the difficulty (which is also a difficulty in parts of the NT).

The comparison above with Joshua suggests another insight. Yahweh's purpose is worked out through Assyria, but Isaiah does not say that this conviction can be generalized, any more than can Joshua's statements about Israel's occupation of Canaan. We cannot infer that all conquering nations are acting as Yahweh's agents. Yahweh is indeed sovereign in the history of nations such as Aram as well as Israel (Amos 9:7), yet Yahweh's involvement with Assyria in connection with Israel's destiny has a unique significance. In this sense, what Yahweh says about Assyria cannot be assumed to apply to other nations. Assyria has the misfortune as well as the good fortune to be Yahweh's instrument in working out Israel's destiny. That makes it open to special scrutiny.

10:16–19 / Therefore being Yahweh's agent will not be the last word in Assyria's relationship with Yahweh, and Yahweh will not be satisfied to use an agent that itself shares all the faults of those to whom it brings disaster, and more. Like Amos, again, Isaiah assumes that even a power that does not have Yahweh's special word to Israel knows right and wrong; and compare Romans 2 (Wildberger, *Isaiah 1–12*, p. 425). As in the woes against Judah, the woe against Assyria leads into a thudding prophetic **therefore** introducing the declaration that action will be taken by **the Lord, the LORD Almighty** (that description again: see on 1:24, where it paralleled "the Mighty One"). The **light** that is a great blessing realizes its capacity to become a curse. God as light can become God as devouring flame. The motifs of trees and fire thus reappear. The Assyrian forest is consumed. The symbol of calamity for Judah becomes the symbol of calamity for Assyria, with the thoroughness of which Judah has been warned (with v. 19 cf. 6:11–13). A more down-to-earth version comes in 37:36.

10:20–23 / So Assyria is reduced to a remnant, in the most negative of senses, with no suggestion of potential for new growth ("remaining trees" in v. 19 was literally "remnant of trees"). But the downfall of Assyria is not enough. If Yahweh is to have succeeded as Wonder-working Planner, that also requires the raising of Israel. Something must happen to Israel's remnant. For a moment this raising is expressed only in somewhat half-hearted form (v. 20). The actual focus remains on Assyria. Perhaps the half-heartedness stems from the ease with which the people could indeed revert to a rejoicing in the nations' downfall that had failed to learn the lesson it needed to learn. So Israel is given two sober reminders of its destiny. It is to rely on God (v. 20) and to turn to God (v. 21).

For Israel, Assyria's significance is to have reduced Yahweh's people to a mere remnant. At least that means Israel stops thinking that it will have the support of this people who would actually put it down. So the effect of Assyria's attack is to push Israel back to reliance on Yahweh. It is Assyria's own "strange work," a converse of Yahweh's (see 28:21). Only a remnant is involved, but that remnant will now recognize the folly of relying on human supports who eventually turn against them (v. 20). Israel will then live up to another interpretation of the name Shear-Jashub as it turns to Yahweh, holder of the designation Mighty God (v. 21) which also appeared in that other name in 9:6. If the notion of a remnant surviving had become some sort of comfort instead of being a threat, verses 20–21 take the idea of a remnant returning and do something new with it that prevents it from being a false comfort. Survival is not enough. It is still necessary that people learn the lesson about false and true reliance (see 30:12; 31:1) or standing firm in faith (7:9; 28:16).

Even more strangely, after this prediction there comes another warning of decimation to a remnant (v. 22). If one reads the book of Isaiah in the way that it invites us on the surface, as a message to Ahaz and Hezekiah's day, then this talk that looks beyond the crisis of the day to destruction for Assyria and a turning on the part of Israel could itself encourage false hopes for the prophecies' implied audience. Everything will turn out all right in the end. Verses 20–21 remind the people again of the severity of the calamity that hangs over them. If historically the chapter's composition reflects a later period, perhaps the new decimation of verses 20–21 is a later one. There is a parallel with the unexpected prospect in Ezekiel 38–39 of another final battle after the people have been brought back to life in their land. There is disaster (at the hand of Assyria) and return to Yahweh (e.g., in the time of Hezekiah and Josiah), but beyond that still more disaster (at the hands of Babylon).

10:24–27 / In the two parallel sequences (10:5–23 and 10:24–11:6) these verses correspond to 10:5–10. They extend Yahweh's encouragement and transfer Yahweh's anger. The **therefore** (v. 24) looks illogical, because the encouragement that begins here does not follow from the warning in verses 22–23 but resumes the promises of verses 5–23 as a whole. Once Ahaz as king had been told not to be afraid of the northern allies (7:4); verses 24–25 invite the people as a whole to share that confidence in relation to the great empire. They are again reminded that they are not really "this people" but **my people** and that they **live in Zion,** the place where Yahweh also dwells (8:18), which is therefore a place of safety. The time when Zion is a place of insecurity (v. 12) is over. This and other terms of encouragement thus echo those in verses 5–15, especially their opening. Now, however, Isaiah speaks of Assyria wielding, rather than being, Yahweh's **rod/club** (v. 24). The **anger/wrath** is still Yahweh's, but it is on the move from Judah to Assyria. The fact that this move will happen **very soon** (v. 25) balances the earlier challenge to Yahweh to hasten to punish (5:19) and the talk of hastening to spoil (8:1).

We are not in a position to check whether God fulfilled this promise to act soon. Indeed it is noteworthy that the text gives us no precise clue as to what situation to relate it to. The Bible customarily invites the people of God ever to live in the conviction that Yahweh's intervention may always be imminent. Yahweh will deliver the people as in the time of Gideon and of Moses (vv. 26–27). Both these moments combined disaster to oppressors with deliverance for Yahweh's people (see 9:4; Judg. 7:25).

10:28–34 / At this point, threat becomes fall. With verse 28 comes another sudden transition, to a vivid account of the Assyrian army making a confident march on Jerusalem. It is a dramatic conclusion to the account of its triumphant progress from Carchemish to Samaria (vv. 9–11). As that sequence does not correspond to any particular historical one, so this is an imaginary picture of the Assyrians' closer advance, which actually took place from the south when it happened—unless this describes an incident of which we are not otherwise aware. It is a canny route for an army to take for the last fifteen miles of an attack from the north, avoiding the main road and the cities it would have to confront there. In part it follows a line to the east of the main road along the ridge, via Ai. Near Michmash it involves negotiating a deep wadi (NIV **pass;** see 1 Sam. 14) and therefore leaving the baggage there (Oswalt, *Isaiah 1–39*, pp. 274–75). Halfway down this route the army camps at Geba, seven miles northeast of Jerusalem, and the next day it is in a position to look down at the city (see on 2:2–5) as it reaches the brow of the hill near modern Mount Scopus.

At this point of high drama, suddenly everything is turned upside down. The arrogance of verse 32 is too much. It provokes a response. Once again Yahweh will suddenly cut down Assyria like an impressive forest (see vv. 16–19). The description of God as **the Lord, the LORD Almighty** recurs from verse 24, thereby constituting a bracket around verses 24–34 emphasizing Yahweh's powerful sovereignty. It is the description that needs to be true if Yahweh is to prove mightier than Assyria. The cutting down to size that threatened Judah and that Judah actually experienced is transferred to the woodcutter (cf. the wording in e.g., 2:11–13; 5:15). The more literal account comes in 37:36.

11:1–9 / Chapter 11 brings together two themes from earlier chapters—the felled tree that might be capable of new growth (especially 4:2; 6:11–13), and the unsatisfactory king with the promise of one who will better live up to the Davidic vision (7:1–17; 9:1–7). In Ephraim it was customary to change the dynasty every few years, like a modern democracy ever changing governments in the strange hope that we will eventually find a good one. It would be surprising if no one in Judah campaigned for a new dynasty there. Unfortunately for such people, Yahweh's promises to David parallel those to Israel, and are thus as irrevocable. Instead, then, the felling and renewing of the people is focused into the felling and renewing of the Davidic monarchy. The latter becomes a means to the former. **Shoot, stump,** and **branch** are rare words that occur only here in this connection (the words are different in 4:2; 6:11–13). The passage is thus not merely recycling a familiar image but developing directly from earlier talk of the felling of trees. Here, for the first time, the implication is that the Davidic tree has been cut down. But it grew from mere **Jesse** in the first place, so there is no reason why it should not do so again. The idea of going behind David to his roots in Jesse to fulfill the promise even points to the possibility of a critique of David himself, whose weaknesses are exposed in Samuel-Kings.

It turns out that this development in imagery is a transitional one. While the implications of this promise could have been worked out in terms of the image of the fruitfulness of a tree, verses 2–3a describe the promise according to a different framework, centering on the image of spirit. When Yahweh's spirit rests on the branch, it bears fruit in the form of capacities to which human beings (including monarchs) generally only pretend. That was true of Assyria's **wisdom** and **understanding** (10:13). It was true earlier of the nations' **counsel** (8:10) and of Judah's **power** (see 3:25; the word lies behind the reference to "warriors" there). The words counsel and power also evoke the attributes of the Counselor and Mighty God of 9:6. It was true of Judah's lack of **knowledge** (5:13) and its misdirected **fear** (7:4; 8:12–13; 10:24). All these attributes have been referred to as belonging to God and/or as mis-claimed by human beings. Now they become real in a human figure. The doubling of the reference to the fear of (reverence or awe before) Yahweh corresponds to that extra stress earlier on misdirected fear (8:12–15). It also emphasizes that this is the feature that explicitly distinguishes true wisdom from wisdom that leaves God out of account (see Prov. 1:7).

The OT Wisdom books do not speak in terms of Yahweh's spirit. The spirit of Yahweh appears in the OT in connection with powerful manifestations of Yahweh on prophets, on the leaders in Judges, and on the first kings. The return to that provision here thus suggests a link with the origin of the monarchy (see v. 1). It was of the essence of this coming of Yahweh's spirit that it was tumultuous and unpredictable, as was the case with Saul. The notion that Yahweh's spirit might **rest** on someone is therefore almost an oxymoron. This idea of resting features in the story of the prophets in Numbers 11:25–26 and suggests a mixing of metaphors designed to make a large theological claim. The supernatural presence of God's gifting might not *have* to be tumultuous and spasmodic. It could be steady and continuous. It is such a gifting that the community needs from its Davidic branch, as it does of any king. The story of Solomon in particular also shows that. Yahweh promises the community such a gifting for this branch, fulfilling Proverbs' own vision of wisdom resting in the minds of people who are understanding (14:33; the same words as here). The branch will be permanently clothed in the kind of wisdom that lives in the world aware that it is God's world.

It is also in keeping with the vision of Proverbs that this wisdom issues in the giving of fair judgment, which corresponds to a judgment that takes the side of the weak and resourceless (vv. 3b–5). Almost every word in these verses takes up phraseology from previous chapters. The branch will put right the failure of the community and its leadership that has been berated in these chapters. The branch will reflect Yahweh's own concerns pictured in these chapters and will take up Assyria's active prosecution of Yahweh's will in punishing wickedness. It will share Assyria's relentless strength but combine it not only with the familiar **righteousness,** but also with **faithfulness.** It is the first occurrence of this noun, which is related to the stress on standing firm in faithfulness in 7:9. Like a uniform, the clothing (v. 5) thus mirrors the person.

The imagery changes again with verses 6–8, though verse 9 then offers its explanation. Context suggests that the talk of harmony in the animal world is a metaphor for harmony in the human world. The strong and powerful live together with the weak and powerless because the latter can believe that the former are no longer seeking to devour them. The end to which verses 6–9 lead thus belongs in the same world of thought as verses 1–5 and fits with other themes from earlier chapters (e.g., 2:2–4). Indeed, the book opened by using animals to stand for human beings (1:3)—also in connection with the question of knowledge, as here.

11:10–16 / Another reference to **the Root of Jesse** facilitates a further transition to a different agenda, namely the restoring of the remnant of Yahweh's people to its land. As Yahweh raised a banner to summon the nations to punish (5:26), so now the Davidic shoot draws the remnant back, standing as a banner to summon the nations to help their victims go home. They will **rally to him** or "seek" him. The promise is ironic, for "seeking" was Judah's problem on the way to its being reduced to a remnant (8:19; 9:13). They will be drawn to the branch as they will be drawn to Zion (2:2–4), and he will have glory for the nations to recognize (cf. 4:2).

After this transition, the theme of the restoration of the remnant is pursued without continuing reference to the Davidic shoot. The passage presupposes a scattering of Israel to the north and east in Mesopotamia and to the south in Egypt and beyond, such as came to Ephraim in 721 B.C. and to Judah later. So widely spread is this remnant that it can be spoken of as extending across **the four quarters of the earth.** It is easy to focus on Babylon as if it was *the* locus of *the* exile. Judah was widely dispersed. The first reaching out (v. 11) was presumably that at the exodus (cf. 10:24, 26; 11:15–16). The second reaching out is then a "second exodus." There has not been one particular moment when all the people of Israel have been brought back to Palestine from the four corners of the world, as is evidenced by the fact that most of the Jewish people do not live there. But the fall of Babylon, Assyria's imperial successors, freed them to return, and subsequent periods of freedom and flourishing in the land have witnessed to God's faithfulness to this promise.

The parallelism of **Israel** and **Judah** (v. 12) suggests that "Israel" refers to Ephraim and that this vision looks for Ephraim's restoration as well as Judah's. In due course Chronicles, Ezra, and Nehemiah draw attention to the presence of people from the north in the Second Temple community, which 1:1 suggested was the reference of Isaiah's prophecies. This interest in both houses, parallel to that in Ezekiel 37, continues in verses 13–14. With daring, the vision looks for harmony between Ephraim and Judah, for a time when hostility and jealousy are at an end. This is a further expression of the dream in verses 6–9. This harmony does not extend to other nations (v. 14), though the concern there is with security and/or with the fulfillment of God's promises regarding the promised land.

When peoples migrate or are transported to other countries, they rarely return. Verses 15–16 recognize that only a miracle will bring the remnant back from Mesopotamia and Egypt, and promise a miracle like that which originally brought Israel from Egypt. The Euphrates is only another river, capable of being turned into a series of dry wadis. The promise of a **highway** constitutes a first statement of a theme that will become vital in this book (19:23; 40:3; 62:10).

Additional Notes §8

10:6 / **Send/dispatch** (lit. "command"): originally Yahweh sends a word (9:8; 55:11), often via a prophet (6:8; 48:16; 61:1), and sends Israel as aide (42:19) and Israelites as proclaimers (66:19). Yahweh can send saviors/deliverers from other peoples (19:20), including by implication Cyrus the Persian (13:3; 43:14). Or the word can be implemented by the exercise of authority over the hosts of heaven (45:12), over weather (5:6), and over disease (10:16). In the OT way of speaking, "it is not necessary to know oneself commanded in order to be commanded" (Oswalt, *Isaiah 1–39*, on v. 7, p. 263).

10:9 / Apart from Samaria, all the cities named are in Aram; all fell to Assyria between 738 and 717 B.C. But they are named from north to south, so that the words picture the Assyrians advancing steadily toward the gates of Jerusalem itself.

10:16–19 / The specific promise of Assyria's downfall was fulfilled only in the next century, when Nineveh fell to the Babylonians in 612 B.C. The emphasis on this promise has stimulated the proposal that it belongs to a strand of material inspired by Isaiah that was produced in the time of Josiah, who brought about religious reform in Judah and Israel (see Clements, *Isaiah 1–39*, p. 113).

10:20 / **Truly** is "in *'emeth*," a word for trustworthiness related to the verb "stand firm in faith" in 7:9.

10:24 / NIV's lack of a heading here after providing one at v. 20 and at 11:1 could mislead the reader. The headings draw attention to themes that are important to Christians rather than drawing attention to the way the sections of the book work.

10:26–27 / **As he did in Egypt:** in Exod. 14:16 it is actually Moses who is commanded to lift his staff. Literally the text here reads "in the way of Egypt" and does not say who lifted the staff then. Perhaps Yahweh's now lifting the staff illustrates the heightening that is often a feature when Yahweh acts again as in the past. It is a feature of typology. For that matter, Judges says nothing of Yahweh whipping Midian, though it is Yahweh who causes the Midianites to slaughter each other. The language of v. 27 follows that of 9:4, suggesting that Midian is the main focus through vv. 26–27, which would explain the odd order in which the exodus is mentioned after Midian—it is an afterthought. In the last phrase of v. 27, NIV "preserves the MT but at the expense of making no sense" (Motyer, *The Prophecy of Isaiah*, p. 119, n. 2). The Hb. for shoulder (see NIV mg.) is similar to that for fatness.

10:33–34 / Out of context this might refer to Judah's leadership, but the context here suggests Assyria, after vv. 16–17 as well as after vv. 28–32 and in a chapter that has otherwise turned from calamity to promise.

11:1–2 / **Branch, Spirit:** NIV's capitalization of these words recognizes their later significance but gives a misleading impression in an OT context. The former is not a technical term; the latter no more deserves an initial capital than expressions such as "face [of God]" or "heart [of God]."

11:6–9 / A literal interpretation of verses 6–8 would also have difficulty in explaining how wolves and leopards can remain themselves if they lie down with lambs and goats. The picture might be a more generally symbolic portrait of order and blessing, no more to be interpreted literally than the geophysical transformation of 2:2–4 (Wildberger, *Isaiah 1–12*, pp. 480–81). But verse 9 points away from this, too.

11:9 / After reference to Yahweh's holy mountain, *ha'arets* more likely denotes the land than the whole earth (so NIV at, e.g., 7:24; 9:19; 10:23).

11:11 / It would be nice to take **Hamath and the islands of the sea** as pointing to the north and west, if the latter are lands across the Mediterranean. With the Mesopotamian countries and Egypt and the countries beyond, these places would then give specificity to the reference to the "four quarters of the earth" in v. 12. But Hamath in Syria is not especially north and we do not know of Jewish settlement across the Mediterranean until much later. More likely **the islands of the sea** are the Phoenician coastland, so that this and Hamath go together, and the phrase in v. 12 is to be taken less literally.

§9 A Song to Sing on the Day of Salvation (Isa. 12:1–6)

After an act of deliverance of the kind that brought the people out of Egypt, one might expect there to be a song to sing like that in Exodus 15, and so there is; indeed, verse 2 virtually repeats Exodus 15:2.

12:1–2 / Israel is challenged to announce its intention to **praise:** the verb is the one that introduces thanksgiving, that praise that gives testimony to what Yahweh has just done for the worshiper, by making public confession of the facts—as also happens when one confesses sin. For many chapters, **that day** has been a day of calamity (2:11, 17, 20; 3:7, 18; 4:1; 5:30; 7:18, 20, 21, 23; only 4:2 is an exception). Now it is the day when the remnant turns to Yahweh (10:20), when Assyria's burden is taken from Judah's shoulders (10:27), when the Davidic shoot draws the nations to restore this remnant to its land (11:10), when Yahweh in person reclaims that remnant (11:11). But above all and beneath all, it is the day when the anger of 5:25; 9:12, 17, 21; 10:4, 5 gives way in accordance with the promise of 10:25. It gives way to **comfort,** the first announcement of another theme to recur later (e.g., 40:1; 49:13; 61:2; 66:13). Here this comfort already reveals itself as a matter both of words and of actions, like anger. But actually the word translated "comfort" has occurred once before, in 1:24. There the verb denoted Yahweh's getting relief from holding in anger; now Yahweh gives relief to those who have encountered this anger. Its recurrence thus tells the same story of transformation as the recurrence of the phrase **that day.**

So chapters 1–12 end with **salvation** (v. 2) as they began with it in Isaiah's name, "Yahweh is salvation." Salvation denotes an act of deliverance. It presupposes a situation of need and a destiny of blessing, but it draws attention to the act that takes people from one state to the other. The experience of Yahweh's deliverance draws from Israel the confession of trust and fearlessness that Yahweh has longed to hear. Israel will now draw the same water of salvation (12:3; 8:6) that they tasted after the Red Sea deliverance (Exod. 15:27; 17:1–7).

12:3–6 / Verse 3 marks a transition from singular "you" to the plural and introduces a second song. What needs saying again needs saying twice, and verses 4–6 parallel verses 1–2. **Give thanks** is that same verb that was earlier translated praise. The second thanksgiving goes beyond the first in making more explicit the inherently public nature of an act of confession, and the verb thus imperatively addresses others rather than cohortatively addressing the self. Since 2:2–4 the nations were destined to know what Yahweh had done and could do, so as to seek Yahweh's involvement in their own affairs. They were destined to know that **the Holy One of Israel** was **great** in the midst of the **people of Zion**. It has been necessary for this to take place by a circuitous route, via the nations bringing disaster to Yahweh's people and then watching Yahweh restore it. But take place it will, for all the world to recognize—because Yahweh is Lord of all the world. In chapters 40–55 the message of comfort and the turn from anger will be declared not as future but as present (e.g., 40:1; 54:8). There Yahweh delivers people from their overlords and fulfills these promises, and these songs can be sung. After that, each time Yahweh does this, they can be sung again.

The phrase "the Holy One of Israel" closes chapters 1–12 as it nearly opened them (1:4). The failure and the destiny of Jerusalem/Zion and the God of justice and faithfulness, of anger and comfort, are these chapters' great subject.

§10 Introduction to Chapters 13–23

Chapter 12 would have made a fine ending to a book, and perhaps it once did. Isaiah has warned Judah of calamity to come, then looked at the other side of trouble to the punishment of the troublers themselves and to the fulfillment of Yahweh's purpose for Israel "in that day." Isaiah 13 then marks a new start. The word **oracle** announces something new; this distinctive title will introduce most of the sections within this next major division of the book, chapters 13–23. To judge from the contents, *massa'* does not necessarily suggest an oracle in the narrow sense of an actual word from Yahweh. It can be (among other things) an imaginative picture, a lament, or a poem—in other words, any kind of prophetic composition. In Isaiah, at least, the word invariably denotes material that relates to Yahweh's dealings with foreign nations. Even 30:6 only proves the rule. *Massa'* is the same as a word for "burden" (see Jer. 23:33–38).

While chapter 10 referred to the fate of Assyria, the focus in chapters 1–12 was Isaiah's own nation. In chapters 13–23 the balance is the reverse. While these chapters allude to the destiny of Judah and Ephraim, it is the fate of the peoples around them that comes into focus. The flow of the text suggests that we can divide the peoples into two sequences of similar length (chs. 13–17 and 18–23), each sequence being subdivided into two parts of similar length. The first part treats the northern powers (13:1–14:27), the second some of Judah's neighbors (15:1–17:14), then the third deals with the southern powers (18:1–20:6), and the fourth and final part contains more material relating to the northern powers (21:1–23:18). In the second and fourth sequences, Jerusalem itself makes an unexpected appearance. A summary statement about "many nations" stands at the center of the arrangement. The prominence of Babylon at the beginning of this section in chapter 13 and Tyre at the end, in chapter 23, reflects their status as the two most impressive powers within the Assyrian empire, to the far northeast of Judah and the nearer northwest. The structure of this section as a whole is as follows:

The Fate of the Northern Powers:		*The Fate of Judah's Neighbors and Jerusalem Itself:*	
Babylon	13:1–14:23	Philistia	14:28–32
Assyria	14:24–27	Moab	15:1–16:14
		Damascus	17:1–9
		Jerusalem	17:10–11

The Fate of
Many Nations
17:12–14

The Fate of the Southern Powers:		*The Fate of the Northern Powers and Jerusalem Itself:*	
Cush	18:1–7; 20:1–6	Babylon	21:1–10
Egypt	19:1–25; 20:1–6	Dumah	21:11–12
		Arabia	21:13–17
		Jerusalem	22:1–25
		Tyre	23:1–17

Why does a Judean prophet speak of the fate of other peoples? Isaiah does not tell us, but other OT material may help us to see why. In Numbers 22–24, when Balaam uttered his words concerning Israel (which was a foreign people for him, though he spoke Yahweh's word), he and his paymaster knew that declaring Yahweh's words of blessing or trouble would be effective. The declaration put Yahweh's will into effect. The likes of Amaziah and Jeroboam knew that it was a serious business when Amos declared a death penalty on Jeroboam (Amos 7:11). These poems in Isaiah 13–23 also put Yahweh's word into effect.

Second, the Moabite king is interested in Balaam's words about Israel because the destiny of Israel is relevant to him. Its trouble means his prospering; its blessing means his loss. In the same way, the poems in Isaiah 13–23 do not concern nations in general, but nations with whom Judah's destiny is interwoven. Bad news for Judah's enemies is indirectly good news for Judah. Bad news for Judah's potential allies is an indirect warning for Judah. It is the latter that dominates chapters 13–23, especially if we read the poem against Babylon in the context of Isaiah's own day.

Third, his experience with Balaam gives the Moabite king the opportunity to align his policies with Yahweh's rather than be ignorant of them, ignore them, or oppose them. Isaiah's poems give the same opportunity both to Judah and to the peoples of whom he speaks. As far as we know, admittedly, prophets who prophesy concerning other nations did not generally deliver such prophecies to those nations or to their representatives or send the prophecies to them. But Jeremiah (see Jer. 27) and Jonah do so, and some of the peoples did hear Isaiah's words about them, even if most did not. In 14:32 Isaiah prescribes an answer to a Philistine embassy, and in 18:1–7 he addresses a Cushite embassy. The direct audience of his words may have been the Judean leadership, but he will have intended that in one form or another the content of his message become the Judean response to this embassy.

Fourth, the poems in Isaiah 13–23 no more confine themselves to cursing foreigners than Balaam's prophecies did. As the foreign diviner found himself compelled to bless Israel, so the Israelite prophet is compelled to bless the nations. This is most explicitly so when Isaiah looks forward to a time when Egypt, Assyria, and Israel can worship together as Yahweh's people (19:23–25). But it is not the only passage where the conviction that Yahweh has a positive concern for the nations surfaces, or where this possibility is flagged before Israel (see, e.g., chs. 15–16). While the NIV headings describe these poems as "A prophecy against Babylon/Moab/Damascus . . . ," there is no word for "against" in the Hebrew text.

Other features of Isaiah 13–23 contrast with the Balaam story. First, Balaam's oracles gave no reasons for Yahweh's intentions regarding Israel. These poems do give reasons for Yahweh's intentions regarding the nations. One reason recurs. It is not their crimes against humanity (contrast Amos 1–2) or their wrongs against Judah (though see 17:14) but their majesty and power that are objectively and subjectively a threat to the majesty and power of Yahweh. They look and think as if they have taken God's place. Their downfall is thus a theological necessity; they have to be put down lest it look as if they are inherently majestic and powerful. The fact that the poems include talk of their downfall indicates that the poems have a role to play in Israel's theological education. It is another reason for their being uttered in Judah. They are designed to help shape Israel's worldview, so that Israel may live in the light of the truth about Yahweh and the nations and not (for instance) come to think that they do have power and majesty like

God's, or think that Yahweh has power only within internal Judean affairs.

Second, the framework of contemporary history dominates the Balaam story more than it does Isaiah 13–23. The Balaam story does look beyond the immediate horizon of Israel's imminent threat to Moab, and it is set in the context of Yahweh's ultimate purpose of blessing and cursing associated with the promise to Abraham. But Isaiah 13–23 keeps moving between the foci of contemporary or imminent historical events and the ultimate Day of Yahweh, the day when Yahweh's original and final purpose will come about, when Yahweh will reign in just judgment and a son of David will reign in just judgment (16:4–5). The concern of Isaiah 8 is the many-watered roar of one great nation, Assyria. The concern of Isaiah 17:12–14 is the stilling of the many-watered roar of many nations.

Third, the Balaam story fits the horizon of prophecies against other peoples that are designed to harness divine power to the defeat of one's enemies. Isaiah 13–23 is not generally concerned with the defeat of peoples with whom Judah is or might be at war. While one or two of the poems, such as that concerning Moab, would fit such a context, it is not required for them and is irrelevant to most of the others. If anything, the complex as a whole points in the opposite direction. It relates to peoples whom Judah might regard as allies, or who might regard Judah as a potential ally, in the context of the tensions between the Assyrian empire and its underlings during the last third of the eighth century B.C.

Fourth, the Balaam story is full of irony as the foreign king seeks to buy words that will curse Israel and ends up paying good money for words that bless his enemy, but Balaam's own words are mostly straightforward in meaning. They are promises of blessing for Israel. The poems in Isaiah 13–23 are more subtle. It would be surprising if the Isaiah of chapters 1–12 merely sought to make Judah feel good by promising the downfall of its enemies. In fact, the poems keep turning into implicit or explicit warnings to Judah itself. The point is implicit not least in the central warning about majesty ("pride") and power, for this is precisely Isaiah's critique of Judah in 2:6–22.

Fifth, the poems are thus subordinate to Isaiah's own agenda, just as Amos 1–2 is subordinate to Amos's agenda. Isaiah's distinctive theme is the necessity for Jerusalem to trust in Yahweh and not to be afraid of peoples who are rebelling against Assyria and pressing Judah to do so (see on 7:1–9). These two themes are related. He knows that Assyria is Yahweh's means of governing the world in his day. These themes underlie chapters 13–23 as a whole. Assyrian records as well as OT material specifically indicate that Babylon, Philistia, Moab, Aram, Ephraim, Cush, Egypt, and Tyre sought to assert independence over against Assyria during the years of Isaiah's ministry, that they allied with each other in doing so, and that they sought to involve Judah in such movements. Isaiah believes it to be bad politics for Judah to yield to their tempting blandishments—not because he is a better worldly politician, but because he knows what Yahweh's priorities and intentions are. Yahweh is going to put down all these nations; it is foolish to put trust in any of them. An implication of his claims regarding the destiny of these nations is a strong faith in the worldwide and absolute power of the God of Israel.

Why, then, does Isaiah include Jerusalem in these chapters? Perhaps it brings out the ambiguity in Jerusalem's position. It is the city of Yahweh. Yet it lives in the world. Insofar as it operates by the world's methods (its own inclination), Yahweh treats it in the same way as other peoples, and so it can tellingly appear sandwiched between Damascus and Cush or Arabia and Tyre.

The subjects of all the poems thus make sense in the context of Isaiah's ministry. Nevertheless their perspective is not confined to those decades. Like chapters 1–12, they also refer to contexts beyond Isaiah's day. These include at least the decline and fall of Assyria itself a century later, the fall of Jerusalem in 587 B.C., and the collapse of the Babylonian empire in 539 B.C. It is impossible to know how much of this is because Isaiah's vision took him on to those events and how much it is because Yahweh also inspired later prophets and expositors to bring Isaiah's prophecies up-to-date. What we can say is that the prophecies describe an arc that spans Yahweh's purpose at work in the world as a whole, over at least two centuries. The prophecies enable us to understand Yahweh's way of working in Israel's world over a long period, and thus in ours.

§11 Poems about Northern Powers (Isa. 13:1–14:27)

13:1 / Babylon here appears in Isaiah for the first time; it is the subject through 14:23. Its prominence in chapters 13–23 may reflect two facts. In Isaiah's day, Babylon was significant as a powerful city that was inclined to rebel against Assyria, like other powers nearer Judah such as Philistia and Egypt, and in collaboration with them. When the prophet Isaiah puts in his last personal appearance in the book, in chapter 39, it will be in connection with a Babylonian embassy's visit to Jerusalem. There will be more behind that than the Babylonian king's desire to congratulate King Hezekiah for recovering from an illness. At the very least the Babylonians were networking, for they shared with Judah the position of unwilling underling of Assyria. They represented the temptation to rebel against the power that Yahweh had put in charge of the middle east for the time being. Babylon is "the prime symbol of successful revolt against Assyrian sovereignty" (Watts, *Isaiah 1–33*, p. 200).

We will also come to see that the story of Hezekiah's openness to the Babylonian embassy leads into the section of the book whose background is Judah's own eventual subservience to Babylon more than a century later. Babylon then became the major power in Israel's life. The prominence of Babylon in this set of poems about other nations in chapters 13–23 also suggests that later situation. S. Erlandsson (*The Burden of Babylon: A Study of Isaiah 13:2–14:23* [Coniectanea Biblica 4; trans. G. J. Houser; Lund: Gleerup, 1970], p. 165; see Additional Note on 13:1–14:23) suggests that perhaps verse 1 was added in such a later context, to draw attention to the fact that Isaiah himself had spoken about Babylon. Perhaps Isaiah's prophecies were collected, arranged, and updated in the sixth century B.C. by people who wanted to preserve his message in such a way as to point to its significance for their own day—though we can only theorize about who these people might have been.

Indeed, it is noteworthy that these chapters about Babylon overtly refer to Babylon only three times. Many of the individual prophecies could relate to anyone. Only the introduction in 13:1 and the notes in 14:4 and 22 refer to Babylon in particular. In 13:2–16, it is not even clear whether Babylon is the victor or the vanquished. While Isaiah himself will have uttered prophecies about the Babylon of his day, it is a plausible view that the other prophecies here did not originally refer to Babylon and that they have been reapplied here to that city. Babylon is the "Assyria" of a century later, so oracles about Assyria would be naturally reapplied in this way.

The focus on Babylon may also reflect even later realities as Babylon comes to be the archetype of national power asserted against God—symbolism that is particularly explicit in the NT Revelation to John. So the Babylon whose fall is described here is not merely the historical Babylon, Israel's conqueror, but also the symbolic Babylon. Its fall signifies the dethroning of every power opposed to God. To look at it another way, given that Babylon comes to have that significance, it is telling that the chapters begin with the city that has this destiny.

13:2–16 / Since before Isaiah's time, Israelites had looked forward to the Day of the Lord, a day when Israel's enemies would be punished and Israel itself would enter into God's fullest blessing. Amos warns about such hopes (Amos 5:18–20), and Isaiah has warned his audience about this day (see, e.g., 2:10–22). In 13:2–13, Isaiah pictures it happening before people's eyes. The portrayal recalls the vivid picture of the Assyrian army's advance in 10:28–32.

We have been told that the oracle concerns Babylon (v. 1), but in what sense? Verses 2–13 do not name anyone. Is Babylon the destroyer, like Assyria in chapter 10, or is it the victim? If the former, is the victim again Judah, so that this is another frightening account of attack on Jerusalem? Or is the victim Assyria, receiving its comeuppance? If Babylon is the victim, who is the destroyer? Is it Judah itself—are the tables truly turned?

While the audience puzzles over such questions, it listens for clues within the words themselves. The oracle starts in the midst of things, like a novel or a film. We hear an army commander issuing the order for his troops to enter a city. We know he speaks from a place of good visibility, but initially we do not know who speaks, who is addressed, who the **them** are who are to be summoned, who the nobles are against whom they come. The oracle thus draws us into its midst without our knowing whether we wish to be so drawn. What if we ourselves should be the victims, or the unwilling warriors?

Verse 3 begins to clarify things. The general is evidently Yahweh. But who are the troops? They are Yahweh's soldiers, identified with Yahweh's cause, manifesting the vigorous gusto a successful army needs if it is to complete a challenging assignment. They are also **my holy ones.** Are these the holy ones of Psalm 89:5–7, Yahweh's heavenly army (see v. 5)? The word is more literally "my consecrated ones" (NRSV), which indicates instead a human army dedicated to the task of fulfilling Yahweh's purpose in the world by making war. The language is similar to that in passages such as Jeremiah 51:27–28 in connection with Babylon. Yet the antithesis should not be drawn too sharply. The OT assumes that events on earth reflect more than merely earthly factors, as is particularly clear when an army wins (or loses) a battle against all the odds. It is not mere human strength that decides these things. The classic story that illustrates this reality describes Moses directing the heavenly forces while Joshua directs the earthly forces against Amalek (Exod. 17:8–13). And here heaven joins earth in manifesting the signs of calamity (v. 10).

The notion that war and holiness can belong together may be a difficult one for us. It is certainly a dangerous one. Most wars are fought in the name of holiness. The collocation of ideas has consistently been appropriated ideologically. Leaders and peoples fight wars that are at least partly designed to fulfill their own desires while they claim to be fighting in the name of God. The OT's implication is that God takes the risk of being involved in that process, in which nations use God's name as they seek to pursue their own ends. In this way God is involved in battles that do put down oppressors and free the oppressed—rather than doing nothing at all, or acting directly from heaven in a way that does not involve human beings at all. War thus becomes one of the activities that most revealingly tests humanity to see whether it will appropriate God to its agenda or whether it is actually "dedicated" to God's.

A further insight on this matter may emerge from Isaiah as a whole, which encapsulates the OT in microcosm. Israel's history demonstrates that war gets no one anywhere, not even God. Violence begets violence; it never ends it. So the battles in Isaiah become more supernatural and less this-worldly (e.g., chs. 24–27) and the achievements to which the book testifies are won by absorbing violence rather than administering it (52:13–53:12).

Although the OT describes Yahweh as being all-knowing in the sense of being able to know all about us, it also describes Yahweh as learning from experience. It is through such a process that Yahweh concludes that creating humanity and yielding to Israelite pressure to appoint a king for the people were bad ideas after all (Gen. 6:6–7; 1 Sam. 15:11, 35). Perhaps the same is true of fighting. Or perhaps it is simply true of the idea of involving humanity in fighting, which Yahweh seems to stop doing. Yahweh in person carries on fighting until the end of the Bible.

So we hear "Yahweh [of] armies" (see on 1:24–25) mustering a great army (vv. 4–5). It is a particularly appropriate way to speak of God when Isaiah is describing the great Day when the forces of heaven and earth are in battle. Once more the prophecy's universal nature emerges in the intended scope of the destruction. It covers "the whole *'erets.*" That could simply mean **the whole country,** but it can as easily mean "the whole earth" (NRSV). For the moment we are again kept in suspense, but the latter scope will become more overt in verse 11 **(the world).** A vision of destruction of one land is in microcosm a vision of destruction of the whole world. Or a vision of destruction of the whole world is made concrete in the destruction of one people, to which verse 1 has alerted us. In verse 6 the NIV margin notes that the word **Almighty** is not "armies," as in verse 4, but *shadday.* We do not know what this name means, but here in Isaiah the point of it is clear, for the word for **destruction** is *shod,* so that the juxtaposition of the two words invites the hearers to see Yahweh as Destroyer by name and as therefore eminently capable of effecting the day of destruction. The response of verses 7–8 is therefore not surprising.

Initially the oracle presupposed the perspective of the army, but now it considers the perspective of its victims (v. 6). The Day of Yahweh is coming upon them (see on 2:10–22). The expression itself combines a universal and a concrete reference. The ultimate day comes in a concrete sense when Yahweh's purpose is fulfilled for a particular people in a particular context. A pattern characteristic of biblical prophecy appears here (see on 2:2). While the Bible speaks as if the end of the world is imminent, the day when this prophecy is fulfilled is not the final judgment, but the moment when God's ultimate purpose receives one of its periodic partial fulfillments in history, as pride is put down and the oppressed are delivered.

Verses 9–11 tighten the screws, emphasizing the cruelty of the battle and the fierceness of the divine anger (see on 5:25–30), but they add a new note. Why is Yahweh so angry? The causes are human failure (v. 9b), badness, wickedness, and perversity (v. 11a). The four words suggest that people have fallen short of God's glory and God's expectations, they are flawed and nasty, they are antisocial and in the wrong, they have deliberately chosen the wrong way. The problem was expressed in their confidence in themselves (v. 11b). It was such self-confidence that triggered the coming of Yahweh's Day for Judah in 2:10–22. A further parallel with the earlier prophecy is that here, too, what is wrong with human exaltedness and confidence is that it belittles Yahweh's exaltedness and authority. Thus the confrontation. **Pride** is the word for Yahweh's **triumph** (v. 3), while **arrogance** is a related word. **Ruthless** is related to the word for "shake" in 2:19, 21 and "dread" in 8:12–13. So the arrogance and pride of the ruthless are wrong because they represent the pretense to be God.

Initially, the oracle described the results of the invasion mostly in material and psychological terms. It meant destruction and **anguish** (vv. 6, 8). But human slaughter has also been mentioned, and this has the emphasis through the rest of the chapter (vv. 12–22). A series of similes and metaphors follows, and a more frightening sequence of literal images redolent of the television news when it is preceded by a warning for the sensitive who might not want to watch. Once more we are also reminded that this is not a mere earthly calamity (v. 13).

13:17–22 / The portrait also now becomes politically specific. The army Yahweh is summoning is that of **the Medes**, further northeast than Mesopotamia. They were historically one of the most powerful warrior nations of the east, though Media was also an area Assyria sought to treat as part of its empire. So this reference narrows the interpretive options for chapter 13 as a whole; Yahweh's agent is neither Assyria nor Babylon. The description of the Medes is not designed to commend them. Indeed, lack of compassion is one of the reasons for Babylon's own downfall (47:6). As with the Assyrians, their relentlessly aggressive instincts will be harnessed to Yahweh's purpose. They are not merely interested in booty (v. 17). They enjoy fighting and killing itself.

Verse 19 at last names the Medes' victim. The city of **Babylon** is a particular embodiment of that human achievement, power, and **pride** (v. 19) that pretends to rival the greatness of God. The

Chaldeans (see NIV mg.), tribes from further south in Mesopotamia, gained control of Babylon in Isaiah's day. The parallels with Yahweh's threats against Judah continue as the prophecy declares that impressive Babylon will become no more than devastated **Sodom and Gomorrah** (see 1:9). Any Judean would have seen that the description of verses 20–22 fitted the long-gone cities by the Dead Sea. The imagination would have boggled at the thought of impressive Babylon reduced to the same emptiness.

Reference here to the Medes and not the Persians, the imperial power after Babylon from 539 to 333 B.C., would cohere with the view that the prophecy against Babylon presupposes the Babylon of Isaiah's day. At that time Media was the great power further northeast which might be a threat to both Assyria and Babylon. Yet it was actually Medo-Persian armies that put down Babylon and released Judeans from their confinement to Babylon in 539 B.C., so "the Medes" could be a way of referring to the Persian empire, just as "Chaldea" was a way of referring to Babylon. This will at least have encouraged a reading of chapters 13–14 against the background of this Babylon's fall. Indeed, Yahweh's intention to **stir up** the Medes will be taken up in 41:2, 25—verses that may see this prophecy's fulfillment in the rise of Cyrus.

The blessings in Psalm 137:8–9 have often offended people, as if believers should not have such desires. This passage enables us to see that the blessings in the psalm are simply prayers that what Yahweh has announced here in verses 16 and 18 should come about.

14:1–2 / Nothing in the book so far clarifies the link between 14:1–2 and what precedes, but chapters 39–52 will do so, and readers a century or so after Isaiah's day would have understood. Babylon's fall will mean Judah's freedom. The worldwide perspective of chapter 13 thus yields to a direct concern with the implications of Babylon's fall for little Judah (see H. Wildberger, *Isaiah: A Commentary* [trans. T. H. Trapp; Continental Commentaries; Minneapolis: Fortress, 1997], vol. 2, pp. 12–15). It will result from Yahweh's compassion for Jacob-Israel. Verses 1–2 start not from reduction to a remnant (like 10:20–23), but from expulsion to an alien land. Thus they promise not increase but return. The language of chapters 39–52 will overlap with the language here (**Jacob-Israel, have compassion, choose,** and the reversal in v. 2 whereby the nations who made Israel captive now become Israel's captives). But this is not simply an anticipatory summary of the themes of those later chapters. The focus there will be more on Yahweh's return to the land. Here, to say that Yahweh **will settle** them in their land is to take up the language of Joshua: the occupation of the land will be repeated. To say that aliens will join them is to say that this occupation will be better than that one, for then aliens were banned. The fact that **their land** remains **the LORD's** land takes the edge off the nationalism of verse 2 and issues the reminder that land cannot really belong to people and be bought and sold by them. It is a theological impossibility.

14:3–23 / At last the links are explicit: Babylon's downfall means Israel's relief and restoration. On the way to that, it means the downfall of the king of Babylon. **How** is the classic beginning for an expression of horror, whether the horror is combined with grief or with satisfaction. The poem is a funeral dirge sung for a king who is at present very much alive. It parallels Amos's funeral dirge for Israel in Amos 5:2, sung when Israel was still very much alive. The last ruler of the Babylonian empire, on the throne when it falls to the Persians, will be Nabonidus, but the point about the poem is not to give a literal description of the fate of a king at a particular moment. Rather, this is an imaginative picture of the fall of the ruling Babylonian power.

First, the dirge imagines Israel relieved of oppression by the king's death, and in a position to exult over God's judgment on wickedness (vv. 3b–8). It pictures the exultation shared by the many peoples whom he had ruled. Again it presupposes that only Yahweh has the right to exercise furious violence and aggressive authority, a conviction that is the protection of ordinary peoples as long as they do not come to be corrupted by power themselves.

Second, it imagines Sheol **(the grave) astir** to welcome the king (vv. 9–11; see on 5:8–24). When people die, physically they go to join their ancestors in the family tomb. Like Greek thinking, Middle Eastern thinking pictures the inner person similarly joining the ancestors and other dead persons in a non-physical equivalent to the tomb. It is a form of continuing existence with other people, but an inactive one, like that of the body itself in the tomb, and with a debilitating side (see v. 11b). The arrival of the king of Babylon will at least relieve the tedium of Sheol, a reality for other once-important people who are experiencing death as the great leveler.

The poem starts again with a new **How** introducing verses 12–15. It tightens the screw on the picture by picturing the king as one who had tried to make himself into God. The point has been implicit throughout. Anyone who wants to exercise power and enjoy prestige is trying to be God. Now it is explicit. Appropriately, the poem utilizes motifs that an Israelite audience would recognize as coming from foreign myths: **morning star, son of the dawn** takes up two titles of Canaanite gods. Babylonian and Canaanite stories spoke of gods who tried to take over the power of the highest god, and the poem here turns such stories into a parable of what the Babylonian king is doing in presuming to exercise God-like authority, force, and prestige—and that over the whole world. He will collapse as readily as does Venus, the morning star, when it falls each day from the height of the sky. While Babylon aspired to lead a rebellion against Assyria in the time of Isaiah, it was not yet the major power it would eventually become, and it seems likely that this poem refers to a later period when the king of Babylon has had the chance to develop the pretensions the poem describes. The situation presupposed is, again, one later than Isaiah's own day.

Verses 15–20a work further with the link between the physical grave and the spiritual Sheol. A king has a more impressive tomb than a commoner (indeed, he has a private one), and a king also keeps his status in Sheol. Death is not, after all, the great leveler. So part of this king's downfall is that this vestige of special position is also denied him. Indeed, he joins those who die in battle and receive no proper burial at all.

For what reason? First, the poem offers yet more clarification of 13:2–13. It was the Babylonian king who **shook the earth** and **made the world a desert,** the process we saw in the vision in 13:2–13. So Yahweh's agent there was the king of Babylon, bringing downfall to the Assyrians. It is he who now receives his own downfall. The pattern follows that of chapter 10, with Assyria replacing Judah and Babylon Assyria. In addition, he **would not let his captives go home** (as Cyrus the Persian will when he overthrows Babylon). Further, and strikingly, the poem declares, **you have destroyed your** own **land and killed your** own **people.**

How has he done that? Verses 20b–23 suggest part of the answer. **The offspring of the wicked,** i.e., "the wicked offspring," is the king himself. He will be forgotten. The Bible does not actually mention Nabonidus, Babylon's last king (Belshazzar, in Daniel, was regent in his day). The king's own offspring will pay for the perversity of the older generation, as children do.

How much are we to learn from such a picture of Sheol about what actually happens after death? There is a playful (though serious) side to the prophet's picture, and it may be that we should not press the details, any more than those of (say) Job 1–2 or Luke 16:19–31. But NT passages such as Matthew 27:52 and 1 Peter 4:6 presuppose the basic OT understanding. The gospel does not change that basic understanding. It adds the news that after Christ's coming Sheol is not the end for people who belong to him.

14:24–27 / This footnote reference to Yahweh's plan for Assyria, the great power of Isaiah's own day (see on 10:5–11:16), is surprising, especially for its brevity. It even lacks the "oracle" heading. In general, chapters 13–23 take for granted the international status quo in which Assyria rules, and implicitly support it by declaring calamity on rebels against Assyria, because Assyria is Yahweh's agent. This brief note perhaps reassures the hearers of the point that chapter 10 has made, that Assyria's day will come. If the chapters were developed after Isaiah's day, this may be a restatement of Isaiah's earlier message regarding Assyria that dates from the time when Assyria's fall was indeed imminent, a century after Isaiah's day, in the reign of Josiah (so Clements, *Isaiah 1–39*, p. 147).

Striking is the stress on Yahweh's coming to a decision and implementing it. Forms of the root *ya'ats* reappear (**purposed, plan, determined, purposed;** see on 5:8–24). Isaiah's language again makes clear that Yahweh's plan is not a detailed determining of every event that happens in history, most of which may well go against the divine purpose. In general Yahweh is not sovereign in world history. Events do not happen in accordance with Yahweh's wishes. Yahweh's plan is a determination nevertheless to achieve a certain purpose in the long run, to establish rule in the world, and a periodic determination to bring about certain specific events (here the eventual fall of Assyria) that will make a particular contribution to that long-term purpose.

Additional Notes §11

13:1–14:23 / On the eighth-century background, see esp. Erlandsson, *The Burden of Babylon*, pp. 163–66.

13:3 / **Those who rejoice in my triumph:** lit. "rejoicers of my triumph," which need not mean they personally identified with Yahweh's cause; it could mean "my rejoicing triumphant ones."

14:1 / The chapter begins with the word *ki*, commonly translated "for" (KJV; NRSV "but"), which makes a link with what precedes (thus the Hebrew Bible has no chapter break here). See on 1:29–30.

14:4 / **Taunt** is an overtranslation: "poem" would be more neutral (KJV has "proverb").

14:12 / **Morning star** is the expression translated "Lucifer" in the KJV—by that time the passage came to be understood as an account of the fall of Satan. In the Babylonian and Canaanite stories that the poem is using it does have a significance of such a kind, but the Bible uses the picture only as a parable about something happening on earth to a human being. Ezek. 28:12–19 applies the same story to the King of Tyre. The Bible contains no account of the fall of Satan except that of his downfall in Rev. 20, but believers wanting their theological curiosity satisfied on this question have often thus misunderstood Isa. 14.

14:13, 15 / **The utmost heights of the sacred mountain:** the same phrase as in Ps 48:2. The word for the utmost heights then reappears as **the depths.** The king aspires to the extremities of heaven but reaches the extremities of the "pit," another term for the place where dead people live.

14:20b / **The wicked** is plural, so the offspring of the wicked are not merely the king's own offspring. "Offspring consisting of the wicked" is grammatically possible, but vv. 21–23 imply that the king's offspring die because of him, not for their own wickedness.

§12 Poems about Judah's Neighbors and about Jerusalem Itself (Isa. 14:28–17:14)

14:28–32 / With this section we move from the great powers to Judah's neighbors, and first to Philistia, its immediate neighbor to the southwest, between the Judean hills and the Mediterranean. *Realpolitik* is urgent here, as the provision of a concrete date suggests. Ahaz died in the 720s B.C., as did the Assyrian kings Tiglath-Pileser III and Shalmanezer V. One of the latter is the "broken rod." A king's death often brings a hiatus of power, and Philistia joined a coalition of peoples also interested in resisting Assyrian authority at the time. Philistia was perhaps pressing Judah to join them (v. 32). So Philistia symbolizes locally what Babylon does far away—a temptation to rebellion.

Isaiah warns Philistia (along with Judeans tempted to think independence with it) that the hiatus will be temporary. The enemy from the north will reappear in due course. This is a literal description of the direction from which the Assyrians would come, but in light of later usage the phrase may also cast Assyria as an embodiment of the traditional "enemy from the north" (see, e.g., Jer. 1:13–15; Ezek. 39:2). There will be no deliverance for Philistia through its political activity as there will be for Judah through its relationship with Yahweh, the God who has real power and is committed to Jerusalem (v. 32).

Many people in Judah believed more in Jerusalem's security than Isaiah did. He would like to see them live by their theology (Wildberger, *Isaiah 13–27*). Indeed, in light of the lament at Moab's hurt that follows, with the invitation and hope in 16:1–5, might he be implying in his proposed reply to the nations such as Philistia and Moab that they can count themselves among the **afflicted people** who **find refuge** in Zion which Yahweh established?

15:1–9 / Chapter 15 begins a poem about Moab. Relationships between Judah and Moab, its neighbor on the east, were as fraught as relationships between Judah and Philistia—and Judah preserved longer memories of strife with Moab. The reference to Zoar recalled an unsavory story about the ancestor Moab's origins within Abraham's extended family (Gen. 19:30–38). Tensions with Moab were part of family relationships, and these can have an extra edge to them. There were more humorous as well as unsavory stories about Judah's relationships with Moab on the way into the promised land (Num. 22:1–25:5). Thus prophecy warned and statute legislated against relationships with Moab (Mic. 6:5; Deut. 23:3; see also Isa. 11:14; 25:10). But the story of Ruth gives a different picture of everyday life where relationships could be quite acceptable.

Moab was not part of the territory promised to Israel, as Philistia was (see Deut. 1:7), but from time to time the two peoples invaded and ruled each other. The Jordan River is the natural border between Israel and Moab/Ammon. The area of the Israelite tribes that settled east of the Jordan was thus particularly vulnerable to Moabite expansion. More significantly, Moab joined with Philistia, Edom, and Judah in rebelling against Assyria in the late eighth century (see *ANET,* p. 287a). The description of calamity on Moab here, like the warning to Philistia, indirectly warns Judah not to overestimate its strength. The description need presuppose no specific invader; it would be enough to recognize the activity of Yahweh's armies (see ch. 13).

Chapters 15 and 16 manifest some sharp transitions (e.g., between 16:1–5 and 16:6–12) which suggest that perhaps they comprise a series of independent poems that were not originally linked. If so, they have been arranged so that two sections of very similar length, comprising laments that close with warning, form a bracket around a shorter section in which Moab expresses its hopes.

Lament for Moab
15:1–8

Warning to Moab
15:9

Moab's Hopes
16:1–5

Lament for Moab
16:6–12

Warning to Moab
16:13–14

Like the poem about the king of Babylon, the bulk of the material about Moab thus takes the form of laments over the disaster that has overcome the people. Like that preceding lament, they invite hearing at a literal level so that we grieve over the suffering of the people. They also invite reading at an ironic level that sees calamity as all Moab deserved. Many, if not all, the places involved formed part of Israel's "promised land" and were in the area into which Moab had expanded. As laments, these chapters are composed of shorter lines than usual, as is visible in the English translation. Specifically, the second half of each line usually has two main words instead of three, so that the poem keeps bringing us up short. We do not know whether there were specific events to which the poems are responding (like 14:28–32) or whether they came from the prophet's creatively imagining what calamity for Moab would be (like the bulk of chs. 13–14).

Verse 1, then, begins a first lament and warning for Moab. As in 13:2–16, the poem begins in the middle of things, in the manner of a film or novel. In imagination, at least, the calamity has already happened. The poem conveys a sense of its actuality and its significance by describing its aftermath. It describes people's reactions to the event rather than the event itself. An army has marched at speed through the country, wasting its land from the south (v. 1) through the center (v. 2) and on to the north (v. 4). Ordinary people are overcome by grief, shock and distress (vv. 2–3, 8). Fugitive soldiers flee down to the Dead Sea and on south into Edom (vv. 5, 7). The famous pastoral wealth of their country is destroyed (v. 6). The story is told in hushed tones from one end of the country to the other (v. 8). Words that recur tell the story: **weep** (vv. 2, 3, 5), **wail/lamentation** (v. 2, 3, 8), **cry/lament** (vv. 4, 5a, 5b, 8). The last resembles the word for the oppressed Judeans' own "cries of distress" in 5:7 and for the Israelites' cry in Egypt (Exod. 2:23). One might compare and contrast the similar divinely-inspired imaginative account of the Assyrian army's advance on Jerusalem in 10:27b–32.

In the drama, poet and hearers stand between what has happened (vv. 1–8) and what will happen (v. 9). We cannot infer whether author and hearers literally stand at that point, or stand before anything has happened (as 16:13–14 does), or even after the whole has taken place (as the setting in Isaiah as a whole would presuppose). It might seem that what has happened is as disastrous as disaster could be, but verse 9 makes it worse. Sometimes a closing promise that some will survive or that Yahweh will restore the people takes the edge off a prophecy of calamity. Far from offering light at the end, this poem declares that there is even more darkness to come for both fugitives and survivors. And the one who speaks is Yahweh in person. We might have reckoned that verses 1–8 comprised the prophet's human lament; see especially verse 5. The closing line invites us to revise our understanding of the whole, for evidently Yahweh is actually the speaker. Apparently the pain is Yahweh's, but so is the intention to bring even more pain.

16:1–5 / In the meantime Moab has to cope with the situation it confronts, and what follows here may offer it the way to evade the threat of 15:9. Again we hear a voice whose identity is initially not clear. In light of what preceded we might take these as continuing Yahweh's words, though by the time we get to verses 3–5 they are the Moabites' own plea. So either Yahweh urges, or the Moabites urge themselves, to seek the protection of Judean rule at this moment when the structures of life in Moab itself have collapsed, the crops have been devastated, and Yahweh threatens that there is more to come. Moabite emissaries brace themselves for the humiliating and frightened journey from their "Rock," **Sela,** the Edomite capital where they have apparently taken refuge. They must make their way across the River **Arnon,** which Judah would regard as its proper border with Moab, down into the barren Jordan cleft and up the mountains on the other side to the outwardly less impressive little hill of Zion (vv. 1–2).

With deep irony, the moment of terrible destruction thus provokes words that acknowledge the potential blessing of that rule of Jerusalem presented in the vision of 2:2–4. Once more, words can be heard at two levels. Perhaps verses 3–5 are desperate flattery or whistling in the wind. With further irony, the prophet will of course mean every word. Moab assumes that the promise in 14:32 is not limited in its application to "his afflicted people," or even assumes that "his afflicted people" may not be confined to ethnic Israel. In fact it makes the same assumption as its most famous daughter, Ruth.

Politically and religiously there was a close relationship between belief in **Zion** as the place where Yahweh dwelt and belief in **the house of David** as Yahweh's regent there. Yahweh was committed to Zion and committed to David (see Ps. 132). Strikingly, the two are not brought into explicit relationship elsewhere in Isaiah, perhaps precisely because they were so easily subject to ideological annexing in Jerusalem. The way Moab speaks of David in verse 5 guards against that danger.

Counsel (v. 3) is their first affirmation of the Davidic vision (see, e.g., 11:2). The expectation that Moab might find protection in the anointed Davidic king's **shadow** follows. With more irony, Judah saw this as its own protection as it lived among the nations (Lam. 4:20), not vice versa. Sheltering the vulnerable and terminating oppression (vv. 3b–4) are further features of Judah's royal ideal now put onto Moab's lips. **Love** (v. 5) is the distinctive word *khesed* that suggests the steadfast commitment that one person will sometimes show to another whether or not they are obliged to do so. **Faithfulness** is *'emeth*, which, like *khesed*, is not a very common word in Isaiah. It suggests human constancy, stability, and sincerity (10:20; 38:3; 39:8; 42:3; 43:9; 48:1; 59:14, 15) that meet with and need to mirror that of God (38:18, 19; 42:3; 61:8). On **justice** and **righteousness,** see on 1:21. The link between these traits and the establishment of the Davidic throne appears in 9:7, though God's original promise to David recurs elsewhere (2 Sam. 7:16). The link between God's love, God's faithfulness, and the establishing of David's throne appears in Psalm 89:33–37 in the context of a lengthy exposition of God's promise to David.

It is a further wonderful irony that Moab should have such expectations of David. Their expectations are Isaiah's own vision for David, but they have not been fulfilled in Judah itself. The Isaianic texts speak of the failure of love and faithfulness and of justice and righteousness. Is Moab being set up for disappointment? Or is putting such hopes on the lips of a foreign people another attempt to shame the Davidic house to fulfill its vocation? How extraordinary that it is Moab that expresses a trust in the secure establishment of David's throne, too. Isaiah has had difficulty in getting David's house itself to believe in it (7:1–17).

16:6–14 / A further section of lament and warning for Moab balances the first. These two thus bracket the statement of Moab's hopes. Chronologically this lament does not follow on the expression of hope, any more than the first lament does. The parallel laments resemble the parallel halves of a line of Hebrew poetry. Like such repetitions, the second version goes beyond the first as well as paralleling it. So verses 6–14 begin by bringing out the reason for the calamity that has come upon the people in the prophet's vision. As usual it is the nation's **pride** in its greatness and achievements (see 13:11, 19; 14:11—NIV **pomp**) that obscures and evades the fact that real "majesty" (the same word) belongs only to Yahweh (2:10, 19, 21; see comment). In the context, verse 6 then forms a comment on verses 1–5, which have amounted to an abandonment of that Moabite pride. Moab has herself acknowledged that **her boasts are empty.** At the other end of verses 6–12, verse 12 likewise forms part of the background to the seeking of verses 1–5.

The **therefore** that follows verse 5 then perhaps implies "so that's why . . . ," because the words that follow, **the Moabites wail . . . they wail together** (v. 7), repeat exactly words in 15:2, 3. Again the poem grieves for the destruction of Moab's rich produce. In imagination it tours the specific places that Judeans knew to be part of the land Yahweh promised Israel, land that was illegitimately occupied by Moab. Here there is more of a focus on the north than on the south. Again the **I** of prophet or God grieves with Moab, here with more overt personal involvement. Again Moab goes to its **high place** (v. 12; cf. 15:2), here with the specific comment that this is pointless—which links with verses 1–5 and 6. Again the lament closes with the warning that things will get worse, here with more specificity and a more explicit claim that it is Yahweh who speaks.

In their location after verses 1–5, verses 6–13 warn Moab that there can be no "cheap grace" in recourse to Zion and David. They have to face the falsity of their pride (v. 6), the reality of their suffering (vv. 7–11), the failure of their religion (v. 12), and the prospect that the future will be even worse than the past (vv. 13–14). Then they need to return to their confession in verses 1–5 and make it a description of their future.

17:1–9 / We move north from Moab to **Aram** (v. 3) or Syria, though the poem speaks of Aram's capital city **Damascus.** The mention of the city corresponds to a feature that runs through this poem and forms a contrast with the poem on Moab. There cities featured, but they were chiefly ciphers for their inhabitants. "Heshbon cries out" meant "the people of Heshbon cry out" and the problem was the withering of their fields (15:4; 16:8). The disaster that had come on Moab was an agricultural disaster; the invader had destroyed the crops, not the buildings. Chapter 17 describes an urban disaster. The Aramean capital stands in ruins. So do **the cities of Aroer** (v. 2), the southernmost point in the territory into which the Aramean empire had extended but which Israel also claimed (2 Kgs. 10:32–33).

Again the disaster is described as something that has already happened, though presumably this is actually another prophecy. This time the poem works by using participles to describe a scene of ruin. Again the technique thus resembles one of film, as if it begins with the camera panning across a silent and devastated landscape. So literally the poem opens, "There is Damascus, stopped from being a city and become a ruined heap, the cities of Aroer deserted. . . ." But then **Damascus/Aroer** becomes **Ephraim/ Damascus** and **Aram/Israelites** in verses 2–3, and the verses that follow focus wholly on northern Israel. First, Aram and Ephraim are treated together, which reflects the *Realpolitik* of Isaiah's day (see 7:1–2 and the comment).

Then Aram is warned that things will be just as bad for them as they will be for Ephraim. Verses 4–6 expound just how bad that will be. It will be like the humiliation of an important person who then also fades away through ill-health, or like harvesting that is also followed by the collecting of the gleanings—except that the tiniest amount will remain, like the most inaccessible olives on the tree or the handful that you ignore because you have so many. Like the references to Jerusalem in relation to Moab in 16:1–5, these references to Ephraim are there because they relate to Aram. But theologically it is disturbing that the fate of another part of Yahweh's people provides the illustration for a foreign people's fate (on Isaiah's concern for Ephraim, see 9:1–7; 11:10–16, and the comment). And the references to Aram and Ephraim are there because of their significance for Judah.

Like Moab, Aram will thus face the failure of its own religion and will turn to the God worshiped in Jerusalem, here described by Isaiah's distinctive title for that God. The critique of Aram's religion announces a theme that will become prominent later in the book, namely that they **made** their gods whereas Israel's God is their **maker**. There is a further verbal effect in the fact that the Hebrew word for **look to** comprises the same letters as "make," though in a different order.

Verse 9 concludes the statement about Aram with a return to where we began, the destruction of the cities, now straight prophecy in the future. With further irony, as their fate is tied up with northern Israel's, so it will repeat the fate of the cities that fell before Israel when Israel entered the land. Again the poem uses verbal effect: the Hebrew words for **strong** and **abandoned**, which come next to each other, are very similar. This similarity contrasts starkly with the differences in meaning. And abandoned and **left** come from the same verb, so that the similarity draws attention to the similarity and difference now: once abandoned to Israel, now abandoned to weeds. As the description of repeated ravaging in verses 5–6 recalls that of Jerusalem in 6:11–13, so this talk of abandonment and **desolation** takes up words from there too. Aram's fate parallels Judah's as well as Ephraim's, and/or Judah is no better and no better off than Ephraim and Ephraim is no better and no better off than Judah.

17:10–11 / It is becoming clear that these poems about other peoples are more complicated than their titles imply. They are more than mere reassurance for Judah that its enemies will get their comeuppance. The point is now even more overt, because suddenly verses 10–11 are directly addressing someone. The someone is feminine singular, and the only one who can be accused of forgetting her **Savior** is Jerusalem herself. Isaiah 17 begins to remind us of Amos 1–2. There the northern prophet condemns the people's neighbors, then Judah, then Ephraim itself. Here the southern prophet condemns the people's neighbor, then Ephraim, then Judah itself. Again the poem utilizes verbal effect. The description of Yahweh as **the Rock, your fortress** resembles the phrase "strong cities." Jerusalem has a more impressive object of trust than Aram's, but it has **forgotten . . . not remembered.** Again, the Hebrew words for remember, **vine,** and **plant** sound very similar, as if to point to the conviction that if there is no remembering, there might as well be no vine planting. These are voluntary acts. Remembering and forgetting are voluntary acts. They mean keeping in mind and putting out of mind. So Jerusalem is as guilty for its forgetting as Aram is for its god-making (v. 8), its literal harvest will be as disastrous as Ephraim's metaphorical harvest (vv. 5–6), and its literal wasting as cruel as Ephraim's metaphorical wasting (v. 4).

17:12–14 / If verses 10–11 suddenly narrow the focus to Jerusalem itself, verses 12–14 suddenly broaden the focus to the raging nations. The section opens not like an oracle; the word **Oh** often opens a declaration of calamity (see Additional Notes on 5:8–24). Even beyond the "Oh," the language follows that of 5:8–24 with its **raging** and **uproar** (there NIV has "nobles" and "brawlers"). But this is not Judah's raging and uproar, and we recall from those earlier chapters how the **great waters** (8:7, the same words) are a figure for the Assyrians. Here Assyria is not named, and the "Oh" relates to **many nations.** It generalizes the promise about Assyria. Indeed it summarizes the general truth that has been implicit in what we have read so far in chapters 13–17 and will continue to see chapters 18–23 illustrate. Further, the many nations are put down not because of their wrong against Yahweh, as was Assyria in 10:5–19, but because they **plunder us**. It is not Assyria's master who speaks here, but Assyria's victims. So this general statement at the center of chapters 13–23 declares the general truth about Yahweh's capacity to put the nations in their place, which the chapters apply in different directions. It thus reminds the people of the truth that will be proved in generation after generation.

Additional Notes §12

15–16 / For further reading see B. D. Jones, *Howling Over Moab* (Atlanta: Scholars Press, 1996).

16:1–2 / **Women** is the plural of the word translated "Daughter" (see on 1:8–9). The Moabite men approach the strong woman, Zion, like weak women.

16:3b–4 / NIV and NRSV close the Moabites' words after v. 4a, but the text does not indicate this, and it leaves vv. 3b–4 floating. If they are prophetic words, in the context their promise still follows on and supports Moab's own words.

16:5 / The word *khesed* will not recur until 40:6 (NIV "glory"), where it denotes the fading nature of all such human commitment; then it denotes God's steadfast commitment in 54:8, 10; 55:3; 63:7, and that of human beings in 57:1 (NIV "devout").

16:7 / **Men:** MT has "raisin cakes" (*'ashiyshey*, see mg.); Jer. 48:31 has "men" (*'anshey*). Raisin cakes were royal bounty (2 Sam. 6:19). They were evidently stimulants (cf. the link with grapes/vines and thus with wine which follows in vv. 8–10) and were eaten both as lovers' food (Song 2:5) and at religious festivals (Hos. 3:1). So Moab laments the loss of much-enjoyed luxuries.

16:14 / **As a servant bound by contract would count them:** i.e., accurately!

17:1–3 / The participles here are followed by imperfect verbs, which usually imply English future, but I take it that in v. 1, at least, this is an example of the Hb. idiom whereby a finite verb continues a participle but the participial meaning is kept—that is, the passage has present reference (see GK 116x).

17:3b / Presumably the idea is "Aram will be reduced to a remnant and will thus experience the same fate as the glory of Israel." Verses 4–6 then explain the latter.

17:5 / **The Valley of Rephaim** is a fertile plain near Jerusalem.

17:9 / NIV transposes clauses and thus changes the meaning. The order is "their strong cities will be like the places abandoned to thickets and undergrowth that people left because of the Israelites." The LXX apparently had a different text, "their strong cities will be like the places abandoned by Hivites and Amorites that they left because of the Israelites." There would be only a slight difference in the Hb. NRSV follows this text. It makes more explicit the comparison with peoples fleeing when the Israelites first came.

§13 Poems about the Southern Powers (Isa. 18:1–20:6)

For three chapters we turn to the far south. Cush covers an area corresponding to the very south of modern Egypt and the northern part of Sudan. A Cushite dynasty ruled Egypt itself at the end of the eighth century, so this poem about Cush is as much a poem about Egypt (cf. 20:1–6).

18:1–7 / This poem begins "Oh," like the preceding poem about the nations in general (NIV translates **woe** this time). This parallel suggests that the embassy from Cush raises issues covered by the generalization that appeared in 17:12–14. It also presupposes yet another form of *Realpolitik*. A Cushite embassy arrives in Judah by sea, presumably seeking Judean cooperation for its control of Egypt, which in itself would involve resistance to Assyria like Aram's and Ephraim's. Reliance on Egypt will be Judah's temptation in chapters 28–32.

Isaiah turns the **messengers** on their heels (v. 2). His words may be more directly meant for the Jerusalem politicians who have the task of actually responding to the embassy. Perhaps he is sending the messengers off home. The people of their area are of famed height and appearance. But the phrase translated **tall and smooth-skinned** is of uncertain meaning, and he speaks more as if sending them off somewhere other than home. The people **feared far and wide** is Assyria (see 10:24), and verse 2b sounds as if it is referring to Mesopotamia. The embassy, then, is sent off to see the Assyrians themselves.

The forces summoned by banner and trumpet (v. 3) are unnamed, as in 13:2, and so are their victims. Assyria might feature on either side. But in any case the point is that Yahweh is in control and human politicking will not be what decides world events. People will see and hear when Yahweh's army responds to the heavenly commander's summoning. For a while the appropriate human stance is waiting quietly (see 30:15; 32:17), because that is what Yahweh is doing, like people waiting for harvest (vv. 4–6). The moment for Yahweh's action will arrive. It will come later than people think (they are seeking to bring it about now), but also earlier than they think (before the due harvest time), with devastating effects for the tree.

A surprising footnote follows the grim depiction of the results of battle. Whoever the people described in verse 2 are, and whether they played some part in the battle or not, they now bring **gifts** to "Yahweh armies," the kind of gifts that constitute homage to a victorious king (the word comes otherwise only in Ps. 68:29; 76:11). The description recalls 16:1–5. The reversals of history bring another nation to acknowledge Yahweh. The description of Zion as **the place of the Name** of Yahweh recalls Deuteronomy's characteristic conceptualization (e.g., Deut. 12:5–12) applied to Jerusalem in the promise to David and the prayer of Solomon (2 Sam. 7; 1 Kgs. 8). A person's name expresses who the person is, so the description of Zion as the place where Yahweh's name dwells is an indirect description of it as the place where Yahweh is present in person.

19:1–15 / It is not surprising that Egypt should feature in these prophecies. It was Israel's old oppressor and would in due course be Judah's biggest temptation. It seemed a resource for protection when Assyria invaded, and it was well-known as a repository of ancient wisdom. It might seem wise to treat Egypt as a resource.

But wisdom is justified by her children, implies Isaiah, and real power lies somewhere else. Judah was familiar with the picture of Yahweh riding on the storm clouds from Sinai to Palestine (Deut. 33:2, 26–28; Ps. 68:7–9, 33) and it knew that Yahweh could always come in such power again when needed (Ps. 18:10). Here the direction of the journey is reversed (v. 1) and so are the results: not fertility but withering (vv. 5–10). Yahweh will bring a repetition of the natural disasters of which Israel read in the story of the plagues in Exodus. Instead of the Israelites being divided against each other, the Egyptians will be (v. 2). Instead of the Israelites being subject to a cruel overlord, the Egyptians will be (v. 4).

As in the poem about Moab, this poem about Egypt contains a number of elements that we may be able to link to actual historical events. Assyria under Sargon defeated Egypt about 720 B.C., for instance, and that defeat might serve as a healthy reminder in the time of Hezekiah a decade or two later. So might the subordination of Egypt to Cushite rulers noted above. But the prophecy lacks the specificity that enables us to be sure of such links, in Isaiah's own day or subsequently. The poem may be based on actual events, but it as likely offers an imaginative picture like the Moab poem rather than one whose detail relates to a specific context.

The exodus story demonstrated the feebleness of Egyptian leadership and religion. Yahweh is greater than Pharaoh and his gods. It is the Lord Yahweh who decides on power issues in Egypt (v. 4). The distinctively Isaianic motif here is the demonstration of the feebleness of Egyptian wisdom. Pharaoh thought he had a corps of skilled political advisers. They told him that was what they were. They had wisdom collected over the centuries. Israel knew it well. At least one section of Proverbs was adapted from an Egyptian prototype, the Thirty Sayings in Proverbs 22:17–24:22. In the conviction that all truth is God's truth, Israel was quite open to learning from the culture and religion of other peoples where that could fill out and fit with what they knew of Yahweh. But this is a dangerous path, and it can lead to an excessive and undiscerning regard for those other resources. So Isaiah attacks reliance on human wisdom, Israelite or foreign.

In Isaiah's vision, Egypt finds itself overcome by internal disorder, external oppression, and natural disaster. As well as its intellectual tradition, the famous asset of Egyptian life was the Nile with its crucial role in Egyptian agriculture, industry, economics, and life. That fails (vv. 5–10). In the moment of disaster its religion and its advisers are helpless. Indeed, these advisers bear responsibility. They have led Egypt astray and made them wander about like helpless drunks (v. 14). If one is to give political precision to the charge, they did not know how to read the Assyrians or the Cushites.

How foolish of Judah, then, to treat Egypt as the great repository of power and sagacity, especially when its calamity comes about not merely because of the inherent inadequacy of its resources but because of Israel's own God, brought here by cloud chariot. Yahweh has been formulating strategies that will be far more effective than Egypt's (v. 12). More chillingly, Yahweh has been involved in making the Egyptian leadership trust in its own inadequate insight and thus in confusing its people (vv. 13–14). One recalls the motif of the closing of the Pharaoh's mind in Exodus. It is as well that we shall soon read of a more positive side to Yahweh's sovereignty.

Egypt's experience of calamity and its response to events parallels Judah's: with verses 1, 2, 3, 4, 13, and 15 compare 7:2; 3:5; 8:19; 7:17; 3:12; and 9:14, respectively—though **palm branch and reed** (v. 15) are especially telling terms in connection with Egypt (Clements, *Isaiah 1–39*, p. 169). Again the prophecy's direct concern is not that Egypt should come to a bad end because of its wickedness or its treatment of Judah, but rather that Judah should not take it too seriously.

19:16–25 / The prophecies relating to Egypt again parallel those concerning Moab in that two sections of threat stand on either side of a central section that envisages the foreign power turning to Yahweh when it faces the fact of its humiliation. It is prose, not verse; it cannot be set out as lines and half-lines and it lacks the parallelism that characterizes verses 1–15.

The passage tells of five features of "that day." First, in verse 16, **in that day the Egyptians will be like women** carries on the theme of verses 1–15 and might be considered with that section. Again we read of Yahweh's **planning** at work. Yahweh's hand is **uplifted** as once it was stretched out at the exodus. But the last people who reacted like women to catastrophe were on their way to Zion (16:2). Losing macho aggressiveness and self-sufficiency can make it possible to be open to God. The words for **shudder** and **fear/be terrified** can be used for trembling and thrill before God (e.g., 66:2, 5; 60:5), while the word for **terror** *(khaga')*, which comes only here, sounds as if it should have something to do with a festival *(khag)*. So while abject fear would be an appropriate enough response to the experiences described in verses 1–15 (as in 10:29; 2:10, 19, 21), there might be more to be said. This will turn out to be a low key beginning to a suite that resounds more and more as we read on through verses 16–25.

The second reference to that day comes in verse 18, with **in that day five cities** will speak Hebrew and swear allegiance to Yahweh. If these words refer to five specific cities, we do not know which they are and why they are mentioned. While a number of Jewish communities developed in Egypt from the time of Jeremiah, and these might have suggested the images for the prophecy, the prophecy goes beyond that. While concreteness of detail in a prophecy can suggest a link with concrete events, we have no evidence of such background in this case (contrast 1 Kgs. 13:2). Of course that may be coincidence—the prophecy might presuppose that its audience knew of facts that are now lost to us. But concreteness of detail can also function to add vividness to an imaginative scenario, and it seems as likely that this is the function of the detail here. In practice that is its function. We then need not look for a one-to-one correspondence with any specific events. The picture envisages Egypt having such a change of attitude to Judah and to Yahweh that some cities, including ones known for their commitment to Egyptian traditional religion, will even adopt Hebrew and take the worship of Yahweh as their city religion. The passage is thus a vivid promise that communities in Egypt will be drawn right into recognizing Yahweh and identifying with Israel. It is Yahweh's way of affirming, for the peoples of Egypt in particular, the promise that all the families of the earth will be drawn to Abraham's people and Abraham's God (e.g., Gen. 12:1–3). This point will become more explicit in verses 24–25.

Thirdly, **in that day** "Egypt will have its own 'salvation history' " (Sawyer, *Isaiah,* vol. 1, p. 176) parallel to Israel's (vv. 19–22). It is difficult to imagine a more radical picture of Egypt seeking and finding Yahweh. In possessing **an altar,** and especially **a monument,** they are worshiping Yahweh the way Israel's ancestors did in Genesis. Subsequently altars were more controlled and monuments (sacred stone pillars) were banned. The Torah's hesitation related to the conviction that these could compromise witness to Yahweh by encouraging people to worship according to traditional ways. The prophecy believes that, in this foreign land, such markers can witness to Yahweh. They will be like the monument (NIV "pillar") that was to witness to a commitment on the part of Jacob and the Aramean Laban to live in peace before their common God (Gen. 31), or like the altar east of the Jordan that witnessed to the fact that people there did have a share in Yahweh (Josh. 22).

So Egypt will be able to cry out as the oppressed seeking deliverance and to find it, rather than being the oppressor who causes people to cry out. Further, Egypt will acknowledge Yahweh as deliverer in the way that Israel did at the exodus, rather than as victor (cf. Exod 6:7 and 7:5). It will express that acknowledgment in worship and commitment in the way Israel was taught to do at Sinai. Yahweh will **strike** as Egypt and Israel were stricken, but Yahweh will also **heal** Egypt as Israel was healed and Egypt was not (Exod. 15:26). Egypt will **turn** to Yahweh as Moses did (Exod. 5:22; NIV "return") and make **pleas** to Yahweh as Egypt and Israel did then (Exod. 8:28–30; NIV "pray"), but this time Egypt will do this for itself and find healing.

Fourthly, **in that day** Egypt and Assyria will be one in life and in worship (v. 23). This was an extraordinary vision since in Isaiah's day Assyria was Egypt's overlord and Egypt Assyria's unwilling subordinate. Then there will be an equal relationship expressed in shared worship.

And finally, **in that day** Yahweh's purpose to bless all peoples will find fulfillment (vv. 24–25). The usual scholarly view is that this "advanced" vision in verses 19–25 belongs to the latest OT period, and that it is an imaginative picture of how Yahweh's promise to Abraham in Genesis 12:1–3 might come to pass. Blessing all peoples had always been Yahweh's purpose. Verses 19–25 simply give contextual expression to the reality of this. That the words **my people, my handiwork, my inheritance** should be attached to Egypt and Assyria and not just to Israel is breathtaking. The recurrence of **Israel** (contrast **Judah** in v. 17) indicates that the prophecy's vision is for the whole nation. The other side of the theological promotion of Egypt and Assyria and Israel's consequent surrender of its unique position is that Israel itself will be one of the international "big three." The blessing's concern for Abraham's people itself still stands.

The prophecy is a spectacular example of one that never came true. It was presumably preserved because of a conviction that it came from Yahweh and expressed the vision to which Yahweh was committed. While Christians may believe that aspects of it have come true in a metaphorical sense as people of all nations come to acknowledge Jesus as Messiah, even then much is left over for the shaping of our own vision and prayer. It therefore invites us to look forward to and to pray for the coming of the day when nations such as Egypt (and we can then add our own nation) revere God, when its cities (and we can add the name of our own city) acknowledge Yahweh, when such nations have a salvation history parallel to Israel's, when the great powers are united in worship, and when the promise to Abraham indeed comes true.

20:1–6 / This final section of chapters 18–20 brings together Egypt and Cush, the two peoples who have been the subject of chapters 18–19, and completes the calamity-promise-calamity pattern that parallels chapters 15–16. It also makes explicit the direct implication that runs through these prophecies: do not **trust** in these peoples or **boast** in them or you will end up **afraid** and **put to shame.** They will let you down, either because they are deliberately deceitful or because they are unable to give the **help and deliverance from the king of Assyria** that you wanted and they promised. Words such as trust, help, and deliverance belong to Yahweh—not to the likes of Egypt and Cush. Earlier in the book, 10:3 and 19:2 ironically anticipate verses 5–6. But those words will be key ones in the account of Judah's dealings with Yahweh, Egypt, and Assyria in chapters 28–32 and 36–37, though the recurrent word for "trust" there is different. Here the word for **trusted in/ relied on** is *nabat*, which means more literally "looked to."

We can link all the peoples in chapters 13–23 to the political events of the late eighth century and to the efforts of Assyria's underlings to gain independence, but chapter 20, along with 14:28–32, provides the most concrete link. Sargon was emperor from 722 to 705 B.C. His own records (see *ANET*, p. 286) relate how Ashdod, one of the main Philistine cities on the coast south of Tel Aviv, led an independence movement against Assyria involving neighboring peoples such as Judah. In the course of it they appealed to Egypt for help. In 711 B.C. (just after the Cushites gained power in Egypt) Sargon's army took and destroyed Ashdod, transporting its inhabitants. That is the fate of which Isaiah warns Egypt and Cush, and the whole **coast**, which might mean Philistia in general, or might mean the whole region including Judah and its allies such as those that appear in these chapters.

Chapter 20 is also distinctive for the window it opens on Isaiah's ministry, which resembles that of Ezekiel with his symbolic behavior. Verse 2 is a parenthesis that provides the background to the chapter. Thus the order of events is:

(a) Isaiah went about in a sackcloth coat for an unstated period, perhaps because this was a prophet's garb (2 Kgs. 1:8), or perhaps as a sign of mourning for events he prophesied;

(b) then three years ago, which would be the beginning of the independence movement, he cast off his sackcloth coat;

(c) for three years he has thus gone about at least coatless—no joke in a Jerusalem winter;

(d) just now the Assyrians' defeat of Ashdod leads to the threat that Egypt and Cush (and other peoples associated with them) will also be transported.

Yahweh thus speaks **through** Isaiah (lit. "by the hand of"), not only via his words but via his actions. He is again **a sign and a portent** (see 8:18). Perhaps he has already been involved in one form of such action, if sackcloth suggested mourning. He now changes it for another, going about as if stripped for a humiliating transportation. In this, God is giving people not merely an illustration of what will or could happen but a sign of being in the midst of actually making it happen. It has the power of a sacrament. God is putting a decision into effect before their eyes.

Additional Notes §13

19:2 / **Kingdom:** a canton or small division of the federal state.

19:11, 13 / **Zoan** is a historic seat at the northeast of the Nile Delta and thus on the Israelite side of the country. **Memphis** is the capital of Lower Egypt, near modern Cairo.

19:16 / References to **that day** (also found in vv. 18, 19, 23, 24) are commonly assumed to be from a period later than Isaiah, and this may well be right, though all sides of scholarly opinion on the matter reflect presupposition and fashion. We lack evidence and criteria for dating the prophecies. As Oswalt notes (*Isaiah 1–39*, p. 374), Clements (*Isaiah 1–39*, pp. 169–70) dismisses the extreme views that the material comes from Isaiah himself or from the second century and decides for a date in the middle, but without giving arguments.

19:18 / "Destruction City" is *'ir haheres,* while "Sun City" (see NIV mg.) is *'ir hakheres.* While this might be a slip one way or the other, Hb. manuscripts sometimes altered names that referred to other religions (e.g., Eshbaal, or "Baal's fire," becomes Ishbosheth, "Man of shame"). This looks like another such example. Sun City is On or Heliopolis, city of the sun god, Re, where Joseph's father-in-law ministered (Gen 41:45).

19:19 / Scholars have looked for specific events with which to link the **altar,** such as the temples of the Jewish community at Elephantine (Aswan) in the fifth century B.C. and at Leontopolis in the second, but none of the suggestions quite work (see Clements, *Isaiah 1–39*, pp. 171–72).

§14 Poems about Northern Powers and about Jerusalem Itself (Isa. 21:1–23:18)

21:1–10 / This cryptic poem about **the Desert by the Sea** forms a small-scale parallel to 13:1–14:23. First, it concerns the fall of Babylon, although this is not made explicit until near the end. The hearers thus remain in suspense. Second, it relates both to the situation of Isaiah's day, when Babylon was one of the powers encouraging the assertion of independence over against Assyria, and to the later context of Isaiah 40–55 when Babylon was about to fall to Persia.

Third, the vision once again starts in the middle of things. Perhaps this was how it came to the prophet. In the winter, strong desert storms sweep north from the Negeb toward Jerusalem, and the vision begins with something like such a whirlwind. What does it stand for? It comes **from a land of terror,** the description used in 18:2, 7: so is this Cush, or Assyria?

The prophet's questions, and ours, begin to be answered in verse 2. **Shown** is literally "told" (so NRSV), which suggests something verbal rather than visual, so the prophet receives some words of explanation of the vision. Immediately and typically, the answers raise as many questions as they answer. **The traitor** sounds like Cush and Egypt again (20:5), or any of the powers of which we have been reading who will not fulfill the hopes Judah may place in them. **The looter** is the word for Moab's unnamed attacker in 16:4 (NIV "destroyer"). Either could also refer to Babylon itself.

Verse 2b suddenly clarifies identities—not by a direct interpretation of what has preceded but by a commissioning of two peoples to act. The hearers have to put two and two together. They might do so by seeing these two peoples as the betrayer and looter. Perhaps these two were supposed to be Babylon's allies, for instance, and have betrayed and looted instead. Or the hearers might see them as agents of the betrayer/looter's punishment.

Elam we know as the location of some exiled Israelites (11:11). Its neighbor **Media** we know as attacker of Babylon (13:17). So we are back in the far northeast. These two are Yahweh's agents in bringing to an end **all the groaning she caused.**

But who is "she"? If Babylon was the subject in chapter 13, perhaps it is here as well, but for a moment we (and the prophet?) are left to inference. Indeed, the words are more open than that, for the phrase is literally "all her groaning," which might just as easily (more easily?) mean "all the groaning she utters." Who would she then be? Again the passage resembles chapter 13, where initially the subject might be (for instance) Assyria, or Judah, or Babylon again, or some other victim of Assyria such as ones we have met—or ones we have not yet met, such as Edom. Once more the fearful prospect of a scene of death and destruction provokes anguished terror (vv. 3–4; cf. 13:8). In the victim city the prophet can see life carrying on as usual (cf. the story of Babylon's fall in Dan. 5). Like someone in the audience shouting out uselessly to the cast in a film, the prophet shouts to warn them of the terror that is imminent (v. 5b).

Then Yahweh speaks. The introduction to verse 6 slows down the action and announces a change of scene. This **lookout** is evidently not on the walls of this city that is unaware of its imminent attack. He is on the walls of the attackers' own city, where people anxiously wait to discover how their army is faring (see Judg. 5:28–30). There is no e-mail or fax. They have to await the first signs of the army returning. Will they come as victors or in flight after defeat?

At last we overhear the report addressed to the lookout which also makes clear what the whole poem has been about (v. 9b). Babylon indeed fell to Assyria in 710, 701, and 689 B.C., and to Persia in 539 B.C. Yet the poem closes with another declaration that can be received in different ways in different situations. To a people **crushed** by Assyria, the prospect of Babylon's fall is bad news. To a people crushed by Babylon itself a century or two later, it is good news.

21:11–12 / After hearing the prophet's vision in verses 1–10, the prophet's hearers might immediately be struck by verse 11a as having a double reference. **Dumah** is an oasis near Babylon which, like Babylon, was subject to Assyrian attack in the eighth century and would itself be concerned about Babylon's fate. The region also experienced Babylonian invasion and withdrawal in the sixth century, not long before Babylon fell. But oracles can be allusive and symbolic, and *dumah* is also a Hebrew word for **silence** (see NIV mg.). Both other times this word occurs in the OT, it refers to the silence of death (Ps. 94:17; 115:17), so it sets a somber tone for the poem. The voice that addresses the prophet (v. 11b) comes from **Seir** in Edom, and the word *dumah* also resembles the word **Edom** (see NIV mg.), which will be addressed with hostility rather than sympathy in chapter 34. So a voice from one place of deathly silence calls to another place of deathly silence.

The city's **watchman** is someone who stands on a watchtower (v. 8). The words are similar in Hebrew, as they are in English, which further invites us to link verses 11–12 with verses 1–10. A watchman's task is especially important during the night, when an enemy might mount a surprise attack, or at least prepare one. Thus the arrival of morning means a sigh of relief. At least that threat is over. But the world-weary watchman is only too aware that another night is always coming. Symbolism perhaps continues in this enigmatic exchange. The question is whether the night of calamity and oppression is over, and the answer for Dumah/Edom is "not finally."

21:13–17 / The word *'arab* (NIV **Arabia**) comes only here, in this poem about the steppe, and could refer to people living on the high desert plain, or it could mean "evening." So again the introduction points in several directions. The scene remains to the northeast from Judah. **Dedan** and **Tema** are oases near Dumah in northwest Arabia. Dedan is mentioned in the records of Nabonidus (see on 14:3–23) and Tema was his capital for a period. Again we are in the midst of an event, perhaps within the same sequence of events as in verses 1–10 and 11–12. There has been a battle and there have been winners and losers. The unidentified losers are exhausted and fleeing and are now without water or food. The oracle urges the nomads of Dedan and Teman to have mercy on them.

Verses 16–17 are in prose and might be a separate prophecy, but they begin "For . . . " (see NRSV; NIV omits), which seems to invite us to take verses 13–17 together. As happens elsewhere in these chapters, these last verses lift the suspense and identify the losers. The exhausted fugitives are the remnants of the powerful forces of **Kedar,** a people rather than a city, one of the most powerful peoples of northwest Arabia. Their kings sometimes ruled cities such as Dedan and oases such as Tema, but they were in turn sometimes ruled by Assyria or Babylon. The passage presupposes the downfall of these mighty ones who in the past controlled the cities that have now, as the tables have turned, been invited to have mercy on them. Of course the victors, Assyria and Babylon, will also have their comeuppance in time.

There is no comment on the sinfulness of these various peoples, for which their defeat would be punishment. The theological point comes rather in the final sentence, which asserts an extraordinary conviction of the sovereignty of Yahweh the God of Israel in the events of far off peoples whose interrelationships have nothing to do with Israel directly. Yahweh is Lord even in the far north and east where Assyria and Babylon operate, so Israel needs to take account of Yahweh's lordship. And the fate of these Arabian peoples again suggests that there is nothing to be gained by allying with Babylon.

22:1–14 / Again the enigmatic title comes from the body of the poem (v. 5), though in this case the location of **the Valley of Vision** becomes explicit (vv. 8–11). We have to accept that many of the poems in these chapters do not tell us their historical background, so that reading them is a little like reading a parable, or understanding a film when you arrive halfway through. While the prophet's first hearers would probably have known more than we do and therefore would have understood his words in a more straightforward, and perhaps more nuanced, way, the written form of the prophecies assumes that we can make sense of them without that knowledge.

We know the general background to this poem from the story of events in Jerusalem in Isaiah 36–37 and more broadly in 2 Kings, though we do not know whether the event that stimulated rejoicing was the particular deliverance described in chapters 36–37. The poem here does presuppose some occasion when Jerusalem has been threatened, besieged, and relieved. This has produced understandable rejoicing, but the story is not over, and eventually the city's destruction will come. The usual critical view is that the poem has been expanded in the light of Jerusalem's fall in 587 B.C., though it is difficult to know precisely which elements originate with which situation. But evidently the passage works with an arc that extends from marvelous deliverance in the eighth century to eventual fall in the sixth century, and invites us to reflect on issues of joy, grief, realism, sobriety, security, practicality, trust, and repentance in the light of that.

But all this we do not know as we begin to hear the words in verses 1–4, which sound like another vision of disaster upon some foreign people. This people is challenged about its uninhibited rejoicing in a deliverance. There are at least two things they are ignoring. The first is its terrible cost and its ignominy (vv. 2b–3). Sennacherib's own records document this with regard to Judah (see *ANET,* p. 288). The second is the fact that there is still a destruction of the people to come (v. 4). The deliverance is only temporary. The expression here seems too strong for this to be simply another way of referring to the deaths in verse 3. Yahweh has not finished.

For Yahweh's **day** (cf. 2:12) will come for the Valley of Vision (vv. 5–8a): the word "for" is there in the Hebrew (see NRSV, and note on 1:29–30). **Tumult and trampling and terror** nicely reproduces an assonance in the Hebrew, where the words also rhyme. This will be a different kind of **tumult** from the one the people indulged in after the city's relief (v. 2). In verse 8a it becomes clear that in this poem the subject and the audience are one and the same. Not only Babylon is a victim of **Elam,** but also Jerusalem (cf. 21:2). **Kir** is another city somewhere to the northeast and part of the Assyrian empire. Kir was a destination of deportation in 2 Kings 16:9–10 and therefore a name to bring a chill to Judean ears. It is not only the far northeast that sees **charioteers and horses** (see 21:7, 9). It is not only there that the **shield** will be needed (see 21:5). It is not only Philistia's **gates** that will weep (see 14:31). What comes on other peoples will come on Judah too.

It looks at first as if the description of **that day** in verses 8b–11 continues the description of a day in the future. But it becomes clear that the day has already come about, when Jerusalem was under threat and the community applied itself to repairing its defenses and water supply so as to enable it to withstand a siege (see 7:3; 2 Chron. 32). The repeated verbs **look** and **see,** which summarize the prophet's critique, bracket these verses. The people asked the right practical questions about their situation but utterly failed to ask the right religious questions—about the significance of what was going on, about "Who" or "Why" as well as "What." It was not just Sennacherib who was threatening them, but Yahweh.

Again the title **the Lord, the LORD Almighty** and the repeated reference to **that day** (vv. 12–13) link with verses 5–8a and 8b–11, but the content of verses 12–13 takes us back to verses 1–4. There ought to have been grief at their losses and their ignominy, at the fate that still awaits them and at their failure to turn to Yahweh, but there is only revelry. They would not have actually said **let us eat and drink for tomorrow we die.** The prophet puts on their lips the implications of their behavior (cf. 28:15). Because they insist on revelry when sober reflection is what is needed, death will be the result. The repetition of the phrase "that day" brings out how the day when Yahweh acts in people's experience now, and the final day when God will act in ultimate judgment and/or mercy, are two expressions of the same reality, the same working. "Now" foreshadows "then"; "then" will fulfill "now."

Verse 14 hardly means that Yahweh would refuse to forgive if they did turn back. The implication is rather that no one can offer atonement for them if they do not turn. It is another sharp way of trying to bring them to their senses and to warn the hearers of the terrible consequences of following their example. Again the warning is grounded in the fact that the one who speaks is **the Lord, the LORD Almighty** (see vv. 5, 12, 15). The title came previously at 3:15, then in a similar cluster to the one here in connection with Yahweh's putting down the Assyrians in 10:16, 23, 24. Jerusalem either has the comfort of this three-titled God for it or the fear of this God against it. Yahweh's warnings to Jerusalem are at least as chilling as those to any other city.

22:15–25 / The message to Jerusalem in chapter 22 includes a message to a politician. We have seen that the background to chapters 13–23 in Isaiah's day is the reign of Ahaz and Hezekiah and that Isaiah's concern with other peoples relates to their significance as potential allies and instigators of independence movements in relation to Assyria. Yet, strangely, Isaiah rarely refers to the kings. In particular, there is a strange "silence" about Hezekiah (Watts, *Isaiah 1–33*, pp. 221–22) from 1:1 to 36:1. When this silence is broken, Eliakim and Shebna appear as the two most significant royal ministers (36:3, 11, 22; 37:3). They act as intermediaries between Hezekiah and the king of Assyria's emissary and between Hezekiah and the King of kings' emissary.

The words **The Lord, the LORD Almighty** introduce Yahweh in the same serious terms as those in verses 1–14, and Isaiah's opening words to Shebna, **What are you doing here?** are the same as his opening words to the people as a whole (see Additional Notes on v. 1). So Isaiah confronts this senior minister with the same solemnity and the same question as he had used with the people. But the focus of the question is different, and bizarre (see v. 16). If the **here** (which actually comes three times, as NRSV shows) and the participles are to be taken at their face value, with further bizarreness the confrontation takes place at the tomb itself where the work is progressing.

There are several elements to Isaiah's critique. First, Shebna thinks he is going to die peacefully in Jerusalem and that it is worth making arrangements for his eventual burial there. Like the people in verses 1–14, he has not seen the seriousness of the threat that hangs over the city. He may commission a tomb, but he will not use it. He will be hurled into a foreign land to die **there** (the word comes twice in v. 18). Some irony attaches to these preparations for death, in the light of the saying in verse 13 and the warning in verse 14. Second, Shebna has abused his position of power to commission this tomb in a place of particular splendor and honor. So he will lose his position (vv. 18b–19). Third, the reference to his splendid chariots adds an extra note of critique that points to the political policies with which he was associated (see 31:1).

So Eliakim will succeed Shebna. Verses 20–24 underline the power and glory of his office, which belong to Shebna at present. It emphasizes Yahweh's commitment to the city and the Davidic line; both will be secure in the hands of Eliakim. The prophecy describes the **place** (cf. 18:7) as **firm,** using the verb that described the city in 1:21, 26 (NIV "faithful"), the people in 7:9 (NIV "stand"), and the city's waters in 33:16 (NIV "will not fail"). Eliakim is the guarantee that such security can be experienced now. But it turns out that, as usual, the prophet's rhetoric has been leading us up the garden path. The declaration has a terrible sting in the tail (v. 25). It is a scene worthy of Ecclesiastes. One senior minister is replaced by another, but he in turn will then be replaced. There is no progress.

So let no one rely on any of them, not least their family who might be tempted to do so. Although Eliakim seems to be senior to Shebna in chapters 36–37, this hardly counts as fulfillment of the threat expressed here. But the association of the two with each other there expresses in another way the point in that last verse. "Politicians: a plague on all their houses."

At last the audience is in a position to understand why we are listening to these prophecies to a pair of Judean leaders. Yahweh had promised that the future could depend on them. But a chain is as strong as its weakest link. The promise will turn into disaster. The city and the royal house are only as safe as Shebna and Eliakim. They will fall, and everything with them.

One might have expected that the chapter about Jerusalem would bring this sequence of chapters to an end. In fact, another follows. One effect of this is to make Judah just another of the Middle Eastern powers whose recalcitrance Yahweh is trying to control. There is nothing distinctive about it (cf. Amos 9:7).

23:1–18 / The fact that the sequence actually concludes with a poem about Tyre gives it an impressive end to match its impressive beginning. Babylon and Tyre are the two significant powers at the eastern and western frontiers of Assyria's empire, its equivalents to New York and Los Angeles.

Once again it is the city's impressiveness that is a key factor in making its downfall necessary. But Babylon, along with Elam and Media, was on the edge of Israel's known world. Tyre was the beginning of a world that Israel knew stretched across the Mediterranean. Chapter 23 thus leads well into the worldwide perspective of chapters 24–27 (Sawyer, *Isaiah,* vol. 1, pp. 204–6). Once more the poem gains its effect not by describing the city's fall but by speaking from the perspective of its aftermath, here the awed reactions that will be appropriate from Tyre's neighbors and trading partners.

Again the title names the subject but the poem itself does not initially do so. So the audience is left in suspense as to who needs to be bewailed. NIV adds "Tyre" in verses 1b and 3 to clarify the meaning (contrast NRSV), but dramatically Isaiah's own audience has to work out who the poem refers to. Once more the opening of the poem does not say who it refers to. It thus leaves open the possibility that it might originally have referred to some other power, such as Sidon, which *is* named. Again the fact that the poem describes Tyre's fall as past does not establish whether it has happened historically or has happened only in the prophet's vision. NIV's understanding of the cryptic verse 13 implies the latter. Babylon has been defeated and Tyre needs to pay heed, though the prophet overtly offers Tyre no way of escape. Babylon's defeat is simply the guarantee that Tyre will also fall.

Tyre is on the Mediterranean coast south of modern Beirut. It comprises a small **island** (vv. 2, 6) half a mile off the coast, with a superb natural harbor, and an overflow development on the mainland. The old city thus had enviable natural security. It was a **fortress of the sea** (v. 4). A sequence of Assyrian emperors tried to capture it in order to bring it into line, with varying degrees of success. Nebuchadnezzar of Babylon also found it too capable of resistance (Ezek. 29:17–18). Presumably the background of this poem is Tyre's assertion of independence from Assyria during Isaiah's lifetime, which provoked two Assyrian attacks. But as far as we know neither led to its capture, certainly not to defeat on the scale presupposed here. Indeed, there is little indication that the prophet envisages military action, unless it lies in the enigmatic verse 13. In due course, in the fourth century, Alexander actually took Tyre only by building a causeway from the mainland, which then silted into a permanent land link.

Tyre was a major maritime and trading power, the leading city in Phoenicia, a crossroads on the trade routes between Asia, Africa, and Europe, the **market-place of the nations. Tarshish** is a port in Spain, one of a number of Tyrian colonies, the furthest imaginable point to the west, and ships of Tarshish are "ocean-going vessels" (see 2:16). The city would thus be the admiration of the Mediterranean and Middle Eastern world. It was an ancient equivalent to Rome or Singapore or San Francisco, well-known to the prophet's hearers by its reputation and for its links with Israel in Israel's heyday (e.g., 1 Kgs. 5; 7; 9).

And the prophet imagines people called to bewail its fall. **Destroyed** may be an over-translation of a verb that need only refer to defeat or loss, but it was evidently a serious defeat. The poem's immediate geographical horizon is on one side the eastern Mediterranean, the island of Cyprus, the first landing point on the journey west from Tyre, and on the other side Tyre's major trading partner, Egypt (**Shihor** is the Nile valley). But the people of Tyre are told to go and find refuge as far away as its daughter city Tarshish itself (v. 6). Ms Tarshish (for the phrase "Daughter of Tarshish," see on 1:8–9) becomes a dependency now deprived of the senior partner she needed for her trade (v. 10).

If Tyre falls, who is safe? Its security was a linchpin of the structure of international trade and travel. So the news causes dismay and anguish in Egypt, another of Assyria's unwilling underlings, as well as in Phoenicia (v. 5). The sea itself grieves the loss of its daughter. The bereavement puts it into the same position as a woman who has never had any children (v. 4). The references to Tyre's neighbor Sidon (vv. 2, 4, 12) in themselves make clear that the calamity is not confined to Tyre but affects Phoenicia in general with its orientation to the sea and its involvement in trade (v. 11).

This sense of bewilderment and fear replaces the quite reasonable pride and exultation that Tyre had felt on account of its antiquity, its international connections, and its power over its own far-off trading colonies (vv. 7–9). As is often the case, the talk of **pride** need not imply that Tyre was inordinately proud of itself. The context, with its references to glory and renown, suggests that its pride is its objective impressiveness, not its subjective arrogance. The word is rendered "majesty" in 2:10–22. Nor does the prophet refer to Tyre's notorious religious influence on Israel through the Tyrian queens Jezebel and Athaliah. The mere fact that it was so impressive and successful meant that it would need to be brought down, because its majesty threatens to obscure true majesty and to encourage false trust (see on 13:9–11).

So Yahweh **planned it** (vv. 8–9). It is another act of the one whose careful, strategic, and effective purpose is at work not only in the history of Israel but also in that of the nations of the world (see 5:19; 9:6; 14:24–27; 19:11–17; 28:29). Failure to clarify how the disaster came about helps to underline the ultimate rather than immediate causes.

Verse 14 rounds off the first part of the poem (cf. v. 1). Verses 15–18 parallel the more positive closures to other poems. Like them, they also raise eyebrows. Tyre's trade is like prostitution and after her long desolation she seems like an aged whore still trying to ply her trade. But now her profits will be holy to Yahweh and will go to Yahweh's worshipers, as in the days of Solomon and Hiram (Sawyer, *Isaiah,* p. 202). So there is hope even for her trade. Yahweh is as free to reverse Deuteronomy 23:18 here as to reverse Deuteronomy 24 in Hosea 1–3. It is also a neat reversal of verse 9. Historically, seventy years takes us from Isaiah's day to the period of Josiah, the collapse of the Assyrian empire, and the relative freedom of Tyre and Judah (Sweeney, *Isaiah 1–39,* p. 309).

Additional Notes §14

21:1 / The reference to **the Desert by the Sea** is a mystery. It may refer to the fact that Babylon was a desert area in the region of Mesopotamia near the Persian Gulf and/or it may take up the word **desert** from later in v. 1.

21:5 / On **oil the shields**, see 2 Sam. 1:21. But we do not know whether (for instance) this was a religious rite, a form of anointing, or an aesthetic act, to make the shields look nicer, or a practical task, to make arrows slide off them.

21:8 / In Hb. **the lookout** (though actually a different word from that in v. 6) is very similar to **a lion** (NIV mg.). The latter makes poor sense here and probably came about as an error in copying by a scribe. Many commentators assume that the lookout is the prophet himself, on the walls of Jerusalem, and that the army in v. 9a is attacking Babylon, but this confuses the picture.

21:11–12 / **But also the night:** the Hb. may mean "but it is still night at the moment." The watchman is then telling the questioner that there is longer to wait yet. **To me** (v. 11) might imply that here the prophet is the watchman.

21:13 / The root word *'arab* originally referred not to an ethnic group but to people who lived on the high desert plain (the word *'arabah* also denotes the arid steppe in the Jordan rift). Only later did the word come to denote the Arab people. But the word also resembles another root and could mean "evening": cf. vv. 11–12. The heading is lit. "an oracle/poem *in* the steppe" or "*. . . in* Arabia," illustrating how the headings are taken from the actual poems. The verse division implies "You caravans of Dedanites will camp . . . " (see NRSV) and implies that this location is the Dedanites' punishment. It is they who have been defeated. This is an easier way to read the Hb., but NIV makes better sense of the passage as a whole.

21:16 / **As a servant bound by contract:** see on 16:14.

22:1 / **What troubles you now:** lit. "What to you now," i.e., "What are you doing here, what's going on?" NRSV's interpretation "What do you mean" makes better sense in the context than NIV, as the people seem exultant rather than troubled.

22:5 / We do not know what **the Valley of Vision** refers to. "Valley" is *ge'*, the term for the steep ravines around the city that form its natural security (e.g., *ge' hinnom*—cf. Gehenna). The "valleys" of v. 7 are the broader vales (*'emeq*) such as the Vale of Rephaim (17:5).

22:6 / The verbs in vv. 5–8a continue to be in the past tense. In translating them as present tense, NIV assumes that the past tense reflects the actuality of the vision to the prophet, but the section might simply continue verses 1–4 or be written in the light of the actual fall of the city in 587 B.C.

22:8 / **The Palace of the Forest:** the many-timbered structure referred to in 1 Kgs. 7:2; 10:17.

22:13 / The words **you say** are not in the Hb. (see NRSV). It is more likely that Isaiah ironically associates himself with the proverb-like saying that expresses the implications of their behavior for the fate he will share (cf. the weeping of v. 4).

22:14 / Here at least Yahweh's word comes to the prophet by something like dictation, to which the prophet listens. The words take the form of an oath: "If this sin is atoned for for you until you die. . . . "

22:18 / The word for **chariots** is actually a slightly different one from that in 31:1. The word here especially suggests a war chariot (in modern Hb. it means a tank).

23:1 / **Destroyed:** for a discussion of whether this is an over-translation, see M. A. Sweeney, *Isaiah 1–39 with an Introduction to Prophetic Literature* (vol. 16 of *The Forms of the Old Testament Literature*; eds. R. P. Kneirim and G. M. Tucker; Grand Rapids: Eerdmans, 1996), pp. 307–8.

23:9 / **Bring low** is lit. "defile" (NRSV): see Ezek. 28:7.

23:10 / NIV emends MT, whose opening verb is the same as that in v. 6 (see NRSV). But the emendation is difficult to fit with what follows. KJV suggests "flow over your land like the Nile." Is that inviting Tarshish to reverse-colonize Tyre (Oswalt, *Isaiah 1–39*, p. 433)?

23:13 / "Every attempt to extract a meaning from the verse as it stands is beset by insuperable difficulties" (J. Skinner, *The Book of the Prophet Isaiah* [2 vols.; Cambridge: Cambridge University Press, 1896 and 1898; revised ed., 1915], 1:190). NIV takes it as a warning to Tyre to learn from the fate of Babylon when it resisted Assyria. NRSV is more literal, "Look at the land of the Chaldeans! This is the people; it was not Assyria. They destined Tyre for wild animals. . . . " The verse then identifies Babylon, not Assyria, as the power that reduces Tyre. It did get nearer to this than Assyria did, but it did not actually take the city (see Ezek. 29:17–18).

23:17 / **Seventy years** (see Jer. 25:11–12) suggests a human life-time and therefore a period that people now living will not see the end of.

§15 Devastation and Renewal for the Whole Land (Isa. 24:1–27:13)

The word *massa'* no longer introduces the prophecies, but not until chapter 28 do we return to the direct, confrontational challenges to the people of God that dominate chapters 1–12. Chapters 24–27 thus stand out from the material on either side. The canvas broadens yet further than it had in chapters 13–23, but the tone of these chapters continues. The prophecy depicts further disaster and devastation, but makes fewer references to specific peoples. The effect is to convey a more terrifying impression of calamity for any city or land (such as whichever one the hearers belong to). Beyond that, this section envisages Yahweh's dealing with powers in heaven as well as powers on earth. It also envisages comfort and deliverance for all peoples on a day when death is swallowed up forever—a more radically new day than any of which we have read so far in the book.

Structurally, the chapters interweave a series of visions of devastation and renewal with a sequence of songs of responsive praise to sing "in that day":

> the land laid waste (24:1–13)
>
>> response (24:14–16)
>
> earth and heaven in tumult (24:17–23)
>
>> response (25:1–5)
>
> the world rejoicing, Moab humiliated (25:6–12)
>
>> response (26:1–19)
>
> Israel protected and restored (26:20–27:13)

At the same time, the visions and the responses link with each other so as to form two sequences on parallel tracks. The theme of devastation in 24:1–13 continues in 24:17–23, whose ending is then the starting point for 25:6–12. The equivocal response of 24:14–16 gives way to unequivocal praise in 25:1–5, whose theme is then taken up in 26:1–19.

Because of their visionary portrayal of world judgment, heavenly conflict, and a radically new day, the chapters have been described as a "Little Apocalypse." "Apocalypse" is another word for a vision or a revelation with an "eschatological" character. The words "eschatological" and "apocalyptic" are used in such varying and often ill-defined ways that they are best avoided. As a form of writing, apocalypses flourished in Israel much later than Isaiah's day. Many come from the period after the last of the OT writings ("apocalypsis" is the Greek word in the title of the NT book of "Revelation"). Many apocalypses focus on world disaster and renewal. The traditional critical view is thus that this material comes from a yet later period than that of the actual arrangement of chapters 13–23, and that these are in fact the latest chapters in the book. But precisely because they refer hardly at all to specific nations or events, there is little hard evidence to go on regarding the question (see also Additional Notes on 26:7–19 below). More clear is the fact that they continue a movement within the book—from a focus on Judah to one on the nations, around to a perspective on ultimate devastation and renewal. But the chapters do not lose the conviction that the world's destiny is interwoven with Israel's. Indeed, by the end the chapters are again narrowing the focus to more of a concern with Israel, and this prepares the way for the return to direct address to Judah in chapter 28.

24:1–13 / The vision of the land laid waste is an artful poetic composition, making effective use of assonance and repetition to bring its point home. The assonance and repetition suggest the repetitiveness and completeness of the devastation the vision describes. At the same time it is again presented as unfolding before the prophet's eyes, as presumably it did: literally "There, Yahweh is laying waste the land . . . . " Perhaps the picture of a land's devastation and a city's destruction reflects calamities that came to a specific land and city, but these have become pictures of the destruction of national and city life in general when Yahweh acts. The event looks more like a natural disaster than a military defeat.

Like other translations, NIV has **the earth** for *ha'arets*, which was its meaning in 23:8, 9, and 17, but in 23:1, 10, and 13 the same word meant "the land." Here in chapter 24 KJV has "earth" thirteen times (including v. 1), but "land" in verses 3, 11, and 13. If you were a Judean hearing the prophecy, you would not be sure which way to understand it. Is this a depiction of disaster on the land of Israel, or on the world as a whole? As the chapter unfolds, the ambiguity deepens. On the one hand, verse 4 also uses the word that specifically refers to **the world**. But then verse 5 sounds like a description of the people of God. Judah cannot simply dismiss this vision as a depiction of calamity that does not affect them. Only when it has faced the possibility that it may be under God's judgment can the people of God dare to think that other people may be under God's judgment.

The concreteness of the picture and the two-sidedness of the word *'erets* bring before the eye a vivid impression of calamity affecting a specific country. This country stands for any or every country in the world. Those who hear this vision cannot evade its point; it is as if *their* land is subject to devastation, *their* city destroyed. The lovely **face** of the land is distorted and defiled (v. 1). Religious status, social status, and even economic status offer no protection from this devastation (v. 2). This reminds us again of Tyre in the previous chapter.

In due course it transpires that the face was not so lovely after all. It was already **defiled** by the people who lived on it. Unless the "land" refers exclusively to Israel, verse 5 expresses a striking conviction that all people live in a pure land within a **covenant** relationship. This parallels the description in Genesis 9:8–17, where God enters into covenant relationship with the whole world. That covenant is purely a commitment on God's part to be faithful to the world. No human response is required to make this covenant "work," for God has discovered that no human response will be forthcoming (Gen. 8:21). Yet the OT assumes that humanity is expected to live in covenant relationship and knows the basic shape of what this involves (cf. Amos 1:9 and the argument of Rom. 1). By virtue of being created, human beings have some understanding about how life is supposed to work and have consequential obligations regarding how they should live their corporate life. Israel's covenant relationship is then an application of the general covenant relationship to Israel in particular. It is designed to benefit the world as Israel becomes a covenant for the people (42:6), while God's prior covenant with the world also undergirds God's special commitment to Israel (cf. Jer. 33:20). This is the first explicit reference to covenant relationship in Isaiah, and it applies to the whole world.

But people have ignored that perspective on their lives and have to live with the consequences. They thus re-enact in their own lives the events that took place at the beginning (Gen 3:14, 17; 4:11; 5:29—though the word for "curse" is different there). They also re-enact the experience of Israel, that living in freedom from that perspective means in the end polluting their land and being reduced to a remnant (v. 6b; the Hb. word for **left** is also found in 4:3; 7:3; 10:19–22; 11:11, 16). Elsewhere other images for Israel are reworked for this city and people (cf. v. 1 with 6:11; v. 13 with 17:6).

So Israel is a paradigm for understanding God's ways of working with the whole world. God makes the world aware of how life should be lived and brings calamity when people do not live that way. Here we have a framework for understanding the position of the nations—they know that they live in God's world with commitments for their own life and for their relationships to each other as members of one family. God invites them to live in the light of that. This is, among other things, the best way to evade the consequences of the curse. The vision of 2:3 is then of the nations' re-learning a revelation they have forgotten.

The curse consuming the earth suggests another model for understanding causality in the world (see on 9:18–21). Once again disaster comes not only as God's act but as the "natural" result of wrongdoing. Violence and sexual immorality, the two main causes of defilement (e.g., Num. 35:33; Jer. 3:1–2), are like pollutants with the power to overflow and destroy. But the talk in terms of curse here suggests an interconnection between these two ideas. It is God's powerful word that determines that wrongdoing finds its inevitable outworking in trouble. The OT talks about God's curse as Paul will talk about God's anger in Romans.

A vision of the kind that appears in verses 1–3, 7–13 appeals to our imagination. It invites us to bring to mind the kind of amalgam of impressions of disaster and its aftermath that tends to form in our minds through television, films, and newspapers. Here is a city reduced to a ruin of rubble, futile hands scrabbling at debris in a desperate search to reach the source of a moan before the person dies, wailing mothers carrying the children killed in somebody else's war.

The prophet takes up the desolation of such experiences in the life of Israel, but he does so in order to point people toward an even worse devastation. The Bible takes the blessings we enjoy in this life (the joy of our relationships with our family and friends, the excitement of knowing the presence of God in our lives) as foretastes and pictures of the joy of heaven (25:6–8 is an example). The Bible also takes the disasters that come upon the world that we know (earthquake, plague, famine, war) as foretastes of and pointers to the last great calamity that will overcome the earth. As we watch the combatants in successive outbreaks of war bombarding each other, or read chilling scenarios of life after a nuclear war, Isaiah 24 invites us to remember, among other things, that these are grim pointers to the last terrible day of destruction of which the Bible speaks.

24:14–16 / In reaction to the vision of wasting, the visionary first hears **voices** all over the earth declaring their response to this scene of ultimate devastation (vv. 14–16a). We are not told to whom the voices belong. They might be angels, or Israelites, or survivors from the nations. Who they are is not the point. It is the content of their response that is important. It consists in worship. The choirs who sing these songs of **glory to the Righteous One** know that the day of calamity is the day when defilement is at last cleansed, covenant-breaking punished, and God shown to be God. Events have exposed the pretensions of the nations to "glory"—two different words in verses 15 and 16. They are words that have recurred in threats of calamity for Israel and the nations whose "pride" (the same word as **majesty** in v. 14) compromises God's glory.

Yet the visionary cannot but be awed by the vision, is unable quite to join in with these songs of joy, and feels a quite different reaction (v. 16b). It is one that involves an overwhelming personal sense of desolation at the horror of wrongdoing and/or the horror of devastation. That reaction was part of what was involved in being a prophet. This was not just a matter of living in the future and escaping into visionary anticipation of calamity and blessing to come, able happily to accept a land's devastation. The prophet was appalled at the vision of what could be seen in the land and what threatened the land, and he shared this feeling with God and people in the prophecy, lest the terrible desolation portrayed in the vision should overtake them.

24:17–23 / Assonance and repetition again add verbal power to this picture of tumult on earth and in heaven, which initially portrays the same threat as that in verses 1–16. But these verses directly address "the inhabitant of the land/earth," individualizing the people as a whole (the word is singular: see NRSV)

as the land itself was individualized in verses 1–16. Before this unspecified quasi-individual, with whom the hearer is challenged to
identify, there opens up a series of disasters as in a nightmare or a
horror film (vv. 17–18a). In Jeremiah 48:43–44 this nightmare
threatened Moab, and in Amos 5:19 a similar one threatened Israel. Here it threatens everyone (Sawyer, *Isaiah*, pp. 209–10).

Then the camera draws back and pictures the scene from a
broader, yet more frightening, perspective. The calamity is not re-
stricted to the plane on which people live. It involves the world
above and below, the world from which come flood and earthquake. The shutters in the sky that normally restrain the waters
are opened to flood the earth (see Gen. 7:11) and the foundation
pillars, on which the earth rests, shake. God stops holding back
the concentrations of dynamic power and energy that surround
human life. Again the assumption is that this is the natural fruit of
rebellion, for the terms of God's covenant with the world are
themselves the foundation on which it rests. They reflect the nature
of the world itself, and when they are ignored, calamity can only
follow. The end of verse 20 follows the wording of Amos 5:2.

In that day, verse 21, suggests the beginning of a new
prophecy. The imagery does change, but the double emphasis on
the world above and the world below continues. The very name
"Yahweh armies" (v. 21, see Additional Note) reminded Israel that
supernatural forces fight on Yahweh's side, but anyone could see
that this does not mean that battles on earth always work out in
accordance with Yahweh's will. Evidently supernatural forces
fight against Yahweh, too. Jewish apocalypses such as those in
Enoch extensively develop this concept (but see also Dan. 10). The
stars and planets are the physical embodiments of such heavenly
powers, as is reflected in the practice of astrology (cf. 40:26); perhaps the sun and moon are or feel guilty by association (v. 23).

As with resistance on earth, Yahweh may be relaxed about
powers that resist in heaven for quite a while, but in due course
will "visit" them (see on 10:1–4). Revelation 20 sees this imprisonment coming about through Jesus' victory won on the cross,
pending the moment of final "visitation." Although Yahweh does
not reign in heaven or on earth at the moment (which explains
why things are as they are) and Yahweh's glory is not yet manifest, nevertheless one day Yahweh will reign in glory (v. 23).

The last line of the chapter is another surprise. We have become used to a picture without names and locations, a picture
whose power derives in part from its anonymity. Now we are

brought back to earth and assured that cataclysm, earthquake, and cosmic conflict are subordinate to a purpose that Yahweh still intends to fulfill in Jerusalem and before its elders, as at Sinai (Exod. 24:9–10). It is a nice reversal of 3:14 and 9:15 (Oswalt, *Isaiah 1–39*, p. 456).

25:1–5 / This time, in this section of worship on earth, the prophet's response contains none of the ambivalence of 24:16b. We have noted that 24:1–13 would not easily let Israel rule out the possibility that the devastated land was its own. Such visions force the hearers to ask questions about themselves and God. One of the significances of verse 1 is, then, to affirm that the speaker recognizes Yahweh's lordship rather than numbering among those who rather affirm their own.

To **exalt** is to "lift Yahweh high" in recognition of the fact that Yahweh *is* "high and exalted" (6:1). The praise makes a verbal as well as a substantial link with what precedes. It follows Yahweh's bringing down of the "high people on earth" (24:4) and "the powers on high" (24:21). It also recalls the Babylonian king "setting his throne up high" (14:13) and Yahweh's putting down the "high ones" of 2:11–17 and 10:12, 33. The act of worship completes the great reversal whereby the arrogation of "height" is terminated.

The testimony follows the standard form of Israelite praise in that it begins with a commitment to **praise** or thanksgiving (see on 12:1) and then gives the reasons for this confession. While verse 1 first states these reasons as a generalization, verses 2–3 and 4–5 explain both the negative and positive sides of these reasons. Each begins with "for," fleshing out the **for** in verse 1 (see NRSV).

We have noted that judgment is an act of sovereignty whereby Yahweh acts *for* the needy and thus *against* the powerful. It is thus both good news and bad news, according to which group you belong to (see on 1:17, 21). So the calamity on city and land that we have witnessed in vision was an awesome wonder and also an act of "faithful faithfulness" (another of the prophet's repetitions). It was another act that worked out the purpose of Yahweh and revealed Yahweh as a politician who can make plans and put them into effect (v. 1, see also on 5:8–24). It was a wonder planned long ago by the "wonder-working planner" (see on 9:6, where the words are similar).

This calamity on a foreign city will make a deep impression on other powerful nations. On the worldwide scenario presup-

posed by chapters 24–27 it is still Yahweh's purpose not merely to
put nations down but to win their acknowledgment and worship
(vv. 2–3). **Peoples** and **cities** are singular. The prophet refers to
one people and one city to make the picture more concrete, recalling the city and people that were devastated in 24:1–13. Both the
individual event and the spin-offs mean that Yahweh has been
acting for the protection of the powerless. Now the prophet describes the grim reality of power and the protective shelter Yahweh gives as the power is dissipated (vv. 4–5).

25:6–12 / It is easy to get confused over whether the OT
is "nationalist" or "universal" in focus. Is Israel preoccupied with
its own destiny or does it care about the world? A passage such as
this does nothing to clarify the matter because it continues to presuppose a different configuration of the question, or to presuppose that the antithesis is a false one.

In the prophet's vision we are back **on this mountain** (vv. 6,
7, 10), Mount Zion (24:23). It is to be the place where Yahweh's
people have their worldwide disgrace removed (v. 8). Their disgrace is their humiliation before the world when they have been
exposed for their false trust and scattered among the scoffing
nations (30:5; 54:4). They will have waited for Yahweh to **save**
them (the word for **trusted** refers to waiting expectantly for something to happen: it is the same word in 26:8, also 8:17). They will
now enjoy that **salvation.** It is a moment when Yahweh prepares
the most sybaritic royal banquet on this mountain, and a moment
when Yahweh will **swallow up** mourning and death. The imagery
in verses 6–8 describes it vividly. It speaks literally of the succulent
dripping richness of the food and of wine that has been allowed to
mature and increase in alcohol content on the lees and has then
been well-decanted (see NRSV). The prophecy's characteristic repetition and assonance further enhances its power. In this context
the talk of swallowing up death suggests the abolition of death
rather than the introduction of resurrection (for which Daniel 12
is the first biblical reference). Not only will the existent pain and
hurt of the loss of loved ones be healed. There will be no more of it.

But the banquet and the consolation are not just for Israelite
elders such as had shared a meal with Yahweh at Sinai (see 24:23)
but for all peoples (vv. 6, 7, 8), as the declaring of Yahweh's word
on "this mountain" was for all (2:2–4). The vision functions in a
way analogous to 19:16–25, where earlier hints that individual

peoples such as Moab and Egypt might turn to Yahweh and find acceptance became explicit promise. Here that is generalized.

It is then extraordinary to find the reverse in verses 10–12, and commentators sometimes deplore the contrast between verses 6–8 and 10–12 (see, e.g., Clements, *Isaiah 1–39*, pp. 209–10). But the NT picks up both without embarrassment (see Rev. 9 and 21). As Yahweh's commitment to Israel and Yahweh's concern for the nations have to be held together, so do Yahweh's concern for the nations and their need to turn. The OT is universalist in the sense that it believes in Yahweh's commitment to all peoples; it is not universalist in implying that all peoples will inevitably turn to Yahweh one day. The prophet's deftness with imagery and repetition returned to a more solemn purpose. Moab ends up swimming in a cess-pit not because it is Israel's enemy but because of the same consideration that underlay the critique of Moab and other nations (including Israel itself)—matters of majesty and height and pride. Verses 6–9 and 10–12 offer alternative scenarios to Israel, Moab, and other peoples.

26:1–19 / The prophet's next proposed response to Yahweh continues the theme of praise in 25:1–5 and also matches the vision in 25:10–12. The opening reminds us of chapter 12 and might make us think that chapter 26 will nicely round off chapters 13–26, but there will be more to follow. This is reminiscent of the way chapter 22 might have seemed the ending to chapters 13–23. The motifs from chapter 12 recur: **in that day, song, salvation** in the sense of deliverance from threat and pressure, **trust, strong** (translated "strength" in 12:2), **lofty** (translated "exalted" in 12:4). Making the comparison helps to highlight the distinctive feature of this new hymn. That is its focus on the city, which derives from its context. In chapters 24–25 the city, and concretely Moab's city with its "lofty" walls (again it is the same word in 25:12), has been vulnerable to earthquake and devastation. Again it is affirmed that **Judah** has a city that does not have that vulnerability. The basis for this strength is curiously unstated. The word "God" is not there in verse 1 (see NRSV), so the point that the song celebrates is the bare fact that this city's walls are effective in providing deliverance. They thus contrast with Moab's walls (25:12—where again Yahweh's act was unmentioned though presupposed).

Another contrast with 12:1–6 is that **we** sing the song—not just "I." Surprisingly, the worshipers then bid their gatekeepers open its gates, not keep them shut, so that the city is open to other peoples who lack such security, just as Yahweh's revelation (2:2–3) and Yahweh's banquet (25:6–8) are open to all. The nation that trusts in its majesty and security (25:12) and ignores that ever-lasting covenant (24:5) has no place there, but **the righteous nation that keeps faith** may enter. Passages such as Psalm 24 and 118:19–20 describe righteous Israelite pilgrims or a righteous Is-raelite king in these terms, and commentators assume that here the righteous nation is Israel. But the concern with the whole world in these chapters (not least ch. 25) points rather to an open-ness to other nations. A nation that is thus of **steadfast mind** in its commitment to Yahweh's ways and that **trusts** in Yahweh rather than in its own prestige and security will find **perfect peace.** The last phrase is another of the prophet's repetitions, literally "peace peace," double "well-being." This will include freedom from war but will also extend beyond that. The promise thus takes up that of 9:6 and applies it to any nation that turns to Yahweh. Verses 4–6 underline the point and again remind of the alternative.

A tone that is quite different from anything we have read in 24:1–26:6, or for that matter earlier in the book, runs through verses 7–19. Verse 7 sums up the implication of verses 1–6 in the form of a saying that might have appeared in Proverbs; the repeti-tion of **righteous** picks up verse 2. **Way** is more literally "cart-track," which makes the statement of faith the bolder. Cart-tracks require some smoothing. But verses 8–19 contrast with the past two or three chapters' bold unquestioning confidence in the vision of God's acting to put down human pretension and to bring bliss to the tearful. Instead of these being seen as clear and unquestion-able realities, there is an owning of the need to live by faith, and a longing to see as realities the events that have been described in vision.

The prayer has four elements.

(a) We are yearning for the acts that will vindicate your name (vv. 8–9). In the context of this prayer (e.g., v. 9b), the object of the people's day-and-night yearning is not an inner experience of God but the witnessing of events that will demonstrate to the world that Yahweh is God. They do not see them yet.

(b) We want your enemies to be made to see (vv. 10–11). These prophecies thus far have seen the world that does not know Yahweh as open to seeing what Israel has been privileged to see— even if the world has needed a shattering experience to make it do that. But there are none so blind as those who will not see, and the prophecy here looks at the world from the other angle. Calamity

may teach people and grace may not do so. The metaphor of fire
(see 66:15–16) presumably derives from the fact that fire was a terrible calamity and thus a means of Yahweh's bringing judgment
(see 1:7; 9:19; 29:6).

(c) We do believe we will see well-being, in light of the ac-
complishments we have already seen (vv. 12–15). Assyria, Babylon, Persia, Greece, Syria, and Egypt counted among the other
lords in the time from Isaiah to the second century. The prayer
presupposes a time such as that of Haggai and Zechariah (and
Isaiah 56–66) when Yahweh has put down one of these lords and
given the nation increase. On the one side this expression of confidence looks back to the picture of the Babylonian king's fall in
14:9–10. On the other it sees the vision of 9:2–7; 44:23; and 54:1–3
as fulfilled (though the language in v. 15 is less similar to these
verses than it looks in the English). This belief in fulfillment stimu-
lates faith in a fuller establishment of the well-being that that vision spoke of. In verse 12a "you will establish" would be as natural
a rendering as "you establish" (see NRSV): it is a statement of hope
based on the experience of verse 12b.

(d) We look for new life in the future, aware of what was not
accomplished (vv. 16–19). Again, verses 16–18 reflect a period
such as that of Babylonian domination. The awareness of achievement (v. 12b) is all but obliterated by the awareness of non-
achievement (v. 18b: the word for **brought** is that translated "accomplished" in v. 12b). Its counter is the further statement of
faith in verse 19. In isolation it might seem a statement about individual resuscitation, but in context it more parallels Hosea 6:2 and
Ezekiel 37:1–11 as a conviction about Yahweh's bringing resurrection to the nation. Yahweh's dew has a miraculously life-giving effect when it falls.

26:20–27:13 / Once more we move back from prayer to
prophecy that again links with the previous sections of prophecy
in 24:1–12, 17–23, and 25:6–12 as much as with the immediately
preceding prayer. But for this closing section the horizon narrows
from the world's destiny to that of the people of God. Israel is to be
protected and renewed.

(a) Yahweh will visit earth. Images from widely-spread
parts of the OT combine to give verses 20–21 their power. Again
Yahweh is coming from heaven (cf. Mic. 1:3). Again this involves
"visiting" human wickedness in wrath, coming to take action so
that it produces its "natural" results, as Yahweh did through and

on both Assyria and Babylon (see 10:3, 5, 12, 25; 13:5, 11). Again that wickedness lies in the prevalence of violent death, like Abel's. Again Israel must take shelter when Yahweh "passes by," like Israelites at the first Passover and like Noah's family in their ark.

(b) Yahweh will visit Leviathan, the serpent-dragon (27:1; see Additional Notes). Yahweh will finally destroy the serpent-dragon: in other words, will finally put down all forces that oppose order and blessing in the world (cf. Satan's fall in Rev. 20).

(c) Yahweh will protect the vine from visitation (27:2–5). In this inversion of the song in 5:1–7, instead of unfulfilled hopes and burning, there are unfulfilled fears and abundant fruitfulness. Yahweh does not want anyone to "visit" this vine (the same verb again: NIV **harm**). Yahweh is **not angry** with it, feels no burning rage (see on 5:25–30, a passage about anger that follows on the first vine song). Yahweh's feelings here thus contrast with the ones expressed there. Anger is not Yahweh's essential nature (see 28:21). That is quite a statement in this angry book. Having previously invited briers and thorns to take over the vineyard, Yahweh now relishes the prospect of a fight with them to protect the people ("Make my day . . . "). Yet apparently the benign feelings extend even to these potential spoilers of the vineyard, if they change their stance. Yahweh would rather be at peace with them, too: it is the principle that has underlain the poems on peoples such as Moab and Egypt. Warmaking is not Yahweh's essential nature, either—also quite a statement in this warring book.

(d) Yahweh will make the vine bear fruit (27:6–11). In 5:24 **root** and **blossom** (NIV there translates "flower") were destined to rot and blow away, so verse 6 promises another reversal. But the people's present experience contrasts with that promise. We can hear Israel's prayers here (cf. Ps. 44). "That talk about being the vinedresser and about fruitfulness is all very well, but you have bludgeoned us in the way the first vineyard song threatened (see 1:5–6). You have slaughtered us (the verb *harag* in v. 7b nicely takes up the occurrence at the end of 26:21, which Israel is proving true; its blood is crying out from the ground). You have contended against us, not for us, as you said you would (the verb *rib* recurs from 3:13a—NIV paraphrases there). You have expelled us from our land. Like the hot desert wind you have carried us off by the **fierce blast** of your anger (*ruakh*), the blast destined for enemies and from which you claimed to protect (11:15; 25:4). Further, 'fierce' was the stance you claimed to take against Leviathan, not us (v. 1), and the 'fierce' nature of the bondage imposed by

Babylon from which you claimed to deliver us (14:3; NIV "cruel" there). You have let people destroy the very means of our worshiping you. The fortified city of Jerusalem is desolate and empty and open to being grazed by animals because all its leadership has been deported (see 1:9; 5:17; Lam. 1:1). You are our maker, our creator, but you have no compassion for us, you show no favor to us."

Yahweh has three responses. Whatever happened to them, the fate of their attackers has been worse: look at fallen Assyria or fallen Babylon or fallen Persia . . . (v. 7). The bludgeoning was designed to achieve something (v. 9; cf. 1:24–31), as the pruning of the vine can mean fruitfulness. The destruction of the means of worship is actually the removal of sin. And the abandonment of the city and the withholding of compassion are deserved. Its inhabitants were stupid (v. 11).

As is evident from the translation, the moves from second to third person and from "perfect" verbs (denoting completed actions) to "imperfect" verbs (denoting actions still in progress; e.g., vv. 7–8) make this a difficult passage. It is not even certain that verses 10–11 describe Jerusalem. When "Jacob" appeared in 17:4, the word referred to northern Israel. Here it might again denote the people of the north, the city then being Bethel (Sweeney, *Isaiah 1–39*, p. 351) or Samaria (Wildberger, *Isaiah 13–27*, p. 592). The purging of that city is then set in the context of the promises in verses 6 and 12–13. Kaiser (*Isaiah 13–39*, pp. 229–31) assumes that the unclarity about the city's identity reflects the prophet's incompetence, but the ambiguity means that chapters 24–27 end as they began. The city of God can never escape seeing itself as treated like other cities, not least the cities it sets itself over against. It is always both challenged and assured about the fall of the city that is characterized by violence, religion, and self-aggrandizement.

(e) Yahweh will gather the harvest (27:12–13). The opening phrase suggests that the final verses are a separate promise, but they continue the theme of verses 2–5 and constitute a fourth response to the complaint that lies behind verses 6–11. They also take further the process whereby material from the opening chapters is expanded upon (see 11:11–16, which brings the opening prophecies to their close). They open like a threat but neatly turn into good news. Yahweh will gather the harvest, reversing the scattering of verse 8, and reestablishing worship that Yahweh welcomes.

Additional Notes §15

24:1–16 / Following are some examples of the assonance and repetition: *boqeq . . . boleqah* (**lay waste . . . devastate it,** v. 1); *k* (like) comes twelve times in v. 2; **borrower/lender** and **debtor/creditor** are forms of the same words (v. 2); *hibboq tibboq . . . hibboz tibboz* (**completely laid waste . . . totally plundered,** v. 3); *'avelah navelah . . . 'umlelah navelah . . . 'umlalu* (**dries up and withers . . . languishes and withers . . . languish,** v. 4). Then in v. 16a the word "for me" occurs three times, and v. 16b comprises five variants on the root *bagad.*

24:17–23 / Further examples of assonance and repetition include: **terror** and **pit** and **snare** (v. 17) *pakhad* and *pakhat* and *pakh.* V. 18a then elaborates the three words in parallel ways. In v. 19, **the earth** is repeated three times, and each verb is repeated in two forms for emphasis. V. 21 has more literally "the army of heaven in heaven and the kings of the ground on the ground." In v. 22 **herded** actually translates a three-fold repetition of the word "gather" and **shut up in prison** is more literally "imprisoned in prison."

25:6–8 / Further examples of the language devices here include: the same word used for **feast** and **banquet,** for **rich food** and **meats** (*shemanim*), for **aged wine** and **wines** (*shemarim*); **best of** is *memukhayim,* **finest of** is *mezuqqaqim.* The same word is used for **destroy** and **swallow up** ("swallow" is more literal); the same root is used for **shroud** and **enfolds** and for **sheet** and **covers.** Other repetitions (**all peoples, on this mountain**) are apparent from the English.

26:1b / The words read literally "a city of strength for us deliverance [someone] will appoint walls and rampart." "City" and "deliverance" are feminine nouns and "walls" is plural so it is difficult (though not impossible) for them to be subject of the masculine singular verb, but adding "God" seems arbitrary. More likely the verb is implicitly passive, which is a possible Hb. usage. Further, "(its) deliverance will be appointed (as its) walls and rampart" makes less sense than "(its) walls and ramparts will be appointed [as its] deliverance." Deliverance is the result of having walls and rampart. It is not identical with it (contrast Zech. 2:4–5, where Yahweh "is" the city's wall; and see also Ps. 48:12–14).

26:7–19 / The material does not give concrete markers that would enable us to link it with specific events, but the description would fit the period before or after Babylon's fall, the event that would free deportees to return to Judah. Oswalt (*Isaiah 1–39,* p. 482) assumes that God inspired Isaiah to project himself into that period and speak about it as if it were past. It seems more natural to assume that God drew people to pray this way at that time and that the chapters have a much less direct relationship with Isaiah's ministry. But this makes no difference to our understanding of their meaning.

26:8 / **Yes, Lord, walking in the way of your laws, we wait for you;** lit. "Yes, the way of your judgments we wait for you": in light of what follows, "the way of your judgments" more likely refers to God's acts that we are looking for than to our own acts (see v. 9b).

27:1 / Middle Eastern myth sometimes sees the power of metaphysical and moral disorder as embodied in the sea, sometimes in a sea monster; cf. St. George and the dragon. In later Jewish thought Satan comes to have this role. In Thomas Hobbes's *Leviathan*, the monster "meant the centre of absolute power" (Sawyer, *Isaiah*, p. 224).

§16 Introduction to Chapters 28–33

We return to the kind of material that occupied chapters 1–12—prophecies and stories directly concerning eighth-century B.C. Judah and Jerusalem. The difference is that much of these chapters relates to a subsequent period, the reign of Hezekiah and the period of his seeking help from Egypt in asserting freedom from Assyrian domination in 705–701 B.C. The fundamental issues in Judah's life remain as they were a few years earlier. Centrally, the question is whether the people will live by trust in the promise of God regarding king and city, treating these as the key to their security and freedom, or whether they will insist on seeking freedom and security in alliances with stronger nations. Only the external politics have changed: Assyria is now oppressive overlord, not savior, as Isaiah had warned would become the case. We know that the period is now that of Hezekiah because of the references to Egypt as potential savior. The king himself is not mentioned until we come to the stories in chapters 36–39.

Chapters 28, 29, 30, 31, and 33 all begin "Oh" (see Additional Notes on 5:8–24), which thus introduces a series of "Ohs" for the people of God (all of similar length) and ultimately for their would-be destroyer:

for a drunken leadership (28:1–29)

for the city of David (29:1–24)

for the obstinate nation (30:1–33)

for a people who rely on Egypt (31:1–32:20)

for a would-be destroyer (33:1–24)

It is a distinctive feature of each of these "Ohs" that the element of threat dominates at the beginning but that the element of reassurance becomes more and more prominent.

threat	28:1–22	reassurance	28:23–29
threat	29:1–16	reassurance	29:17–24
threat	30:1–17	reassurance	30:18–38
threat	31:1–6	reassurance	31:7–32:20
reassurance from the beginning			33:1–24

This pattern corresponds to the balance within chapters 1–12 and within the book of Isaiah as a whole. It requires the people to take Yahweh's warnings seriously but offers them more and more encouragement that disaster does not have the last word.

§17 Oh You Drunken Leaders (Isa. 28:1–29)

28:1–6 / In due course it will become clear that we have left behind the block of prophecies focusing on other nations, but this beginning, describing the fall of drunken Ephraim, does not in itself require that. Ephraim had featured in that material (see 17:1–8) and so had prophecies beginning "Oh" (see 17:12; 18:1). Indeed, we have seen that Ephraim may have been the subject of 27:7–11. Once again, Isaiah is declaring that the Assyrian storm is about to break out.

The warning begins by describing the impressiveness of the Ephraimite capital, the city of Samaria. It sits on a hill that rises gently but firmly from the rolling slopes of northern Israel, and from the top commands a view for miles around of country whose fertility might be the envy of Jerusalem. It had been fortified and beautified with stone and ivory (see Amos 3:15; 6:4–6). With its walls it stands like a garlanded head above the "shoulders" of the slopes that surround it.

But at the end of a banquet, people's tatty garlands are trodden underfoot, and Isaiah sees Ephraim's beauty itself as tatty. Perhaps this is because Assyria has already inflicted its first defeat on Ephraim and its ally, Aram, in 735 B.C.; only time awaits the city's final downfall in 721 B.C. Perhaps the time is earlier but Isaiah can see that this defeat is (theologically) inevitable. Or perhaps what he sees in Samaria makes its splendor now seem tawdry. This city has been beguiled by its own importance (**pride** again: see on 2:10–22). The language is very similar to that used of Babylon in 13:19. The people's own finery mirrors the city's, but they placard it at self-indulgent drunken banquets. We see in modern nations how people in important positions in politics, business, or religion easily fall into self-indulgence. In Ephraim's case, the banquets may well have been essentially religious festivals. This would make that worse, because it involved flaunting their self-importance in the presence of the One who was really important. When the Assyrian storm arrives, the finery will be trodden underfoot.

As in 17:1–8 and other poems in chapters 13–27, calamity is not Yahweh's last word. Once more, Yahweh takes the edge off the nightmare with a promise (vv. 5–6). Although the disaster will reduce Ephraim to a **remnant** (see on 4:2–6; 7:1–9; 10:20–23), they are still "Yahweh's people." Israel's real beauty and glory lie in Yahweh, not in their city or their finery. And people who take on leadership in matters of justice or of defense do not have to be trapped in the fate of their predecessors. Yahweh can be their dynamic and strength to change.

28:7–13 / The critique in verses 1–4 related to people in general, like that regarding Judah in 5:13. But it was the ruling class who had most opportunity for such self-indulgence, and the reference to leadership in verse 6 suggests that the leadership was especially in mind. In modern nations, the besetting temptation of religious leadership is sex. In Israel it was drink (vv. 7–9). The former distorts people's insight, but the latter does so more obviously. Yet what appalls the prophet is not merely that drink makes them get their visions and their counsel wrong. There is something obscene about the very fact that they combine the two. Perhaps they got their visions and their counsel right. They are still disgusting.

It is clear enough that the prophet goes on to quote their mockery of him (vv. 9–10, see NIV mg.). It is not clear whether this mockery is also a fruit of their drunkenness, though it is interesting to imagine a scene at a sumptuous well-wined festival meal, perhaps where an alliance against Assyria was being celebrated (as an answer to prayer?), and where Isaiah delivers one of his critiques of national policy and the well-wined participants put him in his place. Their critique is that his religious and political faith is all too simple.

What we have read so far makes it easy to see why they would respond to him in this way. The prophets have sometimes been portrayed as people who could read the political signs of the times more perceptively than other people. In a sense that is right, but they were able to do so because of the way they took account of the facts concerning God. They then hammered home rather simplistic political messages. Just trust in Yahweh, Isaiah said. That is where **rest** and **repose** lie for people worn down by the pressure of playing off Assyria against their neighbors and vice versa, never being able to be sure that they have backed the right horse (v. 12). If they will not listen to his stupid-sounding message, they will have to learn from even more stupid-sounding foreigners (v. 11), and learn the hard way (v. 13).

First Corinthians 14:20–23 neatly applies Isaiah's words to the function of tongues. Because unbelievers are likely to scoff at this way God allegedly speaks, speaking in tongues becomes a sign that leads to their condemnation.

28:14–22 / Much of the content of verses 7–13 may imply that the prophecy has changed focus from Ephraim to Judah, but the prophet once again works his audience subtly. Only in verse 14 does it become explicit that he is speaking to Judah itself. The effect of the chapter is a little like that of Amos 1–2, where the prophecies of calamity for other nations function to soften up Israel for the prophecy against it.

The warning to Ephraim in verses 1–6 presupposes that Samaria has not fallen, which happened in 721 B.C., but verse 14 sets the warning in a context that relates to the end of the eighth century. Since the warning has thus now come true, so Judah had better take notice of Isaiah's simplistic words. "Samaria is a mirror in which they may read their own character and their own doom" (Skinner, *Isaiah,* 1:222).

Therefore on the lips of a prophet is usually a word to cause a shudder. It heralds the move from accusation to sentencing. Here the pattern is more subtle but the shudder-quotient is as real. The **scoffers** are people who can talk their way out of anything. The words attributed to the leadership (v. 15) are not words they actually said. They did not realize they were entering into a **covenant with death** or making **a lie** their **refuge,** any more than they actually asked people to "prophesy illusions" to them (30:10). But that is the implication of what they have done. They have made some politically wise-looking moves to safeguard the security of God's people by allying with some of those neighbors who were the subject of chapters 13–23 so as to find protection from the Assyrian flood (cf. 8:5–8). But this means they have entered into a suicide pact. "This alliance you are so pleased about, that everyone is talking about: it is an alliance with death." They have thus deceived themselves and entrusted themselves to something that will deceive them by not producing the security they need.

The beginning of verse 16 repeats the "therefore" (see NRSV; NIV has "so"), because we have not yet been given the bad news. Indeed, after a more solemn introduction of Yahweh as the speaker, we are kept in suspense for yet another verse. First the prophet points to the building Yahweh had been doing in Zion. The **cornerstone** has been identified with the law, the temple, the monarchy, the city, the saving work of Yahweh, the people's relationship with Yahweh, the true believing community, Zion itself, the Messiah, faith, the remnant, or the actual promise about the one who trusts (Kaiser, *Isaiah 13–39*, p. 253). The prophet's words are evidently too vague for us to identify the cornerstone, so the point perhaps lies elsewhere, simply in that fact that Yahweh had been engaged in building in Zion. Indeed, more literally Yahweh's words are "Behold, I am the one who laid . . . . " The people's security lay in the fact that Yahweh had been building. This building was grounds for trust. They would not be dismayed (NRSV "will not panic"). But it also meant that Yahweh's **tested stone** set them a test that they had failed. They had not trusted. Verse 16 is therefore part of the prophet's indictment of the people.

The notion of a tested stone then takes the picture in a different direction. Yahweh has ensured that the building's foundations meet the building regulations. The same regulations govern what is built on the foundation. The test, like a **measuring line** or **plumb-line,** is whether or not what is built meets the criteria of just judgment (**justice** and **righteousness:** see on 1:21–23). It is striking to find this concern reappearing. It has featured little since its prominence in chapters 1–5 (but see 9:7; 16:5). Isaiah has two sets of criteria for assessing the life of the people of God. One has to do with attitudes to Yahweh (do people trust?), the other to do with attitudes to society (do they implement justice?). Different contexts may require an emphasis on one or the other, but both are important. If the people fail them, then the calamity they are seeking to avoid will overwhelm them. Jerusalem has made its **bed** and it must lie in it (v. 20).

Judah's strange covenant provokes Yahweh to do a strange deed. The section comes to a powerful close in verses 21–22. Isaiah pictures a great act of God like those in the time of David (2 Sam. 5; 1 Chron. 14). But here God rises up against Judah, not for it. This prophecy leads to one of Isaiah's most penetrating theological comments on the nature of Yahweh and the nature of Yahweh's work with the people of God and in the world. Clearly Yahweh is a tough-minded God who is not afraid to make hard decisions and implement them, not afraid to express anger, and not afraid to hurt people when that seems necessary. But what is Yahweh like inside? What are Yahweh's preferred ways of operating? And what about Yahweh's preferred way of relating to the world? Is Yahweh the kind of boss who is happiest when there is cutting to be implemented and firing to be done? (And is Isaiah that kind of prophet?)

No, says Isaiah. All this talk of bringing destruction, of which his prophecy is so full, is Yahweh's **strange, alien task**. It does not naturally fit the commitment Yahweh has made to Israel. It does not fit the notion of Yahweh's choice of Zion. A medieval midrash reports how someone who had made God angry was told, "You have caused me to take up a trade that is not mine" (from S. Buber's edition of Tanhuma, Balak 69a, as quoted in C. G. Montefiore and H. Loewe, *A Rabbinic Anthology* [New York: Schocken, 1974], p. 57).

It is easy to say "This hurts me more than it hurts you" and not mean it, but at least the statement affirms the priority of blessing over bringing destruction and establishes that theologically love and anger do not have equal place in the divine nature. Yahweh's action on behalf of David is Yahweh's natural work. Acting against Judah is alien to Yahweh. But Yahweh will act that way if necessary.

A further warning to stop thinking that they can talk their way out of the crisis (v. 22) closes off this section where it began in verse 14. The final line first affirms that 10:22–23 is still true (the formulation will be taken up again in Dan. 9:26–27; 11:36). It then also takes up the frightening picture of the destruction of the whole *'erets* from 24:1–20. And, once again, the hearers must picture the destruction of their own land—not someone else's.

28:23–29 / One of the characteristics of Isaiah 1–39 is an ambivalent relationship with pragmatic human insight. Chapter 29 will again attack it, as the source of the nation's death pact. Here human insight provides a parable for God's. Indeed, the prophet speaks exactly like a human teacher, such as the one who speaks in Proverbs. He urges attention, asks rhetorical questions, expects everyday life and the workings of nature to be illuminating for the deeper issues of life, reckons that God's activity is reflected in those ordinary human activities, assumes that life is a whole rather than dividing it into the sacred and the secular. The parable closes with the implication, "If the farmer by God's inspiration knows how to get a crop, how much more does God, the very source of purposeful action and effective insight." With **wonderful in counsel,**

compare 9:6 (and see the closing comment on 5:8–24). The word for **wisdom** is one that occurs once in Micah but otherwise only in Job and Proverbs (e.g., Prov. 8:14). It holds together the idea of insight and the effectiveness that follows from it.

The parable is an example of the tradition that Jesus would take up, and specifically opens up the theme of his parable about a man sowing seed. It is designed to provoke questions, to make people think, to puzzle them into realization, to open them to further teaching, to get them to agree before they quite know what they are agreeing to. One must acknowledge that, to be prosaically succinct, God teaches farmers to use varying techniques of planting and varying techniques of harvesting at varying times for varying crops. So what?

Little in chapter 28 provides the answer. But then, one might expect the interpretation of a parable to follow it, not precede it (as 5:1–6 was followed by v. 7 and further by vv. 8–24, where we have noted that the assertion of Yahweh's purposefulness was also central). So it is here. The whole of chapters 29–32 will combine the assertion that Yahweh plows with the promise that Yahweh also sows, that Yahweh has a time to attack and also a time to defend, that Yahweh uses moderation even with the rougher processes of dealing with Judah. This parable declares, allusively, that there is a positive purpose behind the strange destructive work in which Yahweh is engaged, which parallels the promise regarding Ephraim in verses 5–6. So its message is the obverse of that previous parable in chapter 5.

Additional Notes §17

28:15 / "False gods" (NIV mg.) points to a different understanding of v. 15 as a whole. Out of context it might indicate that people had consciously made a covenant with the god Death, worshiped by the Canaanites. The drunken banquets will then have been occasions when they sealed such a covenant. It is more likely that Isaiah is bringing home his regular critique that the community should not entrust its future to alliances against Assyria (see v. 16a).

28:21 / We could link **Gibeon** with Josh. 10, but why then is this mentioned *after* David? As 2 Sam. 5 and 1 Chron. 14 also link Geba/Gibeon with the Baal-Perazim story, it is simpler to take v. 21a to refer to the one event.

§18 Oh You City of David (Isa. 29:1–24)

29:1–4 / Here alone is Ariel a name for Jerusalem. It means "God's lion," but a similar word means "hero" in 33:7, while "Ariel" sounds the same as a word for the hearth around the temple altar where animals were burnt in sacrifice (see Ezek. 43:15–16). So we hear Isaiah lamenting "God's lion" *or* a hero *or* the altar hearth, and we are not helped a great deal by the next line that makes clear that the term refers to Jerusalem, which David had once besieged. Parabolic communication is again at work. Isaiah has caught our attention. What does he mean?

It is the last meaning, hearth, that especially counts. It suggests a grim parable for Yahweh's intentions. The ongoing **cycle** of worship makes the altar of key significance to understanding the city, but the city is then inclined to think that this round of worship somehow protects it. But one recalls 1:11–15. Yahweh intends that the whole city should become an **altar hearth**. It is as if the sacrificial fire consumes the altar itself. To put it another way, Yahweh intends to **encamp against** the city as David once had (the verb is the one translated "settled" in v. 1). People thought that, along with that cycle of worship in the city of Zion to which Yahweh was committed, they were also protected by their link with the David to whom Yahweh was also committed. Isaiah turns that on its head. David had originally been against Jerusalem, and Yahweh joins him in that. "The inhabitants of the city will be reduced to grovelling ghosts of their former selves" (Clements, *Isaiah 1–39*, p. 236). They are as lost and as pathetic as the Jebusites who never dreamed that their city could be taken (2 Sam. 5:6). In Sheol (see on 14:3–23) people cannot truly communicate. At this point, as at others, their "lives" are attenuated versions of the real lives they once lived. So their voices become even lower whispers than often characterize the dying, little more than a rattle in the throat. Judeans who tried to communicate with the dead, instead of with God, sought to learn their language (8:19). They will now speak it because they belong with the dead. Here the prophet seems to use this language as a metaphorical way of speaking of the "death" of the city, although the prophecy does not give us indications of the period this threat comes from.

29:5–8 / One of Isaiah's extraordinary somersaults follows. It catches us the more unaware because the word for **but** is also the ordinary Hebrew word for "and." Literally he says, "And will be like small dust—[not you, as we expect, but] your many enemies." One would have thought that things had gone too far in verses 1–4. But the moment when everything seems lost is the moment of reversal. Jerusalem's great enemy changes sides and becomes its great defender. Yahweh is coming to visit (the verb used again in v. 6) not Jerusalem itself but its enemies. The fire at the altar hearth will consume its attackers, not the city. The deliverance of which people could only dream (v. 8) becomes reality. Chapters 36–37 tell a story with similar dynamics and Psalm 48 puts the same theological conviction into worship.

The relationship between verses 1–4 and 5–8 raises literary and theological issues. The sharpness of the tension has made scholars infer that the two passages are of different origin. Verses 1–4 would then be Yahweh's words through Isaiah, when such a defeat indeed threatened the city from Assyria, and verses 5–8 Yahweh's words from a century later, when Assyria's downfall actually was imminent. Alternatively, the reference to **many enemies** and **hordes of all the nations** could look beyond any one historical crisis to a "last great battle," in the manner of later prophecies such as those in Ezekiel 38–39. Either way, verses 5–8 come here because the city was indeed unexpectedly delivered in Hezekiah's day, and that deliverance provided a promise of final deliverance.

Regardless of the answer to the literary question, the juxtaposition of verses 1–4 and 5–8 also points to a theological issue. Yahweh must be involved both in chastising the people of God and in defending them. Yahweh must "show himself holy by righteousness" (5:16). Yahweh must also demonstrate that holiness in its other aspect, by keeping a commitment to people once it has been made (cf. Hos. 11:9 where this point is explicit). So Yahweh may go to the very edge of annihilating the people but in the end will not do that. If Isaiah felt this double necessity, he himself may have been responsible for the sharp juxtaposition of verses 1–4 and 5–8. Yahweh will always in the end rescue the people or restore them, as the history of the Jewish people and of the Christian church demonstrates, though perhaps only after letting the situation progress to the very edge. Destruction is always an alien, strange work (28:21). Even if a necessary one, it is not a final one.

29:9–12 / The transition from verse to prose after verse 10 alerts us to the concern of verses 9–12 with two related but different forms of dyslexia. One visual impairment takes the form of an inability to read the signs of the times. To Isaiah it is obvious what is involved in a relationship with Yahweh and what trouble will come through lack of trust. Why can people not see it? It is as if their blindness was willed by Yahweh (see 6:9–10). Once again, urging them to blind themselves is an attempt to break through their blindness. The phrases in parentheses in verse 10 may be interpretive, in which case the passage points to the blindness of the whole people and specifically to a blindness of those who were supposed to enable the other people to see. Jesus' talk about blind guides will make this point again (see Matt. 15:14; 23:16, 24). This is the only passage which suggests that other prophets who preached a different message from his rivaled Isaiah—as was the case with his contemporary Micah (3:5–7) and later Jeremiah (e.g., 23:9–40).

The second vision, in verses 10–12, anticipates another aspect of later prophecy. Seers such as Daniel and John will also have visions that require interpretation. They seem to be **sealed** until someone unlocks them. That is how people respond to Isaiah's **vision.** It is crystal clear and simple, yet they cannot understand it. Understanding a prophet's words requires moral, inner illumination as well as skill in Hebrew.

29:13–14 / In contrast to people who will be aware that they do not understand, there are the people who think they have the measure of God, which is our besetting temptation. They sing the right choruses but their minds are much too small to encompass God. As usual, the "heart" stands for the capacity to think and make decisions (see 6:10; 7:2, 4; 9:9; 10:12). They learn these choruses from good human teachers, but they remain only choruses on **their lips,** even if they re-used Bible verses (v. 13).

So God will blow their little theologies wide open (v. 14). This takes us again to God's "wonders" that demonstrate real **wisdom.** If the words of 28:29 implied that there is a positive purpose the other side of calamity, unfortunately the prophecy goes on to remind us that calamity must come first—unless, of course, the people take some notice. Isaiah has little hope of that, but it is never over until it is over. Sometimes people change their minds and come to new insight because they see the force of some other way of looking at things, and in the light of that give up the old way. Sometimes (like Paul) they have to be shaken to their senses.

29:15–16 / The Hebrew Bible begins a new section with this "Oh" saying. It speaks of yet another kind of people (or the same people during the week)—people who think they can hide. These will again be people who worship Yahweh, but they do so with a schizophrenia that we may again recognize in ourselves. In formulating their political decisions they behave as if they think that the great decision-maker does not know about them. They plan for the future and security of God's people as if they are responsible for it and have the insight to make decisions, rather than as the objects of Yahweh's decision-making. Once more the people presumably do not themselves articulate the statements about this, any more than we do. But these are the implications of the way they behave.

29:17–21 / The day is coming when (in)sight is restored. **Lebanon** will stand for **forest** in general. Even allowing for this, the two-sided picture in verse 17 is at first a further puzzling parabolic image. It turns out to hint in another way that God's wisdom knows the time for both kinds of visitation (see vv. 18–19 and 20–21).

We might be tempted to answer the opening question with a no, since no such event has taken place. Such a reversal would take place a century later than Isaiah's day, and perhaps the phrase **in a very short time** indicates that this promise—expressed as a question—comes from that moment when the downfall of Assyria was imminent, bringing with it as it did new freedom for Judah. But that freedom was short-lived, which reminds us that in Scripture, as in our own lives, every moment when God's kingdom seems to have arrived turns out not to be the last (so far).

As well as promising that verses 9–12 will be reversed, verses 18–19 rework the image of blindness yet again to add a different promise. Since **gloom and darkness** suggest the experience of calamity itself (as in 8:21–9:2), the gift of hearing and sight implies deliverance. This then fits verses 19–21. The people in darkness are needy now, even if they or their forebears were willful. The "humble" are the "poor" of 11:4. The word suggests their humbleness of position or their humiliation rather than their humility. So the downtrodden will find joy in being restored by Yahweh.

Conversely, the exalted will be put down. The **ruthless** we know (see, e.g., v. 5). The **mockers** we also know (see, e.g., 28:14, 22). We thought these two belonged to two different nations. This warning (or the promise for their victims) is that ruthless outsiders and smooth-tongued insiders share the same destiny. Indeed, the latter are now more prominent (vv. 20b–21). Their skill with words is a liability not only in the political affairs of the nation but also in its judicial processes that centered on community legal processes in the square inside the city gate (see, e.g., 1:21–26); "in court" is literally "in the gate" (see NRSV).

29:22–24 / The further promise of this second kind of visitation comes to a close with a literal account of the point that verse 18 made metaphorically. Chapter 29 thus ends as chapter 28 did, as if this book belonged to Proverbs. It thus again illustrates Isaiah's two-sided relationship with the teaching of Israel's sages. He is against their pragmatic insight that thinks the sensible way to formulate policies is to leave God out. He believes in real insight that keeps God at the center. The concrete reference to people who **complain** stands out here. In Proverbs 16:28; 18:8; 26:20, 22 this verb denotes people who criticize other people behind their backs. Was Isaiah perhaps a victim of this (see v. 10)?

Four aspects of verses 22–23 deserve note:

(a) Reference to Abraham (or anyone else in Genesis) is very rare in the prophets. Yahweh will indeed increase the people in accordance with the promise to Abraham; reduction to a remnant is not a permanency.

(b) Like other traditional societies, Judah is a "shame" culture. In modern societies where community breaks down, shame ceases to matter. Where your place in society matters, the removal of shame and the restoration of pride is a powerful promise.

(c) Such restoration of pride is not in tension with awe before God; rather it links with it. People will hold their heads high, but in reverence in the presence of the holy one.

(d) A forced cowing before human might is thus replaced by a willing bowing before divine might: **stand in awe** is the root translated "ruthless" in verses 5 and 20.

Additional Notes §18

29:1 / **Settled** is the verb rendered **encamp** in v. 3 and refers to David's encampment in besieging the city.

29:13 / The LXX text quoted in NIV mg. is the version that underlies Matt. 15:8–9. **"Is made up only of"** is *tehi;* **"in vain"** would be *tohu.* The Greek NT sometimes bases OT quotations on the Greek OT, as modern preachers base biblical quotations on standard translations, without necessarily going back to the original to check the details.

29:21 / **False** testimony is that word *tohu:* the judiciary is as empty as the worship.

§19 Oh You Obstinate Nation (Isa. 30:1–33)

It has made sense to read much of chapters 28–29 against the background of Judean assertion of independence from Assyria and alliance with Egypt in the latter part of Isaiah's ministry, but only in chapter 30 does reference to Egypt become explicit. While the setting might be the independence movement during the reign of Sargon in 713–711 B.C., alluded to in passages such as 14:28–32, we have separate reference to alliance with Egypt in the context of the similar events of 705–701 B.C. during the reign of Sennacherib (see the stories in chs. 36–37). Sennacherib has set out with his army to put his rebellious subjects in their place, and Hezekiah is involved in a flurry of diplomatic activity.

30:1–7 / There is nothing inherently wrong with relying on the help of other nations: Scripture can portray Assyria, Babylon, Persia, Greece, and Rome as agents to achieve God's purpose, so we cannot assume that it is inappropriate. On some occasions, however, such peoples are working against God's purpose, so we cannot assume that it is always appropriate to rely on them. This is one of Hezekiah's mistakes. Judah does not consult Yahweh regarding its foreign policy (vv. 1–2a). The underlying problem is that they are **obstinate children**—their rebellion against Assyria is a result of that attitude. God has kept trying to direct them into the right way, as one does a child or an ox, but to no avail. Yahweh has **plans** or a strategy for current political events (as in 5:19; 14:26; 25:1; 28:29—NIV "counsel"). Judah is stupidly willful to ignore it. **Heaping sin upon sin** perhaps describes the combination of ignoring Yahweh's will on the one hand and on the other looking to Egypt for what they should trust Yahweh to provide.

The terms that describe Judah's expectation of Egypt vividly convey the scandal of their action. Egypt will be Judah's **help** (that translation is rather general: at 10:31 NIV rendered "take cover"), **protection, shade,** and **refuge** (v. 2). In passages such as Psalms 91 and 121 these very words express the expectations that the king is invited to have of God. These psalms elaborate on the connotations of these metaphors. Life sometimes involves being imperiled by the burning heat of the sun or by other dangers, and at those moments Yahweh is like a cleft in whose shadow we find shelter, or a rock on which we climb to find safety from swirling floods, or a mother hen under whose wings we hide. Isaiah assumes that this applies to the pressures of political life as much as to those of personal life. There is near-blasphemy in transferring these metaphors to Egypt.

Furthermore, other gods are as powerless as they are blasphemous (of course, the two are related). Treating Egypt as if it could live up to those metaphors can only mean tears before bedtime (vv. 3–5). Egypt is **useless** (v. 5, from the verb *ya'al*). Variants on the same words are then translated "do not bring **advantage**" or **unprofitable** (vv. 5–6; see also NRSV). Having achieved part of his effect by accumulating different images, Isaiah thus achieves another part by repeating the same word. Egypt is useless. Elsewhere the OT applies the word especially to the other gods that Israel was tempted to worship or admire (e.g., 44:9, 10; 47:12; 57:12). Judah has treated Egypt and those gods as profitable, but they are both equally useless. Although things may look impressive— **Zoan** and **Hanes** are at the northeastern and southern extremes of Lower Egypt, and so stand for the whole country—they will ultimately disappoint. Here words for shame, disgrace, and humiliation are heaped up (NIV uses **disgrace** for two different words) to balance the varying images for protection that were heaped up earlier. The king's courageous political policy was designed to issue in increased international standing for Judah as an independent nation that acknowledged Yahweh alone, not some Assyrian overlord. It will actually issue in humiliation.

The word *massa'* (v. 6; NIV **oracle**) introduced most of the poems about other nations in chapters 13–23. Its use here in introducing the enigmatic poem that follows especially recalls its use in introducing the enigmatic poems in chapters 21–22. Once again Isaiah gets attention by intriguing us. Why are we about to hear a sharp little poem about Negeb wildlife? Is the wildlife the **lions** and **snakes**? Or is it the **donkeys** and **camels**? The word *massa'* looks the same as a word for "burden," and this poem duly looks at the toings and froings with Egypt from the perspective of the beasts of burden who have to **carry** the loads involved ("carry" is the related verb *nasa'*).

There is some irony in the description of the journey in verse 6, which corresponds to earlier warnings of what will follow if they turn their backs on Yahweh (see Additional Notes). The people are destined for a tough journey **through a land of hardship and distress.** The middle of verse 6 describes the land through which the caravan travels, but describes it in terms of the destiny that the nation wishes to avoid.

Perhaps there is further irony in the collocation of **riches/treasures** and **donkeys' backs/humps of camels:** the whole enterprise looks stupid. The point starts to be explicit in the last line of verse 6, which NIV rightly links with verse 7. They are on their way to **an unprofitable nation** (see on v. 5), **to Egypt, whose help is utterly useless** (a different expression from that in v. 5), **Rahab the Do-Nothing.** The scathing dismissal brings the poem to a brilliant climax. To judge from Job 9:13; 26:12, Rahab (not connected to Josh. 2; see Additional Notes) was a figure like the Tiamat of Babylonian stories, a powerful, assertive mythic female force, also comparable to Leviathan (see on 27:1). Psalm 89:10 sees Egypt as the earthly embodiment of Rahab in Israel's experience, and by implication Judah now hopes to see something of that Rahab-like dynamic asserted on its behalf. The fact that figures such as Rahab are always defeated would provide Isaiah with one direction in which to take his rhetoric, but he goes for a more devastating one. The Egypt that had once been the embodiment of Rahab-like power is a shadow of its former self. It is like a monster that has been put to sleep. A famous feature of the Egyptian landscape is the sphinxes, giant animal figures in stone. They could seem threatening, but they could not move. Egypt itself resembles them. It is a "Do-nothing." This "wildlife" is less impressive than the lions, snakes, donkeys, and camels.

More seriously, this is no way to evade the destiny that threatens the nation. Rather, it walks right into it.

30:8–11 / Yahweh has a sign for the self-deceived rebels. In the ancient world one spoke in order to communicate and wrote only to record. Isaiah has used his best oral communication skills and failed. All that is left is to put his words on record so that people will always know. Of course, what we are reading about is actually another exercise in communication. Telling people about this writing is another attempt to get through to them.

The characterization of Judah as **rebellious . . . children** recalls the book's first indictment (1:2). Their resistance to Yahweh's teaching was the background to Isaiah's previous commission to write it down (8:16). They resemble obstinate students who will take no notice of their mentor, who therefore puts into writing the advice they have received so that there can be no dispute about the reasons for their eventual failure.

As in our own day, it might be quite imaginable for Judeans to wish that the whole idea of people having visions would go away (see v. 10a), but our other instinctive desire is that people should have encouraging visions rather than discomforting ones. As verse 10 develops it becomes clear that this is also Judah's desire. They do not want to be challenged about **what is right** but reassured that God is with them. In Isaiah's context this would amount to prophesying **illusions.** Judah was not literally asking to be deceived, of course, but that was the implication of their attitude to their prophets. For most prophets themselves, too, it is easier to be reassuring than confrontational (see Mic. 3:5–7), and prophets do not consciously prophesy illusions any more than people consciously wish they would do so. But there can easily develop a collusion between people and their ministers whereby the latter agree to say what the former want to hear. It is much more uncomfortable when ministers put people face to face with **the Holy One of Israel.** The verses that follow reassert the two reasons for this.

30:12–14 / Firstly, the people need to rely on the Holy One rather than on deceit. The **therefore** corresponds to the one at 28:14: we move here from indictment to sentence. The people's rebelliousness lies in their resistance to being confronted over **oppression** and **deceit** (see 5:8–24 for a similar indictment and warning in different terms). The two are linked, for "oppression" specifically suggests robbery by defrauding (see Lev. 6:1–4, where verb and noun occur three times; also Lev. 19:13), while "deceit" suggests deviousness. The word occurs elsewhere only in Proverbs, so once again Isaiah is asking his hearers to take seriously that strand of Scripture to which they were in any case inclined, and to note that it combines a moral commitment with a pragmatic bent.

Fraudulence and deceit involve a cynicism that seems in radical tension with anything to do with relationships, yet oddly they presuppose trust (NIV **relied on**) and dependence—fundamental features of relationships. Once again blasphemy is involved. Instead of trusting and depending on Yahweh, they trust and depend on oppression by deceit. They trust that they will succeed and that their "gain" will actually profit them. Proverbs indicates otherwise (e.g., 3:5, for both verbs; also 28:24–28).

The manner in which their sentence will be executed also reflects Proverbs' way of thinking. Indeed, the image of indictment and sentencing disappears. We have noted that Isaiah has several models for understanding God's activity in the world (see on 9:18–21). Once more what threatens Judah is not some intervention from outside, but rather the "natural" fruit of its own action. "Sin pays a wage, and the wage is death" (Rom. 6:23, NEB). To put it Isaiah's way, **sin** such as deviousness and defrauding that looks so effective and is hard to uncover is actually like building a **high wall** without making sure that its rocks are of compatible shapes so that they fit together properly. Without anyone needing to interfere, it will collapse. It will do so quite comprehensively because of the way the rocks all depend on each other, like a pot smashed to useless smithereens. Either their deceit will fail or their gain will not profit.

30:15–17 / Secondly, the people need to rely on the Holy One rather than on their own initiative. This second reason the people do not like being confronted by the **Holy One of Israel** also relates to the repeated challenge about where they put their **trust** (NIV "relied on" in v. 12). They **would have none of** the one as they "rejected" the other.

The talk of trust takes us back to the main topic of chapters 28–33. People are concerned about **salvation** and **strength,** about survival and the resources to ensure that. They assume that they are responsible for their destiny, that they cannot simply sit back and let themselves be trodden into the ground by one side or the other in the conflict between Assyria and its underlings. Isaiah says that is just what they must do. The keys to strength and achievement are **rest** and **quietness.** Quietness is what Isaiah had urged on Ahaz (see 7:4). "Take it easy, relax," was his message. It is ironic that "rest" (*nakhat*) is another of the emphases of Israel's own sages, so again Isaiah is urging them to live by their own principles. Elsewhere the word comes only in Job (17:16; 36:16), Proverbs (29:9), and Ecclesiastes (4:6; 6:5; 9:17). The most significant use of the word is in Ecclesiastes, where "rest" contrasts with chasing after wind, activity that will get you nowhere (4:6; NIV "tranquillity"). Ecclesiastes does not believe in doing nothing, but in being realistic about what "doing" can achieve, even when you do not think you have grounds for a robust expectation that God will act. Isaiah misses such realism in Judah; he believes that there is a good basis for such an expectation, but they would have none of it.

Taken in isolation, Isaiah's words would suggest an encouragement to irresponsibility. They have to be set in the context of other exhortations to initiative and responsibility. But Isaiah speaks rather directly to an activist generation like our own that is inclined to behave as if the church's survival or success depends on our plans and programs. Like the challenge to Ahaz to trust, however, this comes in a context where the invitation has been spurned, and God will see that what the people do trust in lets them down.

30:18 / So Yahweh waits for the moment to show favor. The verse begins with another occurrence of the word that usually means "therefore" (see on v. 12) and creates the expectation that we will find here a threatening ending to verses 1–17. **Longs** is the verb subsequently rendered "wait." Following on what precedes, Yahweh's waiting looks as if it has a negative implication. It would be a frightening thing to be told that you live in a time when Yahweh is not **gracious,** another statement designed to shake people to their senses. But the words that follow, **he rises to show you compassion,** make clear that those opening words must have had the positive connotation NIV attributes to them. And it is this note that verses 19–26 will develop. So verse 18 introduces what follows as well as concluding what precedes. It is the chapter's hinge. It represents another turnaround like the one at 29:5. The Hebrew Bible closes a section after it. There is a logic ("therefore") about it, but it is a divine logic, not a human one (cf. NIV's **Yet**). The "illogic" (**for**) continues in the basing of confidence in Yahweh's capacity for judgment. So far that has been a threat to Judah; now it will be its promise. Yahweh has to take the tough stance of verses 1–17, but that is not the end of the story. The moment of favor and compassion will come, and people can therefore **wait** confidently for it. The fact that "wait" is the same word as "longs" suggests that our waiting is built on Yahweh's waiting, and is guaranteed to find fulfillment because of that.

30:19–26 / The transition to promise brings a transition to lyricism. NRSV prints most of verses 19–33 as prose, NIV prints half as prose, while Thomas *(Biblia Hebraica)* lays out the whole as poetry. The lines are not very rhythmic and have little parallelism, but the lyrical nature of the prophecy makes it far from prosaic. Verses 19–26 offer a series of images of a better future.

There will be no scope for weeping because a cry is answered as quickly as it is uttered (vv. 19–20a). There is no unrealistic romanticism about this lyricism. Jerusalem's future is expected to continue to include experiences of **adversity** and **affliction** that would make people **cry for help** and **weep**. They are the terms used to describe Israel's experience in Egypt and in the stories of the "judges" (e.g., Exod. 2:23; Judg. 2:4; 3:9). The promise is that the cry for help will immediately be answered, so as to leave no scope for ongoing weeping. Normal human life involves this alternating of a cry for help and a responsive hearing.

There will be no danger of wandering because the people will have clear guidance (vv. 20b–21). In Isaiah's day the people could not claim that they lacked teachers, but the promise presupposes that the threat that Isaiah has hinted at, that people lose their teachers when they ignore them (see 8:16–17), has been fulfilled. They will now hear their teachers' voices when they are inclined to deviate from the path. The word **teachers** links with the word *torah* and could apply to the teaching of priests or sages, but in this context will refer to prophets' teaching (see vv. 9–10; 1:10; 28:9).

People will recognize images for what they are (v. 22). Isaiah refers only occasionally to the people's inclination to continue in the traditional religion of the country, but this was one of the principal causes of adversity and affliction (see, e.g., 1:29–30; 8:19–22). Images will repel them and they will finally abandon them because they make contact with Yahweh impossible. They will no longer be attracted to them as alternatives to Yahweh or means of relating to Yahweh. Instead of counting among the most valuable things (even if only on the outside), images will count as things you would most easily throw away.

Farming will flourish (vv. 23–24). The Judean hill country was not ideal farming country and would be vulnerable to drought and plague, so the promise of plenty corresponds to a felt need. **Bread of adversity** is replaced by **food** (the same word) that is **rich and plentiful**, and **water of affliction** is replaced by **rain** to make things grow and **streams of water** for plentiful fresh drinking. Obviously the interest here lies especially in such provision for human beings, though the enthusiasm in the picture of the animals' own enjoyment of plenty suggests a horizon that looks beyond that.

Nature will be transformed (vv. 25–26). The prophecy becomes more colorful in its portrayal of nature bursting constraints so that water flows at the tops of mountains, not merely at the bottom where you expect it, and the light of sun and moon is wondrously increased. Two other notes are then struck that look as if they belong to a different symphony, but both again safeguard against romanticism. The reference to slaughter is unexpected and critics thus usually reckon it a later addition. Its effect is to recall the tough closures to the lyricism of Psalm 104 and to forbid us to forget the need for putting down human pretensions to power that the book so often emphasizes (cf. the "tower" in 2:15). The reference to binding and healing likewise recalls the toughness of what Isaiah expects before these moments of new creation, and reaffirms that Yahweh will dress and heal as Yahweh had attacked. It perhaps also indicates the point of the metaphor in verses 25–26, that transformation of nature is a figure for transformation of human life, or at least accompanies it (see 11:6–9).

The background of verses 19–26 is not the kind of crisis that the earlier part of the chapter speaks to, but rather a situation where people who ignored the prophets' messages have experienced God's attack upon them and God's withdrawal from them. God now speaks to them of a new experience of grace and mercy and a new future. Presumably these words therefore come from a time later than that of Isaiah himself, though there are no concrete indicators of a more precise background than that.

30:27–33 / This closing vision in chapter 30, of a day of shaking and shattering and burning, typically begins in a way that teases the audience over which direction it will take. The opening words recall the vision of worldwide calamity in chapters 24–27, again beginning with **See** followed by a participle (lit. "There—the name of Yahweh coming . . . "). The prophet portrays a grim scene unfolding before our eyes. The words also recall the traditional picture of Yahweh coming from afar to act in power (see esp. Deut. 33; Judg. 5; Ps. 68; Hab. 3). These links would suggest that Yahweh comes to act on the people's behalf by putting down other nations. But in those other passages Yahweh comes from Seir/Sinai. Here Yahweh's name comes **from afar,** like the visitation of Judah by Assyria in 10:3 and that in 13:5 (NIV "from faraway lands"). So is Judah victim rather than beneficiary? This would fit the fact that the passage also recalls the picture of Yahweh's angry destructiveness, breathing fire, in passages such as 4:4 and 5:25–30. It is God's people who are usually the objects of God's anger, not other peoples (it is people you love that you get angry with). It would also reflect the description of the rushing torrent in 8:8 (NIV "swirling"). So this language might initially make the hearts of the audience sink as they have another bucket of anger poured over them.

Verse 28b resolves the ambiguity. It is indeed the nations that are the victims, not Judah. The one who comes from afar is not Assyria but Assyria's destroyer. The belief in God's sovereignty in the nations' affairs goes beyond that in chapter 10. Yahweh not only uses their own instinct for self-aggrandizement, Yahweh inspires them in their actions—and thus **leads them astray,** because they come to their own destruction. The way of thinking recalls the motif of the stiffening of the Pharaoh's mind in Exodus. While human beings are responsible for their actions (cf. "Pharaoh stiffened his resolve," e.g., Exod. 8:15), the great Dramatist also inspires the actors to act the part in the play that contributes to the unfolding of its plot.

So the downfall of these nations contributes to Judah's finding freedom. Another parallel with chapter 24 is thus the interweaving of destruction with worship (vv. 29, 32). The **night** festival is presumably Passover, which was celebrated at night. So this is an occasion of death and deliverance like that in Egypt. Indeed, the interweaving also recalls the reference to the day of slaughter in the midst of lyrical promise in verses 19–26—but it is an obverse of that. There the effect was to subvert romanticism. Here we are surprised to find reference to joyful worship (with **flutes** and **harps,** those gentle instruments!) in the midst of **anger** and **destruction.** That could risk encouraging warlovers to think that Yahweh is on their side when this is not so, but it takes that risk in order to encourage the victims of great powers that bondage does not last forever.

Distinctive here is the talk of Yahweh's **name** coming. Yahweh's name, like Yahweh's spirit or word or glory, can almost seem to have a life of its own. We have seen instances (see, e.g., 1:1) of the way in which in a traditional culture like Israel's a name may express who the person is, and so it is with Yahweh's name. The name *is* the person. Where the name is uttered, the person is proclaimed. Where the name is, the person is. Zion is thus the place of Yahweh's name (18:7)—that is, Yahweh's place. But sometimes Israel experiences Yahweh acting in power in a manner that suggests Yahweh was not present before. It thus pictures Yahweh as coming to a situation in power and not as having been present but inactive. In the same way we think of God as always being with us, yet also as sometimes coming to act in power.

Reference to the great power of Isaiah's own day eventually comes in verse 31, but it is subordinate to ongoing reference to the nations as a whole. In the OT and in the NT, individual powers, such as Assyria, Babylon, and Rome, become ciphers for whatever is the great power of the day, and the context suggests that **Assyria** here has that significance. Verses 27–33 indeed portray God's angry final shattering of the world of nations, and the description serves to frighten anyone who belongs to major world powers as well as to encourage smaller nations that chafe under them. A terrible storm with lightning, hail, thunder, and flood suggests the image of Yahweh's destructive fire, thundering voice, and overwhelming torrent. The picture of a funeral pyre prepared for the great leader of the world powers and due for igniting by Yahweh's **breath** likewise should frighten any great leader. Prominence in life is succeeded by prominence in death. It is as if Yahweh is going in for the kind of sacrifice of a human being that Middle Eastern peoples sometimes offered, and the king is Yahweh's sacrifice. The combined pictures here are almost as frighteningly destructive as the threat of Gehenna in the NT.

Additional Notes §19

30:1 / **My Spirit:** better "my spirit" (see Additional Notes on 11:1–2) or even "my will" (NRSV).

30:4 / Following on v. 3 these look like Egyptian envoys, but that makes poor sense. It is more likely that "they" refers back generally to Judah (see v. 2): these are Judean envoys traipsing from one end of Lower Egypt to the other.

30:5 / On **shame**, see the comment on 29:22–23.

30:6 / The words *'erets tsarah wetsuqah* are all taken up from 8:21–22 (NIV "earth," "distress," "fearful"). The last word is a rare one; it already reappeared in 29:2, 7 (NIV "besiege") in a restatement of the threat to Jerusalem. The word for "hardship" also came in an earlier warning in 5:29–30 (NIV "distress") in the company of a description of Assyria as roaring at Judah like a **lion**. A **darting snake** was another figure for Assyria in 14:29 as it threatened Philistia (NIV "a darting, venomous serpent"). Commentators have speculated that the Assyrians had already invaded and controlled the main road to Egypt, obliging the envoys to take some hard off-the-beaten-track route. But this interpretation reads a lot into the verse, and the links with these other passages in Isaiah more likely explain the language.

30:7 / The phrase **Rahab the Do-Nothing** is obscure in detail. The words are *rahab hem shabet*, literally "Rahab they a sitting," thus "They are Rahab—a sitting." Combining the second two words as *hammoshbat* produces "Rahab who has been stilled." This is more straightforward, which may not make it more likely to be correct. There is no link with Rahab in Josh. 2, whose name is spelled *rakhab*, meaning "broad."

30:15 / Although the Hebrew Bible starts a new chapter here, verse 15 opens with the Hb. word "for" (see NRSV and note on 1:29–30), which makes the link with what precedes.
"Repentance" is lit. "turning/returning." Passages such as 10:20–22 and 31:6 suggest that this is a turning (back) to Yahweh as the nation's security. Isaiah did want a turning from war, and his contemporary Micah brings together that phrase and Isaiah's word for "trust," but it is a lot to read reference to turning from war into Isaiah's words here—or even into Micah's (see Mic. 2:8, NIV).

30:19 / The Hb. uses an idiom whereby verbs are repeated for emphasis: lit. "in weeping you will not weep; in being gracious he will be gracious." NIV neatly conveys the tone of the latter, but it is more difficult to find an equivalent for the former. The point is not merely that weeping will cease. The idea is "Far from weeping, how gracious you will find Yahweh to be when you cry." The last clause is also expressed with a vivid succinctness (two words in Hb.), "as-his-hearing, he-has-answered-you."

30:20 / NRSV "Teacher" rather than "teachers" presupposes a respelling of the word from *moreyka* to *moreka*.

30:27 / The verb *ba'* could be a participle ("[is] coming") or a finite verb ("has come"). The word order with the subject first suggests the former. This then is a noun clause. Admittedly Deut. 33, Ps. 68, and Hab. 3 have finite verbs with this same word order. But the introductory "See" (lit. "there") reinforces the impression that this is a noun clause.

30:33 / Jeremiah 7:31–32 gives the background and indicates that **Topheth** was in the Valley of Hinnom just outside Jerusalem. All the other OT references to Topheth come in Jeremiah except for the account of its defiling by Josiah in Jeremiah's day (2 Kgs. 23:10). This and the links with Deuteronomy, such as that reference to Yahweh's name, support the view that this passage comes specifically from the late seventh century when Assyria's fall was indeed imminent (Sweeney, *Isaiah 1–39*, p. 396). In this case, the reference to Assyria would have to be taken more literally.
The focus on the "Assyrian" king and the threat of death can be compared with the pseudo-lament for the Babylonian king in 14:3–21.

§20 Oh You People Who Rely on Egypt (Isa. 31:1–32:20)

In the introduction to chapters 28–30 we suggested that 31:1–32:20 is one unit. Chapter 31 is much shorter than the units on either side, chapter 32 has no opening "Oh" like the rest of chapters 28–33, and taken together chapters 31–32 better fit the pattern whereby chapters 28–30 give increasing prominence to reassuring promise on the other side of threat.

31:1–3 / In powerful fashion these opening verses sum up the thrust of chapters 28–30 as Isaiah tries one more time to reach Judah. There is little that is new or subtle here. Rather, the prophetic preacher recapitulates the point of the sermon in unmistakable terms and words of one syllable before making the appeal in verse 6. The repetitions tell the story: **Woe, go down to Egypt, help, rely on, horses, trust, the Holy One of Israel, stumble, fall, perish.** In addition, **seek help** is a key term repeated from 8:19 (where NIV translates "consult/inquire") and **stretches out his hand** a key phrase in warnings of Yahweh's angry action in 5:25 and 9:11–10:4. The new words in verse 1 (**multitude, chariots, horsemen, look to**) have something different in common. They will all reappear in succeeding chapters (see 31:3; 36:9; 37:24). As well as resuming and taking further ideas from chapters 28–30, verse 1 will turn out to have themes that are taken up in the vision found in the stories about Hezekiah in chapters 36–39.

The reminder that Yahweh, too, is **wise** (v. 2a) takes up 28:23–29, but it is the negative implications of the fact that are worked out here. There Isaiah promised that plowing is succeeded by sowing. Here he emphasizes the harshness of the plowing process. There the capacity to make a plan and fulfill it was good news. Here the fact that Yahweh **does not take back his words** is a threat. As in 30:12–17, the warning about looking to Egypt for **help** is accompanied by a warning to the **wicked** who think that they can rely on the help of evildoers—on sinning their way out of trouble.

The formulation in verse 3a articulates an underlying conviction of Isaiah's in a fresh way by setting up a sharp antithesis. On the one side there are mortals. The word is *'adam,* the regular word for human beings in their humanness, made in God's image but inclined to self-exaltation and destined to be brought down. They are only creatures with breath in them (2:9–22). Parallel to it is **flesh** *(basar),* the stuff common to human beings and animals. There is nothing wrong with being flesh. Unlike the Greek equivalent, the Hebrew word does not imply wrongdoing or worldliness. It is just the ordinary created stuff of which human beings are made, designed to see God (40:5) but in itself perishable like grass (40:6).

On the other side there is **God.** The word is *'el,* the most absolute and dynamic term for God as the holy one who acts in justice (5:16), who is with the people and thereby guarantees their security (8:10; 12:2), who is like a powerful warrior (9:6; 10:21). And God is **spirit** *(ruakh),* like the wind that brings burning judgment (4:4), shakes trees (7:2), scorches seas (11:15), drives storms (25:4), and carries off peoples (27:8), or like the inner dynamic that gives both insight and the power to put it into effect (11:2; 28:6) but is also capable of reducing to confusion or stupor (19:14; 29:10), or like the breath that can utter words that have devastating effect (11:4; 30:28). God can come and dwell among human beings, and God puts the divine spirit within humanity and gives its dynamic to humanity (specifically Egypt!—19:3). But "God" and "spirit" are two words that stand for what distinguishes deity from creation. So it is an act of extraordinary folly to behave as if Egyptian cavalry had any significance independently of divine spirit.

31:4–5 / Isaiah continues to recapitulate the message, this time recalling 29:1–8 with its address to "God's lion" (but here Yahweh has become the lion) and its subtly-achieved move from threat to encouragement, from Yahweh's attacking Jerusalem (it is the lion's prey!) to Yahweh's defending it. The expression **do battle on Mount Zion** is the one that meant "fight *against* Mount Zion" in 29:8.

As well as being like a lion, Yahweh is like a mother bird. Admittedly, the comparison with **birds hovering overhead** is not inherently reassuring. They might be vultures (cf. Hab. 1:8) who

shield their prey for the same reason as a lion. It is only the four words that comprise verse 5b ("shield and-deliver, spare and-rescue") that make it clear that the prophet is playing on the two possible meanings of the preposition and of hovering to shield. The verb "shield" *(ganan)* is a rare one from which are derived the nouns for garden as well as shield. It occurs otherwise only in 37:35 and 38:6, in a similar connection. Parallel with it is the promise to spare or '**pass over**': the quotation marks reflect the fact that this is the only occurrence of the word with this meaning outside Exodus 12, and the verb presupposes that the one who passed over could easily have destroyed. But Yahweh indeed comes to **deliver** and **rescue**, not to kill and consume.

31:6–7 / It is therefore the appeal that comes next. The burden of Isaiah's ministry is that Judah should **return** to Yahweh. It is therefore remarkable that this is the only occasion when he actually bids them to do so. The exhortation will come only once more in the entire book, in 44:22, on Yahweh's own lips. The words are in prose not in verse, and they may be a later contribution to the book. Even so, their distinctiveness in content and style gives them particular impact in driving home the implication of chapters 28–31. Indeed, as we begin to come toward the end of the chapters that relate to Isaiah's own ministry to Judah, perhaps they drive home the implication of all that we have read, for the reminder that Judah has **greatly revolted** takes up one of the words with which the book began in 1:5 (NIV "persist[ed] in rebellion," *sarah*). The word denotes turning away, so it designates the problem in a way that coheres with Isaiah's formulation of the solution. They have turned away. He calls them to turn back. The precise word is a rare one and it has not occurred with this meaning since 1:5; further, at each occurrence it forms part of an unusual phrase. Literally, they have "increased apostasy" (1:5) and "deepened apostasy" (31:6). Their turning away has multiplied in quantity and depth. It is time to turn back. Eventually they are going to have to recognize the emptiness of the direction in which they have turned (v. 7); they might as well do so now.

31:8–9 / So the following verses offer the promise of relief. The sermon goes back to what God will do rather than what we must do. The poetry resumes and summarizes the promises about the defeat of that enemy who threatens Jerusalem. But, following on verses 6–7, these verses provide further context for that exhortation. The people will abandon images because the fall of Assyria discredits them (Sweeney, *Isaiah 1–39*, p. 403).

Talk of Jerusalem as Yahweh's **fire** or **furnace** takes up the image of Ariel (29:1), but it also recalls 1:25. The prophet reworks other threats from earlier in the book. Whereas the Assyrian sword would cause Judah and its allies to fall, to be devoured, and to flee (1:20; 3:25; 13:15; 21:15), now a supernatural sword will impose this experience on Assyria. Whereas Assyrians once rallied to the battle standard (5:26; NIV "banner"), now they flee it. Whereas Judah once looked for a stronghold to protect it (2:21, NIV "crag"), now Assyria has to do so.

Putting the strong young men to forced labor constitutes another neat reversal. Israel's "taskmasters" in Egypt were literally their "masters of forced labor," and forced labor was regularly the destiny of a defeated people in the service of their victors. It is an extraordinary thought that mighty Assyria should become a labor pool for little Judah.

32:1–8 / It has been suggested that verses 1–5 directly portray and support a ruler such as Josiah or Zerubbabel, but there is no explicit indication of this, and verses 6–8 work against it. Whatever years they come from, verses 1–8 contrast with how things actually are in Judah. There is a tradition that Isaiah was in due course martyred. If he uttered this prophecy in public in Jerusalem, it is not surprising. If many of his prophecies have been political dynamite, this one is even more explosive than others. Its implication is that the current leadership of the city is stupid and immoral, and due to be replaced by something very different. We know the trouble Jeremiah got into for speaking in those terms a century later. On the other hand, we hear of no such treatment of Isaiah, and this may link with the essentially positive portrait of Hezekiah and of Isaiah's relationship with him in the stories in chapters 36–39. Further, it is strange that Hezekiah is never named in these present chapters that seem to relate to his reign—unlike the earlier Ahaz, named in chapter 7 and in 14:28.

So chapter 32 begins with a positive statement about the way things will one day be. King and government will exercise just judgment (v. 1, see on 1:15b–20) and thus fulfill their vocation to be protectors to those who need protection (v. 2). There are nice verbal links with what has preceded. The image of a **rock** recurs (cf. 31:9, NIV "stronghold"). The strength that Judah and Assyria had both needed to look for, the people who are in need of shelter will now find. The fearsomeness of the spirit/wind (see on 31:3) also recurs, but now the needy will find shelter from it. Both storm and heat could be life-threatening dangers in Judah. Each person in government will be involved in protecting the weak from the social equivalents.

There is a contextual aspect to this job description for the leadership of the state. Just judgment and the protection of the weak were the things that were lacking in Jerusalem. If the city's problem had lain elsewhere, the prophet's vision for government might have put the emphasis elsewhere. On the other hand, this is commonly the OT's vision for government (see Ps. 72 for a classic expression). It is not a vision distinctive to eighth-century B.C. Judah. That might be partly because a community is always in need of this emphasis, and partly because the temptations of power always push governments in the opposite direction. It offers a striking contrast with the job description for government in modern societies. It is not that our governments are necessarily unjust, but they do not place just judgment and the protection of the weak at the heart of their job description. Neither in Israel nor anywhere else has this promise been fulfilled, and therefore it gives us agenda for prayer.

Without quite saying so, then, the positive promise for the future leaves no doubt that in the present Judah has a problem. The negatives in verses 3–4 move nearer to saying so. By implication, in the present the leadership can see and hear, but it chooses not to look or listen, to God or God's prophet (see 31:1; 28:23) or to the needy. In the present they see themselves as being decisive, but the prophet sees them as **rash** (literally "hasty"; in 35:4 NIV tellingly renders "fearful"). In the present they can no doubt deliver a well-prepared speech, but when pressed about how this all fits their faith in Yahweh, they have a **stammering tongue.** Measured action and fluency of speech are virtues that Israel's sages prized and encouraged. The prophet is thus already using the language of the sages, and once again is turning it back on the people who thought they were experts in it. **Fluent** repeats the same word translated **rash** earlier in the verse. Instead of speaking fluently but stupidly, they will speak fluently but wisely, with the wisdom that starts from reverence for Yahweh.

The nouns in verses 5–7 make the point even more explicit, again in the language of the sages. Isaiah is surrounded by **fool**s and **scoundrel**s. "Fool" is *nabal,* and the story of Nabal in 1 Samuel 25 shows what such a person is. A "scoundrel" or "villain" (NRSV) is someone who is wily, crafty, and deceitful, which again shows that the stupidity that concerns the prophet is a moral obtuseness that is not incompatible with cleverness. It consumes their whole person, words, thoughts, and actions (v. 5a). It draws people away from Yahweh into **ungodliness,** godlessness (v. 5b; cf. 10:6). The word denotes the process whereby someone ceases to belong to the people of God and becomes apostate or profane or heathen. The critique of previous chapters has shown how that works (e.g., 28:7; 29:13–15; 30:1–2, 10–11; 31:1, 6–7). They are the fools who say to themselves "There is no god" (Ps. 14). To put it another way, it draws them into **error,** makes them wander about like drunks not knowing where they are or how to get anywhere (the verb, *ta'ah,* occurs in 3:12, NIV "lead astray"; 9:16, NIV "mislead"; 28:7, NIV "stagger"; 29:24, NIV "are wayward"; 30:28, NIV "leads astray"). Things are bad enough when a society has fools and scoundrels in its midst. It is ten times worse when they are its leaders, called **noble** and **highly respected.** Once again the prophet laments the way they fail their first duty to the weak, both by what they do not do (v. 6b) and by what they do (v. 7b).

Verse 8 takes us back to where we started, offering a definition of true leadership and an implicit promise.

32:9–20 / The position of this address to the women of Judah, leading into the final promises of chapters 28–32, parallels that of 3:16–4:1. A message to the women complements a message to the men. The reference will again be to the well-to-do women, the mothers and wives and daughters of the community's politicians, businessmen, prophets, and clergy. Women in a patriarchal society had little choice but to sit around and look nice (3:16–4:1), doing not a lot that was politically significant, while the men exercised the power. The words for "so complacent/feel secure" (vv. 9–11) reappear in verse 18 where NIV renders them **undisturbed** and **secure,** and it is inappropriate to read value judgment and references to feelings into the words in verses 9–11. These women had the fortune and the limitation that they were not involved in the flurry of activity that has concerned us in chapters 28–31. They had nothing to do but relax with a basket of grapes and dates and risk dying of boredom.

But that is soon to come to an end. Here the focus first lies on calamity that takes the form of natural disaster (vv. 10–13), and the picture might suggest a plague like that of Joel 1, but the devastation of the city (v. 14) implies that once again war is involved and that it is an army that destroys nature. Fine dinner-parties with their buzz and laughter are thus replaced by the dress of mourning, mourning for that devastation that means you can no longer sit in the splendor of your house or palace or in the shade of your vine or your fig tree. **Fruit** is replaced by **thorns and briers,** the **merriment** of people by the merriment (NIV **delight**) of **donkeys** and **flocks.**

Forever (v. 14) . . . **till** (v. 15)! It is a fine contradiction. Admittedly, the Hebrew term "forever" regularly has fewer metaphysical connotations than the English expression, but it does suggest something final and permanent. This calamity will look permanent. It will feel as if it goes on forever. It deserves to go on forever. There is no basis for thinking anything different, except the being of Yahweh for whom the bringing of trouble is not first nature, and the commitment of Yahweh to Jerusalem that means that devastation is unlikely to have the last word. The breath of God (NIV "Spirit" is misleading) will scorch and wither (4:4; 11:15), but it is also capable of renewing. Breath brings life.

The new life will involve the social world as well as the natural world. In isolation, indeed, verse 16 could indicate that verse 15b was an allegory: the picture of a renewed nature symbolized a renewed social world. NIV's introduction of the metaphor of "fruit" into verse 17 might encourage this reading ("result" would avoid that). But the talk on both sides, in verses 12–14 and 20, seems quite literal and rules out this allegorical interpretation. And one might expect the Yahweh who is lover and creator of both the natural world and the social world to be renewer of both. The fact that renewal in one can be used as a metaphor for renewal in the other shows that they are not two separate worlds but two aspects of God's one world that thus work together. The phenomenon recurs in passages such as Psalm 72, which we have noted expresses the same vision of government as verses 1–8 here.

The problem with Judah's present is that its natural world and its social world are out of joint. The fields and land are fine, but scoundrels govern the country. The leadership is living in a relaxed and reposed way, but the moral coherence of the universe that comes from Yahweh means that there is no way this can continue. The subterranean faults must issue in earthquake. Only then can there be an act of new creation whereby proper order is restored and **righteousness** issues in **peace.** Usually *shalom* suggests well-being in a broad sense, but what follows makes it clear that here the English word "peace" conveys the idea. There were features of the life God means for us that the women and men of Jerusalem longed for, sought by their mistaken policies, and thought they possessed: **quietness** and **confidence, peaceful dwelling-places** and **secure homes** and **undisturbed places of rest**. They now become reality. Another **forever** (v. 17) replaces the fearsome one of verse 14.

Verses 19–20 then summarize verses 9–18 with the promise that even though there must be that terrible devastation of the natural world as well as of the humanly-made world, that is not the last word. The final vision (v. 20) looks more like one that belongs to the country than to the city that otherwise features prominently in verses 9–20. It hints that the "earthquake" will make it possible for the community to return to a more natural human life than that of the city.

Additional Notes §20

31:2 / In the context, "the help of evildoers" is more likely the help that evildoers give than the help that other people give them, as NIV implies (cf. v. 3).

31:9 / What "their stronghold will fall" (NRSV is similar) would mean is not clear. The link with 2:21 supports KJV's "he shall pass over to his strong hold," which also allows the verb to retain its more usual meaning and gives good parallelism.

§21 Oh You Destroyer Who Has Not Been Destroyed (Isa. 33:1–24)

We noted in the Introduction that the major copy of Isaiah from Cave 1 at Qumran leaves a space after chapter 33, and this chapter indeed closes off the first half of the book. It does this quantitatively, because we are fairly precisely half way through the book. It also does it thematically and verbally. At one level chapter 33 is jerky and puzzling. The addressees keep changing, we are not clear who is being talked about, and no train of argument develops through it. Its unity, consistency, and coherence come from its expository relationship with all that has preceded. It pairs with chapter 1, which provided an anticipatory summary of the message of Isaiah.

Chapter 33 has two distinctive features when compared with that opening synthesis of Isaiah's themes. One is that in an unparalleled and sustained way it takes up the actual words of preceding chapters and uses this technique to generate its synthesis of the message of the book so far, with a special focus on the immediately preceding chapters. The other is that, instead of focusing on calamity while closing in hope, it focuses on hope while acknowledging calamity. In this respect it also leads into chapters 34–35, which have a similar profile but introduce themes that will be developed later, rather than taking up themes from earlier chapters.

Chapter 33 thus expounds its message of promise by taking up words that promised hope in earlier chapters, and by taking up words that threatened calamity and reworking them so that they also now promise hope. While some words that reappear are common ones that would prove nothing, others are very rare, and the total number of repetitions is exceptional. It is this technique that suggests that the repetitions are significant for understanding the chapter as a whole. The parallels noted below concern only passages where the Hebrew word is the same or is related.

Sometimes NIV uses a different word of similar meaning, which again is noted below where it is harder to work out.

The chapter's expository method has a number of effects. First, by taking up threats from earlier chapters and using the same words to indicate the nature of God's promises, it simultaneously honors the reality of the threats and declares that they do not have the last word. The very power of the threats becomes a resource that gives power to the promises. The divine power attached to the threats becomes a divine power attached to the promises. The depth of the calamity is reversed so that it becomes the measure of the height of the blessing.

Second, the chapter provides the community that reads it with the words with which to make the response to Yahweh that previous chapters have sought. Yahweh has longed for people to turn to their God and has challenged them to put their trust in their God. If they take this chapter on their lips, it constitutes prayers and statements of faith that fulfill Yahweh's longings and meet Yahweh's challenges. The background to this is that the trust that people have previously misplaced is now exposed as the prophet had said it would be.

Third, the chapter often takes up expressions from earlier chapters but uses them with a different meaning. It thus utilizes the paronomasia that appears elsewhere in the book (e.g., 5:7). This has several effects. One is to make readers think and look at things from new angles, in the manner of a parable. Another is to imply connections that we have not thought of. It invites us to believe in a linked wholeness of the real world that lies behind the prophecy, the world of Yahweh. Reality is not a collection of separate and independent bits. It is a whole.

Fourth, chapter 33 makes no concrete historical references of the kind that often appear in this book. The effect of that is to generalize its promises. While they could apply to people in Isaiah's own day, the people of Jerusalem who live in subsequent centuries do not have to perform any hermeneutical gymnastics to see how they apply to them. In this respect, chapters 1 and 33 contrast with much of what stands in between them, where there are many implicit and explicit references to concrete situations. Setting chapters 1 and 33 around chapters 2–32 thus invites readers to see the message of chapters 2–32 as a particular concrete application of the more general points made in chapters 1 and 33. More accurately, chapters 1 and 33 have inferred principles about God's relationship with Jerusalem from chapters 2–32 and present readers with these principles as clues to understanding the material in between. More accurately still, chapter 1 comprises a compilation of "regular" messages of Isaiah's from different times in his ministry, which might have appeared within chapters 2–32 but here introduce his message as a whole. Chapter 33 then comprises a reworking of phrases from preceding chapters that constitute a different kind of whole, summarizing the implications of his message retrospectively.

Another implication emerges from the fact that chapter 33 has a generalizing nature and lacks concrete references to contexts and dates. It makes it impossible to date the chapter. Ever since the end of the nineteenth century there have been commentators who have dated this chapter in the time of Isaiah, Josiah, the Babylonian period, the Persian period, and the Greek period—in other words, every possible time from Isaiah to the end of OT times. This is not the only section of Isaiah of which that is true, and there is no reason to think that this situation in the study of Isaiah will ever change. The material itself simply does not provide the data upon which to base dating. This kind of historical approach cannot lead to compelling conclusions. We have to study the chapter as it is, as an exposition of what hope means in the light of what has preceded, without knowing its date.

33:1 / The "Oh" (NIV **Woe to**) addressed to a destroyer-betrayer marks continuity with preceding chapters and might momentarily make the audience steel itself for another picture of its own calamity. Instead there comes the beginning of the reversal that runs through the chapter. The "Oh" addresses a **destroyer** who is involved in **betraying** (see 21:2; NIV "looter"). In chapter 21 it likely refers to Babylon, which would make sense here in connection with the Judean deportation there. But Assyria has usually fulfilled the role of destroyer, though it has been shared by Babylon and others (13:5, 6; 15:1; 16:4; 22:4; 23:1, 14). Potentially it applies to any attacking power. "Betraying" (see also 24:16) suggests a nation that fails to fulfill the hopes people have in it. Again, betrayal was a characteristic of many large and small nations that appear in this book and later in Israel's history. Indeed arguably it is the essential characteristic of nations that Isaiah especially strove to get Judah to face. Whoever the destroyer/betrayer, it will drink its own medicine.

33:2–4 / The "Oh" in chapters 28–32 has been spoken sometimes by Yahweh and sometimes by the prophet. Verses 2–3 make clear that here prophet, or prophet and people, speak. They turn from addressing the destroyer to addressing the one who will bring about the destroyer's downfall. At last the words are the ones Yahweh has longed to hear: **be gracious to us; we long for you** (see 30:18–19). There Yahweh was waiting to be gracious and a blessing was declared on people who longed for Yahweh. Isaiah had promised that they would see Yahweh's "arm" coming down on Assyria (30:30). They now ask Yahweh to be their **strength** (the same word). "Morning after morning" they were to experience Yahweh's scourge (28:19). Now they ask that **every morning** they should experience Yahweh's deliverance. In a place of distress they had been told that they would be saved if they relied on Yahweh (30:6, 15; also 25:9). Now they call Yahweh their **salvation in a time of distress.** The tumult of the nations has terrified Judah (29:5–8, NIV "many/hordes"). Now they acknowledge that this **thunder** (the same word, *hamon*) of Yahweh's **voice** will terrify Assyria, as Yahweh promised (30:30–31). Now Judah's foes **flee** as once its own leaders did (22:3). Isaiah had promised that Yahweh would **rise up** to show the people compassion (30:18). They acknowledge that this is happening. Yahweh had promised there would be a scattering, driving storm (30:30). They see **nations scatter.** Judah had been warned about plundering (e.g., 8:1–4) and about its fruit harvest (32:10). Now the nations are warned that their **plunder** (see on v. 23) **will be harvested** (the latter word occurs only once more in the entire OT). The nations had been warned about their thirst remaining unsatisfied, and Judah had been warned about not satisfying the thirsty (29:8; 32:6). The reference to when people **pounce** uses a similar word to the word for "thirsty," though with a different meaning.

33:5–6 / Yahweh is now confessed rather than addressed. Another key theme in earlier chapters has been the declaration that Yahweh will be **exalted,** rather than the human resources in which people trusted (see 2:11, 17; 12:4). The actual word also came in 26:5 and 30:13. Human beings dwell in dust (26:19) and Yahweh brings down those who pretend to live on high (24:21; 26:5). Yahweh **dwells on high,** whence spirit is poured down (32:15). Whereas Zion is currently filled with silver and horses and images, Yahweh **will fill Zion** with just judgment. Yahweh has been their **sure foundation** in doing things planned long ago (25:1, NIV "faithfulness"). He is thus the sure foundation. Whereas Tyre will not be able to hoard its profits (23:18), Yahweh will be the people's **rich store** (the same word). The **wisdom and knowledge** to find the way of **salvation** in their time of crisis has been the recurrent topic of chapters 28–32. Yahweh will be that resource. They have spent their **treasure** on what has actually been a foolish quest for such deliverance (30:6). The key is real reverence for Yahweh (NIV "fear") instead of the superficial reverence they manifest (29:13, NIV "worship").

33:7–9 / That promise for the future contrasts with the hardship of the present. The word for **brave men** comes only here, but it looks very like the word Ariel (29:1). It is these brave men and not just the powerless who **cry** (see, e.g., 5:7) because of what they see and experience **in the streets** (5:25; 10:6; 24:11), like Moab (15:3). The **envoys** (30:6) who had worked so hard for **peace** now only **weep,** and weep **bitterly**—though that was what Judah had chosen (5:20). But we know that Yahweh will achieve peace (32:18) and bring an end to weeping (30:19). The **highways** that Yahweh had promised (11:16; 19:23) but that had been the scene of a significant confrontation (7:3) are **deserted,** as the whole land was destined to be (1:7; 6:11—both times the related noun). Contrary to their expectations, the scourge has indeed reached them (28:15), so other travellers have stopped moving, like Rahab (30:7). They had bidden their prophets to give up their path and stop talking about the Holy One (see 30:11). Now people have stopped going on the paths. They thought they had a **treaty** (28:15, 18) but it is broken, like the one they broke themselves (24:5). As people **despised** Yahweh's teaching and provision and word, but not yet their images (5:24; 8:6; 30:12; 31:7), so people have despised their **cities** (see mg.; 1:7; 6:11; 32:14, 19). Their lack of respect for the potter (29:16) now becomes a lack of respect for humanity in general, though that is a fulfillment of warnings (2:11, 17) and a deserved reversal (28:14; 29:13). The same word for "humanity" that lies behind **no one** comes in all these passages.

So **the land mourns and wastes away:** the words repeat 24:4. **Lebanon is ashamed** similarly recalls 24:23 (the word for "moon" is very similar to the word for "Lebanon"). It **withers** like the reeds of the Nile (19:6, the only other occurrence of the verb in the OT). Lebanon and **Bashan** were part of the warnings in 2:13, Lebanon and **Carmel** in 29:17 (NIV "fertile field"), Carmel and desert (cf. **Arabah** here) in 32:15–16, forest in 29:17 and 32:15 (cf. **Sharon** here). The trees dropping their leaves or fruit recalls 32:10.

As a whole, verse 9 thus repeats 32:9–14 and restates the need for 32:15–16.

33:10–12 / Yahweh here arises to act. The fact that Yahweh would **arise** to act was a threat in 2:19, 21; 28:21; and 31:2, but now it is good news. For Yahweh's being **exalted,** see on verse 5. Yahweh's being **lifted up** contrasts with the exaltation of the mountains and trees (2:12–14; 30:25) and recalls 6:1. **Chaff** and **straw** take up 5:24 (the first word occurs nowhere else in the OT), as does the **fire** that **consumes** them. But see also 29:6 and 30:27–30, which also incorporate the **breath** that overwhelms (there it is Yahweh's). The people also repeat the experience of 26:17–18: they **conceive** and **give birth** to wind/breath. They are **burned** like the cities in 1:7, as if to **lime** rather than merely to remove dross and leave pure metal (1:25), burned like the **thornbushes** of 32:13 that have now been cut down for burning.

33:13–16 / In 32:9 **listen** was the summons to Jerusalem's women regarding what Yahweh was about to do. Here it summons citizens who now live **far away** (see 6:12) as well as such who are **near** (cf. 29:23, the word "among them") regarding what Yahweh has **done** (a common word, but see the significant repetitions in 29:16), which is pictured as past. It is time they acknowledged Yahweh's **power** as their strength (the same word in 30:15). The **sinners in Zion** recall the sinful nation of 1:4 with their sinful hands, stained by blood and images (1:18; 31:7). They **are terrified** in the way that 2:10, 19, 21 envisaged. **Trembling grips the godless** (cf. 32:6) like the lions of 5:29. The **consuming fire** recurs from 29:6 and 30:27, 30.

The repeated question **who can dwell** and the characterization that follows in verses 15–16 then take us in a different direction, because in the form of the words and in the general content it takes up Psalm 15 as well as earlier material in Isaiah. The two different words for **dwell** in verses 14 and 16 *(gur, shakan)* correspond to the two words in Psalm 15. The people acknowledge that they cannot fulfill the psalm's prescription and cannot enjoy that dwelling to which the prescription points. **Extortion** recalls 30:12 (NIV "oppression"), **bribes** 1:23 and 5:23, **murder** (lit. "bloods") 1:15 and 26:21, **shuts** the eyes 29:10 (these are the only two occurrences of this expression in the OT), **on the heights** 32:15 (22:16 is also a particularly neat link), **refuge** 30:13 (the participle "high"), **mountain** 22:16 (confirming that earlier ironic link) as well as 31:9 and 32:2, **fortress** 29:7, **bread** and **water** 30:20, 23, **not fail** 22:23, 25

(NIV "firm," with irony again). Thus the section begins with Yahweh exhorting the people to listen and respond, and in the bulk of it they do this by acknowledging that Isaiah's critique is fair and that they have failed to live up to the specifications of the psalm.

33:17–19 / In this vision of a restored leadership the promises contrast with the fall of the king's underlings in chapter 22 and with the prophet's explicit and implicit critique of the monarchy itself. The promise that their **eyes will see** their leaders recalls 30:20 (though "see" is now *khazah,* not *ra'ah*), while the ideal **king** specifically takes up 32:1. **Beauty** once more replaces branding (3:24); but beauty was a standard expectation of a king (e.g., David in 1 Sam. 16, Absalom in 2 Sam. 14, the king of Tyre in Ezek. 28). In contrast with the confines of little Judah, the ideal will also be realized in a **land that stretches far**. The expression is no longer a threat (cf. 30:27, and related words in 5:26; 6:12). **In their thoughts** that had likewise gone far away from Yahweh (29:13) they will **ponder the former terror** like the lion that caused it (31:4, NIV "growls"). **The one who took the revenue** occurs only here in the OT; **officer** is Shebna's title in chapters 36–37, though not in 22:15. In the context, the terms look more like titles of enemy officers. There may be an irony in the promise that these enemy officers will have disappeared, as Shebna has been warned he will fall. Seeing the king will thus contrast with having to see the **arrogant people** who had invaded them, the people **obscure** in their speech (translated "deep" in 30:33, "greatly" in 31:6), of **strange tongue** (see 28:11).

33:20–24 / This vision of a restored city repeats the double invitation to **look** and **see** from verse 17 (NIV there "see" and "view"). The eye turns to the other of the two objects of Yahweh's love and choice that Judah especially treasured (cf. Ps. 132). **Zion/Jerusalem** is the **city** of David (29:1; also 32:13), the **tent** of David (16:5). It was the subject one verse before the reference to the king in 32:1 (31:9, also 4–5; 28:14, 16; 29:8; 30:19). Here fighting, fire and furnace give way to enable it to become a **peaceful abode** such as Yahweh had imperiled but then promised to restore (32:18; see also 32:9, 11, NIV "complacent"). Its **festivals** are no longer dismissed (1:14). The word for **will not be moved** occurs only here, but it looks very like the word Zoan (19:11, 13; 30:4) in the country that Judah thought was key to security. **Its stakes will never be pulled up,** unlike Eliakim's (22:23–25). Its **ropes** are no longer deceitful (see 5:18); instead of being **broken** they will be as secure as their former attackers' footwear (see 5:27).

The city will be **a place of . . . rivers and streams** like the ones that Egypt was to have spoiled (19:5–8), **broad** like the one into which Shebna was to be cast (22:18, a rare idiom). It will be troubled by **no galley** of the kind that Tarshish possessed (23:1, 14) **with oars.** The word otherwise occurs in the OT only at 28:15 (NIV "overwhelming"), where it is followed by the verb here rendered **sail** (there "sweeps by"). No **mighty ship** will attempt to confront the **Mighty One** (see 10:34). Yahweh will not merely replace the inadequate **judge** (1:26; 3:2) and **lawgiver** (10:1; 22:16 "chiselling" is a form of the same word because laws are "set in stone") and **king** (32:1). Yahweh will take their place, and of course **save us** (19:20; 25:9; 30:15).

So the sea-powers are ridiculed. Their mighty ships are useless. Their **rigging** (the "ropes" of v. 20) **hangs loose** (the word for the "abandoned" fortress in 32:14). Their **mast** and **sail** (see 30:17 "flagstaff/banner") are no longer functioning properly. The mast is not **secure** (cf. 28:2, 22, NIV "strong/heavier"). The sail is not **spread** (cf. 19:8, NIV "throw"). Instead of collecting **spoils/plunder** (8:1–4; 10:2, 6; and see v. 4) they will be **divided** as spoil (see 9:3) even by the **lame** (an adjective from the verb translated "pass over" in 31:5). In contrast, **no one living in Zion** (see on "dwell" in v. 16) **will say, "I am ill"** (a complete reversal of 1:5–6). **Those who dwell there** (literally "the people that dwells there," cf. 30:19; 32:18 "live") commit **sins** (e.g., 1:4, where the word people also comes; 5:18; 6:7; 27:9; 30:13). But these will be **forgiven.** Contrast 1:14 (NIV "bear") and the terrible plea "do not forgive them" in 2:9, which is now reversed, and see on verse 10 above (where "lifted up" is the same verb).

So the chapter closes by bringing together reminders of what God has promised for Zion through the book, which will bring healing, security, and flourishing that contrast with the loss it has suffered through its unfaithfulness.

Additional Notes §21

33:2 / For the verb "long for" used here *(qawah)*, see 25:9 (NIV "trust"); 26:8 (NIV "wait for")—also Isaiah's longing in 8:17 and Yahweh's own in 5:2, 4, 7.

33:4 / NIV adds **O nations;** the Hb. text does not explain the "your" or the word "plunder" with its sudden change in who is being addressed. The Syriac, Targum, and Vulgate apparently had a text that divided the words differently and lacks the word "your" (see NRSV). V. 4 then follows v. 3 smoothly.

33:8 / The fact that the preceding chapters often refer to cities but never to (plural) **witnesses** supports MT (NIV mg.). The Qumran text, which NIV follows, provides the word one might expect in the context if one ignores the fact that the chapter consistently links with what precedes.

§22 Streams Turned into Desolation, Desert into Pools (Isa. 34:1–35:10)

While chapter 33 looks back and reworks the message of the book so far, it does so in a way that points forward and emphasizes the wondrous reversal and restoration that Yahweh will bring about. Since the second half of the book is more renewal-focused, chapter 33 thus also anticipates this material. Chapters 34–35 then mirror chapter 33. They have one eye to what has preceded, but they more explicitly point to what will come, introducing us to themes to be developed in the second half of the book. We will see that chapters 36–39 are stories that talk about Isaiah and were therefore hardly written by him, while chapters 40–66 presuppose a later context than Isaiah's day and are presumably the words of later prophets.

34:1–3 / A vision of Edom's judgment begins with a summons to sacrifice. The nations are summoned to court—but not to a trial, where they would have at least the theoretical chance to defend themselves (cf. passages such as 41:1–4). Their guilt is assumed. The court meets purely for the determination of punishment. There is a gruesome contrast between the summons of **the earth and all that is in it** here and the one that will come in 42:10–12. Contrast also the summons that involves the nations and heaven and earth as a whole in, for example, Psalms 67 and 96–100.

When the OT speaks of God's **angry . . . wrath,** we have noted that Israel itself is usually the object of this anger (e.g., 30:27–33). On the other hand, it is usually foreign nations that are the victims when Yahweh speaks of "total destruction" (*kherem*; but see 43:28). This is the term used of Joshua's destruction of the Canaanites (see also 11:15; and 37:11, perhaps ironically). Yahweh claims them as if they were a sacrifice like the whole offering which was totally burnt because it was totally given over to God. But it is also the case that we get angry when someone does wrong to people we care about, and Yahweh's anger here links with the nations' harsh treatment of Israel such as we have heard about in previous chapters and will hear more of in succeeding ones (and see v. 8).

34:4–5a / **Stars** and **starry host** (v. 4) is the word translated **armies** in verse 2; the reference is presumably to heavenly forces that stand behind earthly forces (cf. 24:21). The destruction of verses 1–3 is not confined to the worldly powers themselves. There is also devastation in the heavens. But this turns out to be a preliminary to the focus moving in a different direction.

34:5b–8 / We return to earth and find that Yahweh's sword has turned its attention to Edom, now under judgment and offered in sacrifice. Judah's southeastern neighbor was conspicuous by its low-key treatment in chapters 13–23 (see 21:11–12; also 11:14). Elsewhere Edom is a prominent object of prophetic attack (see Jer. 49; Ezek. 25; Obad.), while Lamentations 4:21–22 expresses Judean feelings about Edom after the fall of Jerusalem. Edom/Esau was of course the twin brother that Jacob-Israel loved to hate. But Israel's own version of its story in Genesis interestingly shows an awareness that Esau generally behaved at least as well as Jacob in the context of that troubled relationship, even if he was to live by the sword (Gen. 27:40). Now he is to be devastated by it.

No reasons for Edom's devastation are given and nothing we know about the history of Edom and its relationship with Judah would explain the fierceness of this chapter unless it is the mere fact of recurrent conflict through the monarchic period. The chapter has been the basis for inferring conflicts between Judah and Edom in the Persian period, but this is a hazardous process. Perhaps Edom is already a symbol for national power asserted against God and against the people of God. In rabbinic writings it comes to stand for Rome and for the heir to Rome's power, Christendom (see, e.g., M. Jastrow, *A Dictionary of the Targumim, the Talmud Babli and Yerushalmi, and the Midrashic Literature* [2 vols.; New York: Pardes, 1950]). The passage then constitutes another warning to international or multi-national powers concerning their inevitable destiny.

Verses 5b and 8 form a bracket around this section. They again make explicit that God's gruesome act is an act of **judgment** in the strict sense, the executing of a court's verdict. The "judgment" commonly refers to people in power ensuring that the powerless get their deliverance and vindication (e.g., 32:1, 16; 33:5, NIV "justice"). This suggests that the prophet sees the people as Edom's victims and sees this judgment as their deliverance. That becomes explicit in verse 8. **Vengeance** (judicial recompense; see on 1:24) and **retribution** indicate the conviction that there is some justice to be sorted out with Edom. And **to uphold Zion's cause** implies not the instinct to support my country, right or wrong, but rather the conviction that Zion is in the right.

Inside this bracket, however, the "total destruction" of Edom again indicates that through this event Edom is being totally handed over to God (see on v. 2) and the verses that follow develop the metaphor of slaughter as sacrifice. It is as if Yahweh's metaphorical **sword** is the knife with which the priest cuts up animals for **sacrifice**. The soil in **Bozrah** (known from archaeological work to have been a big city, perhaps the capital) and the rest of the country is thus pictured as soaked in **blood** and **fat** in the way the soil of the temple altar area would be. But **wild oxen** and **great bulls** are not sacrificial animals, and such animals are used as figures for powerful human beings (e.g., Ps. 22:12; Lam. 1:15), so verse 7a pictures the fall of the Edomite leadership and military.

34:9–17 / Once again the images of judgment and sacrifice give way to the image of devastation, as we saw between verses 1–3 and 4–5a. Here the devastation consists in natural disaster in Edom. While Yahweh is no doubt assumed to be the agent of disaster, there is no mention of this (NIV's reference to "God" in v. 11 is an interpretive addition; cf. NRSV). The land is devastated as if by a volcano or a nuclear accident, in the manner of Sodom and Gomorrah. It becomes for ever lifeless and impassible, habitable only by the hardiest of birds (vv. 9–11a). It is as if God has used the state of the world before creation as the blueprint for planning what Edom should now be: **chaos** and **desolation** (v. 11b) are the frightening onomatopoeic words of Genesis 1:2, *tohu wabohu* (NIV "formless and empty"), which sound as meaningless as the scene they conjure. There is nothing for the rulers to rule and, in any case, no rulers to rule it (v. 12). The cities in which they lived are **overrun** by **thorns, nettles,** and **brambles,** and become home for **desert creatures** instead of human beings (vv. 13–15). Yahweh has definitively determined that these creatures should thus gain permanent new homes, and put it into writing; they have the title deeds (vv. 16–17). While the historical Edom went into decline three centuries after Isaiah's day, it is a mercy to it that the declaration in chapter 34 has never been implemented on it.

35:1–2 / In a sharp and unexplained transition, the picture of a movement from garden to devastation is succeeded by five pictures of transformation. As pictures they need to be appreciated with the aid of the imagination.

Chapter 35 begins by envisioning an opposite movement to the one we have just imagined—from desolation to fruitfulness. The unnatural devastation of chapter 34 is different from the **desert, parched land,** and **wilderness** of chapter 35. These three terms denote natural features of the Middle Eastern landscape, the area where the rainfall is too slight for crops or trees to grow but not too slight to provide shepherds with enough natural vegetation to pasture their sheep. It is austere and tough. But each spring the desert blossoms in grass and flower wherever the winter rains bring new growth. The poem starts from that natural annual flowering and imagines a wondrously enhanced version of it whereby the wilderness will **blossom** and **burst into bloom.** The same word occurs three times: the desert will burst, burst, burst. In the way that meadows naturally sprout wild flowers such as the crocus, the desert will sprout forests and woods like those of Lebanon, Carmel, and Sharon instead of the scrub bush and acacia which is all it can usually support. Cedar and pine, vine and olive abound. The brightness and flourishing will be like a smile, indeed a **shout** of **joy,** on the face of the landscape.

Will joy lead to blossoming or blossoming lead to joy? Verses 1–2a express it both ways, perhaps reflecting the fact that in experience both orders are possible, or perhaps reflecting a sudden holistic bursting out in more than one form. And who are "they"? Is the expression indefinite ("people will see . . . ")? The fact that the word is emphatic ("those") makes this unlikely. Is it "those" of whom we are about to read in verses 3–10? But then we would expect "these." Is it Lebanon, Carmel, and Sharon, or the desert creatures of chapter 35, or the people of Edom themselves perceiving that this miracle reflects the work of God? Whichever is the case, evidently the miracle of the **glory/splendor** of Israel's God exceeds this new manifestation of the **glory/splendor** of Lebanon/ Carmel/Sharon.

35:3–4 / This second scene moves from fear to hope for people whose lives have collapsed and who sit head in hands, fearful, anxious, depressed, lonely, tired, despairing. They have (literally) "hasty hearts": they are always jumping up in fear. They can see no future, no end to this thralldom. Then the same people have their burden lifted, with confidence replacing fear, hope replacing despair, energy replacing fatigue. What makes the difference is the awareness that their God is coming. The promise resumes that of chapter 34 from an explicitly Judean viewpoint. Judicial recompense (see on 34:8) will indeed mean the deliverance of the victims of wrong. The promise for the future can make strength possible in the present. The picture applies to people who have fallen to the calamity Isaiah has warned about, but because it does not relate itself specifically to only one such experience, it therefore stands as an ongoing promise to God's people.

35:5–6a / A third scene moves from silence to shouting as it pictures handicapped people: someone who cannot walk, a blind person, a deaf mute. Then the same people are able to run and see, to hear and speak. There are at least four ways of reading this picture. It suggests God's concern for people with these particular needs (see Jer. 31:8) and God's promise that they have a special opportunity to join in the joy of this day of transformation. It suggests a further way of portraying the experience of Israel as a whole, imprisoned by disaster and calamity, unable to know freedom of communication or movement (see 42:16). More solemnly but also encouragingly it suggests the ongoing moral state of the people of God (see the description in 29:10, 18 and 42:18–19). And it also suggests the state of the world to which the people of God is called to bring that freedom (42:7). The translation **shout for joy** obscures the point. There is no word for "joy" there. The verb simply refers to the ability to make a noise at all, for that is the miracle!

35:6b–7 / The fourth scene returns to the wilderness, where the transformation of people reflects that of the landscape from desert to pool. It is a different transformation from that of verses 1–2. Normally the land is parched and brown. Neither human beings nor animals or plants can easily live there. Then suddenly the terrain is the same, but transformed somehow. It is water supply that makes the entire difference. The bubbling of people mirrors the gushing of waters that turns wilderness into wetlands.

35:8–10 / The fifth picture, one of returning home, is more of a drama. It does not tell us the outline of the story in the first line, as the first four do. There is a **highway:** so travel is envisaged, but what kind of travel? It is a "holy way," so perhaps it is the road that leads to the shrine. Certainly it demands that the people who walk it be people who could enter there without defiling it (for the word "unclean," see 6:5; 52:1, 11). But what constitutes defilement? Stupidity is here the answer—the moral obtuseness such as leaves God out of account, which Isaiah often attacks. Positively put, the visa requirement is that you belong to Yahweh's **redeemed/ransomed.**

Both verbs (*ga'al* and *padah*) gained their meaning from the customs of everyday life. Family relationships impose family obligations. If someone within your family gets into trouble, it is your responsibility to give your all to make their life livable again and to restore them to their place in the community (see Additional Notes). "Redemption" suggests the acceptance of such family obligations. Both these obligations involve money, and "ransom" puts this financial question in the forefront of consideration. It involves paying the price required to free an animal or a person who for some reason "belongs" elsewhere (e.g., Lev. 19:20; 27:27).

These everyday words provide pictures for what Yahweh does in restoring Israel from the losses that come to it in the course of its life. The people were like members of Yahweh's family to whom Yahweh accepted a family obligation to do whatever it took to make their life livable. Or they were like people who had come to belong elsewhere and needed someone to negotiate their freedom. They thus become the redeemed/ransomed. The second word has occurred before (1:27; 29:22). The first will become a favorite word in chapters 40–55 (see on 41:14). The appearance in parallelism of the nouns "redeemer" and "father" in 63:16 underlines the family background of *ga'al*.

At the end of the line that refers to the redeemed/ransomed, while we are still thinking about the significance of those two magnificent words, a telling verb is slipped in. The point about this processional way is that it is the road on which these people **return.** When this verb is applied to Israel, usually in Isaiah (and elsewhere) it denotes returning to Yahweh. So this drama presupposes the fulfillment of the vision of 1:27 (with its reference to the ransomed; the "penitent" are the "returners"). It also presupposes the fulfillment of the condition of 6:10 (with its concern about the blind and deaf and the stupid), of the promise of 10:21, and of the command of 31:6.

This return also means that the people will **enter Zion,** which rather suggests it is an outward as well as an inner return, geographical as well as spiritual. The meaning is perhaps implicit in the name of Shear-Jashub (see 7:3) and in the warning of 10:22. It is the return that 11:11–16 promised without using this word, a return of people scattered like the people at the Tower of Babel and decimated almost like the people of Sodom and Gomorrah. They still exist in far off places, and Yahweh has promised that redemption/ransoming is not merely a past event. Returning to Yahweh and returning to Zion have become two sides of the same coin.

So now we are in a position to work out where this processional way leads. It is not just a road through a city, because it is the kind of road where there might have been wild animals. It is a long road, through potentially hazardous territory. But it will be protected, for the sake of those accredited travellers, to take them to **Zion.** And the close of the drama ties the whole chapter together. They arrive there shouting, like the transformed desert and the no-longer-mute (**singing** is the same word as "shout for joy" in v. 6a). Scattered over the four corners of the Middle Eastern world, they have nothing to shout about, but arriving at Zion they will have reason to make a noise. **Everlasting joy will crown their heads** as forests and woods crown the tops of the desert mountains and as these rejoice. **Sorrow and sighing will flee** from the hasty-hearted and fearful. It is a strangely negative way to end, but perhaps it does so because that is where the people are, and the negative promise is the most welcome one.

This lyrical picture of God's salvation looks beyond any concrete historical experience. As it stands, chapter 35 has no more been realized than chapter 34, and it thus remains as a promise regarding God's ultimate purpose. While it would be an exaggeration to say that it contains the message of chapters 40–55 in a nutshell, each of its motifs is taken up there. Jesus then also takes up some of its motifs and applies them to his own ministry (Matt. 11:5). These two examples of the use of chapter 35 elsewhere provide interim fulfillments of its vision and illustrations of what other such interim fulfillments might look like. In our own experience, when we see God replacing desolation by fruitfulness, fear by hope, silence by shouting, or desert by pool, and when we see believing communities finding their way back to God and back to the place of God's purpose for them, we see this vision finding another interim fulfillment.

Additional Notes §22

34:1–35:10 / It is a matter of dispute how far chs. 34–35 sow seed thoughts that will be developed later and how far they are a summary of what is to come that was actually written retrospectively. Like the dispute over the date of ch. 33, this disagreement is unlikely to be resolved, but it does not affect the fact that chs. 34–35 do introduce us to later themes.

34:5 / The verse begins "for" or "when" (see Additional Notes on 1:29–30), and the word **see** usually marks the beginning of a sentence. That suggests we should link the first line with what precedes. This also gives coherence and completeness to vv. 4–5a as concerning Yahweh's action in relation to the heavenly army, with v. 5a pairing with the middle line of v. 4 as a bracket around the intervening two lines. "The people I have destroyed" then presumably means "the people I have doomed to destruction" (cf. NRSV). The Hb. is lit. "the people of destruction." The events in this chapter are all future, even when verbs in the past tense portray them.

35:9–10 / For examples of redemption see the obligation regarding someone who falls into poverty in Lev. 25:25–55 and that regarding someone without immediate family in Ruth 3–4.

§23 Hezekiah's Great Political Crisis Confronts Him (Isa. 36:1–37:7)

We may be surprised to find the introduction to the second half of the book in chapters 34–35 followed by four chapters of prose stories about Hezekiah, the last of the kings of Isaiah's own lifetime. One reason for this surprise is that they also appear in 2 Kings. As with 2:2–4, we do not know which is the more original version. But Isaiah is prominent in the stories and they incorporate some of his prophecies, so it is reasonable enough that they should appear in the book called Isaiah. There are several other locations within the book that would seem more natural than this one. Yet their placement here adds to the sense in which chapters 34–39 as a whole face two ways. The stories are more retrospective than prospective, but as well as looking back to Hezekiah's kingship, they end with the prospect of Judah in Babylon (39:5–8). They thus lead into chapter 40 more concretely than any other chapter could. But their retrospective focus means that, together with chapters 34–35, they form intertwined hooks that bind the two parts of the book tightly together.

In the company of other little peoples on the western edge of the Assyrian empire, Hezekiah had asserted independence from Assyria in 703 B.C. King Sennacherib therefore led an army to put these peoples in their place. His own records relate how he did so (see *ANET*, pp. 287–88). First, he reestablished authority in northern cities such as Sidon, Achzib, and Akko, replaced the king of Sidon with his nominee, and imposed tribute. This frightened into submission the kings of places such as Ashdod, Beth-Ammon, Moab, and Edom, though not of Ashkelon, whose king was therefore deported to Assyria while the city was forced to pay tribute. Continuing down the Mediterranean coast, Sennacherib conquered and despoiled cities such as Beth-Dagon and Joppa, and he defeated the combined Egyptian and Ethiopian force that had responded to a call for help from Ekron. Sennacherib goes on, as to Hezekiah, the Judean, he did not submit to my yoke. I laid siege to forty-six of his strong cities, walled forts, and to the countless small villages in the vicinity, and conquered them. . . . Himself I made a prisoner in Jerusalem, his royal residence, like a bird in a cage. I surrounded him with earthwork. . . . Thus I reduced his country, but still increased the tribute. . . . Hezekiah himself, whom the terror-inspiring splendor of my lordship had overwhelmed and whose irregular and elite troops that he had brought into Jerusalem, his royal residence, in order to strengthen it, had deserted him, did send me later to Nineveh, my lordly city, together with thirty talents of gold, 800 talents of silver, precious stones . . . and all kinds of valuable treasures.

In broad agreement with this account, 2 Kings 18:13–16 relates how Sennacherib captured all the fortified cities of Judah; when Hezekiah acknowledged that he had done wrong in rebelling and asked him to withdraw, Sennacherib imposed a tribute of three hundred talents of silver and thirty talents of gold. Paying this involved the surrender of all the silver in palace and temple and in stripping the gold overlay from the temple doors and doorposts.

Comparing Sennacherib's account with those in Kings and Isaiah reveals that he omits the fact that he did not actually conquer Jerusalem. But he did procure its surrender. Comparing the account in Isaiah with Sennacherib's and with that in Kings reveals that Isaiah 36–37 omits the fact that Hezekiah did surrender. The account in Isaiah 36–37 and that in 2 Kings 18–19 are largely word-for-word the same, but 2 Kings 18:14–16 does not appear in Isaiah.

While it might be that the defeat and the deliverance happened on separate occasions, this is not the impression that we receive from the way the story in 2 Kings 18 unfolds. More likely, the differences reveal the nature of the story each narrator wished to tell. This was an event that could be seen as either a defeat or a deliverance—depending on how you told the story. Isaiah 36–37 invites us to listen to the story for a lesson on how a person of faith best handles a political crisis, and it therefore emphasizes the deliverance.

The version in 2 Chronicles 32 further complicates the reading of Hezekiah's story. There Hezekiah is unambiguously a hero who behaves just as Isaiah would wish. Although the same is true in Isaiah 36–37, we have already read chapters 28–33 with their implicit critique of Hezekiah as the king responsible for the policies that Isaiah attacks in those chapters. There is an ambiguity about the OT's account of Hezekiah's character and about his achievements. Perhaps that reflects an ambiguity about Hezekiah's actual character and achievements. Different accounts, therefore, can be illuminating in their selectivity for different audiences in different situations with different needs.

36:1–3 / Sennacherib begins his campaign by achieving the easy targets. **Lachish** is actually the most impressive of these lesser cities. Its remains form a huge mound or "tell" in the lower hills near the coastal plain to the southeast of Jerusalem. It is thus nearer than Jerusalem is to the route down the coast that an army would take. From there he sent one of his senior staff to Jerusalem to attempt to procure Jerusalem's surrender. He did not want to have to lay siege to the city, which would cost him time and resources and would cost Hezekiah, too. The minister took an impressive military force to underline the point.

Water is a key factor in the siege of a Middle Eastern city (cf. ch. 7). In building a city one customarily chose an elevated position for security, but this meant that the site would not have a spring. Although Jerusalem is lower than some of the mountains around, the original Mount Zion sits on a rocky spur that gave it considerable security on three sides. It needed humanly-devised defenses only to the north, although by Hezekiah's day the growth of the city westward across one of the valleys that once protected it complicated this matter of defense.

Mount Zion also possessed a flourishing spring, the Spring of Gihon, which flowed from the base of its spur. Hezekiah had already been responsible for a monumental engineering project that involved digging a tunnel through the rock of the spur to bring the water from the spring inside the city walls, where it gathered in the Pool of Siloam. That eastern side of the city symbolizes Hezekiah's achievements in seeking to ensure his city's security. There the Assyrian stands to confront the king, at the very spot where Isaiah had confronted Ahaz, which reminds both the king and the story's audience of the confrontation in chapter 7. The army has disappeared from the scene (physically there would be no room for it in this location). The Assyrian stands alone like Isaiah (with no son).

As the Assyrian replaces Isaiah as the man who will address the Judean leadership, three of the king's staff replace Ahaz. Presumably king might go out to king, but a king's representative deserves only the other king's representative. As someone whose formal title was palace administrator, Eliakim perhaps had a similar post and significance to the Assyrian **commander**. The latter's title is an Akkadian word (Akkadian was the language of Assyria) transliterated into Hebrew as *rab-shaqeh*, which seems to denote "chief cup-bearer" (see Gen. 40:1; Neh. 1:11). It thus looks like an honorary title for a senior member of the king's political staff, like "palace administrator."

It was Eliakim who Isaiah had said would replace Shebna as a key figure in Jerusalem political affairs (22:15–25) and he has now apparently done so, as he is named first among the three Judean officials. Shebna is now a lesser figure, though more a secretary of state than a typist. He is there along with Joah, whose title **recorder** is also that of a senior minister of state (see 2 Sam. 8:16; 20:24; 1 Kgs. 4:3). So the Assyrian king's representative brings his master's message to the Judean king's representatives.

36:4–10 / The great king's representative then speaks. When Isaiah had confronted Ahaz, he had addressed him as the Great King's representative who has been given his Master's words to pass on, and who speaks with all that master's authority. "This is what the Sovereign Yahweh says" (7:7) were thus his words of introduction. The commander speaks in the same way, as he begins his unconscious parody of a prophet's challenge, **this is what the great king, the king of Assyria, says.** Historically, the parallel works the other way around; a prophet speaks the way a king's representative speaks, because that is what a prophet is. Now the movement is reversed.

His subject is **confidence**: literally, "What is this confidence with which you are confident?" The word recurs five more times in verses 5–9. It is Isaiah's own subject. Hezekiah has no doubt been attempting to build up morale in Jerusalem by encouraging his people to believe that resistance is a realistic policy. Sennacherib will not risk trudging up to Jerusalem to deal with it, especially now that it has Egypt as an ally. But, he asserts, these are **only empty words**—literally "a word of lips," mere sounds that come out of the mouth. They do not count as real **strategy and military strength** (v. 5).

Here too the commander speaks like Isaiah, who must be smiling if he is peeping out of a window at the event. "Strategy and strength" were exactly what the king was supposed to be expert in (see 11:2; NIV "counsel and power"). Isaiah's plaint in connection with Hezekiah's day in particular was that the state was thinking through "strategy," but without taking Yahweh into account (30:1, NIV "plans"). Now an Assyrian politician repeats the prophet's accusation that they did not really know what they were doing. Isaiah had declared that Yahweh was the key to military strength (cf 28:6, NIV "strength" for "battle") and that they did not know where real "strength" lay (30:15–16). Now an Assyrian politician also repeats that accusation. Isaiah had declared that Egypt was too feeble to be depended on in a crisis (31:3). Now an Assyrian politician repeats that observation as well. Not only will this crutch collapse under you. It will wound your hand in the process (v. 6). Verses 8–9 underline the point. Judah thinks the key to safety is **horses, chariots,** and **horsemen;** the Assyrian subverts that belief in his own way, as Isaiah had in his (31:1).

There is a second strand to the Assyrian's confrontation, and again it sounds as if he is not merely Sennacherib's puppet but also Isaiah's and Yahweh's. **You rebel against me,** he says (v. 5). The "me" is his master, Sennacherib, but the words are also the words of a prophet for whom the "me" is Yahweh. This accusation opened Isaiah's book in 1:2, though using a different verb. The actual phrase used here recurs in this connection in Ezekiel 2:3. Rebellion against Assyria *is* rebellion against Yahweh, because Assyria is Yahweh's agent (10:5). The argument will recur when Jeremiah sees Babylon as Yahweh's agent a century later. If he is rebelling against Yahweh, Hezekiah cannot claim to be relying on Yahweh. Isaiah might be smiling wryly again, for relying on Yahweh was exactly what Isaiah wanted Hezekiah to do, but he agrees with the Assyrian that trust in Yahweh would not make rebellion successful.

The Assyrian commander adds the clever and interesting argument that this trust is impossible because of the way Hezekiah has been treating the worship of Yahweh (v. 7). Isaiah might be quizzical about this observation. His uneases about the people's worship of Yahweh have been of a different order. To put it another way, he also feels some distaste for the high profile of worship in the Jerusalem temple, but on a different basis (see 1:12–17). Where these chapters recur in 2 Kings, the Assyrian's argument resounds with more irony, for 2 Kings 18 has just commended Hezekiah for the religious reforms to which the commander refers.

His Isaianic coup de grâce comes in verse 10. It is the point that underlies that observation about rebellion. It was not the Assyrian king's own idea to invade Judah. It was Yahweh's. He comes as Yahweh's agent to bring destruction to Judah. "Yahweh told me," he asserts. Once more, Isaiah nods. Once more, the Assyrian ironically repeats the words of the prophet, acting as if he were the prophet's lackey (see 10:6).

36:11–17 / A moment of wondrous humor follows. The Assyrian king's spokesman has delivered this politically challenging and theologically penetrating speech with its fine climax. The Judean leaders respond like buffoons. They behave like the politicians they are, caring nothing about the issues with which they have been confronted and worrying only about the political fallout of implementing a freedom of information act (v. 11). But the commander knows exactly what he is doing (v. 12). The facts are on his side, and when that is so, it is worthwhile making sure that your opponents' citizenry know all about them. Although his first speech was addressed to the politicians, it could be overheard by ordinary people. His second speech directly addresses the people.

Through verses 13–17 he puts no foot wrong. He rubs their noses in the implications of the political and theological situation that we have just been considering. As he urges them not to believe Hezekiah that Yahweh can be trusted to deliver them, they too can remember the message that Isaiah has been seeking to drive home. They know that he too has declared that reliance on human resources and foreign allies in order to resist Yahweh's purpose does not become a winning game-plan because you garnish it with statements of religious conviction. On the other hand, surrender will mean peace in the short term, and the chance to start a new life in the middle term. There is presumably some irony here. Further, Judeans would know of the way that their brothers and sisters in Ephraim had been transported to Assyria, and were still in the midst of that, to judge from Ezra 4:2.

36:18–22 / So far so good. Then the commander makes his comprehensive, fatal mistake. He moves from questioning the competence of Hezekiah to questioning the competence of Yahweh. He moves from "Yahweh will not deliver you" to "Yahweh cannot deliver you" (vv. 18–20). The move is equivalent to the one that lies behind Isaiah's direct assessment of Assyria in 10:5–11. Assyria was the means whereby Yahweh acted in Judah, but Assyria had no more use for these foreign religions than for the foreign peoples' armies and the countries themselves.

We hear nothing of the people's response, and not enough of the Judean politicians'. We do not know whether the latter's outward expression of grief means that they are simply appalled by the Assyrians' hard line, or by the insulting of their king, or by the blasphemy of their God. We can imagine Isaiah's mixture of horror and a strange relief that things have been brought out into the open in such a way that Yahweh will be goaded into action despite Judean stupidity, if not through its repentance.

37:1–4 / Again there is some ambiguity about the outward expression of Hezekiah's grief. Initially his preoccupation is that **this day is a day of distress and rebuke and disgrace,** and once more we might imagine Isaiah responding "Yes, quite rightly too, trouble is just what Assyria was supposed to bring" (e.g., 8:22). In rebuking Judah, the Assyrian politician was again taking up Isaiah's ministry. Hezekiah is now doing what Isaiah longed for him to do. Instead of turning to Egypt to get them out of trouble (30:6), he is turning to Yahweh. As the situation parallels that in chapter 7, so Hezekiah's response begins to contrast with Ahaz's. Hezekiah is modeling how to cope with a crisis.

That word "disgrace" begins to point to the Assyrian's fatal mistake, for although the word can be used to signify contempt of the people of God (which was what they deserved), it characteristically denotes actual contempt of God. It usually signifies Judah's contempt for Yahweh (1:4; 5:24, NIV "spurned"), for usually God's people, not the world, is the object of God's anger (30:27–33). Like anger, spurning or despising belongs in the context of a relationship. Assyria has made the mistake of becoming like Judah.

The point is explicit in verse 4. Going beyond bringing "disgrace" to Judah (30:5), the Assyrian king and his lackey have dared to **ridicule** (the same word) God. Their **rebuke** therefore invites reversing. So the appropriate response is not argument (see 36:21) but prayer. The Assyrians have crossed a line. The matter is out of the politicians' hands and into the prophet's. The image of Jerusalem as Judah reduced to a remnant (v. 4) recalls 1:8–9.

Hezekiah sends his priests with his officials to see Isaiah, but at this point, at least, prayer is more the prophet's business than the priests'. A prophet was one who took part in the deliberations of a higher cabinet than those of Jerusalem or Nineveh, and was therefore able both to report its deliberations on earth and to intervene in those deliberations in heaven. And this particular prophet has long been occupying the theological high ground in the stance he has taken in relation both to kings and to priests, and anyone else who was around. It is theological high ground that now counts.

37:5–7 /   The word of Yahweh now comes, for Hezekiah's instinct was the right one. It rather sounds as if Isaiah knew what had been going on. If he had not been there listening on the wall, presumably there would have been a line of people keen to report events to him. He has therefore had a chance to listen to God about the matter. His response is twofold, corresponding to the two issues raised by the Assyrian and by Hezekiah's message. First is Yahweh's characteristic **do not be afraid** (see 7:4 in the Ahaz story; also 8:12; 10:24; 35:4), which addresses Hezekiah's concern about trouble and the fate of this mere remnant. But like the commander's words and Hezekiah's own, the response soon centers on what has emerged about attitudes to Yahweh (v. 6b). So the second part of the response is a specific promise of what will happen to sort out the one who has unwisely provoked God (v. 7).

Additional Notes §23

For the debate on the historical issues raised by chapters 36–39, the question whether the Kings or the Isaiah version is more original, and the significance of the chapters in this context, see, e.g., the study in B. S. Childs, *Isaiah and the Assyrian Crisis* (Studies in Biblical Theology Second Series, 3; Naperville, Ill.: Allenson, 1967); R. E. Clements, *Isaiah and the Deliverance of Jerusalem: A Study of the Interpretation of Prophecy in the Old Testament* (JSOTSup 13; Sheffield: JSOT, 1980), pp. 72–89; Ackroyd, *Studies in the Religious Tradition of the Old Testament*, pp. 105–92; C. R. Seitz, *Zion's Final Destiny: The Development of the Book of Isaiah: A Reassessment of Isaiah 36–39* (Minneapolis: Fortress, 1991), pp. 48–66.

36:1 /   **Fourteenth year:** since Hezekiah came to the throne in 725 B.C. and Sennacherib's campaign took place about 701 B.C., this would be ten years too early. The date seems to be a slip, but we do not know how or when the slip came about.

36:4 /   On **confidence**, see the verb in 12:2; 26:3–4; 30:12; 31:1; 32:9, 10, 11, and related nouns in 14:30; 30:15; 32:17, 18 (NIV also translates by "trust," "rely on," "depend," "secure," "security," "complacent," and "safety").

§24 Hezekiah Responds to His Great Political Crisis (Isa. 37:8–38)

It will be a while before Yahweh will carry out the threat in verse 7. In the meantime, verses 8–35 go over similar ground to that just covered, and especially 36:18–37:7. Once again, Sennacherib sends a message to Jerusalem rather than coming himself. Once again he expresses contempt for Yahweh. Once again Hezekiah goes to the temple. Once again Isaiah sends him a message bringing Yahweh's word of judgment and reassurance. As the story unfolds, the dramatic tension increases as we wait to see how and when Isaiah's word in verse 7 will be fulfilled.

While the outline of events is the same, this second sequence is by no means mere repetition. In the manner of Hebrew parallelism, each major section heightens the point. We hear Sennacherib himself speak. We hear Hezekiah himself speak. We hear Isaiah speak at much greater length. And we hear of what happens in fulfillment of his word.

37:8–13 / First Sennacherib makes a mistake parallel to that in 36:18–22. We now discover what stopped Sennacherib from coming to Jerusalem in person. At first he was still in the midst of completing the conquest of the other Judean towns (v. 8). Then he had to give his attention to more urgent business, for Judah's Cushite/Egyptian allies were at last **marching out to fight** (v. 9). That makes it the more important to keep Judah in its place. But there are two problems with his message to Hezekiah. One is that it deconstructs. If there is no hope for Judah and its allies, why is Sennacherib having to give such urgent attention to Judah's chief ally? His minister's claim in 36:6 now reads somewhat ironically.

More seriously, his words succinctly restate the contempt for Yahweh in 36:18–20 and embody the self-confidence of 10:8–15. Even with the Cushites mustering, there is dramatic time for some subtlety. Unlike his minister, Sennacherib goes straight to the point and straight to the king, but he too echoes Isaiah's theme of whom they **depend on,** and ironically assumes that they are taking the stance that Isaiah urged. He speaks of countries that the Assyrian kings had defeated, **destroying them completely.** It is the sacrificial verb from 34:2 (cf. also 34:5), and we know it is actually Assyria's own destiny. But worse, he allows himself a frightening blasphemy. **Do not let the god you depend on deceive you.** Is Yahweh any better than the gods of the other peoples whom Sennacherib has defeated? Where are all those people in verses 12–13? We do not know, and that makes the point. But Sennacherib has thrown down the gauntlet to Yahweh.

Wherein lies the distinctiveness of the God of Israel? People have often sought to identify a difference in Israel's vision of God—for instance, Yahweh is involved in history as other gods are not, or Yahweh is transcendent in relation to nature as other gods are not. It may be that such distinctives can be identified, though they have a way of disappearing when one examines them. Israel's claim is not that its view of God is different, but that its God lives up to the theological claims made for this God. This God actually exists and actually acts with the power that all peoples attributed to their gods. It is this claim that Sennacherib disputes.

37:14–20 / In a response parallel to that in verses 1–4, Hezekiah again models how to cope with a crisis. Chapters 28–32 have implied that Hezekiah left a lot to be desired as king, but at least he knows what to do with a threatening message. He understands that prayer involves bringing things to Yahweh's attention. Arguably this is not merely the beginning of prayer, but the essence of prayer. Showing Yahweh the letter is an act of prayer. Words then follow.

The words of his prayer contain five elements. First, they acknowledge who God is (v. 16). Yahweh is God known in Israel, God sovereign over nations, God the creator. Such acknowledgments at the beginning of a prayer incidentally reaffirm, for the sake of the person who prays, the true nature of reality, how things really are—especially in the face of pressures to believe that they are otherwise. But the words address God not the self, and their central purpose is thus to remind God, "You know who you are." These are the characteristics, then, to which the person who prays appeals in prayer.

Second, the words seek God's attention. They ask God to listen and look—not at the person praying, but at the events he is praying about. They are the verbal equivalent of showing God the letter. In particular, they draw God's attention to another reason for being concerned with what the person praying points to (see v. 17b).

Third, the words of the prayer face facts and speak of facts. The nature of the laments in the Psalms is to go on at great length about the facts of pain and loss. Verses 18–19 are this prose prayer's equivalent. They have no hesitation about pointing out to God what is going on. Even if in theory God knows all about it, attention needs to be gained and motivation engendered.

Fourth, the words make a request (v. 20a). Typically in OT prayer, the actual request forms a much briefer section of the prayer than is the case with Christian prayers. Characteristically, they ask God to look (v. 17) and to act (v. 20a). How deliverance is to come can be left to God.

Fifth, the words of the prayer remind God of the supreme reason for acting (v. 20b). The reason is the equivalent to the Christian appeal "for your glory's sake" or "for your name's sake." They assume that God wants what the person praying does—that the world should come to see that Yahweh is indeed God, God with a capital "G" (cf. v. 10, though this is a distinction possible in English but not in Hebrew).

37:21–29 / There is a sixth characteristic of OT prayers: they receive answers. It is often a prophet who brings them, though perhaps only a king can expect to receive his answer via a prophet of Isaiah's status.

Here the word of Yahweh against Sennacherib comes, as it did in verses 5–7. We have noted that there is a difference between the dramatic audience of a prophecy and the audience that is intended to hear it. Verses 21–29 complicate this. At the first dramatic level the words address Sennacherib, but even within the drama they have a second audience. They are uttered for Hezekiah to hear. There is no reference to their ever being sent to Sennacherib. All he receives is silence (cf. 36:21). We might perhaps also envisage two actual audiences for the prophecy. One is the people of Judah who are to read this book of prophecy. The other is people like ourselves for whom it was preserved as being of significance beyond that first historical context.

Yahweh's word starts where Hezekiah is. It pictures Ms **Zion** watching Sennacherib disappear, not merely relieved but proud and scornful (v. 22). It closes with the facts that make the humiliation of Sennacherib possible. Hezekiah's God has the intelligence that is needed (v. 28). The word for **rage** denotes not so much anger as the powerful thrashing about of a raging bull, while the word for **insolence** denotes the relaxed confidence that was Judah's own destiny, but only because it had Yahweh on its side (32:9, 11, 18; 33:20). Yahweh has the power to disturb the comfortable as well as to comfort the disturbed and to treat Sennacherib the way a hunter treats a wild ox on the way to putting it in the royal zoo (v. 29). It is a scenario to encourage Hezekiah at a moment when the pride and scorn are on Sennacherib's side.

In between verses 22 and 29 comes the familiar double critique of Sennacherib which makes the scenario not merely possible but inevitable. Sennacherib has forgotten who is God. His achievements have made him talk and think as if he is (vv. 23–25). He has behaved as if he could stand tall and look God in the eye. It is the standard temptation of national and international powers. He has taken no account of the fact that his achievements were part of a broader picture whereby God's purpose was being achieved in the world. He has looked at them on too narrow a canvas (vv. 26–27). Again there is both an encouraging and a solemn perspective there for national and international powers to take into account.

37:30–32 / We have noted that Yahweh has been speaking to Hezekiah when he has been speaking against Sennacherib (v. 22). Here are words that directly address Hezekiah. As usual, a prophet's words do nothing to make life easier. They promise a sign, but it is a sign that will be visible only in the future (cf. Exod. 3:12). In the present Hezekiah has to carry on living by faith, or start to do so. In order that this should be living by faith, there is no sign in the present.

Further, there will be nothing immediately supra-natural about this sign. Yahweh does not promise a miracle that will instantly restore the community. Restoration will follow the natural pattern. It will take a year or two to recover from devastation, destruction, death, and depopulation and get back to normality. But it will happen (v. 30). The function of the promise of God is to establish that it really was Yahweh who had acted: Yahweh so often says what will happen, then makes sure it happens, and is then in a position to say "You see, I said it and it happened, so it must have been me, mustn't it?" Yahweh does not rely on the less convincing practice of offering merely retrospective explanations.

Indeed, the sign-ness of this event may lie somewhere else than in the not-very-remarkable event itself. The promise about having something to eat is literal. Without that, nothing else is possible. But the fact that the community can once more **take root below and bear fruit above** (v. 31) is also a sign in itself. The fulfillment of the one is the guarantee of the other, because Yahweh promises to make it so. Hezekiah is invited to make that a matter of faith, too. That **a remnant, a band of survivors** should become a flourishing community again could not be taken for granted. Communities die out. The **zeal** of Yahweh Almighty will see that this does not happen.

The French sociologist and theologian Jacques Ellul comments, "How simple and vital is this sign!" We would call it a return to normality, but actually normality is

> war and murder, famine and pollution, accident and disruption. When there is a momentary break in the course of these disasters, when abundance is known, when peace timidly establishes itself, when justice reigns for a span, then it is fitting, unless we are men of too little faith, that we should marvel and give thanks for so great a miracle, realizing that no less than the love and faithfulness of the Lord has been needed in order that there might be this privileged instant. (*The Politics of God and the Politics of Man*, pp. 178–79)

37:33–35 / This final word from Yahweh about Sennacherib is of more immediate cash value, of dangerously concrete checkability. It is a more prosaic, down-to-earth equivalent of the prophecy of Isaiah in 29:1–8 and 31:4–5. Even if Jerusalem is taken to the edge of the abyss, it will be held from falling.

It is a prophecy to which we have to keep listening until the final word. We will miss something if we leave before the closing credits. One reason that Yahweh will act is clear enough from all we have been reading. Sennacherib has impugned the person of Yahweh as the real God. In his actions he has behaved as if he himself were God, and in his words he has declared that Yahweh is not. It is therefore not surprising that Yahweh acts **for my sake.** Nothing has prepared us for the fact that Yahweh also acts **for the sake of David my servant.** At least, nothing in this story has prepared us for this, but these words do take us back to Ahaz facing a similar crisis and similar faith-issues, where he was both spoken of and addressed as "the house of David" (see 7:2, 13). That is the challenge and the strength of the king of Judah. Yahweh made a commitment to David (2 Sam. 7) which Yahweh will honor. Indeed, in verse 35 the essentials of Isaiah's theology come together: the person of Yahweh, the city of Jerusalem, the promise to David, the theological necessity of deliverance.

37:36–38 / The modern reader may come here to the end of this story with a sense of horror. Nothing has prepared us for verse 36. Yet everything has prepared us for this. Isaiah has spoken continually of the death and destruction of foreign peoples and their armies (e.g., 30:25, 28, 30–33; 31:3; 33:1, 12; 34:1–8). The words may seem harmless because they are only words. But if the words do not become reality, what is their point? One of the OT's consistent starting-points is the reality of how things are in the world. Death and destruction characterize the OT because these things characterize the world. The OT believes that Yahweh is a God involved in the world, and therefore that Yahweh is involved in the death and destruction. The implications are frightening, but not as frightening as the assumption that the world story proceeds without God's involvement, without the possibility of God's intervention, and without meaning.

So what happened? There are three ways of answering the question, and the reader's own philosophical and theological position will determine the choice. One is to say that this is a legend, a dramatization of the conviction that God does deliver Israel and does bring down the proud aggressor. It is as harmless as the words. The second is to say that some natural disaster overtook the army. A hint in the Greek historian Herodotus suggests an epidemic in the camp. This account compares with the explanation of the Red Sea event or the parting of the Jordan by a strong wind or a landslide. It assumes that something extraordinary happened and sees the reference to Yahweh's angel as an Israelite theological interpretation of the event. The third possibility is to say that this is a supernatural event that happened exactly as the text depicts, noting that hesitation to accept the text at face value reflects a modern problem with whether God can be supernaturally active in the world. I do not personally know which of these alternatives is right. It does not seem to make a difference to the significance of the story.

Additional Notes §24

37:8–38 / A common critical view has been that these are two versions of the same events. Instead of trying to combine the two into one story, the text puts the two versions of the story one after each other. The effect is rather like that in Gen. 1–2, where two creation stories are placed one after the other rather than being interwoven. The usual conservative view has been that here there is no reason why the two sequences should not relate two separate events.

37:38 / Assyrian records relate no further visit of Sennacherib to Palestine and tell of his murder by his son twenty years later (cf. vv. 37–38).

§25 A More Equivocal Response to Two Further Challenges (Isa. 38:1–39:8)

The background of these two further events is, again, Judah's rebellion against Assyrian sovereignty. Yahweh's promise of healing for Hezekiah also includes deliverance from Assyria (38:6), and an alternative chronology to the one presupposed in the Introduction does have Hezekiah living on for fifteen years after the Assyrian invasion, until 687/686 B.C. But a number of considerations suggest that the events in chapters 38–39 took place before those in chapters 36–37. This promise of deliverance belongs more plausibly before the dénouement in 37:36–38 than after it. The embassy from Merodach-Baladan, which followed Hezekiah's illness and recovery (39:1), must have taken place before Sennacherib's invasion. He was king of Babylon from 721 to 710 B.C., was then removed by the Assyrians, but regained power in Babylon in the period of the widespread revolt against Assyria in 703 B.C. of which the events in Judah in Hezekiah's day were part. His embassy to Jerusalem was the kind of event that provoked the invasion. All this makes it natural to see the events that lie behind chapters 38–39 as a whole as preceding those that lie behind chapters 36–37.

One can see more than one reason for the stories being arranged out of chronological order. It is not a mistake. One is the longer time frame of chapter 38, which looks fifteen years forward beyond the Assyrian crisis to the end of Hezekiah's reign. Chapter 39 has an even longer time frame and a more specific reason for its location. It looks beyond Hezekiah's reign to events that will take place a century later. These events in the place to which chapter 39 refers will be the specific background to the prophecies that begin in chapter 40.

There is an equivalent theological significance in the arrangement. We have seen that chapters 36–37 are unequivocally positive about Hezekiah. In his relations with Sennacherib he never puts a foot wrong. Chapters 38–39 are more ambivalent. In chapter 38 he both claims a consistent faithfulness to Yahweh and also acknowledges that Yahweh has had consciously to take notice of all his sins (vv. 3, 17). In chapter 39, his revealing all to the embassy is at best an ambiguous act. Whether or not Isaiah's response is seen as a rebuke and whether or not Hezekiah's reaction seems cynical (vv. 5–8), there is no doubt that the closing verses of the story are dominated by a down note that also prepares the way for what follows.

To put it another way, the first pair of chapters about Hezekiah portray a king of Judah more positively than any king is portrayed anywhere in the book, and thereby provide a vision of hope for the future. Hezekiah is the very embodiment of the kind of king Judah needs and one day will have, by God's faithfulness. The portrait is thus an idealized one. There, the need is not for a portrait of Hezekiah "warts and all" of the kind that chapters 30–31 have implied could be drawn. The need is for a symbol of hope for people who were often depressed by the reality of kingship and by the reality of how history turned out for Judah. But the second pair of chapters undermines that and raises the question whether hope for such people must lie somewhere else than in its monarchy, for if Hezekiah (like David) has feet of clay, can any human king ever realize the vision?

There is a further pastoral significance in this arrangement. How can people who go through the experience of defeat and deportation retain faith in God's power and purpose? A story such as this also offers one form of help for living with that experience. It never indicated that events were out of control. They were always within God's purview. Indeed, the following chapters look beyond the experience of loss and deportation at the hands of Babylon to a time when Babylon will get its comeuppance and King Cyrus of the Persians will make it possible for the treasures and the people to return and the city to be rebuilt—as happened beginning in 539 B.C.

38:1–8 / It is difficult to avoid the assumption that prophecy involves speaking about the inevitable. But this story, among others in the OT, reflects the opposite assumption. Prophecy unveils what will happen "if/unless." The if/unless is rarely stated, but prophet and recipient know they are there. Here Hezekiah's personal experience parallels his political one in the previous chapter. It involves a crisis for Hezekiah, an intervention from

Isaiah, and a prayer by the king. The order of events is not the same, though once again the prophetic intervention is unsought. This makes the point that prophecy cannot be controlled, even by the king. Indeed, it is especially important that the king cannot control prophecy. In chapters 36–39 Isaiah brings four messages to Hezekiah, although he does not ask for any of them. The first, in 37:6, proves the rule because it is a response to a request from Hezekiah, but the request was a request to pray.

Hezekiah knows how to respond to a threatening word from God as well as how to respond to a threatening political crisis (vv. 2–3). Like Abraham or Moses, he asks God to have second thoughts. Prayer assumes that knowing God's will makes it possible to seek to get it changed. It also assumes that there ought to be a link between the lives we live and the destiny that unfolds for us. In the light of what we know of Hezekiah we may feel that there is some irony in his claim for himself, and it is noticeable that Yahweh's response (vv. 4–6) does not include an explicit acknowledgment that he has spoken truly. Conversely, of course, many faithful people who pray for deliverance from a fatal illness do not receive it. Perhaps the additional promise of the king's and the city's deliverance from Assyria hints that Yahweh's attention lies elsewhere (and perhaps whether God grants what people pray for often reflects a larger purpose). The basis for Yahweh's grace lies not in Hezekiah's faithfulness but rather in his and the city's political need.

The sign that follows constitutes another parallel and contrast between Hezekiah and Ahaz. Yahweh gives both kings gratuitous signs, but Hezekiah's is designed to encourage someone who is walking Yahweh's way, whereas Ahaz's is designed to halt someone on a different path.

38:9–20 / If Hezekiah's prayer (37:15–20) reflects the dynamic of OT prayer as embodied in the Psalms, his thanksgiving here does that more systematically. A number of passages from the Psalms appear at appropriate moments in OT narrative (e.g., 1 Chron. 16). This may mean that the prayer was composed with the narrative and later included in the Psalter, but it is more likely that the stories quote the hymns than vice versa. As this thanksgiving does not make any specific reference to Hezekiah's experience, presumably it was taken from the liturgy by Hezekiah or by the author of the chapter as an expression of the kind of way Hezekiah would appropriately have prayed. The phrase **a writing of Hezekiah** is more literally "a writing for Hezekiah."

The thanksgiving has three elements. First it looks back to the experience of affliction and of urgent prayer (vv. 10–14). It protests the prospect of dying long before one's "three score years and ten" because this will terminate a relationship with God and with people (vv. 10–11). It sets forward two pictures of what death is like (v. 12) and another of how God has behaved (v. 13), vivid in their imagery and in their portrayal of death as something that was actually happening. It recalls the actual prayer that sought relief from this distress (v. 14—see the reference to crying and moaning).

Second, it recalls the way God responded. This is most specific and most clear in verse 17b. It had seemed as if death had closed in, but **in your love you kept me from the pit of destruction.** The testimony that further **you have put all my sins behind your back** implies an awareness of the failure that chapters 28–32 reflected. The preoccupation with death here makes clear to anyone who was inclined to overestimate Hezekiah that he is a mere mortal, and it prepares the way for the somberness of the message that will follow in chapter 39.

The preoccupation with death continues into the third element in the thanksgiving, a commitment to an ongoing life of praise (vv. 18–20). The living are able to live that life as the dead cannot. Indeed, here that constitutes the greatest deprivation of death, even for those who belong to God's people (Christ's death and resurrection will change all that, of course, but those events lie in the future and will not benefit the dead until the moment described in 1 Pet. 4:6). Conversely, living a life of praise is the great privilege and distinguishing feature of existence in the house of Yahweh as opposed to the abode of the dead. Behind that is the fact that the dead have no opportunity to keep proving the faithfulness of Yahweh and therefore to keep being driven to praise, while the living (not least someone like Hezekiah) have ongoing opportunity to experience Yahweh's deliverance and therefore to be so driven to praise.

38:21–22 / Chapter 38 closes with two footnotes for the curious. "So did Hezekiah just get better miraculously?" Actually, no. Isaiah believed in medicine as well as prayer, prayer as well as medicine. "And did he actually ask for a sign?" Actually, yes; it will almost be as if the sun is coming back to summon him to the house of God. While a boil might not seem life-threatening, in OT thinking it would suggest leprosy, which would be a very serious

matter and one that certainly made it impossible to **go up to the
temple of the** Lord (Sweeney, *Isaiah 1–39*, p. 499).

One would have expected these two footnotes to be inte-
grated in the main story, as they are in 2 Kings 20. The effect of
omitting the first was to make Hezekiah's story structurally parallel to Sennacherib's—though opposite in content. The effect of
omitting the second was to make Hezekiah's story structurally
parallel to Ahaz's—though, again, opposite in content.

39:1–8 / In chapter 39, a drama foreshadows a crisis. We
have noted in the introduction to chapters 38–39 that Merodoch-
Baladan's friendly gesture belongs in the context of the political
events that led up to the Assyrian invasion. It will have been designed to encourage Judean solidarity with other peoples who
were seeking independence from Assyria (see on chapters 13–23).
And presumably that is part of the background to verse 2 here:
the Babylonians are discovering what resources the allies have
available. They will not be available for long: see the verses in
2 Kings 18:14–16 which do not appear in the version of that story
in Isaiah 36–37.

Giving the Babylonians their conducted tour is at best an
ambiguous act. It might have been a way of impressing foreigners
with what Yahweh had done for Judah: compare the story of the
Queen of Sheba (1 Kgs. 10), though that may have its own ambiguity in the light of where the story of Solomon leads (1 Kgs. 11).
But in the context of Isaiah it looks at least as much like the Judean
leadership's accustomed trusting in its material assets and military hardware. The leadership allows Babylon to treat Judah the
same way as it treated Egypt, or Judah treats Babylon the same
way as it treated Egypt (30:1–7; 31:1–3).

The threat in verses 5–7 then implies another way of hand-
ling the necessity that Yahweh should be faithful and that Yahweh
should take note of wrongdoing. Yahweh might allow Jerusalem
to go within a whisker of disaster but then deliver it (so 29:1–8;
31:4–5). Or Yahweh might deliver it now but let wrongdoing reap
its toll in the future. Judah had both those experiences between
the late-eighth century and the mid-sixth century B.C. When we
have read on in the book, we may reread chapter 39 in the light of
the latter experience, which the chapters that immediately follow
presuppose. Another irony then appears in Hezekiah's innocent
displaying of all the treasures and resources of Judah to friendly
envoys from Babylon. Indeed the irony is already revealed by the

prophet's words. This far-off ally which could surely never be a threat to Judah (Hezekiah will have thought) will actually turn out to be a bigger threat than Assyria. One day these treasures of Hezekiah's (or any that survive the Assyrians) and his very family are themselves to end up in Babylon. Daniel 1 specifically takes up these motifs.

In 38:1–3 the prospect of his own demise had led to anguished prayer for a change of mind on God's part, and in 38:19 Hezekiah had spoken of making known Yahweh's faithfulness to one's children. It is difficult not to be struck by the ready acquiescence in the prospects his children now face and not to see spectacular cynicism in his contentment in 39:8 with a faithfulness (**security**) that applies to him but has no application to his children (v. 7, **descendants**).

Additional Notes §25

38:8 / The same approaches may be taken to the sign as to 37:36: it is a "legendary" story (see Clements, *Isaiah 1–39*, p. 291), it was an unusual natural event (see Oswalt, *Isaiah 1–39*, p. 678), or it was a "miracle" (see J. A. Motyer, *Isaiah: An Introduction and Commentary* [vol. 18 of Tyndale Old Testament Commentaries; ed. D. J. Wiseman; Downers Grove, Ill.: InterVarsity, 1999], pp. 234–35).

38:15–16 / NIV plausibly treats vv. 15–16 as also part of this testimony to God's deliverance, but the language is difficult and NRSV translates vv. 15–16 as a continuation of the prayer in vv. 10–14. Either way, the striking feature of the prayer as a whole is its preoccupation with death (see Oswalt, *Isaiah 1–39*, p. 683).

§26 The Gifts of Comfort and Energy (Isa. 40:1–31)

So Isaiah 39, set in Isaiah's own day, envisages the future deportation of Judeans to Babylon. Isaiah 40–55, however, is set in the time after this deportation has happened. It does not say "In days to come God will send a message of comfort to people who have been punished," in the manner of a passage such as 30:19–26. It says, rather, "God is now comforting you who have been punished." The traditional view is that these chapters were written by Isaiah ben Amoz, and we may assume that God could have revealed to Isaiah the message to be addressed to the people in Babylon 150 years after Isaiah's day. But the way the chapters themselves speak suggests that they are rather words of comfort that God gave in the here and now of suffering through the pastoral ministry of a poet whom God called to be a new Isaiah for people who had long been under judgment. Chapter 39 helps us to make the transition from the end of the eighth century B.C., when Isaiah ben Amoz lived and ministered, to the 540s B.C., when God gave the new message of grace and mercy that people now needed to a "Second Isaiah." For reasons explained in the Introduction, we will sometimes call him or her "the Poet."

This first chapter comprises a double introduction to that message. In verses 1–11 the prophet hears voices initiating the process of restoration and is drawn into their ministry, in the manner of chapter 6. Verses 12–31 actually initiate this ministry, which will turn out to be more argumentative than we might have expected.

What the prophet overhears in verses 1–11 can be seen as a chiasm. The opening and closing sections link, as do the second and fourth, while the central one declares the aim and basis of the event.

A A commission to speak to Jerusalem (vv. 1–2)
   B A voice calls for the creating of a way (vv. 3–4)
      C The purpose of it all (v. 5)
   B' A voice says "call out" (vv. 6–8)
A' The message for Jerusalem (vv. 9–11)

40:1–2 / In the aftermath of Jerusalem's fall to the Babylonians in 587 B.C., people who were left in Jerusalem expressed their grief in a series of poems that became the book of Lamentations. A kind of refrain recurs through the first of these poems, "there is none to comfort her" (Lam. 1:2, 9, 17, 21; cf. 16). The city is like a woman who has lost husband and children and sits desolate like Job on his heap of ashes. She has sat this way for nearly half a century. Now a voice declares **Comfort, comfort my people.** The time for the plaint in Lamentations is over.

And the one who speaks is **your God.** In a chilling declaration in Isaiah's own day, Yahweh had declared "You are not my people, and I am not your God" (Hos. 1:9). The covenant relationship is over. (We might prefer to think of it as suspended, but Hosea's formulation is more shocking than that.) It ceased for Ephraim in 721 B.C. and it ceased for Judah in 587 B.C. Now Yahweh reverses the declaration and speaks in a way that presupposes that the relationship still holds after all. The words "my people" and "your God" can still be uttered.

To judge from the parallelism of verses 1a and 2a, it is "Jerusalem" that is identified as "my people," and 52:9 will confirm this. We can assume that the prophet's audience is in Babylon, as this is the impression that will emerge as these chapters unfold, but throughout chapters 40–55 the poems have a double focus. They (probably) speak to people in Babylon, but they often speak about Jerusalem or to Jerusalem (esp. in chs. 49–55). The focus of the Babylonian community lies there. The city's destiny is their destiny. They cannot sing Yahweh's song in a foreign land, and they are committed to remembering Jerusalem, painful though that is. They consider it their highest joy and want God to remember it, too (Ps. 137). Now Yahweh declares, "I have remembered it."

So Yahweh commissions some tender speaking to it. The expression is literally "speak to Jerusalem's heart." We have noted that the heart in Hebrew thinking is more the mind than the emotions, and the comforting of Jerusalem involves giving it some facts to chew on. There are three facts, though they are the same

fact re-stated in three different ways. First, Jerusalem feels that it
has been going through a period of **hard service:** the word is that
for an army, so it suggests the toughness of military service. Job
used it for his experience of affliction and pain. It is like a prison
sentence. Unlike Job's, it is a sentence that was deserved, as Lamentations grants. But now, secondly, **her sin has been paid for.** The
city's desolation, its subjection to Babylon, and its abandonment
by its God have gone on long enough. From the viewpoint of
Judeans in Babylon, more importantly, Ms Jerusalem has been deprived of her children for long enough. Indeed, **she has received
from Yahweh's hand double for all her sins.** Precisely what that
doubling means is not clear. It is perhaps a hyperbole. But its implication is clear enough. Enough is enough.

40:3–5 / The voice that calls for the preparation of Yahweh's **highway** (and the further voice in v. 6) is perhaps responding to the commission in verse 1, but verses 1–11 do not identify
these voices. All we hear is what these voices say. It is the content
of the words rather than the identity of the speakers that matters.
This voice resumes the picture of the **wilderness** in chapter 35,
with its highway, but gives it a different twist. This is not in the
first instance a road for Israel to travel but a road for Yahweh to
travel. In verses 9–11 it will become more explicit that Yahweh is to
make a journey back to Jerusalem (but bringing the exiles, too)
and part of the background to this picture may be the conviction
that Yahweh had left the city in 587 B.C. (see Ezek. 10–11). But the
background prior to that is the picture of Yahweh's coming from
afar through the desert to act in power on the people's behalf
(30:27–33). Once again Yahweh will come in this way. As is often
the case when God does something that parallels an earlier act, this
new work will not merely resemble the first but exceed it. Yahweh
will have a supernaturally-contoured highway to speed this journey, and Yahweh's glory will be perceived by all people **together.**

40:6–8 / But what pronouncement is possible? Another
voice commissions another proclamation and meets with a response like the one Isaiah gave when he heard Yahweh asking for
someone to go speak to the people (ch. 6). But in content the response is as different from Isaiah's as the commission was, and
paradoxically so. Isaiah had volunteered to proclaim bad news.
Isaiah's successor here resists the idea of proclaiming good news.
There are underlying similarities between the situations: both
prophets have to confront a people who will resist their message.

The words in verses 6b–7 are this new Isaiah's explanation for finding the commission unwelcome (so C. Westermann, *Isaiah 40–66: A Commentary* (trans. D. M. G. Stalker; Old Testament Library; Philadelphia: Westminster, 1969), pp. 41–42). The prophet knows that all the people **are grass,** grass withered by the hot breath of Yahweh's wind. So how it is possible to preach to them, expecting a response?

Verse 8a accepts that the assessment is entirely accurate, but verse 8b points out that there is something else to take into account.

40:9–11 / What are the grounds for comfort (vv. 1–2)? Where was Yahweh's road to lead (vv. 3–5)? What were the contents of the proclamation (vv. 6–8)? Verses 9–11, which bring to a climax the introduction to the Poet's ministry, answer all of these questions. The proclaimer who is addressed is now feminine singular. She is fulfilling the women's task of proclaiming good news to her community after a victory (e.g., Ps. 68:11). The city's sovereign is returning home victorious. What victory has he won? This is not yet explicit: it is characteristic of this Poet to unfold themes gradually and teasingly. On the other hand, we are told in passing that Yahweh's return also incidentally means the return of Yahweh's people. They come as the booty Yahweh won in the course of that victory. And then we are told in passing that this God is not only victorious warrior but caring shepherd (v. 11). Both facts are good news for Jerusalem and in Babylon: the refugee Jewish community is to go home in Yahweh's baggage.

40:12–17 / The rest of chapter 40 undergirds what will follow: Yahweh can and will act for you. Two questions underlie verses 12–31. How powerful is Yahweh? Verses 1–11 have already presupposed that the reason for Jerusalem's fall was Judah's wrongdoing, but the Assyrian king's minister of state has verbalized in chapter 36 the alternative understanding that would have been whispered in Judean hearts more and more as years passed. Perhaps the reason was that Yahweh was no more powerful than the other so-called gods whose peoples had been the victims of Assyria and now of Babylon. And even if Judean wrongdoing provided entire justification for the fall of Jerusalem, what is to be said about the city's ongoing desolation and these people's ongoing exile in Babylon? Are they cast off like the people of Ephraim?

The Poet answers the question about Yahweh's power with a fourfold affirmation of it, and then applies that affirmation to the question of Yahweh's commitment. The affirmation concerns Yahweh's power in relation to nations, divine images, rulers, and heavenly powers. A balancing pair of affirmations asserts the power and incomparability of Yahweh as creator. A number of rhetorical questions introduce each of the positive statements—they are the kind of questions to which the questioner knows the answer and believes the audience also knows the answer. They sound as if there is something to discuss but they presuppose that, in their hearts, audience as well as questioner know that there is nothing to discuss. The questions in verses 12–14 and 21–22 ask: Yahweh knows about creation: do you? Verses and 23–24 consider implications regarding Yahweh and the nations/kings. The question then becomes, in verses 18 and 25, "So to whom can you compare God?" And verses 19–20 and 26 respond with the implications regarding images/other gods. Finally, verses 27–31 apply all of this in the affirmation that this God gives strength to you. We will look at each of these affirmations in turn.

Verses 12–17, then, specifically address the creator and the nations. In isolation, the answer to the questions in verse 12 might be "Yahweh": they could form the basis of a powerful picture-presentation of the way God went about creating the world, like a builder calculating the dimensions of the task and weighing out raw materials. Indeed, the audience would have been familiar with the way the religion of its Babylonian overlords pictured the gods measuring the waters of the sea and holding the lands of earth suspended from the heavens as **in a balance** (see *ANET,* pp. 332, 387). But verses 13–14 suggest that the answer is more likely the same as it will be to all these other rhetorical questions in verses 12–26—"no one." The polemic works in a different direction. Babylonian stories described creation as a collaborative project on the gods' part (actually more of a conflictual one). Yahweh needed no aid in the task.

The references to Yahweh's **counselor** and to the **right way** to go about the task suggest that the words refer to more than merely creation as a long ago event. The first word (lit. "the man of his counsel/plan," *'etsath*) recalls Isaiah's emphasis on Yahweh's capacity to effect a purpose in historical events. The second *(mishpat)* is the word usually translated justice. In the Poet's thinking, creation is the first of God's great acts in history. Creation and history belong to the same activity. So God's sovereignty in creation is one with and establishes God's sovereignty in politics. Verses 15–17 therefore follow naturally. They do not imply that the nations do not matter. They matter enough for it to be important that they come to acknowledge Yahweh. The verses do imply the nations' feebleness.

40:18–20 / It is a distinctive feature of OT religion that it consistently prohibits images of Yahweh. According to Deuteronomy 4, the basic problem with them is not that God is spirit but that they can only be misleading in the way they represent Israel's speaking and acting God. They are bound to be silent and immobile and thus cannot actually be God-like. But biblical and archaeological evidence make clear that the prohibition on images worked no better than other biblical injunctions, perhaps because images meet a deeply-felt human need for something to look at and focus on in one's religious faith. People who use icons and other images need to consider the significance of this point. And the great divine images of Babylon would reinforce the temptation to Judeans to want to use images—whether of Yahweh or of Babylonian gods, in worship. A moment's thought, the Poet suggests, makes clear that they are a nonsense.

40:21–24 / The Poet returns to the questions about Yahweh's power as creator and applies them, in a more specific direction, to the rulers. In the last decade of Judah's independent history, fifty years previously, Babylon had deposed and transported first one and then another Judean king, Jehoiachin then Zedekiah. They and their offspring, the theoretical heirs to David's throne, remained under house arrest in Babylon. Babylonian emperors ruled the world. The Poet asks whether the audience really believes that. Doesn't Yahweh as creator rule the world? That puts Babylonian rulers in their places as firmly as they themselves put Judean rulers in their places.

40:25–26 / Theologically, Babylonian people no more believed that their images actually were gods than Christians who use images have the equivalent beliefs about them, though one can easily slip into that belief. Theologically, the Babylonians believed in beings of great power in heaven. The movements of the planets, which represented them, reflected the way these beings shaped destinies on earth. Again this was evidently a temptation to the Babylonians' Judean subjects, just as it corresponds to a belief held by many people in the modern world. But what are these planets? They are subordinates marshaled by Yahweh, not one of whom dares to be late on parade (v. 26b). Imagine entertaining the

thought that Yahweh might be the same class of being! Compared
with Yahweh, the Babylonian gods are feeble.

40:27–31 / Another type of rhetorical question asks why
the community thinks of Yahweh the way it does. Their (alleged)
words (v. 27b) resemble those of a lament, except that the most significant feature of a lament is missing. The words do not address
Yahweh. Rather, they talk *about* Yahweh. It is a devastating sign of
how deep their depression has gone. The community would have
no problem giving a straight answer to the Poet's question. There
were ample grounds for the conviction that Yahweh had abandoned them and cared neither for their **way** nor for their **cause**
(*mishpat* again). The Poet is calling them to look behind that present depression to the convictions about Yahweh that they surely
still affirm. They are called to set their **hope** on the fact that the
God in whom they believe is the one who as creator is sovereign
in political events. "Hope" means not hope against hope but convinced expectation that has grounds for it. Such hope means that
the weary find new resources of energy and perseverance, because they know that they have a future. In this particular case,
the grounds lie in God's power as Creator. This fact about the past
and the present gives grounds for hope in the future. Creator-
power is thus applied to weariness.

The Poet's characteristic designation of the audience is the
double expression **Jacob . . . Israel** (v. 27), and we will often use
this designation. It may refer directly to the Judean deportee community in Babylon and/or to the Judean community back in Palestine. Either way, the prophet's audience is (and we will thus often
refer to them as) Judah or the Judeans. But this little community is
the embodiment of Jacob-Israel, God's people as a whole. "Jacob-
Israel" functions rather like the word "Church": it is a symbol for
God's people as a whole, though embodied (non-exclusively) in
the community the Poet addresses.

Additional Notes §26

40:3 / NIV mg. offers an alternative punctuation that conforms
the translation to Mark 1:3. NIV main text follows the MT's punctuation.
The parallelism makes clear that the main text punctuation is right. The
NT follows the Gk. translation of the OT, which omitted "in the wilder-

ness" (see next NIV note). "In the desert" could then be taken as denoting the place of the calling rather than the place of the preparing. The NT's quotation is just as apposite on the other translation (both the preaching and the preparing happened in the desert). More significant is the fact that in the NT the preparing is a human act, whereas here it is God's act. There, too, the NT is following the standard Jewish understanding of its day, as its application of the OT often does. The Qumran community had established themselves within sight of the scene of John the Baptist's ministry to seek to fulfill this vision. Mark declares that John is the real fulfillment.

40:6 / For "and I said," MT has "and he said" (so KJV), but the verb is odd (strictly it means "and he will say") and who is the "he"? NIV and NRSV thus follow the Isaiah manuscript from Cave 1 at Qumran and the LXX, which both have "and I said."

40:9 / The translation in NIV mg. appears in NRSV, but the idea of Zion/Jerusalem climbing a mountain is an odd one. Further, in 52:7–10, which in several respects takes up the themes of 40:1–11 near the end of chs. 40–55, Zion/Jerusalem is again the recipient of good news, not the proclaimer of it.

§27 Fear Not, Servant Israel (Isa. 41:1–20)

Chapter 41 opens and closes with the first of a number of courtroom scenes that appear in chapters 40–48. In each scene, Yahweh challenges the nations to come to court to settle a dispute over who is really God. The English chapter division implies that these belong together, but as the prophecies further unfold it becomes clear that they are similar beginnings for two parallel sequences of prophecies. In this first sequence the nations' helplessness and their inability to find strength to cope with the crisis that confronts them (vv. 1–7) contrasts with Yahweh's offer of strength to Jacob-Israel (vv. 8–16). Yahweh will express support for Israel by transforming nature in such a way that people will recognize Yahweh's hand in what happens (vv. 17–20).

41:1–7 / Who is really God (v. 1)? This question comes about due to the need to explain the arrival of a conqueror from the east (v. 2–4a). Jewish tradition assumed that this conqueror was Abraham (see Gen. 14 for this side to Abraham). Modern critical tradition sees the conqueror as Cyrus the Persian, who in the 540s B.C. was completing an impressive military campaign through the middle east that would terminate in the conquest of Babylon itself in 539 B.C. It is typical of these chapters to leave the prophecy open to being read either way. The prophet is involved in a task of persuasion that involves convincing an audience of a rather implausible and unwelcome thesis (that Cyrus is Yahweh's agent in restoring the Judeans to their home), and like Isaiah himself, the Poet works gently toward points that will seem scandalous. But the implication of the ambiguity is that Cyrus is an Abraham-like figure.

There are further implications involved in this ambiguity. We have read chapter 40 against the background of the last days of the Babylonian empire and the imminent release of Judeans there, but there was no reference to Babylon. Traditional Jewish and Christian interpretation as represented by commentators such as Ibn Ezra, Rashi, Luther, and Calvin could thus vary on whether and how far they saw the prophecies as relating to the situation of Judeans in Babylon and/or to the messianic age. The chapters work by moving from the general to the particular. It is for this reason that the prophecy refers quite vaguely to **islands** and **nations,** and there will be no explicit reference to Babylon or Cyrus for some time. In the meantime, the prophet works with uncontroversial theological generalizations that the audience will not need to dispute but that will constitute a foundation for later, controversial and unwelcome specific claims. For us, one result of this approach is that we are able to apply the generalizations to the different political and ecclesial situations of our own context, like the general portrait of restoration in chapter 33.

One aspect of the difference between NIV's alternative renderings of verse 2 requires discussion here. The Hebrew word *tsedeq* and its relative *tsedaqah,* which have both appeared in earlier chapters, are even more important in chapters 40–55. The word *tsedeq,* in particular, suggests God's intent to do what is right by Israel by bringing it to its destiny. Specifically, this entails delivering Judah from its bondage to Babylon and vindicating it before the world. The fact that Cyrus's conquest of Babylon will play a key part in the fulfillment of this commitment means that the notions of fulfilling a right purpose and of winning a military victory come to be closely associated with each other. Thus translators may render *tsedeq* "righteousness" or "victory," though neither is very satisfactory. The former loses the dynamism of the word, the latter loses its theological significance. Further, neither makes clear the essentially relational nature of the basis on which Yahweh does the right thing by the people, and on which people do the right thing by each other.

Verse 4b states the conclusion to which Yahweh urges the court. It is the first of a series of claims on Yahweh's part to a sovereignty that extends as far as can be envisaged through time and space. The claim undergirds that other implicit claim that the long-ago achievements of Abraham and the up-to-the-minute achievements of Cyrus are part of the implementation of the same sovereign purpose.

For the Judean community, the rise of Cyrus is thus good news. For other peoples it brings frightening political convulsions. So what are they to do? Judah has the religious resources to cope with the situation, the Poet believes. Other peoples do not. The section thus closes by portraying the fearful helplessness of the nations. All they can do is encourage each other to **be strong** and get on with making a new god or two, preferably one that **will not topple**. It is bad for morale when your god falls over.

41:8–16 / These verses further reveal Yahweh's commitment to servant Israel, which banishes fear. That frightened erecting of new images constituted an attempt to provide the gods with their means of being present with their worshipers. Israel had no need to go in for such projects because their relationship with God worked the other way round. God had taken the initiative in adopting Israel as **servant**. That is a position that demands a commitment on their part (as 42:1–4 will note), but before that it is a position that denotes a commitment on God's part. David was Yahweh's servant (37:35): that was a guarantee of Yahweh's commitment to him and therefore to his city. Now the Poet declares that the people as a whole are Yahweh's servant. Yahweh is committed to them not merely for David's sake, but for their own sake. David had been Yahweh's chosen, but before that the people as a whole were Yahweh's **chosen**. Yahweh had been behind bringing Abraham from the east, and the people are Abraham's descendants. They are Yahweh's friend as Abraham was ("no longer do I call you servants, but friends" [John 15:15]), brought from afar as Abraham was. They need to be reminded who they are. They have not been **rejected**, like David's predecessor Saul. Once again a plaint of Lamentations, a frightening question it raised (5:22), is turned around. Yes, Jeremiah had said they were rejected (6:30) but he was explicit that this applied to the generation of his day (7:29; note 31:37; 33:24–26; and Lev. 26:44). The word is different from that in 40:27 ("disregarded"), but the thought is the same.

So they can be bidden, **do not fear** (v. 10). Like the description as servant and chosen and not rejected, these are words for a king. We have a number of examples of Babylonian prophets' exhortations to a king not to fear, as well as accounts of this exhortation addressed to Ahaz and Hezekiah in chapters 7 and 37. Once more Yahweh is thus according Jacob-Israel kingly status. Jacob-Israel will find in Yahweh the strength that the image-makers sought in vain. The image-makers have to make sure that their images do not fall over. Yahweh will make sure that Jacob-Israel does not fall over. Yahweh's commitment to servant Israel banishes fear.

Yahweh had promised David that the outworking of his position would be deliverance from his enemies, and Yahweh now restates this promise for the people as a whole. As far as we know, no one was raging against the Judeans in Babylon. There is no need to rage against a **worm** (v. 14). It is actually the Babylonians themselves who need a promise like that in verses 11–12. The consternation expressed in verses 5–7 was not groundless. But the threat to Babylon was not a threat to the Judean community there. Indeed, the threat promised their freedom. It is the nature of the promise to David that leads to the expression of the promise to Israel in the manner of verses 11–13. Yahweh is affirming that whatever applied to David applies to them as a community. As verses 11–13 unfold, there is a neat line-by-line sharpening of the metaphorical promise. Their enemies will be ashamed, they will perish, you will not be able to find their bodies, it will be as if they never existed.

In verses 14–16, NIV varies the translation (**Do not be afraid** replaces "Do not fear"), but Yahweh's words are the same in verses 10, 13, and 14. God's grace is such as not to mind repeating the things that we find hard to believe. That description of Jacob-Israel as a **worm** hints that this is a necessity. This is not an insult on God's part but a quoting of their own self-perception. It is the way people might describe themselves in a lament (see Ps. 22:6). Their self-perception, even if accurate, is no barrier to Yahweh's acting, and that is why they need not fear.

This is so because their **Redeemer** is **the Holy One of Israel**—or vice versa. These are two of these chapters' key descriptions of Yahweh. The second title is familiar. It was Isaiah's own distinctive description of Yahweh, with its background in his vision in chapter 6. In the context of his ministry it conveyed the deep threat that stood over Judah. They are involved with an awesome, transcendent, majestic God, and their disdain for this God means that they are in deep trouble. The Poet is now in a position to turn this logic on its head. The awesome, transcendent, majestic God had become involved with them, and in the context of their need that is awesome good news. This God is **your** Redeemer (v. 14).

"Redeemer" (*go'el;* see on 35:8–10) is a family word. It denotes someone who is close to you in the structure of your family who therefore has a moral obligation to support or defend you when you are in need. The classic need is poverty and debt, which might mean selling yourself into "slavery" (indentured labor): you commit yourself to work for your creditor until you have paid your debt. This next-of-kin is then under family obligation to make his own assets available to free you from such slavery (see Lev. 25). Hence the English "redeemer." But in other circumstances the obligation of this next-of-kin might be to offer to marry someone who is otherwise vulnerable and alone (see the story of Ruth) or to insist that justice is done when someone is murdered (Num. 35). In this way, the next-of-kin's task is to restore the community's equilibrium that enslavement, poverty, aloneness, and bloodshed all threaten. The Holy One regards Jacob-Israel as a member of the family, and in fulfillment of the commitment that this relationship entails is prepared to expend resources and energy in defending Jacob-Israel from enemies, protecting them from danger, and restoring them to freedom. That is why Jacob-Israel has no need to fear.

Yahweh will then see that the worm becomes a more powerful earth-mover (vv. 15–16a). The text does not identify the **mountains and hills.** In 40:3–5 they were the obstacles that separated Yahweh from Zion, and it would fit well if they had the same significance here. And as the earlier leveling will mean all people seeing Yahweh's glory, so this leveling will mean that the audience will **rejoice** and **glory** (a different word) in Yahweh as—**the Holy One of Israel** (v. 16b).

41:17–20 / Once again the Poet recalls the way the community prays, as people parched with thirst looking for water but unable to find it, as people who believe that Yahweh has forsaken them (cf. Ps. 22; 42; Lam 5:20). Once again Yahweh promises to be one who answers such laments, with an abundance that far exceeds what they asked for or needed. There is enough water not merely to quench their thirst but to transform their environment. Yahweh's action is characterized by a wild extravagance that will once again bring all **people** to recognize that this sovereign creativity reflects the work of **the Holy One of Israel.**

Additional Note §27

41:2a / The line reads literally "Who stirred up from the east *tsedeq* [he] calls him to his/its feet." We noted in the Introduction that poetry gains much of its power from its denseness, which itself comes in part from omitting the little words. NIV's two translations are thus both possible ways of construing the spareness of the Hb. The fact that the word *tsedeq* comes first in the clause makes it hard to expect the reader to work out that the word "in" needs to be provided, but equally "to his/its feet" does naturally suggest service, so a cross between the two renderings is more natural: "Who stirred up from the east one whom *tsedeq* calls to its service?" The idea, then, is that the conqueror has been called to work for the fulfillment of a righteous purpose, and the question is, Who is it that has brought this about?

§28 Servant and Covenant (Isa. 41:21–42:17)

Again Yahweh challenges opponents to come to court to argue out who is God (41:21–29). Again a passage about Yahweh's servant (42:1–9) follows this court case. Again this leads into praise and a vision of Yahweh transforming nature (42:10–17). While the three sections parallel the preceding set of three, they take matters much further.

41:21–27 / It was explicit in 41:1 that the first challenge was addressed to the nations, and NIV assumes the same here. But as the passage unfolds (see vv. 23–24), it becomes clear that Yahweh is now summoning the gods themselves. The topic for debate has also changed. It is now not "Who makes history?" but "Who can interpret history?" Who can explain the significance of what has happened or say what is going to happen? **The former things** (v. 22) is an all-embracing expression that can reach back at least to the beginnings of Israel's story in Abraham but can also apply to recent political events and the revolution they herald for Babylon. It thus corresponds to the question in verses 2–4a. **The things to come** (v. 22) refers to the outcome of these events in the near future, the fall of Babylon and the freedom of Abraham's people to repeat their ancestor's journey. The capacity to make sense of history in the sense of the ability to show how events form part of a purposeful pattern is the capacity that provides evidence regarding who is God. The gods' inability to make sense of events or predict where they are going is the evidence that they are no-gods. They are helpless and silent.

Verses 25–26 then resume the assertion of verses 2–4 and the question of verse 22. Yahweh further claims to be the only would-be God who can make sense of events. Specifically, Yahweh alone had announced them ahead of time. That is itself an evidence for that earlier claim to be the one who initiated those events.

When did Yahweh do that? If Abraham is still in the picture, then the claim refers back to Yahweh's original commitment to Abraham, the giving of a promise that Abraham would go to another land and become a mighty people and a blessing to the world. Israel's long story, announced and then initiated by Yahweh, is evidence that Yahweh is God. But Cyrus is also in the picture, and the verses may imply that his rise is part of the same purpose. Since it is part of the outworking of Yahweh's commitment, the prophets are suggesting that it was implicitly contained within that commitment when it was announced to Abraham. More specifically, the prophet Isaiah and other prophets had promised that Babylon would not be the end of Israel's story and had declared that Babylon's own day would come. Indeed, 13:17–22 has already announced the fall of Babylon to—the Medes. So Yahweh has ample grounds for claiming that the rise of Cyrus fits easily within the pattern of actions undertaken and words spoken over a long period (v. 27). The Babylonian gods and their prophets can make no such claim, so verses 28–29 reiterate the conclusion in verse 24.

42:1a / Following the description of the commitments Yahweh makes to servant Israel (41:3–16) is a description of the commitment that Yahweh's servant makes (42:1–9). **Here is my servant.** Where? In what direction is Yahweh pointing? The matter has been of huge controversy, especially since the time of Bernhard Duhm, who wrote an epoch-making commentary on Isaiah in 1892. Duhm suggested that this passage, along with three others about Yahweh's servant (49:1–6; 50:4–9; 52:13–53:12), constituted a group of four "Servant Songs" that did not originally belong in their present contexts and needed to be interpreted in relation to each other and independently of those contexts. The basis for this view is the tension between the description of Yahweh's servant in these passages and the references to Israel in its feebleness as Yahweh's servant that appear on either side of the present passage and elsewhere.

Unfortunately Duhm's separation of these four passages from their context has exponentially increased the difficulty of interpreting them. His suggestion has led to a dead end and must be buried (as was done in T. D. Mettinger, *A Farewell to the Servant Songs* [Lund: Gleerup, 1983]). While there are difficulties involved in interpreting the four passages in their context, they are much less than the difficulties of interpreting them without a context.

The four passages are no more "songs" than other parts of Isaiah 40–55 (certainly less so than a passage such as 42:10–12) and no more lyrical and heightened in tone and expression than other parts of Isaiah (such as 43:1–7; 49:15–21; 54:1–17). As poetry, these four passages are thus not distinctive from other parts of chapters 40–55, though they are on the whole more lyrical and heightened than the other passages about Yahweh's servant. We will see that while this does reflect some differences of meaning between the passages, it does not suggest that they are out of place in their context.

So where do we look for Yahweh's servant? The book of Isaiah itself suggests four directions. In 20:3 Isaiah was Yahweh's servant. In 22:20 Eliakim was Yahweh's servant. In 37:35 David was Yahweh's servant. In 41:8, 9 Jacob-Israel was Yahweh's servant. If we look a little way beyond this book, we find Jeremiah designating the Babylonian king Nebuchadnezzar as Yahweh's servant (Jer. 25:9).

Now in post-OT usage the term "the Messiah," like the word "God," can have only one referent. Jews and Christians would disagree about who the referent was, but not about the word's being a designation for one person. Duhm assumed that the same was true of the term "Yahweh's servant" in his four passages, but the earlier chapters of Isaiah mentioned earlier (along with usage in Jeremiah and elsewhere) show that this is mistaken. A number of individuals may be designated "Yahweh's servant." The context has to tell us who is the referent.

So is the servant the prophet who speaks in these chapters, the one whom we call the Poet? In 49:1–6 and 50:4–9 the context indeed points in this direction: the servant speaks as an "I," and we know who the "I" is in these chapters. Here in 42:1–4, on the other hand, the context tells us it is not the prophet, because Yahweh's servant is "he," not "I." We might hypothesize that the passage has been inserted by someone who intended it to refer to the prophet but did not make this clear (so Whybray, *Isaiah 40–66*, pp. 70–71, following Duhm). But it seems more appropriate to assume that an author told us enough to make things clear, at least until we discover that this assumption does not work.

Is the servant some other person, as it was Eliakim in 22:20? There have been many theories of this kind and people are still producing them. Putting together elements from his four passages, Duhm thought the servant was a rabbi who had leprosy.

But, again, such theories ignore the context and guarantee only unprovability.

Is the servant David or David's successor? This has been the common Christian view, and Christians will believe that *the* son of David was the supreme fulfillment of the servant vision (cf. Matt. 12:17–21). But, again, the context does not point the audience in the direction of initially understanding the servant in this way. The immediate context offers more pointers to understanding it as a reference to Nebuchadnezzar or his contemporary equivalent, Cyrus. He was in the picture in 41:21–29 and will be called Yahweh's shepherd and Yahweh's anointed in 44:28–45:1. On the other hand, treading on people (41:25) and not breaking bruised reeds (42:3) are in some tension with each other, and as these chapters unfold, so will be a distinction between the role of Cyrus and the role of Yahweh's servant.

We might have had to move further in trying to resolve those tensions were it not for the explicit description of Jacob-Israel as Yahweh's servant that also came in the previous chapter. Further, we have seen that the structuring of the material in 41:1–42:17 as a whole associates 42:1–9 and 41:8–16 with each other. Indeed, verse 1 refers back to the parallel description of Jacob-Israel as Yahweh's servant, as if to say "You recall that servant (41:8, 9), the one I uphold (41:10), the one I chose (41:8, 9): let me tell you more about that servant." The implication is that 42:1–9 describes Jacob-Israel's role. Jacob-Israel is Yahweh's servant, and this is Yahweh's servant's role. It remains to be seen whether Jacob-Israel will actually fulfill this role or whether there is more to be told of this story. . . .

42:1–4 / The description of Yahweh's servant, then, first reprises the description in 41:8–10 with its emphasis on Yahweh's commitment to the servant in the context of pressures from elsewhere, adding only (but significantly) the expression of Yahweh's delight in this servant (v. 1a). But in 42:1–4 all that is merely the preamble. The substance of the verses concerns the servant's commitment to Yahweh in the context of needs from elsewhere. In this connection, the two key recurrent words in chapters 40–42, *ruakh* and *mishpat*, "spirit/breath/wind" and "justice/judgment/decision," immediately come together in verse 1b. The hot breath of God had withered the people and could carry away the nations, whose images are mere breath/wind. But the spirit of God, of which no one gets the measure and which God shares with all the world, rests upon this servant (40:7, 13 [NIV mg.]; 41:16, 29; 42:1, 5). God could not be taught how to make a decision, even though Israel believed God had forgotten how to do so. That God now commissions this servant to bring a decision to the world (40:14, 27; 41:1; 42:1, 3, 4).

Within verses 1–4, the threefold repetition of this word *mishpat* suggests that it is the key idea. The role of Yahweh's servant focuses on issuing a decision that implements Yahweh's just purpose in the world. A king's servant proclaims the king's decisions and policies and thereby implements them. If the king says prisoners are free, then prisoners are free: the jailers obediently open the prison doors. In a parallel way, Yahweh's servant proclaims Yahweh's decisions and policies and thereby implements them. These verses do not state the content of the policy (but see vv. 5–9), though aspects of the way the servant's work is described offer some hints.

In implementing his commission, Yahweh's servant does not **cry out** (v. 2). The cry is that not of a street-corner preacher but of a person in pain (cf. 5:7). Why should this point be made? It will become clear that Yahweh's servant will not actually receive the instant acquiescence of a king's servant. He will pay a price for his ministry. But further, the difficulty of Israel's fulfilling the task begins to be apparent. Since Israel is itself crying out under the burden of feeling forgotten by Yahweh (40:27), how can it minister to other people overwhelmed by burdens? Specifically, Yahweh's servant will support bent reeds rather than trampling on them and will fan flickering flames rather than dousing them (v. 3a): but Israel *is* a bent reed and flickering flame, so how can it fulfill this role? Yet more pointedly, this servant will **not falter or be discouraged** until he has faithfully implemented Yahweh's policy decisions. The statement is pointed, because the verbs are the same as those in the previous verse (literally, "he will not flicker or break").

Yet the servant's task is clearly Israel's task—or Zion's. For back at the beginning of the book in 2:2–4 Yahweh had envisioned the nations streaming to Zion from where Yahweh's *torah* would come forth. Now **the islands will put their hope** in the servant's *torah* (note also the contrast with their at-a-loss-ness in 41:5–7). On Zion Yahweh would make a decision for them (the verb "judge," which is related to the word *mishpat*), a judgment that would mean the end of war (another reason for the healing nature of Yahweh's servant's work?). In a sense, all that verses 1–4 declare is that Yahweh's servant is now to implement the vision of 2:2–4.

42:5–9 / Verses 5–9 begin with the chapter's first use of the "messenger formula" that indicates that someone speaks with the authority of a commission from the king. But the Poet regularly avoids using this formula "straight." The one who speaks is "God, Yahweh." The first word is *ha'el*, as absolute a term as Hebrew had available to express the idea that Yahweh is *the* God. The rest of verse 5 then expands on this, describing Yahweh by means of participles that provide backing for what follows: here the participles focus on Yahweh's being God of all the world.

The challenging ambiguity of verses 1–4 then continues in verses 6–9. Yahweh resumes the address to **you**. The word is singular. So who is the "you"? Is it the servant of Yahweh who has just been described? The role verses 6–7 describe could be a restatement of that in verses 1–4. But verses 1–4 were not addressing that servant, and the prophet does not tell us that Yahweh now addresses him. The "you" cannot be the "you" of 41:21–29 (which was plural). The last singular "you" was Jacob-Israel in 41:8–16, who has presumably been the implicit addressee throughout. In other words, in verses 1–4 God was saying to Jacob-Israel, "You know you are my servants? Well, this is what my servant is destined to be and do." That might have made the people ask, "Does that really mean that this is God's vision for us?" In verses 5–9 God tells Jacob-Israel directly that this is indeed so. It declares a vision for Jacob-Israel which goes far beyond 41:8–16.

The book called Isaiah never uses the word **covenant** in anything like its usual sense until chapter 54 (the previous occurrences were 24:5; 28:15, 18; and "treaty," 33:8). Perhaps the word had been subject to too much ideological appropriation by people who relied on it too much, as is the case in our own time. And perhaps it was then too painful a word when its underlying theology collapsed with the collapse of Jerusalem itself, which showed that "covenant" was not a guarantee that Yahweh would never let such an event happen. Now the Poet re-mints it in a startling way. As Abraham was to "be" a blessing to the world (Gen. 12:2), so Jacob-Israel is to "be" a covenant for people and a **light** for nations.

The parallel with the promise to Abraham perhaps suggests that Jacob-Israel will fulfill this role in the same way as Abraham did. He did not have to go and preach. What God would do in fulfilling promises would draw the world to pray for similar blessing. So 42:5–9 builds on 41:8–16 by implying that Yahweh's delivering them from their enemies and smoothing the way for them to go home will also function as a sign of Yahweh's commitment to bring other people out from prison into the light outside. Precisely how that is to happen, or what it means, the Poet does not say. Perhaps Yahweh has given just the seed of a vision along these lines, and that is all we can be told. Verses 8–9 offer further retrospective support for the vision. Yahweh must be revealed to the world rather than people mistakenly glorifying no-gods. Yahweh's past acts in fulfilling past declarations of intent provide grounds for believing that Yahweh can and will also fulfill this declaration.

We need some convincing, because there is an uncomfortable correlation between the role described in verses 1–4 and that in verses 5–9, and we have seen reason to doubt whether Jacob-Israel is up to the demands of the former.

42:10–17 / The invitation to praise announces that we are coming to the end of a section of the book, and/or draws attention to the significance of what we have just read. This praise thus parallels chapter 12, though it also contrasts with it. That was a promise to the people of Judah about the prospect of rejoicing in the hearing of the nations in what Yahweh is going to do for it. This is a declaration of the way the world itself can begin praising Yahweh now for the things Yahweh is in the midst of doing for people in darkness. The praise in chapter 12 began like a thanksgiving psalm but ended like a hymn of praise. This begins like a hymn of praise, praise that rejoices in what God always is, but ends more like a thanksgiving—rejoicing in what God has just been doing. But it is a paradoxical thanksgiving, because the things to give thanks for still lie in the future (vv. 13–17: this also applies to the verbs in v. 14b, which are the same as the other verbs translated as future).

It is also a paradoxical thanksgiving because the fact that Yahweh is to thrash about like Goliath is not usually what counts for good news. It only seems so to the powerless who need a champion who will put down the powerful and free the prisoners from the darkness of their imprisonment. And this is what the verses promise. For people in that darkness, imprisonment seems to have lasted forever, and you wonder why Yahweh is so slow to arise and act. Yahweh acknowledges the fairness of that wondering (v. 14a) but says the moment has come. The rise of Cyrus and the tumult it heralds are the sign and the result of the rising of Yahweh from inactivity, shrieking like a woman in labor. The world is to be turned upside down, but that is good news. The turning of desert into pools of water in the corresponding promise at the end of 41:1–20 is complemented at the end of 41:21–42:17 by the turning of pools of water into desert, but the blind and lost will be guided home through darkness and difficulty.

Who is this promise for? The context has implied that the blind and lost may be Israelites as well as others. The only people who cannot claim the promise are people who trust in images (v. 17), which gives food for thought for both Israelites and other people.

Additional Notes §28

41:22 / NIV's marks around "your idols" signify that it has added this word. It has also apparently assumed a change in the form of the verb, which in MT is third person. Literally, the text simply says "They must set forth": the verb is repeated from the previous line. Cf. NRSV.

41:25 / Media is to the north of Babylon, while the Persian empire as a whole is to the east, so Cyrus might be portrayed as arriving in Babylon from either direction. From a Palestinian perspective he came from the east but would arrive from the north (because he had to go round the "Fertile Crescent"). But the latter direction also suggests the image of the "northern foe" of passages such as Jer. 1–6 and Ezek. 38:15; 39:2.

41:27 / Critical scholarship has usually assumed that the prophecy of Babylon's fall in chs. 13–14 itself comes from the mid-sixth century B.C., but the claim in v. 27 comes home more sharply if prophet and community know that prophecy as having come from some time before their day. On the problem of the text of v. 27a, see the comment in the Introduction on "Text."

42:1a / In verse 1, the LXX actually reads, "Jacob my servant . . . Israel my chosen. . . . " That is an interpretation that reads the text in keeping with the context, but it does involve an addition that makes the text itself more univocal than it actually is. Typically for these chapters, MT is more subtle.

42:6 / "People" would usually suggest Jacob-Israel itself, but it referred to people in general in v. 5, which provides the theological undergirding for v. 6.

§29 The Restoration of a Blind and Deaf Servant, I (Isa. 42:18–43:21)

After the parallel sequences of prophecies in 41:1–20 and 41:21–42:17 have come to their natural end in praise, a new pair of sequences begins. First Yahweh directly confronts Jacob-Israel about its capacity to fulfill the servant role (42:18–25). Then Jacob-Israel is reassured that nevertheless Yahweh, the one who brought the community into being, is still committed to it (43:1–7). Further, its calling to be Yahweh's servant still stands, and beyond that, Yahweh intends that it shall also function as witnesses for Yahweh in the legal battle over who is really God (43:8–13). Fourth, Yahweh explicitly declares the intention to defeat Babylon for Jacob-Israel's sake (43:14–21). After this fourth unit Yahweh returns to confronting Jacob-Israel. At this point a sequence parallel to 42:18–43:21 begins and develops these points further.

These chapters unfold themes gradually, somewhat like a novel or a film in which character and plot unfold gradually so that only later do you see the significance of hints that appeared near the beginning. For centuries, commentators have commonly assumed that the prophecies that begin in chapter 40 were intended for the deportee Judean community in Babylon in the sixth century B.C., but there is no explicit indication of that anywhere. People have been consciously or subconsciously reading chapters 40–42 in the light of what precedes (39:1–8) and what follows. We are right to do that, but we need also to see how the Poet actually works, moving from the vague and general to the concrete and explicit. It is part of the Poet's technique to try to win a hearing for a message that, in its concreteness and explicitness, will be hard for the audience to swallow.

42:18–25 / The problem lying under the surface since chapter 40 at last comes out into the open. Although Jacob-Israel is Yahweh's servant, it cannot fulfill the role of that servant. The servant avoids contracting the weaknesses of those he ministers to

(vv. 3–4). This servant has those weaknesses aplenty (vv. 7, 19, 22). Isaiah has amply fulfilled his commission (6:9–10). The community has gone through the terrifying experiences of defeat and deportation but has not understood the meaning of these **many things** (vv. 20, 25). Yahweh's servant is himself blind and deaf.

The opening imperatives (v. 18) might constitute the summons to another court scene, and the argumentative form of verses 18–25 as a whole supports this. It is an innovative court scene in which Yahweh for the first time appears as defendant, not plaintiff (Westermann, *Isaiah 40–66*, p. 109). Jacob-Israel has brought Yahweh to court with the accusation that Yahweh handed the people over to looters. The defendant's response is to turn the accusation back on the accusers. Yahweh wanted to make Israel a model community in which the wisdom of the *torah* was manifested to the world. Destroying Jerusalem and deporting people to Babylon obviously worked against that purpose (vv. 21–22), but it was necessary because of the community's resistance to the *torah* it was supposed to embody. So Yahweh grants the charge but asserts that there was good reason for the action. Any guilt lies with the plaintiff (vv. 24–25a).

43:1–7 / Everyone knows what follows a declaration of guilt such as that in 42:18–25. They know it from community life and they know it from the way the prophets apply the image to Israel's life with God. After the declaration of guilt comes the sentencing. Insides tremble as ears wait for the thunderous "therefore" (see, e.g., 1:24; 5:13, 14, 24, 25).

It never arrives. The logic of grace takes over, and the declaration of failure instead introduces a "fear not" oracle, the kind of commitment given to a king under pressure rather than the kind of declaration made to a criminal about punishment. This prophet would have taken the same stance as Isaiah about the people's failure and about whether punishment needed to be the message earlier; 42:18–25 has made that clear. But the wise farmer indeed knows that there is a time for plowing and a time for planting (28:23–29). Even though the ground remains hard, in this case, it is clear that more plowing is going to achieve nothing. Does God or prophet think that mercy will succeed where judgment fails? If so, succeeding chapters in the book will disabuse them.

If the community finds it difficult to believe in mercy rather than judgment, then the opening descriptions of Yahweh in the participles of verse 1a and in the past verbs of verse 1b provide the theological grounds for it (see also vv. 3a and 7). This logic is the same as was in effect when Moses reminded Yahweh that someone who has put their hand to the plow had better not look back. If he does, people will scorn this farmer as one who knows little about farming. Yahweh listened, had a change of mind, and has not forgotten. That commitment to Jacob-Israel makes a permanent demand on God. It means that Yahweh even goes with the people in the floods and fires of Yahweh's own punishment that the people are currently experiencing (v. 2; cf. 5:24; 8:5–8). No doubt Yahweh also accompanies through the floods and fire of undeserved affliction, but in this context deserved affliction is more to the point (see 42:25). As a result, Yahweh's own presence will actually neutralize the forces of destruction that Yahweh unleashed.

The verbs in verse 3b are perfect, and KJV was surely right to translate them as past. They refer to God's past act of bringing Israel out of Egypt and delivering it at the Red Sea, the event that constituted its creating and forming, its original redeeming and summoning (v. 1). Having done that, then, Yahweh is quite prepared (in keeping hand to plow) to do it again (v. 4). It is illuminating to compare this pair of "fear not" oracles with the previous pair in 41:8–16. Verses 1–3a have much in common with 41:8–13, as do verses 5–7 with 41:14–16. Verses 3b–4 then stand out. The specific content of their reminder of Yahweh's past acts and promise of future acts that builds on the past has no equivalent in the earlier passage.

The resumptive "fear not" oracle in verses 5–7 makes clear once again that the horizon of these chapters is not merely the little Judean community in Babylon. This new act of deliverance exceeds the first: this is the only place in Scripture where God says "my daughters" (except for Paul's alluding to this passage in 2 Cor. 6:18). The women share with the men in a family relationship with their Father in the present and in restoration in the future.

43:8–13 / At first, the command in verse 8 resonates with that in 42:18. It might sound like another sharp scorning of the fact that the one called to be servant is blind and deaf and a commanding that Jacob-Israel's obtuseness be exposed. The return to the court setting in verse 9a increases that possibility. So Jacob-Israel is to be arraigned before the world, as they were at the very beginning of the book (1:2). But then the prophecy takes a new, yet familiar, turn. It transpires that the court is turning its attention from the dispute between Jacob-Israel and Yahweh and reverting to the case Yahweh had initiated against the nations, the question of who really controls history. The nations have been summoned as the accused, not as witnesses. Indeed, they are now challenged to produce some witnesses who can testify to their (or their gods') having announced events such as the rise of Cyrus and the coming fall of Babylon. That would demonstrate that they had been involved in planning and executing a purpose over the centuries.

Yahweh then directly addresses Jacob-Israel itself with the astonishing words **you are my witnesses** (v. 10). It transpires that the reason for bringing the blind and deaf into court is to tell them that they have an important role there. The blind are commissioned to be witnesses.

We have recalled the time at Sinai when Yahweh wanted to abandon Israel and start again. Israel's later abandonment of its side of the covenant commitment that led to Samaria's and then to Jerusalem's fall might indeed have led to Yahweh's having a further inclination of that kind. If Yahweh could not get out of the relationship with Israel, one might alternatively have imagined Yahweh in some way keeping Israel as covenant partner but finding some other agent in the world. Perhaps that might have been abandonment in another guise, in substance if not in form. For whatever reason, characteristically Yahweh moves in the opposite direction instead. Israel has not been very good at its job, so Yahweh enlarges its remit. It becomes Yahweh's witnesses in the court case that was initiated in chapter 41. They **have eyes but are blind.** But at least they have eyes, so perhaps those eyes can be opened. And thus they continue to be **my servant whom I have chosen.** No, Yahweh is not taking the road of finding another servant, despite the evidence against this servant in 42:18–25. Yahweh is persevering with Jacob-Israel as servant. Putting "witnesses" and "servant" together also thus helps to establish how Yahweh's servant fulfills the role described in 42:1–4.

We are familiar with the use in religious contexts of the idea of being a "witness" for God and of giving one's "testimony," but the expressions have lost their legal significance. This language presupposes that there is a case to be argued and evidence to be presented. The evidence lies not in subjective experience, which is not in a law court's concern, but in objective fact. There are events in the world that may seem to make little sense. Indeed, world history as a whole may seem to make little sense. But the Jewish people, and then the Christian church, possesses God's announcements of intentions and God's interpretations of actual events, and these provide the keys to understanding the enigmas of history. Isaiah 40–55 presupposes that this evidence needs pressing in public court, and that its force will be recognized—not least because there are no rivals to Yahweh who can offer a convincing and satisfying set of answers to the enigmas that otherwise confront the world.

A further surprise follows in verse 10b. One might have expected that Yahweh chose Jacob-Israel as witnesses so that the world would come to acknowledge Yahweh. We have presupposed as much in considering the implications of the court case metaphor. Instead, Yahweh says that the object of so choosing Jacob-Israel is that the people themselves should come to acknowledge Yahweh. That longstanding purpose was the one Yahweh could not go back on. And their call as witnesses now has as its own aim the convincing of the witnesses themselves. Their being called to bring other people out of darkness will be the means by which they themselves are brought out of darkness, by which their eyes and ears are opened. Yahweh goes on (v. 10b–13) to spell out the content of their witness and the evidence that is to convince them. These are the facts about Yahweh that their own history has proved to them. Yahweh has long been speaking and then acting, and thereby has been both sovereign in history and proving sovereignty in history. They know it, and they know that it is not true of other so-called gods. They must come to acknowledge it.

43:14–21 / In the present situation, the evidence that Yahweh is God is the fall of Babylon. Having already declared the intention of bringing it about and having named the Medes as its agents (chs. 13–14), Yahweh now declares that this intention is in the midst of being implemented. Literally, Yahweh says not "I will send" but "I have sent": by declaring this Yahweh is putting the deed into effect. It is no longer in the future; it is already actual. This earth-shattering effect that causes panic in the world's financial markets is **for your sake,** for the sake of the little demoralized Judean community, because **the Holy One of Israel** is **your redeemer.** To buttress this short oracle in verse 15, with its implausible undertaking, Yahweh reminds people again, in four epithets, who is speaking—Yahweh the Holy One is also **Israel's creator** (cf. v. 1) and **king.** The last is the converse of describing Jacob-Israel as Yahweh's servant. Yahweh is not merely king of the

universe but king of Israel, and therefore not only able to bring
about an event like the one being described but committed to
doing so because a servant is a servant and can rely on the master's commitment.

I will send to Babylon. . . . Whom? The verb has no object.
The human means of freeing the people is not so very important.
But the lack of an object has another significance. Once more we
see these chapters unfolding themes slowly. This is the first reference to Babylon itself and its downfall. We will not learn the
means of that fall until an equivalent point at the end of the next
series of prophecies, in 44:24–45:8. Here the focus is on the effect
of the event. Babylon sat on the river Euphrates, down which
ships plied their trade, but these will now become the means of
people's attempted escape rather than of the city's business.

Once more, the section of promise in verses 14–21 comprises two parts. In this second part beginning at verse 16, there is
another chain of participial descriptions of Yahweh reminding us
who is the one who is about to give the following undertaking
(vv. 16–17). There are many passages in Isaiah 40–55 that might
refer back to the exodus, but here the language is more explicit
than usual. There is no doubt of the occasion when Yahweh made
a way through impassable waters for one people and then directed the pursuing army (behaving as its own general) into what
turned out to be a trap.

In the very story of Israel's deliverance from Egypt, Yahweh
had bidden Israel to structure its life around the remembrance of
that deliverance (Exod. 12). Now Yahweh says (no doubt with
some hyperbole), "forget it" (v. 18).

Chapters 40–55 often draw an antithesis between former
events or events of old and new events or coming events. The
phrases can have several meanings, and characteristically the Poet
often does not make clear which meaning applies, preferring to
let them run into one another. All belong together as part of the
ongoing purposeful story of Yahweh's announcing an event and
then bringing it about. So the **former** events here in verse 18 may
be creation, or the forming of Israel, or the fall of Jerusalem, or the
initial achievements of Cyrus. The coming events are the completion of those achievements in Babylon's fall, and the restoration
and renewal of the Judean community. Here a **way in the desert**
(v. 19) succeeds the old **way through the sea.** The desert is
not merely the literal desert that separates Babylon from Jerusalem, but the equivalent to that desert through which Israel had

wandered long ago, in which they had experienced Yahweh's miraculous provision of water. So it will be again (vv. 19–20). These are not merely waters to transform the desert but waters to sustain the people through it. The result will be that the animal world honors Yahweh (v. 20a). But the section comes to a climax with the reminder that it is Israel's calling to honor Yahweh (v. 21). Once more, the praise of Yahweh brings a section to an end, as in the Red Sea story itself (Exod. 15).

Additional Note §29

43:14 / **Babylonians/Chaldeans** (mg.): see on 13:17–22. For **fugitives** NRSV has "bars": this involves changing one vowel in MT. It thus pictures the Persians breaking down the bars of the city gates when they took it. Either reading makes sense. **In the ships in which they took pride** is literally "in the ships their cry." NRSV "the shouting . . . will be turned to lamentation" takes the word for "boats" as another word which looks the same but means lamentation, and then takes the "cry" as a pained rather than a proud one. Again, either understanding makes sense.

§30 The Restoration of a Blind and Deaf Servant, II (Isa. 43:22–44:23)

After Job and his "friends" have spent chapter after chapter arguing with God and with each other as to the meaning of the calamities that have come to Job, God appears and puts Job in his place at some length (Job 38:1–40:2). Job submits, and might have expected this was the end of the story. Instead, as one imagines Job's groan, God starts again (Job 40:6). There is a parallel dynamic in the new beginning here at Isaiah 43:22. It seems that 42:18–43:21 reached a fine climax with Jacob-Israel on its way home through the wilderness and about to fulfill its destiny in the praise of Yahweh. But with 43:22–28 Yahweh starts again and goes through a parallel critique to that of 42:18–25. Fortunately, 44:1–5 then also corresponds to 43:1–7. With 44:6–23 is a renewed affirmation that Jacob-Israel is destined to be Yahweh's witnesses, corresponding to 43:8–13. The passage is of much greater length because it incorporates the most systematic of the critiques of images (or image-makers). The equivalent to 43:14–21 then comes in the 44:24–45:8, but because that is also the beginning of a further sequence of prophecies, we will consider 44:24–45:25 as a separate section.

43:22–28 / So we revert to the situation in 42:18–25. Jacob-Israel has brought Yahweh to court (see v. 26). Again the charge underlies the closing words of the oracle: Yahweh has defiled the community's spiritual leadership, indeed treated the whole people as if they were Canaanites to be consigned to ritual destruction, and made them an object lesson in calamity rather than the object lesson in blessing they were supposed to be (v. 28). Perhaps verse 22 also implies that for these long years in Babylon they have been casting themselves on Yahweh in prayer seeking to gain relief from their bondage, and failing.

Once more, their attempt to put Yahweh in the dock backfires. To begin with, **you have not called upon me** (v. 22a). The word order is "not upon me have you called." The implication of the word order emerges from a comparison with 40:27, where we noted that they did not so much complain to Yahweh as complain about Yahweh. That linked with a weariness that Yahweh promised could be dealt with (40:28–31). Here Yahweh again refers to that weariness. They had grown tired in their faith (even before the fall of Jerusalem?) and had not been calling for Yahweh to be their aid and deliverer. Nor, for that matter, have they had to weary themselves with all those sacrificial offerings that the Torah required, because by taking them to Babylon Yahweh had made that round of sacrifices impossible (vv. 23–24a).

As well as taking further the motif of weariness (v. 23b), Yahweh here reintroduces the motif of servanthood, for **burdened you** is literally "made you serve." Although Yahweh has designated Jacob-Israel "servant," the costly demands of this form of service have actually been suspended for half a century. Perhaps lying behind these statements are further elements in the community's accusations of Yahweh before the court: "you have treated us so badly despite all those centuries of prayer and sacrifice and service." "Well," says Yahweh, "however that may be, in recent years you cannot claim that. Indeed, if we look back over those centuries, on the contrary it was you who were making me serve you—wearying me with your wrongdoing" (v. 24b). In 42:18–25 Yahweh had declared that Jacob-Israel could not fulfill the role of servant. In this parallel passage Yahweh declares that indeed the community has reversed the master-servant role.

That might raise the question how it is that Jacob-Israel continues in being at all. Verse 25 explains: Yahweh has been willing to turn a blind eye to the way Jacob-Israel behaved, **for my own sake.** That statement corresponds to the comment in 42:21 on Yahweh's concern to commend to the world the revelation embodied in Israel's life. Yahweh is not going to be put off from fulfilling that purpose merely by Jacob-Israel's attempt to reverse the master-servant relationship.

So Yahweh is quite happy to argue matters out in court. Yes, Yahweh brought about the people's downfall. But there are things to be said about why that was (vv. 27–28: the first father is perhaps Jacob).

44:1–5 / But Yahweh is still committed to Jacob-Israel as servant. As 43:22–28 corresponds to 42:18–25, so 44:1–5 corresponds to 43:1–7. Once more one might have expected a legal charge like that in 43:22–28 to lead into the "therefore" which introduces a sentencing, but once more Yahweh instead proceeds **But now.** Once again, Jacob-Israel is reminded about its origins and promised Yahweh's **help** (*'azar*). It is a rather feeble word in English, but in Hebrew (v. 2a) the word has some of the resonances of "salvation." Once again Yahweh bids Jacob-Israel **do not be afraid** (v. 2b). But that "but now" in verse 1 leads more immediately into another reaffirmation to Jacob-Israel that it is **my servant,** the one **I have chosen.** Verse 2b repeats both statements. All this repetition is designed to have an effect on the audience. The chapters have been underlining the shortcomings of the community that it has been hiding from itself. We hide things from ourselves because we cannot face or handle them. The reaffirmations may enable people to see that they can face these truths about themselves because they can handle them. They do not, after all, mean that people have to be afraid, that Yahweh has cast them off.

As in 43:1–7, a series of promises follows. These promises are here the further grounds for the community not to fear that they have no future. Here, at least, the pouring of abundant water on dry land (v. 3a) is a figure for the pouring of Yahweh's blessing on the community itself in such a way as to make it grow. The imagery of verse 4 might suggest the purely numerical growth of the shrunken Judean community, but verse 5 adds the sense of growth in commitment. In isolation, verse 5 might be taken to refer to proselytes joining Yahweh's people, and later chapters will indeed speak of foreign peoples coming to acknowledge Yahweh. But the present context more likely has in mind Judeans themselves owning their commitment. The charge in 43:22–28 has made clear that the community's trust in Yahweh and commitment to Yahweh are at a low ebb. The pouring out of Yahweh's breath on the people as if it were a liquid like water will bring about both physical growth and spiritual regeneration. People who have been ashamed to own their commitment to Yahweh and their membership of Israel will now do so.

44:6–8 / Thirdly there follows a passage (44:6–23) that corresponds to 43:8–13, though in length it goes off the scale in a magnificent chiasm.

A The redeemer's exhortation to the witnesses (vv. 6–8)
  B The indictment: image-makers' folly, images'
    uselessness (vv. 9–11)
    C Image-making, hunger, and thirst (v. 12)
      D Carpenter and wood: execution (v. 13)
        E Carpenter and wood: preparation (v. 14)
      D' Carpenter and wood: execution (v. 15)
    C' Image-making, feasting (vv. 16–17)
  B' The indictment: image-makers' folly, images'
    uselessness (vv. 18–20)
A' The redeemer's exhortation to the servant and the
  cosmos (vv. 21–23)

Against that background of Israel's weariness with Yahweh and its turning Yahweh into its servant, verses 6–8 begin by re-affirming the second of the intentions in 43:8–13. Alongside the reaffirmation of Jacob-Israel's position as servant (v. 2) is the reaffirmation of its calling to be witnesses (v. 8). In the ongoing case between Yahweh and the other so-called gods, the responsibility of the community is to set out the powerful evidence, embodied in its own experience and history, concerning who Yahweh is, as powerful sovereign.

In the succinctness of the self-description in verse 6 Yahweh moves beyond anything expressed in previous claims. The Poet introduces it as the words of **Israel's King** and **Redeemer** and Yahweh **Almighty**. Yahweh's own claim is to be **first** and **last; apart from me there is no God.**

The first claim implies something about Yahweh's nature, though it relates more directly to Yahweh's relationship with events in the world. The chapters often speak of first or former events and new events or coming events, and declare Yahweh's sovereignty in relation to these. Here is the absolute statement that lies behind such claims. Yahweh alone has been behind world events from the beginning (creation, the call of Abraham, the exodus) to the end (the fulfillment of Yahweh's intention to restore Jacob-Israel and be recognized by the whole world). Yahweh is indeed First and Last. The statement recalls that in Exodus 3, where Yahweh tells Moses that the very name "Yahweh" suggests "I am who I am" or "I will be what I will be." It is not a statement about abstract being, but rather a promise that Yahweh will be there with the people acting in whatever way is needed. And there is no one else who is in a position to make that claim. "Apart from me there is no God." No one else has been at work over the years in that way.

The Poet has often been described as perhaps the first, and certainly the greatest, exponent of monotheism in Israel. This description may be accurate, though it skews the point that the Poet makes. "Monotheism" is a stance over the question of how many gods there are. In relation to questions raised by Greek philosophy, it offers reassurance that there is a principle of unity in reality. Reality is coherent, and the cosmos is under the control of one will—not fought over by many. In the OT and NT the question focuses more on who is God than on how many gods there are. The background is not a philosophical question but the rival claims of a number of deities or sets of deities. The Poet is the greatest exponent of the claim that Yahweh alone is God.

The characterization of this one God as **Rock** constitutes another link with Deuteronomy 32, where the description occurs six times. "Their rock is not like our Rock," Moses declared (v. 31). No, says verse 8. Indeed, there is no one compared with Yahweh who is worth calling "Rock."

44:9–20 / The bulk of this section comprises the most extensive of the passages scorning the images of gods, or rather the makers of such images. The prohibition on making images of Yahweh had a prominent place in Israelite faith. But the instinct to make images of one's god is a deeply-seated human one, and archaeological discoveries indicate that throughout their history, Israelites made images of Yahweh (see on 40:18–20). In Babylon, the community was surrounded by people who had images of their gods, many of them large and impressive, and given a prominent place in worship. It is entirely imaginable that Judeans should have been inclined to worship Yahweh in the same way as these other people. It is also entirely imaginable that they should have been tempted to worship these Babylonian gods themselves, for they had seemed to manifest their superiority to Yahweh. After all, their devotees had destroyed Yahweh's house in Jerusalem.

In contrast to the great critique of images in Deuteronomy 4, the focus of the critique in Isaiah 40–48 is on the way images are made. Indeed, it is actually scorning the image-makers themselves. NIV rightly lays out the passage as poetry. It is actually doggerel verse, poetry whose down-to-earth-ness matches the feebleness of its subject. It is a mystery to the Poet that the image-makers cannot see the point (v. 9). Yet there is also a fierce bite to the polemic.

Although images do not deserve to be taken seriously, they have to be taken very seriously indeed, because they do terrible religious harm in the way they mislead people about the nature and identity of God. Their makers must therefore pay a terrible price for the way they lead people astray (v. 11).

The center of the portrayal (vv. 12–17) is a superficially straight and factual account of how you go about making an image. The account starts with the end of the process, with what people could see in the image-makers' workshops (vv. 12–13), and works backward to the start of the process—the planting of a tree (v. 14). And, of course, a tree is useful in a number of ways. You can use part of it to burn for cooking or warmth and make part of it into—a god (v. 15). The passage assumes that further comment is unnecessary. But in case the initial description does not speak for itself, the Poet repeats it with more detail to make sure that we get the point (vv. 16–17).

Verses 18–20 then correspond to verses 9–11, completing the bracket around the factual description that makes explicit the judgment on this foolish process. Yes, it is a mystery to the Poet how people can be so stupid.

44:21–23 / This outside bracket in turn corresponds to verses 6–8 and directly addresses Jacob-Israel. It urges the people to keep **these things** in mind—which might be the preceding material, but what follows suggests that it is more likely that the phrase refers to the facts about themselves in verses 21–22. First, the affirmation that Yahweh calls them to be witnesses (v. 8) is complemented by the affirmation that they are also still Yahweh's **servant** (v. 21). Then Yahweh deals with the problem of Jacob-Israel's sin (v. 22a), which has been overt at the opening of this section and of the previous one (42:18–25; 43:22–28). It is the problem that receives increasing attention as these chapters unfold. These two facts—that they are still Yahweh's servant and that Yahweh has swept away their sin—can then be the basis for the chapter's only direct exhortation to the people to **return** to Yahweh. By implication, in having divine images made for them they would be turning away from Yahweh. This is so whether the images are images of other gods or images of Yahweh. Images that supposedly represent Yahweh cannot do so. They can represent only a (non-existent) humanly-made god. Images cannot save (v. 17), whereas Yahweh is one who redeems (vv. 22, 23). The further exhortation to the whole cosmos to worship brings the double sequence 42:18–44:23 to a close, as the similar exhortation in 42:10–17 brought the double sequence 41:1–42:17 to a close. We have admittedly not found a passage to correspond to 43:14–21. That will now follow, but it will take on a life of its own. In the meantime, 42:18–44:23 as a whole has mercilessly insisted on the inadequacy of Jacob-Israel. It has compassionately declared Yahweh's intention to restore and renew the community rather than cast it off. It has graciously affirmed that it will still be retained as servant and in particular as witness in court to the fact that Yahweh is sovereign in history. It has specifically announced the imminent downfall of Babylon. And it has devastatingly exposed the stupidity of the image-making that tempts the community.

Additional Notes §30

43:22 / There is no **not** in v. 22b. NIV assumes that the force of the **not** in v. 22a carries over. As in English, this is possible but not very natural (cf. NRSV). Difficulties in understanding vv. 22–24 have arisen from assuming that they refer to the people's relationship with Yahweh before Jerusalem fell, but it is difficult to make sense of the verses on this assumption.

43:28 / The future verbs presumably describe the event of the fall of Jerusalem from the perspective of God's determining to destroy it during the period when the people were committing the sin described in v. 27.

44:2 / We do not know why Yahweh here uses the title "Jeshurun" instead of "Israel," but the most significant thing about the title may be that it otherwise occurs only in Deut. 32:15 and 33:5, 26. It is one of a number of links between Deut. 32–33 (esp. Deut. 32) and Isa. 40–55 that suggest that Deut. 32 was one of the chapters which inspired Isa. 40–55 and to which the Poet directs the community for a theology and a message that could inform their own. It deserves reading in this connection.

44:21 / The verb reads "you will not be forgotten me," which is as questionable Hb. as it is English. MT sometimes combines different words, presumably when different words appeared in different manuscripts. Here the two forms would be "you are not to forget me" and "you will not be forgotten." Both are relevant in the context. "There is to be no forgetting" would preserve the ambiguity.

§31 Cyrus, Yahweh's Anointed Shepherd (Isa. 44:24–45:25)

We have noted that the two sections on the restoration of a blind and deaf servant (43:22–44:23 and 42:18–43:21) paralleled one another, but that the former lacked an equivalent to the last paragraph (43:14–21). This parallel ending now follows, in 44:24–45:8, with its lyrical postscript (45:8) marking it as an ending. Yet 43:22–44:23 did have a different sort of lyrical postscript (44:23). For 44:24–45:8 also marks a beginning. It makes an announcement whose significance 44:24–45:25 as a whole explores. First, it handles the opposition that it expects the announcement to receive within the community (45:9–13). Then it points up the positive implications of the announcement for Israel (45:14–17) and for the world (45:18–25).

44:24–28 / At one level, verses 24–28 are merely an introduction to 45:1–8, without a point of their own. Structurally, that is, they comprise an introduction to Yahweh's words in verse 24a followed by a long self-description on Yahweh's part that occupies verses 24b–28. Such a self-description is designed to buttress some point that Yahweh wishes to make. This self-description thus corresponds to the ones in 43:14a, 15 and 43:16–18 in the parallel section, which in turn buttress the points made in 43:14b and 19–21. But the point Yahweh wishes to make comes only in 45:1–8. On the other hand, 45:1–8 has its own resumptive introduction (45:1a), as if to draw attention to the fact that in substance 44:24–28 has made its point. It has described Cyrus as Yahweh's shepherd. It has simply made it within the form of that self-description. There is more to this self-description than one might have expected. To put it another way, the introduction previews the point. This begins an attempt to get around the defenses of an audience that is not expected to find the message easy to accept.

So once more the one who speaks is the one who redeems Jacob-Israel in the present and who formed it in the past. The description invites the community to prepare itself for good news. Yahweh's self-designation is first as the creator (v. 24b). The description treats creation initially in rather factual and down-to-earth terms ("maker of all") and then more imaginatively (creating is like someone spreading out their tent). Creation being a past event, NIV naturally translates the verbs in verse 24b in the past, but then has present verbs in the following verses that refer to Yahweh's ongoing activity. But the verb forms themselves are all participles. So, more literally, Yahweh says "I am Yahweh, maker . . . , stretcher . . . , spreader . . . , foiler . . . , befooler . . . , overthrower . . . , turner . . . , carrier . . . , fulfiller . . . ". The implication is that Yahweh is, in the present, just as much creator as fulfiller. One of the characteristic emphases of these chapters is that it is precisely as sovereign creator that Yahweh is involved in the community's life in the present. Creation is not only an event in the distant past that set the world going. It was also a nearer past event that set Israel going, and it is a present event that recreates Israel. Israel needs something sovereignly creative to be done for it, and as sovereign creator their God can do it.

In chapter 40, the implied link between creation and present events was that both are the context in which Yahweh expresses sovereign power, and the juxtaposition of verses 24b and 25 suggests this again. The ongoing history of the world reflects its creator's sovereign activity. As chapter 41 then emphasized, other so-called gods and their aides are therefore in no position to know what is going to happen in that history or to make sense of what has happened. So when they attempt to do so, they fail (v. 25a).

Babylon had a vast array of experts in reading the signs of the times as they appeared in the movements of stars and planets and in anomalies in nature. They had a vast library that recorded relevant precedents and judgments. Biblical religion does not rule out the possibility of God's activity being reflected in such ways, as the arrival of some of these experts to acknowledge the birth of Jesus suggests. But it denies that God's activity can be read off from such events by the simple application of empirical insight. Even the experts in Matthew 2 found their way only to the right general area. They needed the Hebrew Scriptures to tell them more precisely where the Messiah might be expected to be born. Philosophy may tell you some important things, but it will leave you helpless before the specific. If the experts try to be specific, God may put them in their place. In Babylon in the 540s B.C., current events are confounding the experts. There were no precedents or

signs that had announced the rise of Cyrus or that could help to
explain its significance.

And that is where prophets come in (v. 26a), as would be the
case in Matthew 2, again as chapter 41 has implied. Philosophy
and the insights of world religions can tell us many truths about
God and the world, but they cannot tell us the gospel. They cannot tell us the specifics about the central thread of God's purpose
in the world that gives meaning to the whole. We discover that
truth only through Yahweh's servants and aides. Significantly,
predictions is the word *'etsat* (KJV "counsel"; see 5:19). Yahweh's
agents are privy to the plans that Yahweh is implementing in the
world, and they are therefore in a position to explain these plans
to Israel and to the world. The unfolding of events according to
their predictions vindicates the truth of their explanations. When
they say that Israel will escape from Egypt and move to Canaan,
or that Ephraim will fall to Assyria, or that Assyria will then fall
to Babylon, or that Jerusalem itself will fall to Babylon, or that
Babylon will fall to the Medes, then their words will be fulfilled
because they issue from involvement in the strategy Yahweh is
implementing.

The participial expression continues in verse 26b but its
form changes slightly to signal a change in the content. Three
times in verses 26b–28a Yahweh speaks as "*the* one who says" (NIV
omits "the one"). The change is a move from the general statement of Yahweh's sovereignty to specific and concrete statements
of how Yahweh now intends to exercise sovereignty. First, there is
to be a restoration of the fabric and the population of Jerusalem
and the other Judean cities. It may be that we should not be too
down-to-earth in reading between the lines of verse 26. There lies
behind it a poet-theologian's vision of what Jerusalem and Judah
were supposed to be, as much as a newspaper-reader's knowledge of how things actually were. Factually, it is unlikely that the
capital was a pure ghost town, and there is no need to assume that
the Poet wishes to pretend that it was such. Its ordinary people
had not been deported, but whoever lived there lived in a city that
had been devastated by the Babylonian army. The bustling excitement and thriving business and religious life of a capital city had
hardly been restored. The population had more likely drifted
away than increased. Jerusalem needed physical rebuilding and
new life-blood. An unexpected third colon (or unit of verse) in this
line promises the restoration of **their ruins**. Because it rounds off
the line as a whole, this likely refers to both Jerusalem and the

other towns. It puts the main emphasis on physical rebuilding, a note that verse 28 will take up again.

Such rebuilding and restoration might seem as implausible as other aspects of the vision these five chapters have presented. As later readers, we know that Jerusalem was indeed partially restored over the next century. Our image of Jerusalem is also shaped by our awareness of the way the city expanded and developed over subsequent centuries. It is therefore easy for us to find God's promise entirely plausible. But before the event, it would have been easier to imagine that Jerusalem was in the midst of becoming another of the abandoned ruins of history. Yahweh's words would be hard to believe. The mythic language of verse 27 thus undergirds them. This restoration is not an unprecedented act on Yahweh's part. The one who speaks is one who has always had power over the forces of disorder and chaos that threaten to overwhelm. Yahweh exercised that power at creation, and again at the Red Sea, and is therefore capable of exercising it again.

Yahweh's third statement (v. 28a) has been long delayed, apparently because it will take even more believing. In relation to the sequences that have preceded, we have noted that 44:24–45:8 corresponds to 43:14–21. The latter included the first explicit reference to Babylon itself, for all Babylon's implicit presence throughout 40:1–43:13. Now there comes the first explicit reference to the figure who has also long been implicitly present, the one who is to bring about the community's deliverance and restoration. Yahweh is also the one **who says of Cyrus, "He is my shepherd and will accomplish all that I please."**

Shepherd is a standard Middle Eastern image for a king, and not long ago Ezekiel 34:23 had promised a day when Yahweh would "place over them one shepherd, my servant David." Once reaching the point of being explicit about Cyrus's place in Yahweh's purpose, the Poet holds nothing back. Cyrus is to fulfill the role that Yahweh has elsewhere attributed to a new David, namely, he "will accomplish all that I please." He will be the means of putting Yahweh's plan into effect.

Specifically, he will issue the edict that makes possible the restoration of city and **temple** (v. 28b). Here alone does the Poet refer to the temple, though it plays an important part in the first part of the book (e.g., 2:2–4; 6:1–13) and in the last part (e.g., 56:3–8; 60:1–7). In keeping with that, the restoration of the temple is very important to Ezekiel the priest. Isaiah 40–55 otherwise focuses on the city itself. But the word translated "temple" is literally "palace" (not the usual "house of God"), so it hints at the great king Cyrus's building a palace for a greater King, and at a reversal of 39:7.

45:1–8 / The opening, **this is what the LORD says,** then, resumes from 44:24 and suggests that now we will hear Yahweh's actual message. Some further affirmation of who Yahweh is (e.g., 44:24a) often expands such an opening. Here in the bulk of verse 1 Yahweh instead glosses the name of the addressee. Before that, however, it is one of the Poet's own opening words that makes the audience miss a heartbeat and means that it is just as well that the rest of verse 1 will reappear in verses 2–7. We are too busy for a moment assimilating the fact that Cyrus has been described not only as Yahweh's shepherd but as Yahweh's **anointed.**

The fact that this word *mashiakh* came to be the standard word to express Jewish and Christian hopes for a future redeemer, *the* Messiah, means that the application of the word to Cyrus indeed sounds scandalous. But within the OT itself the word's regular use applies it to the Davidic king, so it is also scandalous in that context. Once again the Poet declares that what Yahweh once intended to do through a Davidic king will now be achieved through this pagan conqueror.

That introductory gloss on the name Cyrus designates him as the agent whom Yahweh supports (**whose right hand I take hold of**) and declares where this will lead in terms of military success—the successes that Judeans and Babylonians were hearing about, which will come to their climax in Babylon's fall. The actual words to Cyrus repeat the undertaking regarding military success (vv. 2–3a) and commission and support: Cyrus is taken by the hand, called by name, and strengthened just as Israel is (vv. 1, 3, 4, 5). The words add the note that this revolution in Middle Eastern political affairs is all brought about **for the sake of Jacob my servant, of Israel my chosen** (v. 4a): the megalomania of this Poet would seem outrageous if history had not vindicated it by the fact that countless peoples for whom Cyrus means nothing recognize Jacob-Israel's significance. Whereas Cyrus does not recognize Yahweh now, Yahweh's aim includes his coming to do so (v. 3), and Yahweh's acts through him will also lead to the people's coming to recognize Yahweh (v. 6). Again these two aims parallel God's aims in connection with Jacob-Israel (e.g., 41:20; 43:10): the scandal is increased.

In a formal sense Cyrus did come to recognize Yahweh (see Ezra 1:1–5), but archaeological discoveries from Babylon include an inscription by Cyrus on a clay barrel called "the Cyrus Cylinder" in which he enthusiastically attributes his victories to the Babylonian god Marduk. Admittedly the Cyrus Cylinder was likely ghost-written by Marduk's adherents, but Cyrus was prepared to be all things to all gods. If Yahweh's aim in verse 3 was to receive more than Cyrus's formal recognition, then Yahweh was apparently disappointed in this respect (although not in the aim expressed in v. 6). It would, of course, be no new experience for Yahweh to fail to receive someone's acknowledgment. This had been Yahweh's experience over the years with Israel, as it has been with the church.

The content of people's acknowledgment of Yahweh receives yet another new formulation in this connection (v. 7). It may seem easy to see God as author of light and bringer of *shalom*. The presupposition of this verse's radical belief in Yahweh's sovereignty is that Yahweh is also author of darkness and disaster, the darkness and disaster that have overtaken Judah and that are about to overtake Babylon. To say **there is no other** (v. 6) is to deny that there are many gods who share in such responsibility, as Babylonians believed, as well as to deny that there are two forces of light and darkness, as Persians believed (and Christians often have). There is no power beyond Yahweh.

Verse 8 recalls 44:23 in marking a conclusion and the significance of what it follows, but it is not a hymn of praise but a commission by Yahweh to the cosmos to set about fulfilling the intention that has been announced. Yahweh has **created it:** God's acts in history for the deliverance of Israel are God's acts of creation (though so are God's calamities: see v. 6).

45:9–13 / We have noted several times that the Poet's way of speaking implies the expectation that people will have problems with the message. That now comes out into the open. The community cannot believe that God would do what the Poet says God is doing. Using a pagan emperor like Sennacherib or Nebuchadnezzar to bring trouble to Israel because of its wrongdoing is one thing. How could God use a pagan emperor like Cyrus to bring blessing to Israel in fulfillment of the role that God had long ago given to the Davidic king?

We have already read a number of the answers to this sort of question. This kind of action is in keeping with what prophets such as Isaiah have said. True, Yahweh's agent ought to be one who acknowledges Yahweh, and the idea is that Cyrus has the chance to do so. The community may or may not find such answers satisfactory, but in the end, Yahweh claims the power to make decisions about how to run the world whether Jacob-Israel likes them or not. In the NT we find that Paul follows the same form of argument: I will offer you some arguments, but in the end God is God (Rom. 9:20–21).

In Isaiah God is the **potter,** whereas you and Cyrus are only the pots God is making, even bits of broken pot among other bits (Isa. 45:9). God is **father** or **mother,** whereas you and Cyrus are only the **children** God is begetting or bearing (vv. 10–11). God is creator of the whole cosmos and is applying the creator's sovereign energy, through Cyrus, to the restoring of Jerusalem and the freeing of the exiles in Babylon so that they can go home (v. 13). Would they not be wise to let God decide how to achieve this?

45:14–17 / One of the tricky issues in the interpretation of Isaiah 40–55 is the relationship between a "nationalist" concern and a concern for the whole world. Indeed this is an issue in the Bible as a whole (see comment on 25:6–12). It is possible to portray the "universalist" stance in such a way that the "nationalist" tone of a passage such as verse 14 is difficult to relate to it. It is equally possible to be so struck by the "nationalist" tone of a passage such as verse 14 that you feel compelled to tone down the apparent generosity to the world that is shown elsewhere. Here there is no doubt about the glorious re-establishment of Jacob-Israel. Verse 14 is further motivation for the community to accept the idea that Cyrus's upcoming victory is Yahweh's means of blessing them. Far from Cyrus gaining from his victories, they themselves will (v. 14). Once more the promises to the Davidic king apply to Jacob-Israel as a whole (cf. Ps. 72). But that is only a reassertion of their original application to all Abraham's people, for the recognition at the end of verse 14 is the fulfillment of Genesis 12:3b. Recognizing Israel and recognizing Yahweh are interdependent. "Universalism" and "nationalism" complement each other ("universalism" in this context denotes a concern for the whole world to know Yahweh, not a conviction that everyone will be saved). There is a parallel in the church's convictions. On the one side, we have a universalist conviction—we believe that God wants the whole world to be saved. On the other, we have an exclusivist conviction—we believe that this happens only as people come to believe the message that the church preaches.

English translations close their quotation marks at the end of verse 14, but there is no indication of a change of speaker, and this leaves verses 15–17 floating in the air. More plausibly, the LXX assumes that verses 15–17 continue the acknowledgment of the nations in verse 14. Interpreters have often taken the words in verse 15 as a general statement about God's mystery. Either way, verse 15 probably reflects the meaning that attaches to statements of God's hiddenness elsewhere in the OT (e.g., Deut. 31:17–18; Ps. 30:7; 89:46). As Israel sometimes protests, God has been hiding (though in this case because of Israel's wrongdoing). But now God is saving and revealing. The nations acknowledge that Yahweh alone is God and that Israel will always be Yahweh's special people. They acknowledge that Yahweh is the one who hides, but also the one who saves.

45:18–25 / Yahweh's concern with Israel and with the nations is taken further and brought to a climax. Yes, Yahweh is the one God, God of the whole world (v. 18). Yes, Yahweh has especially **spoken** to Jacob-Israel. Further, Yahweh has not so spoken "in hiddenness" (v. 19, NIV "in secret"): the Hebrew word comes from the same root as that in verse 15. If there have been times when Yahweh has been inaccessible, there were special reasons (such as Israel's wrongdoing). Yahweh is not elusive by nature and Yahweh has shown Jacob-Israel quite clearly the true purpose Yahweh is pursuing for them: **truth** is *tsedeq* (see on 41:2), while **right** *(mesharim)* is a variant on the word for making a level or smooth path for the journeys of Yahweh and the exiles in 40:4 and 42:16 (cf. the parent verb, *yashar*, in 45:2, 13).

There is thus some slightly unexpected confrontation of Jacob-Israel in verses 18–19. The beginning of verse 20 implies some imminent parallel confrontation of the nations, for the words suggest another challenge to meet in court. But it transpires that Yahweh summons only people who are the mere **fugitives from the nations,** people who have gone through Babylon's oppression or Cyrus's attacks. Events (will) have shown that they and their images have nothing to say and that Yahweh alone can account for what is going on and claim responsibility for it (v. 21). But the claim to be **a righteous God and a Savior** turns out to be made for their benefit and not merely for their confounding, for the call **turn to me and be saved, all you ends of the earth** (v. 22) follows it. The call expresses most explicitly Yahweh's concern for the whole world.

Yet the context makes clear that this implies no resolution of that tension between universalism and nationalism. First, the ultimate object of this call is the recognition of Yahweh (vv. 23–24). It is not clear whether the ragers who are shamed are the same people as the fugitives who are saved, or whether shame is an alternative destiny to salvation, or whether the ragers are the Judeans of verses 9–11: no reader can relax and avoid saying "Is it I?" But for all the openness of the invitation of verse 22, the chapter ends with the promise that **Israel will be found righteous and will exult.** And we recall that the Judean community is the audience throughout these prophecies. The most exalted of the declarations concerning other peoples is an indirect declaration concerning its exaltation.

Additional Notes §31

44:24–28 / I have oversimplified the comment on participles. "Almost as a rule the participial construction beginning a sentence . . . is continued by means of a finite verb," but the latter continues the participial meaning (GK 116x; see Additional Notes on 17:1–3). Thus here grammatically "befooler," "turner," and "fulfiller" are imperfect verbs, but they continue the participial statement.

44:26–27 / The link between verses 26 and 27 looks less direct in English than it does in Hb., for **ruins** and **be dry** come from different verbs, but they look the same—both are spelled *khareb.*

44:28 / The temple had not been razed to the ground, and **let its foundations be laid** might give the wrong impression. Thus NJB suggests "will be refounded."

45:7 / KJV's "I make peace, and create evil" is misleading. The word *ra'* covers anything "bad." It thus can refer to moral evil, but the context makes clear that here it refers to trouble or calamity.

45:13 / Of course Cyrus conquered Babylon and freed the Judeans for what he could get out of it. The point in the last line is perhaps that there is a higher purpose involved in these events than the one of which Cyrus is aware.

§32 The Fall of the Gods and Their City (Isa. 46:1–47:15)

So Yahweh has declared Babylon's destiny to fall to Cyrus. Now, before the prophet's eyes, the Babylonian gods make the reverse of the journey that the vessels from the Jerusalem temple had made (ch. 46), and the prophet bids the city itself accept the humiliation of its defeat and the end of its exercise of power in the middle east (ch. 47). One might infer that the situation has moved on and that the city has now actually fallen, but as the chapters continue to unfold this does not seem to be the case. Portraying events as if they are happening and addressing the city as if it has fallen are yet other ways of asserting the certainty of these events and thus seeking to persuade the Judean community to believe in them and live by them.

46:1–7 / **Bel** and **Nebo** are two of the most prominent Babylonian deities. The name Bel is an equivalent to Baal, meaning "Lord." Babylonian theology applies the name to Marduk as leader of the gods. Nebo was Marduk's son and apparently patron god of the royal dynasty, to judge from names such as Nebuchadnezzar and Nabonidus. While Nebo's name thus appears in that of the current Babylonian king, Bel's name appears in that of his regent Belshazzar (see Dan. 5). The prophet might have named these two, as Isaiah named Sennacherib and Merodach-Baladan and as Jeremiah named Nebuchadnezzar. It is possible that the use of the gods' names contains a reminder of the two leaders whose own names incorporated them. But the focus is on the gods themselves. These gods have been a prominent subject in earlier chapters (e.g., ch. 41) as Yahweh has challenged them and their devotees to give some evidence that the gods have the power their devotees attribute to them. Now for the first time they are named, as Babylon itself and Cyrus were named for the first time in the preceding sections.

The only reason for naming them is to portray their humiliation, the event that will prove the case that the prophet has been arguing. Everyone was used to seeing the images of the gods carried about in procession, not least from one city to another (Nebo's actually resided in Borsippa, ten miles down river from Babylon). The prophet's vision is a mockery of such a procession, a procession that this time leads into exile. It is a bold image. After all, some people doubtless claimed that Yahweh had been just as unable to prevent Jerusalem's fall and the destruction or removal of the objects that stood for the divine presence in the temple. The prophet has provided an explanation for Jerusalem's fall that makes it an expression of Yahweh's sovereignty rather than a denial of it. But Marduk's priests will be able to do the same for Babylon's fall, blaming it on Nabonidus's neglect of Marduk. However, the prophet would claim that offering such explanations after the fact looks lame in comparison with the relationship between Yahweh's speaking and events. This relationship has provided evidence of Yahweh's lordship over centuries of events.

The carrying of divine images in procession was reckoned to glorify them and was an occasion of great celebration and splendor. The prophet turns it into a parable of their weakness. Gods are supposed to **carry you,** especially in a crisis. What use is a god who then has to be carried? Instead of being impressed by these images, the Judean community ought to let the parable point to their weakness and Yahweh's strength (vv. 1–4). What use is a god that is fixed securely in its place so that it can no more move than do anything when you need it (vv. 5–7)?

46:8–13 / Another new form of specificity now accompanies the specificity of the reference to Bel and Nebo. It is a charge that addresses the community as **rebels, stubborn-hearted,** and **far from righteousness.** Once again, there is no need to assume that the situation has moved on and that this statement presupposes a concrete negative response to previous prophecies (though this might be so). For this specificity fits the pattern of the way the chapters work in other respects. From the beginning, the prophet's rhetorical method suggests the assumption that the audience will be unresponsive. Only now does the prophet state that assumption explicitly. The two charges of stubborn rebelliousness recall the story of Israel in Exodus-Numbers, though the actual language is different.

After the first charge, the prophet challenges the community to face the truths about Yahweh in a summary of what we have read so far. These are the truths that the community has to face. Yahweh has been demonstrating a sovereignty in events over a long period (v. 9a). That sovereignty demonstrates that Yahweh alone is **God**. The contrast with the helplessness of the Babylonian gods to help themselves, let alone to help their devotees (v. 9b), implicitly underlines the point. The fact that Yahweh alone can give a satisfactory interpretation of the span of world events as a whole (v. 10a) proves this. To put it in contemporary terms, the 540s B.C. in Babylon see a clash of meta-narratives. Two worldviews are confronting each other, two understandings of history as a whole. The prophet's conviction is not that Babylon's is true for Babylon and Judah's for Judah but that Judah's alone is an adequate meta-narrative within which to look at the little narratives of the day. In relation to the present, that proves that Yahweh has the power to make decisions and implement them (v. 10b). The decision that Yahweh has made is to bring the conqueror from the east, in keeping with the paradigm that goes back to Abraham (v. 11a). What Yahweh has said, Yahweh will do, in keeping with the pattern of the past (v. 11b).

The second charge, in verse 12, resumes the one in verses 8–9a and thus completes a bracket round verses 9b–11 but also introduces a climactic summary in verse 13. The audience is far from righteousness (v. 12). At first that sounds like a moral condemnation. But Yahweh goes on, **I am bringing my righteousness near.** If we are not sure what that might mean in the context, parallelism helps us, as is often the case: **my salvation will not be delayed.** Yahweh's righteousness (here *tsedaqah*) is Yahweh's acting to do the right thing for Israel in the light of Israel's place in Yahweh's purpose, so that Yahweh's "righteousness" and Yahweh's "salvation" are closely related (see the comment on 41:2). Perhaps the community is far from righteousness in a moral sense, though that point is not made elsewhere in these chapters. It is certainly far from righteousness in the sense that it is resistant to Yahweh's righteous purpose for itself, resistant to Yahweh's plan of salvation for it. It might like to be delivered from its oppression, to experience Yahweh's righteousness, but it refuses to accept the way Yahweh is bringing about that deliverance and implementing that righteousness. Here more than usual one can sense the prophet's frustration with a situation in which the community is too stubbornhearted to see the solution to the problem it so wants to be solved.

Prophet and Yahweh join in trying to take the community by its shoulders and shake it to its senses. *Won't you see that my act of salvation is here? Won't you recognize it for what it is?* As is often the case, we must keep paying attention to the very end in the prophet's poem. Yahweh intends to grant this salvation to **Zion** (v. 13). The name Jerusalem appears rarely in chapters 40–48, but even these chapters live by the vow in Psalm 137:5 and periodically make the fact explicit. The last time we saw this was in 44:28. The prophet lives among the first generations of those who say "Next year in Jerusalem," and the prophet is the kind of person who would mean it in the manner of the Zionist pioneers of the late nineteenth century who indeed returned to the Land when they had the opportunity. For the Judean community in Babylon, an essential element in the promise of restoration is that Yahweh's attractive presence will return to Zion. They themselves will return in Yahweh's train (see 40:9–11).

47:1–4 / The book called Isaiah quickly introduced us to Ms Zion (1:8), the personified city abandoned and desolate. As further background to the prophet's ministry, Lamentations 1–2 has comprehensively bewailed her fate. She has been taken from honor to the dust, subjected to loss and grief, covered in humiliation and weeping. Isaiah 47 imposes the same fate on the agent of her suffering. Ms Babylon takes Ms Jerusalem's place.

Like 14:3b–21, these verses go through the motions of mourning the death of someone who is actually very much alive and whose prospective death the Judean community does not mourn at all—indeed the death lament becomes a taunt. One might compare Jesus' taunt against towns such as Capernaum (C. C. Torrey, *The Second Isaiah: A New Interpretation* [New York: C. Scribner, 1928], p. 368). Like many of the poems about other nations in chapters 13–23, for the Judean community this poem is both promise that its oppressor will be put down and warning not to take this oppressor too seriously. And like other OT prophecies (including ch. 46), it does not correspond closely to what actually happened in the course of the event that one might reckon fulfilled it. It is not like an anticipatory account of the actual fall of Babylon. One significance of this is that here, as elsewhere, "Babylon" is both the historical empire and the embodiment and symbol of oppression, which it becomes more overtly in Revelation.

Four times the poem issues an exhortation or command to Ms Babylon and follows it with the reasons (vv. 1–4, 5–7, 8–10,

11–15). This chapter more systematically develops the picture of
city as woman than does Lamentations. At the moment, the city is
like a woman of power and refinement. She is to become instead
an ordinary working woman, fulfilling the ordinary tasks of a
peasant, with nothing dignified about her.

The descriptions of her as **tender** and **delicate** (v. 1) "conjure
up the idea of luxury, the refinements of the court, the elegant life
of carefree enjoyment" (Westermann, *Isaiah 40–66*, p. 190). She is
everything that the most ambitious Judean might want to be. It
is all about to disappear. This first section (vv. 1–4) gives no specific reason for that negative transformation, though toward the
end it begins to offer pointers. The dethroning is an act of Israel's
Redeemer (v. 4): it is a necessary precursor of restoring the Judean
community and restoring Zion. We recall that the prophecy is formally addressed to Ms Babylon, but the actual audience for which
it is designed is that Judean community itself. But Babylon's humiliation is not merely a matter of arbitrarily removing an obstacle
in the way of fulfilling Jacob-Israel's destiny. The humiliation is an
act of punishment (**vengeance,** see on 1:24–25a). It is something
Ms Babylon deserves. The prophet has not yet told us why.

47:5–7 / A second time Ms Babylon is told to be ready for
her dethroning, but here the words become more metaphorical.
They suggest calamity and its aftermath. Ms Babylon is to experience the **silence** and **darkness** that Zion has experienced (for silence, see, e.g., 23:2; Lam. 2:10; and for darkness, 8:21–9:1; 42:6–7;
Lam 3:2, 6). And now one reason for the punishment becomes explicit. It parallels but contrasts with Isaiah's critique of Assyria (see
10:5–19). In bringing trouble to Judah, Ms Babylon had been the
executor of Yahweh's own wrath, but she had not merely acted in
pride but acted without **mercy.** It is telling that a city personified
as a woman should be so accused, for mercy or compassion is a
woman's natural attribute (the word mercy is related to the word
for the womb). It suggests the feelings of a woman for her children, but they are feelings that a woman might also be expected to
feel for others, such as the **aged** (v. 6). Ms Babylon had so enjoyed
exercising power (like a man?) that she had lost the capacity to feel
compassion like a woman. She has given up her womanliness and
will suffer a woman's fate (see vv. 1–3, 9). Portraying Babylon as
a woman makes it possible to make the point that Yahweh expects mercy to be part of political talk. "In the end, even the empire stands or falls in terms of God's resilient commitment to

mercy. Ruthless power cannot circumvent that resolve of God" (Brueggemann, *A Social Reading of the Old Testament*, p. 119).

47:8–11 / Each section in chapter 47 sounds some note that the following section then develops. As punishment was announced in the first but explained in the second, over-confidence was noted in the second (v. 7) but is now further explained. It can often be the case that people and communities in power think that their position is invulnerable, though other people and communities in power do see the writing on the wall (this image, of course, belongs to Babylon: see Dan. 5). That reminds us once again that the prophet is speaking to Babylon's subjects, for whom their mistress certainly looked invulnerable. Statements such as those in verses 7a, 8b, and 10b express how Ms Babylon looked to the Judeans. It is for their benefit, then, that verses 8–9 offer another version of her womanly transformation. As well as moving from authority to servitude, she will move from the security of wifehood and the joy of motherhood to the insecurity of widowhood and the loneliness of bereavement (v. 8).

47:12–15 / The third section, verses 8–11, also announced a further theme that this final section now develops. Another feature of Babylonian life that threatened to impress the Judean community was the vast Babylonian expertise in reading signs—signs in the sky such as the way in which different planets came into collocation with each other (v. 13) and signs on the earth in forms such as abnormal animal births (see on 44:25). We have noted that Babylon had accumulated extensive libraries recording precedents and events that their vast companies of experts could consult in order to interpret events. On their basis they could also then suggest ways of averting threatened calamity, including rites such as prayers that accompanied the destruction of figurines representing an enemy. If the calamity then failed to happen, this would "prove" that the system worked and reinforce belief in it. It was this religion that constituted Ms Babylon's false confidence. She thought she could control her life, her destiny, and her future, but she is about to find out that she has deceived herself. The system is about to receive its decisive test. As the prophet has said again and again, an event is about to overtake Babylon which its religious resources could neither predict nor account for nor avert. The resources in which Ms Babylon trusts will fail her. All that **counsel** (v. 13) to which she has access is useless alongside

Yahweh's counsel. Far from saving Babylon, the city's experts cannot even save themselves.

Additional Notes §32

46:1 / The Hb. is more literally "their idols became for/into a
creature and an animal," which the translation then tries to make sense
of. NIV mg. follows the LXX, which makes easier sense but is not necessarily right.

47:2–3 / Much of the description has been taken to denote
sexual abuse or rape. This is a common enough feature of war, but the
words are not ones commonly used in this connection and in the context
they more likely suggest the undignified exposure of someone who
simply has to get down to work. She will have (for instance) to trudge
across the Babylonian countryside with its irrigation ditches—though
the reference to wading through streams may hint at the metaphorical
sense in which she is going to find herself in deep water (cf. 43:2).

47:8 / The word for **wanton** suggests the enjoyment of good
food and other pleasures of life. It need not imply excess. Ms Babylon had
simply been in a position to live well, but will be so no longer.

§33 Now Is the Time for Response (Isa. 48:1–22)

Since chapter 40 the Poet has been involved in a battle to win the community's acceptance of a message about deliverance and blessing; the Poet has sounded increasingly hysterical as it seems that this battle will never be won (see, e.g., 42:18–25; 43:22–28; 45:9–13; 47:8, 12). Chapter 48 brings the confrontation and the challenge to its climax. It follows chapter 47 very strikingly, for chapter 48 addresses Jacob-Israel as confrontationally as chapter 47 addressed Babylon. It is almost as if Jacob-Israel was in the same danger as Babylon. The dynamic might even recall that of Amos 1–3, where the prophet warns of disaster to come on Israel's neighbors, only at the end to turn on Israel itself.

The key elements in the prophet's scandalous vision of Yahweh's purpose are all now on the table. The prophet has named Cyrus and Babylon and portrayed the fall of Babylon's gods and of the city itself. All that is to be said about these matters will have been said by the end of chapter 48. There will be no more reference to Babylon and Cyrus, no more asserting that Yahweh alone is God, no more overt arguing with the Judean community—indeed little more reference to Jacob-Israel. The sermon now looks for a response. "With the idols eliminated (44:24–46:13) and the political power of Babylon shattered (ch. 47), there remains the principal obstacle to the new exodus, Israel itself" (R. Lack, *La symbolique du livre d'Isaïe*; Analecta Biblica 59; Rome: PBI, 1973, p. 106).

48:1–2 / Chapter 44:1–5 invited us to envision a day when nominal acknowledgment of Yahweh would become the real thing, but the passage left open the identity of the people who apparently needed to come to a genuine recognition of Yahweh. It is now overt that this is how the prophet sees the community as a whole. Their pedigree is impeccable, their public commitment to Yahweh is well-known, their lives are based in trust in Yahweh, and their eyes are fixed on their home in Jerusalem. Yet **not in**

truth or righteousness (v. 1) is written over their entire religious life. The dynamics of this message exactly correspond to those of Isaiah's (e.g., 1:10–20). For all the seriousness of their inward commitment backed by outward confession, their faith has a fatal flaw.

48:3–6a / The flaw is different from that which Isaiah saw, though there is an underlying link between them. Isaiah would go on to urge the people to stop living their life in contempt of the fact that Yahweh was active in that life and in the affairs of the nations, working out a moral and religious purpose. This conviction that Yahweh is at work and that the community can know what Yahweh is about underlies the Poet's message as a whole. Their abandonment of truth and righteousness consists in their refusal to recognize what Yahweh has been (i.e., what the prophet has spent eight chapters trying to convince them of). Over their history Yahweh has been telling them what would happen and then bringing it about (vv. 3, 5a, 6a). With some cynicism, the prophet speaks as if the sole reason was to stop their attributing events to their images (v. 5b).

The talk of the evidence Yahweh has given of being sovereign in history recalls the court scenes that have been a prominent feature since chapter 41. Verses 3–6a clarify the fact that in those court scenes the overt protagonists were Yahweh and Babylon or Babylon's gods, but the real tension lay between Yahweh and the Judean community. It was the latter that Yahweh really needed to convince. The time for indirectness is now over. Yahweh speaks straight. It was the Judean attraction to images of God or images of the gods (a feature of Judean religious life in earlier Judah and in Babylon) which needed shattering (v. 5b). Like Isaiah's own account of his commission in 6:9–13, the straightness of the language in verse 4 has the potential both to shock people into disproving it and to explain to a later generation why no one listened (and indirectly to urge that later generation to do so).

48:6b–8 / In keeping with that pattern that appears in earlier confrontations, having recalled telling them about events before they took place, Yahweh is now telling them of the next act in the play in which they have central parts. The prophet is never afraid of a little rhetorical inconsistency, and here instead of affirming that these events have been announced long ago (evidence that Yahweh is God), declares that they have not been announced before (otherwise they would only meet a bored sigh: for how long-running has been the story of rebellion, see Exod.

32). Both statements, of course, are true. There were prophecies that promised restoration and even declared that the Medes would put down the Babylonians, but the detail is new.

48:9–11 / In prophecy of the monarchic period, the logical outcome of a devastating critique such as that in verses 1–8 is a declaration that disaster is now to overwhelm the community. But we have reached this point before (see especially 42:18–25; 43:22–28) and know that neither Yahweh nor the Poet can live with that logic (see 43:1–7; 44:1–5). This is not the result of mere softness. Yahweh will muzzle wrath **for my own name's sake, for the sake of my praise** (v. 9), **for my own sake** (v. 11, repeated): **How can I let myself be defamed? I will not yield my glory to another.** It would be superficially more comforting for the community to be told that Yahweh will stay with it because of love, but it is at least as sure an argument when Yahweh remembers the logic that Moses had pressed at Sinai (see Exod. 32:11–13). The reference to the circumstances of Israel's forming in Egypt (v. 10) fits with that link.

48:12–19 / We have noted the way in which parallelism between whole units such as 42:18–25 and 43:22–28 accompanies parallelism within lines in Hebrew poetry. Here in chapter 48, verses 12–19 stand in a parallel relationship to verses 1–11. They begin with the exhortation to Jacob-Israel to **listen,** and they repeat it twice more as the prophet seeks yet again to grasp Jacob-Israel by the lapels verbally and shake it into a response. Once again verse 12 goes on to refer to how Jacob-Israel was **called.** This time the reference concerns how Yahweh called them rather than how they called themselves. Once again verse 12 recalls who Yahweh distinctively is, with a summary that is even more punchy and succinct than any that has preceded. Once again the passage goes on to recall what Yahweh has done that is distinctive, with verse 13 first summarizing the point about Yahweh's authority as creator that goes back to 40:12–31. Then verses 14–16a summarize the themes of chapters 41–47—with the example of Yahweh's speaking and acting being the story of Cyrus and Babylon, which establishes that Yahweh alone is God. While the summary is again thus punchy and succinct, it also manages to be innovative and even more scandalous. Cyrus is now Yahweh's **ally.** But the word is the one translated "friend" in 41:8. It adds to the scandalous epithets in 44:28; 45:1.

Like verses 1–11, the section goes on in verses 17–18 to confront Jacob-Israel directly with the clash between what it is called and how it has behaved. Here that takes the form of a handwringing expression of regret: **if only**. . . .

They are extraordinary words for a God to utter. The book called Isaiah often portrays Yahweh as a God of huge power. Indeed, this very section has done so. When Yahweh speaks, the very heavens stand at attention (v. 13). When Yahweh decides to do something, it happens. Yet Yahweh's relationship with Jacob-Israel is the exception to this rule. Other peoples may occasionally resist Yahweh's purpose, though they then soon pay the penalty (as the previous chapter declared). The people of God (Israel or the church) is able to continue resisting God over the centuries with some degree of impunity. It does lose in the short term, failing to find the promises to Abraham fulfilled in its life (v. 19a). Indeed Yahweh looks over the precipice of its ultimate destruction, and invites Jacob-Israel to do so (v. 19b). But we have again and again heard how impossible it would be for Yahweh to go back on the commitment to achieving a purpose in the world through this people. We heard this most recently in verses 9–11, in all their toughness. This commitment to Jacob-Israel reduces Yahweh to an "if only" before its recalcitrance, like that of parents angry and grieved at their (adult) children's waywardness and their consequent unhappiness, but unable to force them to live the way the parents would wish, and unable to cease being their parents.

48:20–22 / The final three verses repeat the pattern of this chapter a third time, exhorting the people to leave Babylon. It is an unexpected third time, because parallelism by definition works with couplets. Yet OT poetry includes some triplets (indeed vv. 1–11 included seven). They often mark a significant moment or draw attention to something (see, e.g., the promise in 43:14b and the aim in 43:20b–21). In verses 1–11 the triplets included the first line (v. 1a), the second line with its devastating ending (v. 1b), and the last line (v. 11). So here the third section in this chapter is unexpected and marked. As the second was shorter than the first yet heightened it and increased the tension, so the third is even shorter than the second, yet also heightens it and increases the tension once more.

Once again, following the pattern, the section begins with a command. Indeed, as the commands of verses 1–11 were multiplied in verses 12–19, so verses 20–22 multiply further the commands from verses 12–19, and also variegate them. "Listen" thus became "Listen . . . come together . . . listen," which now becomes **leave . . . flee . . . announce . . . proclaim . . . send . . . say,** so that this string of urgent imperatives dominates the section.

One wonders what kind of command is "leave." Hebrew is familiar with commands that express permission or promise, and the exhortation to leave Babylon might be read as an invitation that will not need issuing twice. Yet they will not rush to go "back" to this country that most of them have never seen, and the poetry so far has implied that (as the prophet saw it) they were both mournful at their lot and unwilling to see the current crisis as Yahweh's means of giving them new opportunities. So perhaps the imperative is a serious command.

As the first two sections referred to what the people were called, so this final one utilizes the key description by which they were called, Yahweh's **servant Jacob.** As the first sections recalled Yahweh's acts in the past, so this one recalls the provision of the first exodus (v. 21). As the first two sections linked those earlier events with the current new events, so this final one declares that now Yahweh **has redeemed** that servant Jacob.

Solemnly, as the first two sections moved from command to critique, this third section closes by confronting **the wicked** and warning that they will experience no *shalom* (cf. v. 18). Out of context, verse 22 might appear to refer to Jacob-Israel's enemies or to an element within the community, but in the context this looks like a final challenge to the community as a whole to choose restoration and fulfillment rather than the fate of the wicked who resist Yahweh's purpose and Yahweh's word. Verses 20–21 and 22 offer people two alternative scenarios.

As a whole, then, chapter 48 brings climax and resolution while also making it clear that there is further agenda that also needs to be addressed. It leaves us with Jacob-Israel teetering on the edge of the moment when Babylon falls and the Judean community there is free to return to Palestine, but it leaves us unsure whether the community will ever see events the prophet's way and go.

Additional Notes §33

48:1–22 / In his great commentary, *Isaiah 40–66*, Claus Westermann declared that the moment when Babylon was about to fall summoned Second Isaiah "to the task of proclaiming salvation, and nothing but salvation" to the people (p. 9). Isaiah ben Amoz had lived in a time when calamity had threatened the community and it needed to be brought to its senses and driven back to Yahweh. Second Isaiah lived in a time when calamity had overwhelmed the community and Yahweh now wished to comfort it. But this distinction must not be drawn too sharply. The ministry of the prophets in the time of the monarchy contains many a promise of Yahweh's renewal and blessing, and OT critics used to regard all these as the work of people like the Disciple, but this oversimplifies matters. In a parallel way, confrontation is an important feature of Second Isaiah's ministry. In ch. 48 Westermann regards the confrontational elements as a later expansion by someone other than Second Isaiah, but one weakness of that approach is that it neglects and obscures the fact that confrontational elements run through chs. 41–47. Westermann also sees the notes in ch. 47 as later additions.

48:10 / NIV's verbs in the perfect tense suggest that the refining is the one that has been going on in Babylon, but the context rather suggests that verse 10 refers to what went on in Egypt. Either way, the point is that Yahweh's smelting work on the people has failed to produce any silver.

48:16b / By its verse division MT links this with what precedes, but NIV rightly perceives a disjunction from vv. 12–16a. There Yahweh spoke, and v. 16a pairs with v. 12 as a bracket round the subsection. The I of v. 16b is the prophet, who is now beginning the introduction to vv. 17–19 in an especially emphatic way, putting Yahweh's authority firmly behind the straight words that follow.

§34 To Restore the People and the Land (Isa. 49:1–50:3)

So 49:1–6 is a major turning point. So far the Poet's focus has been Jacob-Israel. Henceforth it will be Jerusalem-Zion. So far the addressee has been Jacob-Israel. Henceforth it will be Jerusalem-Zion. So far Yahweh's promise has thus concerned the fall of Babylon and the end of the Judeans' enforced residence there. Henceforth it will concern the restoring of the city that virtually none of the exiles have ever seen. Once more there is no need to infer that time has moved on or that the people are already back in the city. While that might be so, it is just as plausible to imagine the prophet continuing to exercise a ministry in Babylon. Chapters 49–55 are just as relevant to the people there as are chapters 40–48 to people in Judah.

Further, there is an element of continuity between chapters 40–48 and 49–55 that perhaps points toward the latter's being the continuation of one ministry. We have seen that the issue that has come more and more to the surface in chapters 40–48 is that the problem that needs solving for the Judean community is not merely in the realm of geography—what are they doing having to live in Babylon? Nor is it merely a problem in the realm of politics—what are they doing having to live under Babylon and what is happening as Babylon's power in the middle east collapses? It is a problem of mind and spirit—what has having to live there under those pressures done to them and how can it be undone? That problem continues to set the agenda in chapters 49–55, even while the focus on the surface changes.

49:1–6 / **Listen to me** sounds like Yahweh. But it goes on, **the LORD** called me before I was born. So who now speaks? Read in the context, 49:1–6 becomes entirely intelligible as the prophet's further testimony, following on 40:6–8.

Like Isaiah's own testimony to his call (see ch. 6), this testimony comes after some chapters, not at the beginning of the prophet's words (the initial account came in 40:6–8). Like Jeremiah's testimony to his call in Jeremiah 1:4–5, it begins at the very beginning, with a designating before birth. Yahweh had called this baby forth from the womb in order to fulfill a prophet's calling (v. 1b). Yahweh had prepared the prophet ahead of time for the moment when it would be appropriate to speak the sharp and effective words that would implement Yahweh's purpose (v. 2). As had happened at the creation when God spoke and things happened, so a prophet was the means of God's speaking and thereby putting an intent into effect, and Yahweh had readied the prophet for that moment. It is another aspect of that feature of Yahweh's work that these chapters have so emphasized, that over centuries and over decades Yahweh has been exercising sovereignty and demonstrating sovereignty by deciding to do something, making the plans for it, and then doing it.

So far so uncontroversial. The next half-line gives us more to think about. At some stage, the prophet tells us, Yahweh **said to me, "You are my servant."** In one sense there is nothing surprising about this. Isaiah had been designated Yahweh's servant (see 20:3), as had prophets in general (see, e.g., Amos 3:7). In the present context, however, the expression raises questions. *The* servant of Yahweh has been a major focus of chapters 41–48, and we have learned that:

> Jacob-Israel is Yahweh's servant (41:8–9)
>
> Yahweh's servant has a specific role to fulfill (42:1–4)
>
> Jacob-Israel cannot fulfill that role (42:19)
>
> Nevertheless Jacob-Israel is still Yahweh's servant (43:10;
>   44:1–2, 21, 26; 45:4; 48:20)

The patterning of these allusions to the servant is noteworthy. For nearly four chapters (41:8–45:4) they were a focus of the prophet's work. Then for nearly four chapters (45:5–48:19) everything was quiet and one might wonder what has happened to this theme and the issues it stood for. Then, at the very end of chapters 40–48 we are reminded of them and thereby reminded of the unsolved problem they have raised: Why is it that the prophet claims the position that belonged to Jacob-Israel?

The companion half-line reassures us that we have asked the right question. **"You are my servant, Israel, in whom I will display my splendor."** It is often the calling of some individual to embody the calling of a nation or a group. In due course Jesus will do that for Israel. But, before his day, the prophet has already seen God's finger pointing and been aware of a call to accept this role. Perhaps there is a further link with Jeremiah here, and perhaps reflecting on Jeremiah's ministry helped the prophet to see what God was doing, for in his day Jeremiah was called to be the one person who manifestly lived out what it meant to be Israel. Once more (we may infer) it is precisely because the people as a whole cannot or will not live out their calling that the representative is called to do so.

Back in 40:6–8, when first told to preach, the prophet was unsure whether to believe Yahweh's word and thus with some irony gave us a hint of identification with Jacob-Israel, which also found it difficult to believe. With further irony (v. 4a), the prophet acknowledges having experienced the same uncertainty in those attempts to preach described in chapters 40–48. The words may remind us of Jacob-Israel's own in 40:27 or of the fragility of the people to whom the servant ministers in 42:3–4. Is this servant not up to the task either? But uncertainty is not the end of this retrospective. Whereas Jacob-Israel's words in 40:27 confined themselves to the conviction that Yahweh no longer paid attention to the people's "cause," in contrast verse 4b declares the continuing conviction that this servant's "cause" is in Yahweh's hand (NIV here translates the same word by the phrase **what is due to me**). God is indeed bringing **my reward** (see 40:10). God will bring fruit from the servant's ministry.

So there is a certain parallel between the experience of the servant prophet and that of the servant people. Each threatens to wilt under pressure. A further parallel now emerges. Yahweh's response to the wilting of the people was not only to reaffirm their servant position but to enhance it—they are to become Yahweh's witnesses in the great debate over deity (43:8–13; 44:6–8). Yahweh's response to the prophet's uncertainty about one task is also to add another to it. The task that has underlain chapters 40–48 was **to bring Jacob back.** The task was not primarily to bring the Babylonian community back to Palestine, but to bring it back to Yahweh. It was to bring it back to the conviction that Yahweh was sovereign in the world, back to finding strength in Yahweh, to believing in Yahweh's superiority over other so-called gods, to believing in Yahweh's commitment to it. "Return to me," Yahweh had therefore urged at one climactic point (44:22).

The servant has been exaggerating the burden of that task. So Yahweh adds another. **To restore the tribes of Jacob** is, after all, a rather small-scale responsibility (!): **I will also make you a light for the Gentiles,** so that **my salvation** comes **to the ends of the earth** (v. 6). Nothing in the aim here is new. Being a light to the nations has been the task of Yahweh's servant since 42:6. Yahweh commanded Jacob-Israel only a few verses previously to proclaim to the ends of the earth that Yahweh has redeemed servant Jacob (48:20). And in between these two passages Yahweh urged the ends of the earth "turn to me and be saved" (45:22; see also 40:28; 41:5; 42:10; 43:6). What is new is the more explicit awareness that the prophet is integral to bringing this about. It can hardly be that the task of being light to the world is taken away from Jacob-Israel. That would go against the often-reasserted commitment of chapters 43–44. But the prophet is integral to the achievement of that aim. The point is now explicit, thereby raising the stakes on the success of the prophet's ministry.

This helps to clarify how the two tasks in verses 5–6 relate to one another. The word "also" in verse 6 is an interpretation on the part of NIV, but a plausible one. Yahweh is not saying that the servant prophet is to give up the first task in favor of the second. At least this is not what happens, for chapters 49–55 continue to seek to bring the community back to God. Nor are the two tasks separate and independent ones. Yahweh enables the prophet to see more clearly the significance of seeking to draw Jacob-Israel back to God. Fulfilling this ministry will also bring about the fulfillment of a second mission. The way in which any minister is engaged in mission is by fulfilling a ministry to the congregation that itself has the task of mission.

Admittedly we must be wary of anachronistic understandings of the word "mission," which another NIV interpretation might encourage. The last line of verse 6 reads more literally "to be my salvation to the ends of the earth" (NRSV has "that my salvation may reach. . . ."). There is no implication here that people or prophet have to go out on a mission to **bring** God's **salvation** to the world (contrast 66:19). The sun does not go anywhere when it sends out light, and neither does Yahweh's servant. If prophet ministers and Yahweh acts, the world will see and respond. And it has. The fact that we are reading Jacob-Israel's book is a result.

49:7–13 / Verses 7–13 continue the theme of servanthood, rejection, vindication, and the faithfulness of God, but take it in a new/old direction. Talk of transferring the vocation of servant from people to prophet could be dangerous. It could suggest megalomania on the part of prophet (I once heard the principal of a Jewish seminary say that he was inclined to call in the psychoanalyst when a student talked of feeling called by God to be a rabbi). More importantly, it could suggest that Yahweh has forgotten the undertaking to persist with Jacob-Israel as servant notwithstanding its unreliability. Verses 7–13 begin with the recollection that Yahweh is still **Redeemer and Holy One of Israel,** an important reminder for God, prophet, and people. These verses address one **despised** and **abhorred,** the **servant of rulers.** This is presumably the Judean community itself. For while we have had no indication that the prophet was treated thus, this description does correspond to the community's self-perception (see, e.g., 41:8–20). It may well indicate the way it described itself when it prayed (so Westermann, *Isaiah 40–66,* p. 214). The last phrase is the most painful. Far from functioning as servant of Yahweh, the community is merely servant of heathen overlords. The initial promise of restoration here, then, corresponds to the promise to the community in 45:14–17.

Yahweh goes on to promise that the servant of rulers will become **a covenant for the people** (v. 8). The phrase recurs from 42:6, where it described the role of Yahweh's servant and accompanied the phrase "a light for the Gentiles." That last phrase has just reappeared in 49:6. In other words, we again find the double description of the servant from 42:6 here—divided between verses 6 and 8. The total effect is to reaffirm that Yahweh is indeed still committed to the community's fulfilling the servant role, through the prophet's ministry. It is destined not to be the servant of rulers forever, but to be the servant of Yahweh.

It is by restoring **the land** and freeing **the captives** that Yahweh will make the community a covenant for the people and a light for the nations (vv. 8b–9a). The logic is parallel to that in verses 5–6, though the content of the promise is also significantly different. There Yahweh will make the prophet a light for the nations by restoring Jacob-Israel to God. Here Yahweh will make the community a covenant for the people by restoring Jacob-Israel's land and restoring the people itself to its freedom. All these tasks will play a part in the fulfillment of Yahweh's purpose. Not surprisingly, all correspond to God's promise to Abraham, which involved land, people, relationship, and being a blessing. And Yahweh promises that the released people will be well-provisioned on their journey back for the reallocation of their inheritance (vv. 9b–11).

We have presupposed throughout the study of chapters 40–49 that the prophet's special focus is the Babylonian community, but periodically we are reminded not to make this too exclusive a focus. The prophet has a worldwide perspective and from time to time reaffirms that. Judeans had been transported to or had taken refuge in other parts of the world that surrounded their own land, especially Egypt, and the return of Judeans from Babylon is but one aspect of Yahweh's restoring the community as a whole to their homeland (vv. 12–13)—in order to restore the land (v. 8), whether or not they felt homesick.

49:14 / So Jerusalem's long-lost children are to return home. We now have to ask: how does that look from mother's angle? We begin to find an answer here, in **But Zion said.** . . . We have noted that chapters 40–48 center on Jacob-Israel, a term that suggests directly, though not exclusively, the Judean community in Babylon. At the same time, those chapters occasionally referred to Jerusalem-Zion, a reminder that this is that community's home and destiny. Chapters 49–55 center on Jerusalem-Zion. Instead of telling Jacob-Israel "you are free to go home," they tell Jerusalem-Zion "your children are on their way back home." This implies no change in the prophet's actual audience and no change in the audience that can overhear the prophet's words. The community in Babylon can now imagine its own return to Judah from another angle as the prophet directly addresses the community in Jerusalem.

But the prophet's new audience suffers from just the same crisis of morale, faith, and hope as the old one. Verse 14 corresponds exactly to 40:27. Ms Zion feels like a wife whose husband has left her.

49:15–21 / Yahweh's first response is to invite her to see him as more like a new man than an old philanderer. Indeed, Yahweh also knows what it is like to be a **mother** with a child **at her breast** and knows how a mother's child can never cease to be her child however old it becomes, so how could Yahweh forget this child? Her portrait stands on Yahweh's desk all the time, reminding Yahweh of her brokenness (v. 16). Yes, her own **children** will come **back** to her and will surround her in such numbers that she can hardly embrace them all and can hardly believe that she has such a wondrous family. The picture in verses 19–21 plays with the literal reality of city and inhabitants and the symbol of mother city and the children she provides for and protects, with the symbiotic relationship between each of these.

49:22–26 / How can this happen? Yahweh will beckon with a finger and the gentile nations such as have been responsible for separating mother and children will undertake their reuniting, and faith and **hope** will come back (vv. 22–23). Is that really possible? Yes, if Yahweh is involved (vv. 24–26). And the end result will be insight for the whole world and not merely for Israel (v. 26). The formulation makes particularly clear that the prophet's focus lies in the restoration of Ms Zion, for whom the recognition of Yahweh by the nations is good news, because what the nations are recognizing is what Yahweh has done for Ms Zion.

50:1–3 / There is another objection that Yahweh can hear in the heart of Ms Zion. Surely it is a matter not merely of a husband whose love has grown cold but of one who has actually divorced his wife and/or sold their children into slavery, as the laws imply could easily happen in hard times. The implication of the questions here (v. 1) is that the cause of the children's sale was not their father's financial embarrassment but their wickedness. This was also the cause of their parents' **divorce**—their father was no longer prepared to live with this web of family relationships. There is then no external obstacle to a change of mind on Yahweh's part. And Yahweh's continual "coming" to them (v. 2a) is the evidence that **mother** has not been finally abandoned and that Yahweh wants to re-establish the family relationship. The question is not whether Yahweh has finally abandoned them but why they are so unresponsive to that desire for reconciliation. Yahweh has the will and the power to take the action that is necessary to restore Ms Zion (vv. 2b–3).

Additional Notes §34

49:1–6 / R. N. Whybray rightly comments,

> in view of the fact that in the prophetical books generally the subject of speeches in the first person singular, when it is not Yahweh and not otherwise indicated, is normally the prophet himself, it is remarkable that this identification should have been contested in this case by so many commentators. (*Isaiah 40–66*, p. 135)

There are perhaps two reason for contesting it. Until the late nineteenth century, Christian interpretation saw it as a messianic prophecy. In some sense it is that, though it is remarkable that the only actual quotation from it in the NT applies it to Paul and his associates rather than to Jesus (see Acts 13:47). If the passage is the prophet's testimony, Paul's application of it fits rather well. Then, at the end of the nineteenth century, Duhm set the scholarly world on the wrong track for a century by declaring that this passage, along with three others, did not belong with the rest of chs. 40–55 and needed to be interpreted separately (see the comments on 42:1a). Along with those other passages, 49:1–6 then became contextless and impossible to interpret. There was no way of knowing who the "I" was. In following Whybray's commonsense approach to the "I" here, we should perhaps note another oddity about Claus Westermann's great commentary *Isaiah 40–66*, though it is one he shares with many other interpreters of these chapters. Near the beginning he declares that we know "practically nothing" about their author. "Only once, and even then only for a moment," in 40:6–7, does the prophet emerge from hiddenness. Otherwise "there is absolutely nothing in the nature of a direct allusion to the prophet" (pp. 6, 8). He can say this only because he follows Duhm in separating passages such as 49:1–6 and 50:4–9 from their context, and taking a passage such as 48:16b as an unintelligible accidental addition to the text.

49:7–13 / Although NIV links v. 7 with vv. 1–6, v. 7 and vv. 8–13 have in common that Yahweh speaks in both, whereas the prophet spoke in vv. 1–6. If v. 7 is a kind of response to vv. 1–6, that response continues in vv. 8–13. One indication of this is the opening phrase in v. 8, **This is what the LORD says.** Further words almost invariably qualify this in Isaiah 40–55 (as in v. 7, indeed); 45:14 is the only exception. The brief introduction is more understandable if it simply resumes that longer one in v. 7. The double structure of vv. 7–13 as a whole, then, parallels that of a passage such as 43:14–21.

NIV implies the view that God is now addressing the servant who spoke in vv. 1–6, and this makes good sense of some aspects of vv. 7–13. But the section begins simply "the LORD says" not "the LORD says to me," and it is difficult to make good sense of the whole on this view. The overlaps rather correspond to the overlap between the people's servant calling and the prophet's interim fulfillment of such a calling. More likely Yahweh is addressing the community.

NIV's translation of vv. 8–9a links with its understanding of v. 7, because it implies that the person addressed is the one who "restores," "reassigns," and "says." This is impossible if that person is the people, though it is almost as difficult to see how the servant of vv. 1–6 could "restore the land." More likely Yahweh is the subject of those verbs, and vv. 8–9a need to be translated along the lines of "I will make you to be a covenant for the people, restoring the land, reassigning its desolate inheritances, and saying . . . " (so, e.g., GNB, NEB).

49:23, 26 / The imagery of subjection and defeat may be less humiliating and repelling than it first looks. Joseph and Ruth bow with their faces to the ground before Jacob and Boaz (Gen. 48:12; Ruth 2:10), and licking the dust may then be simply another way of saying the same thing. C. C. Torrey (*The Second Isaiah*, p. 387) compares the recurrent "he kissed the ground before him" in *1001 Nights*. Consuming their own flesh and blood reverses both Lam. 2:20; 4:10, 21 and the metaphorical usage in passages such as Isa 9:12, 19–21. Here the metaphor suggests internecine strife or people rushing to their own death (cf. Eccles. 4:5).

49:24 / MT says "Can plunder be taken from a warrior or captives be rescued from a righteous one?" The righteous warrior might be Yahweh, or Babylon as the agent of Yahweh's judgment, or Persia as Babylon's conqueror. Vv. 24–26 as a whole suggest Babylon. Presumably assuming the last, NIV has made the singular into a plural and followed other traditions (see mg.) in reading "fierce" for "righteous" as in v. 25, rather than reckoning that MT's "righteous" is the "more difficult reading" (and therefore the more likely to be original), which these other traditions have instead assimilated to v. 25.

50:1 / The air of finality about 49:26 and the change of conversation partners in 50:1 are perhaps what led to the English chapter division here (there is no new chapter in MT). But the subject remains the same for 50:1–3.

§35 Four Wake-up Calls and a Departure Call (Isa. 50:4–52:12)

In 50:4 the subject suddenly changes again—in two senses. The grammatical subject is once again a human "I" rather than a divine "I," and the thematic subject is the pressure upon this human "I." In both respects the passage parallels 49:1–6, and it will emerge that 50:4–52:12 forms a sequence parallel to 49:1–50:4, analogous to double sequences we have noted earlier in chapters 40–55. The arrangement of sections is not as tightly parallel as in earlier instances, but the parallelism again means that the second sequence develops issues raised in the first. Here, as there, that involves discussion of the role of Yahweh's servant (50:4–11 as 49:1–6), but here the destiny of Zion and the way the destiny of the Babylonian community relates to it (51:1–52:12 as 49:7–50:3) receive more attention. The first subsection introduces a motif that runs through the section: there are four double occurrences of the verb "waken/awake" (50:4; 51:9, 17; 52:1). There is no reason to resist taking the obvious view that the "I" in 50:4–9 is the prophet, as in 40:1–6. Before the notion of "servant songs" sidetracked the interpretation of Isaiah 40–55, commentators could assume so.

50:4–6 / So, morning by morning, Yahweh wakens. Verses 4–9 do not explicitly identify "Yahweh's servant" as the speaker, though verse 10 implies that equation. The speaker's characteristic way of referring to God perhaps also implies this, for the title "sovereign Yahweh" is correlative to "servant of Yahweh." The expression forms a loose verbal link with 49:22. The title comes twice in the first subsection of this testimony, which also introduces the motif of awakening: **he wakens . . . wakens** (v. 4). Over the past two chapters (indeed over the past eleven) the prophet claims to have been exercising **an instructed tongue.** Here the relationship between God and prophet is more like that of teacher and pupil than that of king and messenger, though the end result is the same. One point about the analogy is the link with 8:16. The Poet is one of those "disciples": the word comes twice here, translated in NIV "instructed" and **one being taught.** The Poet is a "Second Isaiah," indeed (W. Grimm with K. Dittert, *Deuterojesaja;* Stuttgart: Calwer, 1990, p. 360). Perhaps the prophet literally received a new message from God on waking every day, in which case the vast bulk of these messages were not put into this book. More likely, the picture of being awoken every morning to learn is part of the metaphor of teacher and pupil. But it does function to make the claim that the teacher has consistently instructed the pupil. It also prepares the way for the further use of the "awakening" motif in chapters 51–52. The God who is in the awakening business also issues wake-up calls via the one who has been awoken.

We have been reading of the audience's loss of faith and hope. It is **weary** (cf. 40:28–31). The prophet's gift to sustain weariness is a **word,** the word that those foregoing chapters have expounded. This present testimony continues from that in 49:1–6, which spoke of the original divine summoning to this ministry. Here, 50:4–9 speaks of the ongoing divine resourcing. And the prophet has behaved like a model pupil, attentive to the Teacher's every word rather than resistant like the nightmare pupils who sometimes appear in Proverbs (v. 5).

The temptation to resist came from the cost that issued from attentiveness (v. 6). Someone disliked the message enough to attempt to silence the messenger. Now we have had plenty of indication that the community resisted the prophet's message, but its members have been characterized more as depressed and incredulous ("faint," indeed) than as actively hostile. Where we have read of hostility and aggression, it has been on the part of the community's Babylonian overlords. It is easy to imagine that their hostility should have become focused on someone who was encouraging the community to believe that Babylon's attacker was its deliverer.

50:7–9 / The title "sovereign Yahweh" comes twice more in this second part of the testimony. The language in verse 6 could have referred to formal or semi-formal official proceedings of arraignment, and that language continues here. Earlier chapters have put the Babylonians and their gods on trial and ridiculed them for their inability to offer any theological account of what was happening politically. Evidently it is possible to imagine the trial and the ridicule working both ways (we do not know where to draw the line between the literal and the metaphorical). But the prophet is sure of vindication. When the relationship between master and servant first appeared in 41:8–16, we noted that it suggested the security of the servant, who had the master's support. What applied there to the community applies here to the individual. That is one point about the recurrent "sovereign Yahweh." That God **helps me** (vv. 7, 9): the verb occurred three times in 41:8–16. The events that will bring the people freedom from Babylon will also bring the prophet vindication before Babylon. Incidentally (or perhaps consciously), this servant is modeling a stance in relation to Babylon and a confidence about Yahweh's imminent acts and their implications. The community as a whole has been invited to this stance and confidence.

50:10–11 / It is the third part of this "servant song" that refers to the **servant** rather than the sovereign. Presumably the testimony in verses 4–9 addresses the same audience in the Judean community, but only now does this become explicit. It is not immediately clear whether the speaker is Yahweh or the servant (or even a Disciple), though by the end the first seems most likely. The question who within the community are people who revere Yahweh hardly implies that the prophet accepts a situation in which some will do that and others do not. It is more likely that it implicitly challenges the whole community to be that kind of people, to take the stance the prophet takes.

The center of verse 10 reminds us once again of the descriptions of the community as people in darkness, their lives overwhelmed by calamity. The servant has modeled a response to that experience and challenges the people to imitate it. The very different **you** of verse 11 are the attackers who have been described in verses 5–9, who are also the attackers of the community as a whole. Presumably they are only rhetorically present. The warning to them is directly intended to be heard by, and to encourage, those they attack. The difference in the description of their fate in verse 9b draws our attention to the fact that both deal in metaphors. People who play with fire will find it turns back on them. The imagery will later develop into the notion of Gehenna, but it has not done so yet.

51:1–3 / Three times in verses 1–8 Yahweh bids the people to pay heed (see vv. 1a, 4a, 7a). Further imperatives follow each bidding, verbs urging them to look (vv. 1b–2 and 6) and then not to be afraid (v. 7b). It is those last urgings that at last bring out

that verses 1–8 are really a "fear not" oracle, like passages such as
41:8–16. These verses address a people afraid of the future and
afraid of their foes, and the verses offer the people reasons that
this fear can be overcome.

There might seem to be some irony about the opening description of them as people **who pursue righteousness** and **who
seek the LORD,** though there may be less than the English translation implies. "Righteousness" *(tsedeq)* is Yahweh's commitment to
do the right thing by Jacob-Israel—it is Yahweh's act of salvation
looked at from another angle (cf. v. 5), so "pursuing it" suggests
longing for that act of deliverance. Like the talk of being "far away
from *tsedaqah*" in 46:12, it is not a comment on the people's ethical
stance. Similarly, "seeking Yahweh" is not a general devotional religious activity but a pressing of Yahweh to act on their behalf (cf.
e.g., Ps. 40:16; 69:6, with the parallelism). The speakers are the
people who in 40:27 and 49:14 give expression to the conviction
that Yahweh has abandoned them. Those passages suggest that
the people are not necessarily pursuing and seeking in the firmest
of faith, and here both the need to call for their attention and the
nature of Yahweh's words in verses 1b–2 confirm that.

Initially, the challenge to look to the rock would suggest
looking to Yahweh. The people were born from this rock (Deut.
32:18). But it then emerges that here the rock is Abraham and the
quarry is Sarah. In a sense this makes little difference: the point is
that what Yahweh did with Abraham and Sarah is grounds for believing that Yahweh could do something similar again. The decimated community far off from the promised land is hardly in a
less promising state than a childless pair of old people who have
never been to that land at all. The promise of Ms Zion's comfort, the
renewing of her wasted city so that it becomes a garden city, and
the renewing of her population so that the lamenting people sing
and the absent people join in, reinforces the point that Yahweh is
able to do the seemingly impossible. Once more the promise presupposes that the destiny of the Judean community in Babylon
and the wasted city are two sides of one coin.

51:4–6 / Now comes the actual promise of Yahweh's
righteousness/salvation, a promise to **my people/my nation.** Before these verses are over they have promised not only that it will
come **speedily** but also that it will **last for ever** and **never fail.** The
assumption that these prophecies belong to the period just before
Babylon's fall would vindicate that word "speedily," and this will

have been one reason that this prophet's words were preserved when those of other prophets were not. With regard to the promise that this salvation will last for ever, we need to grant that 587 B.C. was not the last time Jerusalem fell and not the last time Yahweh's people suffered defeat, decimation, or scattering. On one hand we might need to infer that the promise concerns how things could be, but that as with other promises of God the people need to meet it with a trusting and committed response. Yet not every future reversal can be plausibly attributed to the people's own failure, so we may also need to trust that this is a promise expressing God's intent for Jacob-Israel's ultimate destiny—whether or not a particular generation finds it fulfilled. The fulfillment of the first promise (that deliverance indeed came, and came speedily), as well as the continuing survival of that people, are evidences that such a conviction is not just hope against hope and that we may dare trust this prophet.

The motif that unexpectedly dominates verses 4–6 and occupies the center of verses 1–8 as a whole is a reminder that all this relates to the world and not just to Yahweh's people. The arm that will bring down Babylon for Judah's sake will also thereby bring to the rest of Babylon's empire the beneficent results of Yahweh's ruling in world affairs. For them, too, the darkness of oppression will give way to the light of freedom. For them, too, hopes that have long seemed vain will be fulfilled.

In other words, the vision of 42:1–4 (and behind that, the vision of 2:2–4) will be fulfilled. Many of the words are the same as the ones that appeared there. **The law** is *torah,* teaching or revelation (see 1:10). **Justice** is *mishpat,* the kind of judgment that is good news because it means that Yahweh is acting authoritatively and decisively on your behalf (see 1:17). Once again **the islands . . . hope** for Yahweh, as in 42:4. These peoples **look to** Yahweh as Jacob-Israel "looks to" Yahweh (40:31, *qawah:* NIV "hope"). As Yahweh grants Jacob-Israel new strength, so these other peoples can face the dissolution of the world—the political world or the material world (cf. 41:1–7). The testimony in 49:1–6 reminded us that the nations remain central to Yahweh's concern, to the people's significance, and to the prophet's ministry. Like the church, in its everyday life Jacob-Israel has its focus on its own destiny and does not think about the world, and God goes along with that. That is part of accepting us as we are—in this case, with our narrow, self-centered vision. But from time to time God reminds the church of its significance and invites it to raise its eyes and take into account

God's concern for the whole world, and from time to time in these chapters God does the same for Jacob-Israel.

51:7–8 / The third exhortation to listen introduces a third description of the audience. They are people who know *tsedeq,* people who recognize Yahweh's saving intention, **who know what is right.** They are people who have received the revelation of Yahweh's purpose, or **law.** Once again, the fact that Yahweh has to bid them to listen hints at a certain irony in the description, and the exhortation that follows underlines the irony. These people who know about that purpose and claim to believe in it are actually as fearful as other peoples (again, cf. 41:1–7). So the passage comes to a climax with a reminder of the exhortation not to be afraid, and of the reasons for confidence (cf. 41:8–16). As the reminder of Yahweh's worldwide concern (vv. 4–6) takes up the concern of the testimony in 49:1–6, so this reminder of the possibility of standing firm under pressure also takes up the testimony in 50:4–9. The prophet has proved it is possible. The same theological considerations, the same promises, make it possible for them to stand firm as well. The argument from the future, the promise of what will be, complements the argument from the past found in verses 1–3.

51:9–11 / We can often look behind these prophecies and see the prayers Israel was praying, and that is so here. One characteristic feature of the people's prayers of lament is the charge that God seems to have fallen asleep and needs to wake up to its fate (e.g., Ps. 44:23–26). So here we find the urgent "wake up, wake up, arm of Yahweh!" The long years of Babylonian domination suggest a long sleep, and it is time Yahweh came out of it. Another recurrent feature of these laments is recalling Yahweh's past acts (e.g., Ps. 44:1–8). That recollection is painful because it owns the contrast with the present, but the very act of remembering also assumes the potential that the future holds. It affirms that God could act, because God has done so before—we are not asking for something beyond God's capacity. It says to the congregation, "God could do it" and to God, "You could do it." Here there is a similar recollection.

It begins with the slaughter of **Rahab,** taking up motifs from Middle Eastern creation stories. The Babylonian version of that story, called "When On High" (*Enuma Elish;* see *ANET,* pp. 60–72, 501–4) involves Marduk, the same person as Bel in 46:1, killing a rebel goddess called Tiamat and cutting up her body in order to use it as raw material for creating the world. In other versions of such stories, creation involves killing a monster (cf. Job 40–41; also St George and the dragon, and the Leviathan of Isa. 27:1). In yet other versions, creation involves gaining mastery of the tumultuous powers of the **great deep** (cf. Gen. 1:2). All that might suggest that verses 9–10a refer back to Yahweh's sovereign acts of power in creating the world. For the recollection of that exercise of Yahweh's power would indeed count as something to reaffirm that Yahweh could act powerfully and creatively in the community's present—a reminder for both God and people.

Yet the recollection in verse 10b clearly relates to Yahweh's act of power at the Red Sea, and that sends us back to re-read verses 9b–10a. There, too, Rahab was defeated (see 30:7). There, too, the **waters** were **dried up.** At the very least, verses 9–10 look at the creation event and the Red Sea event as pictures superimposed on one another. They are two analogous acts of power and love. In combination they offer even more powerful evidence that God can do what is now needed. The evidence no doubt encourages the congregation, but using it in a challenge addressed to God implies that it should also encourage God to gird up his loins and act. Verse 11 then affirms that God will, as it continues on from 35:10 as if to say, "You know that visionary, imaginative portrayal of Yahweh's act of deliverance and renewal and restoration? This is a moment when you will see it become reality."

But who speaks in verses 9–11? Commentators usually assume that this is the voice of the prophet urging Yahweh to wake up. But on both sides (vv. 1–8 and 12–23) it is Yahweh who speaks, and there is no indication of a change for verses 9–11. Now it might be that the prophet assumed that we would have the wit to recognize that verses 9–11 represent a human voice. But on the only other occasion someone says "Awake, awake" in the OT, she is speaking to herself (Judg. 5:12), and it would be typical of the Poet to use familiar speech in a creative way, having Yahweh recollect the events of the past and reflect that it is indeed time to wake up (in 42:14 Yahweh has already admitted to an inactivity that could look suspiciously like sleep). So instead of merely overhearing the prophet urge Yahweh to wake up, as they would themselves urge in their prayers, the people have the extraordinary encouragement of overhearing Yahweh determining to do so, and promising that the moment has come for the fulfillment of that picture chapter 35 portrayed.

51:12–16 / Here, then, Yahweh either responds to the urging of the people in verses 9–11 or, on the understanding just suggested, turns from letting people overhear a conversation within God to direct address. The considerations of verses 9–11 are now brought into relationship with the problem in the community's life to which verses 1–8 had once again spoken. They **live in constant terror every day because of the wrath of the oppressor.** Perhaps the Babylonians were more hostile to alien groups in their midst as Cyrus tightened his pincer around Babylon. That is often the dynamic of those circumstances. But perhaps much of the threat lay in the Judeans' imagination. Either way, they are bidden to remember:

(a) that Yahweh is their comforter (v. 12). "Comforting" may sometimes be a matter of words (as in 40:1), but more characteristically it also points to the actions that give substance to the words, and here that makes sense. To say "I am your comforter" is to say "I am your deliverer."

(b) that humanity is essentially transient (v. 12). The Babylonians are about to have their own experience of that, and the Judeans need to remember it and not fall into the trap of thinking that they have discovered the secret of eternal life. The fact that they knew their own grass-ness (40:6) ought to make that easier. Time is on their side, in the sense that Babylon's power cannot last.

(c) that whereas mortality is the problem their oppressors will not acknowledge, deliverance from death will soon be their own experience (v. 14).

(d) that their maker is also the world's creator and controls those dynamic and potentially destructive forces of creation that are also embodied in the destructive experiences that have come to the community (vv. 13, 15, 16).

(e) that Yahweh commissions and protects the people as well as the prophet (v. 16). It is a recurrent assumption that the prophet fulfills the role of servant only on an interim basis. The role belongs to the community. Recalling their commissioning and protection helps to make that point once again.

(f) that Zion is Yahweh's people, and that this fact closely links with the fact that Yahweh is the world's creator (v. 16).

51:17–23 / Throughout these prophecies in chapters 40–55, as far as we can tell nothing has changed. In outward circumstances the situation of the Judean community in Babylon and the situation of the city of Jerusalem remain the same. The Babylonians continue to be overlords. Indeed, they perhaps act in more oppressive ways. The city walls still lie in ruins. Yet in the prophet's mind everything has changed. God has declared that the moment of revolution and renewal has come. City and community have to start living as if that is so. This does not mean pretending that it is so, nor even living as if it is so in order to make it so. It means living in the light of the fact that it is indeed so, in the conviction that the rise of Cyrus is the evidence that it is so. Yahweh has uttered that wake-up call within the Godhead. Yahweh now utters the same call to Ms Zion.

Once again Yahweh's call reflects the content of Zion's laments, not least as we know them from Lamentations. In doing so, it suggests a series of self-portraits.

(a) I am a guest who has been poisoned (v. 17). At a celebration the host will share a cup of blessing with the invited company, but this cup has turned out to be poisoned. It makes the person who drinks it burn inside and collapse. For Yahweh's fury, compare for example, Lamentations 2:4.

(b) I am a mother who has been bereaved (vv. 18–20). Here the actual words of Lamentations 2:19 recur. In her vulnerability a mother needs her (grown-up) children to look after her. This mother has watched her children die or be deported. They too have drunk her cup of poison.

(c) I am a wife who has been abandoned (vv. 21–22). The one who speaks is your Lord. The precise form of the word occurs only once elsewhere in the OT, in Psalm 45:11, in words addressing a bride and describing her groom. Once more, Zion's husband is promising to come back.

(d) I am a slave who has been humiliated, perhaps raped (v. 23). Most of the occurrences of the verb "torment" come in Lamentations (e.g., 3:32, 33: NIV "bring grief/affliction"), though here the emphasis is on the human agents rather than on Yahweh's own tormenting.

First, then, Yahweh acknowledges the reality of these four portraits, not merely according to how Jerusalem felt but according to how things actually were. To acknowledge them is to move the relationship on, but it hardly does so enough. The basis for the call to wake up lies in the fact that the moment of reversal has now come.

Yet there is no positive portrait of that reversal—guest enjoying banquet, mother surrounded by children, marriage renewed, servant restored. Those images occur elsewhere, but here the focus is on the passing of the poisoned chalice to other people who will now stagger and fall. To put it another way, this passage correlates to chapter 47. Ms Babylon's fall terminates Ms Zion's subjection. The promise recalls the ending of Psalm 137. It would suit our post-Enlightenment liberal sensibilities if the passage did not suggest that one people's humiliation was the necessary correlate of another's restoration, but this expectation was true to events. On the other hand, the prophet will soon go on to envision an entirely different way of seeing the relationship between humiliation and restoration that has more far-reaching significance (see 52:13–53:12).

52:1–6 / The grounds for the preceding wake-up call were negative. The oppressor is being put down. Here are the correlating positive grounds. The converse of the picture in chapter 47 is clear. From the humiliation to which Ms Babylon goes, Ms Jerusalem rises in dignity and authority, to become powerful queen, sacred minister, and independent woman. If the **uncircumcised and defiled** are one group, as they sound, they denote Israelites rather than foreigners, for "defilement" is something that affects only Israelites, and Israelites can of course be metaphorically uncircumcised (e.g., Jer. 4:4; 6:10). Once again Yahweh declares that the time has come when puzzling inactivity is to come to an end, asking **"What do I have here?"** NRSV has "What am I doing here?" "What was I doing here?" might be better. Yahweh is finally recognizing that something must be done.

52:7–10 / For a long time Yahweh has been speaking and exhorting. Suddenly, the prophet is speaking and describing the coming of the reign of God. In vision (or rather "audition"), the prophet has heard **feet** racing across the mountains, the feet of a messenger bringing news of how a city's army has been faring. The prophet has heard the messenger declaring excitedly that the battle has been won, and (with that collapsing of time that happens in a film or a dream or a vision) has even heard the lookouts on the city's walls proclaiming that they can see the victorious king returning with the army (vv. 7–8). The prophet then commissions further proclamation from the very ruins of the city itself (v. 9a), responding to what has already happened in the vision (v. 9b), which will soon happen in history (v. 10). The image of Yahweh as creator or spouse or friend thus gives way again to the image of Yahweh as battling king, victorious warrior. But there is no actual description of this warrior. We hear tidings of the event rather than seeing it (as Ezekiel 1 describes Yahweh's throne and clothing rather than describing Yahweh's being).

The picture pairs with 40:1–11, and the two passages form a bracket around what lies in between, but these verses are also rich in their relationship with other Scriptures. They take the particular image in verse 7 from Nahum 2. The prophet declares, "You know that promise in Nahum? Its moment has arrived." The verses also take up the declaration in Psalms 98–99 that Yahweh reigns, and they declare that this is now a reality reflected in actual events. It has long looked as if Yahweh was not reigning. Events will now demonstrate that Yahweh is acting as king. When the NT in turn says of the significance of Jesus that the moment of God's reign has now come (e.g., Mark 1:15), it is thus continuing a process of using Scripture to illumine events as they happen. The restoration of the Judean community constituted a foretaste of the full implementation of Yahweh's reign rather than its final implementation, and the same will be true of the coming of Jesus. The foretastes give grounds for believing that completion will come.

52:11–12 / As in several preceding units, and in the very first of the Poet's words, Yahweh begins again with an urgently repeated command: "Get out, get out!" It is related to "Comfort, comfort" and "Wake up, wake up." Because Yahweh has heard the exhortation to awake and has acted to comfort the people, it is time for their awakening to become movement. The words repeat the bidding of 48:20–21. Yahweh is once again directly addressing the despondent ex-inhabitants, rather than the personified city. As their ancestors once left Egypt and their parents left Jerusalem, so they are to leave Babylon. In the manner of typology, the new event is like the earlier ones foreshadowing it but different and better. This is not merely a departure but a procession. It needs to make sure it avoids the stain which attached to the previous departure (cf. Lam. 4:15), and which for that matter in due course affected the people after their departure from Egypt when they soon made themselves images. And it is no hurried flight for safety but a procession under the protection of that victorious king of verses 7–10.

Additional Notes §35

50:4–9 / See, e.g., J. Calvin, *Commentary on the Book of the Prophet Isaiah* (trans. W. Pringle; 4 vols.; Grand Rapids: Eerdmans, 1948), vol. 4, pp. 52–60.

51:7 / There is a superficial clash between the description of the people as those who have Yahweh's *torah* in their minds and the assumption in Jer. 31:31–34 that a new act of Yahweh will be needed if people are to be like that, but the two passages are using the word *torah* in different ways. Jer. 31 is referring to the requirements of the covenant and to the conviction that the people need something new if they are to begin to live by them. Isa. 51 is referring to the teaching in this book concerning Yahweh's purpose for Israel and the nations, which the audience, at least at one level, knows well.

51:9–11 / For an insightful look behind these prophecies to the prayers that Israel has been praying, see Westermann, *Isaiah 40–66*, pp. 240–43.

51:15 / The description of Yahweh as one who **churns up** the sea is odd. Normally the sea churns on its own and Yahweh's power lies in quieting it (see v. 10; and e.g., Ps. 93). More likely the verb indeed means "stills" and the line describes Yahweh as one who "stills the sea when its waves roar."

51:17 / To be strictly accurate, the verb form differs from that in v. 9 (hitpolel rather than qal), but the difference is stylistic—rather like a move in English from "awake" to "wake up." The first form reappears in 52:1.

§36 A New Revelation of Yahweh's Arm (Isa. 52:13–53:12)

Like 48:20–21, the end of the previous section, 50:4–52:12, both suggested closure and questioned it. The comment about the impossibility of *shalom* which followed 48:20–21 led into the new twist to the servant motif in chapter 49. The point is less explicit at the end of 50:4–52:12, but the implication is again that not all the prophet's agenda has been handled. Everything is in place for the restoration of the community to Jerusalem and for the restoration of the city itself—but what of the community's morale and faith, its commitment and hope, and what of its servant calling that is now long-unmentioned? Once again there is a new twist to the servant motif, and once again its implications are worked out for the city (ch. 54) and the people (ch. 55).

This section begins with similar words to the ones that opened chapter 42 (NIV there had "here is my servant"). These are the two passages which describe rather than identify Yahweh's servant. Chapter 41 had identified the servant as Jacob-Israel, so the effect of 42:1 was to say "You know that servant I was just talking about? Well, here is a description of what is involved in being such a servant." There was then a tension between the content of the person-description and job-description and the identity of the servant. We might suspect that the already-appointed candidate was not up to the task, but having been appointed, it was not possible to be dismissed. Rather, the appointee needed to be enabled to grow into the job.

There are overlaps with the logic here in chapter 52. Again, preceding sections have identified Yahweh's servant. The Poet has told us about being appointed to fulfill the role, though in such a way as to make us also suspect that there is something interim about this arrangement. The original candidate still has the letter of appointment to the permanent post but may have forgotten where it was put. Once again, however, having told us who the servant is in 49:1–6 and 50:4–11, these chapters now tell us what is involved in being the servant. Once again, the third-person form contrasts with the form used when the servant was identified. In chapters 41–42 "you are my servant" led into "here is my servant." Here "I am Yahweh's servant" and "who obeys the voice of my servant?" (49:1–6; 50:4–11) leads into "here, my servant . . . "—though this time the prophet has indeed used the third person for self-reference in 50:10. This makes it easier to see 52:13–53:12 as describing the prophet-servant in the third person. But once again we are simultaneously invited to identify the servant and also not to do so. What follows contains elements that might have been suggested by the way the prophet's servanthood had worked out, as well as elements that might have been suggested by the experience of Israel, the original servant—but as a whole it fits neither of these. It goes beyond what we have been told of the prophet's experience, while the description in 53:2–9 is hardly a description of Israel.

Our puzzlement at the picture partly reflects the fact that "description" is too prosaic a word for it. What we have here is a vision. Admittedly any job description is a vision, a vision of what someone hopes and longs and believes needs to be achieved and could be achieved if the Archangel Gabriel applied for the post. It is also a vision in the more traditional sense. With the inner eye the prophet has seen something. A picture has come into the prophet's mind. It is a static scene, but a scene that forms a still from a movie. Indeed, the movie is still being made. The prophet hears the director describing where this scene belongs in the movie as a whole. Yahweh speaks of what will come afterward and also of what has preceded (52:13–15; 53:11b–12). Inside this explanation is a response by people who have witnessed the earlier events that the movie portrays (53:1–11a). This response speaks of what has already happened as well as of what is to come afterward, though it does so in the opposite proportions, with more focus on the past—appropriately, because only the director can speak with great confidence about future scenes.

Both voices describe not merely the externals of the action but its meaning. What they do not speak of is the story's reference—what in the "real world" this vision corresponds to. The internal meaning of the movie is clear enough. Who the movie is about is never explained. And off the set, as we have seen, the indications are ambiguous. As happens with movies and with visions or poems or psalms or prophecies, the effect is to invite the audience or congregation into the scene, so that we may discover for ourselves what it signifies for us and how it involves us. The Director is content for us to do that, prepared to take the risk that we do something odd with the scene, as the price of involving us. The Poet has to be content with the Director's doing that. When the poem is unclear about what it refers to, this does not mean that the Poet was not very skillful. The poem probably tells us all that the Poet knew (unless the Poet, too, thought that it would be best to hold some information back in order to make us do the work). A person who has a vision will often not know what it refers to. Its interpretation then has to come from someone else—perhaps the person who recognizes himself or herself in it. For Director and Poet, this vision/poem/job-description/person-description was perhaps the last shot in the attempt to break through to an audience that had half-shut ears and eyes.

The openness of the pronouns in the vision left it open for audiences to find their place in it. When subsequent generations of Jews looked at this scene, they found themselves in it, though they left the portrayal of exaltation for the Messiah. When the first Christians looked at this scene with the risen Christ, they knew that Christ had been the realization of this vision, and the vision then helped them to understand who he was. They also knew that it was God's vision for them (see, e.g., Phil. 2; 1 Peter 2:21–23). As is often the case with a vision or a poem, there is no need to limit it to only one such referent.

One way to understand the vision itself is as the correcting of a series of mistaken assumptions and convictions. In each set of three verses, the corrective statement comes first, after which we discover what the particular misapprehension was.

52:13–15 / First, then, is the assumption that this servant's humiliation is permanent. On the contrary, it is to be reversed. The nature of the servant's disfigurement in the vision is not explicit. The point lies in the assumption that someone who is Yahweh's agent will look the part (see, e.g., 1 Sam. 16:12; Ps. 45:2). Someone whose appearance is not merely unattractive but actually repulsive can hardly be Yahweh's servant. But this one will end up as exalted as God: with verse 13 compare 6:1 (D. R. Jones, "Isaiah—II and III," in *Peake's Commentary on the Bible* [ed. M. Black and H. H. Rowley; London: Nelson, 1962], p. 527). And he will end up acknowledged as who he is.

53:1–3 / The second mistaken assumption is that this servant could be ignored. On the contrary, he embodies the power of Yahweh. It is no longer Yahweh who speaks, though the identity of the "we" who speak in verses 1–11a is not explicit. It is hardly the nations and kings of 52:15, because they tell us that they had not heard a message, nor therefore had they delivered one. Nor does verse 1a fit on the lips of the prophet's community at present, because they had heard the message but had not believed in it and were therefore hardly in a position to lament general disbelief. Most likely it is a statement of the response to Yahweh's servant ministry that God is promising the people will in due course offer. But with this "we" the prophet also identifies with the community, as in verse 8b ("my people"; cf. 42:24, but also other phrases such as "our God").

Since we do not know for certain who speaks, as usual we must respect what the prophecy says and what it does not say. The point lies more in the content of the testimony than in who utters it. The vision witnesses to the truth of what Yahweh has just said. Those who speak were indeed initially aware only of this servant's unimpressiveness, insignificance, rejection, and hurt. Exactly why he was rejected is unstated, though the order suggests that he suffered because he was rejected rather than vice versa. His experience corresponds to the prophet's own experience as Yahweh's servant, rather than to Job's.

53:4–6 / The third incorrect assumption is that this servant was suffering as a consequence of his sin. On the contrary, he was experiencing other people's suffering when he did not need to. **Infirmities and sorrows** could suggest illness and the language here could imply that he was stricken by the kind of skin disease that Leviticus 13–14 discusses. But elsewhere (e.g., v. 7) the vision suggests that the servant's suffering came from the attacks of other human beings, and more likely this is also so here. The servant was maltreated and injured, wounded and **crushed**, attacked and violated. We assumed that this was God's punishment of him, but we have come to realize that this was not so.

One aspect of this is that he was sharing in our experience of being wounded and crushed for our wrongdoing—the kind of experience that Jerusalem's fall and the deportation to Babylon had brought. The implication is that there was no reason for him to do that—he did not deserve it. This in itself does not require that the servant suffered *instead of* the people. They also suffered, but they deserved it.

But verses 4–6 imply more than an undeserved sharing of the suffering that came to people in general. They imply an undeserved experience of suffering that other people did not experience. For there was another sense in which he suffered because of their rebellion. Their resistance to Yahweh made them attack Yahweh's messenger, whose message they believed to be false. He thus experienced **punishment** for the role he had to fulfill. The word "punishment" *(musar)* is not a legal one but suggests the chastisement of a child or a student by a parent or a teacher in order to teach a lesson. He gets beaten like a child or a student so that other people may learn from it.

The supreme significance of his going through what they went through as well as what they did not go through is thus that this **brought us peace** and healing (v. 5). We do not yet know how this happens, though the implication may be that watching him go through that somehow brings about a breakthrough of insight and thus a breakthrough of transformation. With the word *shalom* the prophet takes up the unresolved problem with which 48:22 closed. The speakers know their own transgression and iniquity (or at least the prophet knows it on their behalf). They know that their history up to the state's fall demonstrates an inclination to go their own way rather than to follow the direction Yahweh lays before them. They know that they are the kind of people for whom there is therefore no *shalom,* no peace or well-being or wholeness. They (or the prophet) now affirm that this servant is the key to their becoming that sort of people, and that this has come about through his being afflicted just as they were, but without deserving it.

53:7–9 / The next two realizations go beyond that. The fourth mistaken assumption is that nevertheless he was presumably as much a sinner as anyone else. On the contrary, he was extraordinarily self-controlled in word and deed.

There were Judeans who had been committed to Yahweh's ways who had nevertheless been inevitably drawn into the suffering of the state's collapse and the deportation to Babylon. Jeremiah is the one who is best known to us, and verses 7–8 follow Jeremiah 11:19. While Jeremiah was certainly no deceiver, he could not claim to be someone who kept his mouth shut. So the servant of this vision is like Jeremiah—only more so. Like Jeremiah he has been treated in a way that ignores regular standards of law. Unlike Jeremiah, he has eventually paid a price not merely in terms of deportation but in terms of death. Unlike Jeremiah, one of the devices designed to terminate his life eventually worked, and he has ended up with **rich** and **wicked** people (the term from 48:22) such as the ones who lost their lives when Jerusalem fell. Like Jeremiah, he has paid this price as a result of the ministry he sought to exercise to his own people, and like Jeremiah he has shown none of the deceitfulness of the well-to-do wicked leaders of Judah (see Jer. 5:27; 9:6–8). Unlike Jeremiah, he uttered no word of hostility or aggression in response to his treatment. Who is this man?

53:10–12 / The fifth assumption was that the servant was therefore a self-appointed martyr. On the contrary, his suffering came about by Yahweh's **will**. That immediately modifies two earlier observations. First, in a sense the people had been right all along when they inferred that Yahweh was bringing about the servant's suffering, and that this came about as a result of wrongdoing (v. 4b). Where they were wrong was in assuming that it was his own wrongdoing that he was suffering for. That people often suffer for their own wrongdoing is standard OT and NT thinking (e.g., 1 Cor. 11:29–30), but the story of Job shows that one must not assume this always to be the case. Second, even when people came to realize that he was taking up their sufferings and pains (v. 4a), they had not said all that needed to be said. Behind the servant's action (or passion) lay the master's will.

But what were Yahweh and the servant trying to achieve through this act of identification? The answer is that it constituted **a guilt offering,** though in detail the words here are difficult to construe. You offered a literal guilt offering when you had accidentally committed some infringement of Yahweh's rights or trespassed on Yahweh's domain. It was like a fine whereby you recognized this trespass and thus made recompense (see, e.g., Lev. 5–6). The passage presupposes that Israel's behavior that led to the collapse of the state and the deportation of its leadership had constituted a massive and deliberate such infringement or trespass. The offering system that Yahweh had ordained was not designed to cope with wrongdoing of that kind, but Yahweh was of course free to determine what would cope with it, and had determined that the servant's suffering would fulfill that function. The servant submitted himself to Yahweh in going through massive undeserved suffering in order to serve Yahweh. This would compensate for the massive affront to Yahweh constituted by the people's rebellious life in which they would not submit themselves or to serve Yahweh and therefore made themselves liable to the suffering they experienced.

We may well ask why Yahweh could not simply forgive the people, and whether requiring self-sacrifice on someone else's part to make this possible is not immoral. The vision's initial emphasis on the servant's initiative forms part of the answer. He was not a victim coerced into self-sacrifice but a person who offered himself. Another angle might be that Yahweh has been demonstrating such willingness to forgive for centuries and it seems to have got no one anywhere. People's willingness to take grace for granted has grown rather than diminished, and they have still not found *shalom*. Related to that is the fact that there is no such thing as simple, cost-free forgiveness. Forgiveness involves the wronged party's absorbing the cost of the offense instead of requiring compensation. That is what Yahweh has been doing over the centuries. Yahweh has always been offering a metaphorical guilt-offering in heaven. What the servant does is to externalize that, incarnating it before people's eyes. It is this that makes him the revelation of Yahweh's arm (v. 1).

To put it another way, **he bore the sin of many** (v. 12). The language is again that of Leviticus 5 (NIV renders "be held responsible"). So whereas people normally have to bear responsibility for their own wrongdoing, this servant has taken responsibility for other people's. He took up a role like that of the priests who bear the people's sins when they minister (Lev. 10:17), or like the goat in the Day of Atonement ritual that bears the people's sins away (Lev. 16:22), or like a husband who bears responsibility for his wife's guilt (Num. 30:15). Like the priests, he thus **made intercession for** the transgressors. And he was willing to take this initiative in the conviction that it might make the difference, might bring about the people's *shalom*, might be fruitful (vv. 10b–12a).

The statement that **my righteous servant will justify many** looks like a self-contradictory and scandalous one. The job of a servant of Yahweh such as a judge is to justify the innocent and to declare wrongdoers guilty. Perhaps the prophet refers to God's doing right by the needy in the sense of taking them to their destiny. This has been the meaning of such language in passages such as 45:25. Or perhaps an ellipse is involved here, the idea being that the righteous servant will bring about such a change in

people that they will be transformed and will therefore be able to
be treated as righteous rather than as wrongdoers. More likely the
idea is not that he will justify the wrongdoers but that he will
show the wrongdoers that he himself is indeed just (Westermann,
Isaiah 40–66, p. 267). The courtroom language links with verse 8 in
particular, but also with the implicitly legal context of the chapter
as a whole. The servant has been treated as a wrongdoer when he
was not, either by association with people who were guilty or in
the belief that he was himself a wrongdoer. He has accepted that
treatment, bearing their iniquities with them when he did not
need to do so (the language is the same as Lam. 5:7). But in
the end, the way he exercises his insight (**by his knowledge;** cf.
52:13a), in bringing about their *shalom* and healing, also brings
about his own vindication.

Additional Notes §36

52:13–53:12 / For an exposition of 52:13–53:12 as describing
the prophet, see, e.g., R. N. Whybray, *Thanksgiving for a Liberated Prophet*
[JSOTSup 4; Sheffield: JSOT Press, 1978], p. 25). Whybray assumes that it
must have been written by one of the prophet's disciples, but the last
time the prophet-servant was referred to in the third person (50:10) it
was the prophet who was speaking. I assume that God gave the prophet
this vision as a description of the prophet's own ministry and experience
(partly past, partly future), but that it also points up links with Jacob-
Israel's experience and calling.

For more on the openness of the pronouns in this vision, see
D. J. A. Clines, *I, He, We, and They: A Literary Approach to Isaiah 53*;
JSOTSup 1; Sheffield: JSOT Press, 1976.

52:15 / The usual expression would be "he will sprinkle [water
or whatever] over many nations." Only here is the recipient of the sprin-
kling the object of the verb. NRSV follows a speculative suggestion regarding another meaning of the verb ("startle") based on Arabic; cf. NIV mg. It
fits the immediate context better, though the sacrificial references later
make **sprinkle** less surprising here.

53:1 / The word for **message** means tidings that we hear, not a
message that we preach (cf. NRSV "what we have heard").

53:4 / **Infirmities** is the word for "injured" in 1:5. For **sorrows,**
NRSV has "diseases," but the word's regular meaning is pain (NRSV
renders the same word "suffering" in v. 3). Matt. 8:17 takes it to mean

"diseases," but NT use of OT passages does not always follow their precise or original meaning.

53:10 / The verb in the second line is unusual in this context and its form is ambiguous, so that the clause could mean "if you appoint his life/person a guilt-offering" (cf. mg. and NRSV) or "if he in person appoints a guilt-offering." NIV's paraphrase reflects how difficult the idea is that Yahweh would be addressed for this one clause, when elsewhere Yahweh is the speaker or is spoken of in the third person. Further, the key passage about the guilt-offering *('asham)*, Lev. 5–6, keeps using the word for life/person/self *(nephesh)* in connection with the guilt-offering: see, e.g., 5:15, 17 (NIV renders "a person"). This supports the understanding "he himself appoints a guilt-offering." But the meaning remains obscure. NIV's **though** is odd. The word usually means "if," and this leads more naturally into what follows.

53:12 / **Many** and **numerous** (NIV mg.) are more likely right, as this fits the use of the word for "many" elsewhere in the chapter. These are the people whose restoring to wholeness constitutes the fruit of his ministry.

§37 An Invitation to Sing (Isa. 54:1–55:13)

Once again a return to a focus on Ms Jerusalem follows the servant passage, as happened after 49:1–6 and 50:4–11. There were hints there that Ms Jerusalem's restoration was the correlate of Ms Babylon's humiliation in chapter 47. Chapter 54 is the systematic exposition of that theme. The prophet takes up five images of Ms Jerusalem which once again resume the themes of the people's prayers (we are like a childless and abandoned woman, the victim of angry abuse—literally, we are a battered and insecure city) before coming to a striking conclusion.

54:1–3 / First, the childless woman becomes a mother. How can you ask a woman who is unable to have children to sing with the joy of a mother (v. 1a)? Because the loss is about to be made abundantly good (v. 1b). Ms Jerusalem is about to be one of those mothers who has grieved over being childless for years and then conceives sextuplets with the aid of a fertility drug. She will be unable to stop talking to the TV cameras. In Israel's story, the motif of the childless woman who conceives against all the odds is an important one. The **tent** imagery gently underlines the reference back to the stories in Genesis. The people had their origins in that kind of act. It is tempting to believe that such acts of God belong only in the past, in the Bible, in the great days, but Yahweh has not stopped being that kind of God (cf. 51:1–3, though there Abraham is more in focus than Sarah). **More** is the same word as the "many" of 52:14, 15 and 53:11, 12, which suggests that the many for whom the servant has suffered are the many children of this elderly new mother. Verse 3b suggests a repetition of the story of Israel's original occupation of the land: **dispossess** is a key verb in Deuteronomy (e.g., 1:8, 21, 39).

54:4–8 / Next, the abandoned wife loses her shame. **Do not be afraid** is a familiar exhortation in these chapters, but characteristically the Poet now takes familiar words in a new direction. In a modern Western culture the image here would no longer work. The solution for a Western woman today who has had her husband walk out on her is to learn to be her own person, perhaps with the help of her sisters, and a man who has walked out in a fit of temper can by no means assume that he can walk back in. In a traditional culture, **reproach** continues to attach to a woman who could not hold onto her man. Yahweh speaks as if it were a case of walking out in a fit of temper, though other passages have made clear that there were deeper problems than that. Husband Yahweh could point to many reasons that his wife's behavior made walking out seem the only possibility. The assertion of power (**Maker, Almighty, Holy One, God of all the earth**) in verse 5 is all very well, but Ms Jerusalem knows what it is like to be on the receiving end of that power. It is not enough for those titles to be attached to the word **husband** (*ba'al,* literally "master" or "owner"): again, the picture presupposes a patriarchal understanding of marriage). They need to be attached to the word **redeemer,** that relative who has no power over you but does have a moral obligation to care about your welfare especially when you are in trouble. The word recurs in the last phrase of verses 4–8. Only here does it come twice in proximity.

But Yahweh wisely goes beyond that. In 47:6 Ms Babylon was criticized for lacking the womanly virtue of compassion. Here Yahweh claims this virtue in spades: **deep compassion, with everlasting kindness I will have compassion** (vv. 7–8). The implication is that Ms Jerusalem has grounds for asking some hard questions before having her man back, and Yahweh is anticipating those questions. So in the section as a whole, Yahweh has both given the impression of having behaved in the manner of a patriarchal husband and also made clear that this self-description does not do justice to all that Yahweh claims to be. In the light of her experience, Ms Zion perhaps looked at Yahweh as a "typical" patriarchal husband. Yahweh does not then behave like the average husband or wife in the aftermath of a marriage breakup, putting all the blame back onto the other party. Yahweh does not deny appearing to be like a patriarchal husband but also invites her to realize that there is a great deal more to all that Yahweh is.

54:9–10 / Now the victim of anger is reassured, "I won't do it again." Once more, a modern woman would have some reservations about such reassurances. This is exactly what abusive husbands say before resuming abuse. Yahweh seeks to win trust by several means. The first reaches behind the story of Abraham and Sarah to the story of the great flood. Yahweh can claim to have kept the oath taken there, and associates the commitment to Ms Jerusalem with that kind of commitment. It is from the flood story that the image of a **covenant** comes. Genesis might have described that as a covenant **of peace,** but it does not. In Isaiah, the word makes for another link with the description of the servant's work (see 53:5). Yahweh indicates the seriousness of this commitment to the people by the lengths to which the servant would go as the embodiment of Yahweh's power (53:1b). That might be another ground for Ms Jerusalem's not fearing that power (see on v. 5). Here the point is that it was a commitment that issued in well-being for the people, and Yahweh invites Ms Jerusalem to take that therefore as a reliable promise. In that context Yahweh once again reasserts **compassion** and **unfailing love** (the same word translated "kindness" in v. 8).

54:11–14a / The battered city is now splendidly restored. Yahweh continues a personal form of address but now speaks to the city and promises it will be rebuilt—in a different kind of stone. **Taught by the LORD** is literally "disciples of Yahweh." The word is the one that described the prophet in 50:4. This again makes the point that the prophet's position is designed to be one that is shared. The prophet models the people's vocation and promise. The fruit of their discipleship is *shalom* and *tsedaqah* (vv. 13b–14a): presumably it is this fruit that the precious stones signify.

54:14b–17a / Further, the oppressed city is securely protected. The fear of verse 4 reappears, and its deepest grounds become explicit. The person the city has had to fear is not a mere human attacker but Yahweh, and the security it needs is not merely safety from the likes of Babylon or Persia but security in relation to Yahweh. If it has that, everything else will follow. Without security in relation to Yahweh, all the physical security in the world will not matter. With security in relation to Yahweh, all the physical vulnerability in the world will get no enemy anywhere.

54:17b / The section from 54:17b to 55:13 concludes the work of the Poet with a series of climactic invitations and promises. Jacob-Israel and the Babylonian community were the main focus through chapters 40–48, though the poems began with Zion-Jerusalem and also subsequently reminded us of its importance. Through chapters 49–54, in contrast, the city Jerusalem has been the main focus, though the chapters began with Jacob-Israel and occasionally addressed the people in the plural (see 51:1–8). The Poet's work closes with a final address to the people in general, which thus pairs with 40:1–11. So while the initial concentration on Jerusalem gave way to a focus on Babylon, now the predominant Babylonian focus gives way to a concentration on Jerusalem.

It is in 54:17b that the prophet begins to address the people in the plural once more, instead of addressing the woman/city. This suggests that 54:17b is the introduction to chapter 55 rather than the close of chapter 54. In this introduction the prophet once again promises the people *tsedaqah*. We might also have expected a repeated promise of *shalom*, but the Poet typically surprises us with a different and better, more thought-provoking and faith-building link. Alongside the promise that all Ms Jerusalem's children will be Yahweh's disciples, like the prophet, is the promise that all will enjoy the fruits of being Yahweh's **servants**, like the prophet. In its last appearance in chapters 40–55 the word "servant" is plural, making explicit that this is a position that belongs to people in general and is not to be confined to a prophet any more than to a priest or a king. **Declares the LORD!**

55:1–5 / The community is longing for nourishment, for upbuilding, for the restoration of morale, for a conviction that it has a future. The prophet knows that the message of chapters 40–55 is the one that will meet its needs, and here he makes one last appeal to it to come for that nourishment. It is not clear whether verse 2 refers to literal expenditure on other religious resources such as the making of images, or whether its language is simply part of the detail of the picture that is not to be pressed.

Verses 3b–5 sum up the content of the message. Once God had made a covenant with David, that famous servant of Yahweh. Other prophets promised that this commitment to David would find expression in the re-establishment of the Davidic monarchy, and periodically something like this happened. It happened in the period after the Maccabean crisis in the second century B.C., and Christians saw an expression of this fulfillment in the fact that the world's deliverer came from David's line. The Poet takes a different tack. As Psalm 89 points out, Yahweh had not kept the promises to David. But these promises will be fulfilled not in another individual David, but in the life of the Davidic people. That, after all, was God's intention from the beginning. Having kings was

God's second-best according to 1 Samuel 8–12, and God has now been proved right as monarchy has been discredited. It is another way of expressing the promise that the people will fulfill the role of Yahweh's servant.

55:6–13 / Now, therefore, is the time when Yahweh will act. The people can have that future only if they turn to Yahweh for it, and face up to their being **the wicked** who otherwise have no *shalom*. The verses that follow will indicate that the logic of this statement is different from what we might at first expect. The expression "seek Yahweh" refers to prayer for Yahweh to act (in 31:1 NIV translated this verb *darash* as "seek help from"). It is thus paralleled by **call on him.** The characteristic form that **wickedness** takes in chapters 40–55 is resisting the message about how Yahweh intends to restore the exiles and the land, and it is this resistance that the people need to turn from.

Logic is involved here. The word **for** follows four times in verses 8–13 (NIV omits it in vv. 9, 10, and 12: cf. NRSV, and see Additional Notes on 1:29–30). Three assertions are involved. All are familiar. First, Yahweh's way of running the world and fulfilling a plan for it is indeed very different from the one that the Judean community would have adopted (vv. 8–9). They would never have worked through Cyrus. They are going to have to give up their perspective and work with Yahweh's. Second, on the other hand they can be sure that Yahweh succeeds in fulfilling a plan (vv. 10–11). Once Yahweh's mind is made up and spoken, things happen. These two verses form a bracket with 40:6–8 around chapters 40–55 as a whole. Third, that means there can be joy and *shalom* for the listeners (vv. 12–13), not least because the renewal that the land will enjoy will ever stand before the world and before Yahweh as a reminder that the land is never to be devastated again.

§38 Back in Palestine: Yahweh's Vision for an Open Community (Isa. 56:1–8)

We have come to another transition point in Isaiah, and to the opening of its last major section, traditionally known as Third Isaiah. The work of the Ambassador and the Poet give way to the work of the Preacher, whose account of being anointed for this task comes in the central chapter in 61:1.

So far chapters 1–33 have focused on Yahweh's dealings with Judah during the latter part of the monarchy. They have challenged Judah about the religious and social failings of its life. They have warned it about calamity to come but promised restoration beyond that. Chapters 34–39 then prepared the way for a message that focuses more on encouragement than warning. In a context of calamity, chapters 40–55 sound a note of hope, even though the people found the message of Yahweh's deliverance as implausible as the message about calamity. What happens next?

It is usually reckoned that these last chapters in the book relate to a period later than the work of the Ambassador and the Poet. They imply a setting back in Palestine, and it is assumed that this is the Persian period, when Cyrus had completed his conquest of the Middle East. If the setting of chapters 40–55 is the Judean community in Babylon, then no doubt the Poet would have been among those who returned to the land in the process that began after the fall of Babylon (see Ezra 1), even if this necessitated crawling the whole way on broken glass (as someone has put it). Perhaps chapters 56–66 include some of the Poet's further work and/or some prophecies from Isaiah himself. But the fact that they manifest similarities with the work of both the Ambassador and the Poet may rather suggest that these later chapters are the work of a prophet or prophets who are heirs to both these earlier figures. They continue their work, and sometimes preach on texts from them. They discuss how to live with the Ambassador's challenges (you must do right) and the Poet's promises (Yahweh will do right).

56:1–3 / The first eight verses of chapter 56 present Yahweh's vision for an open community and put the combined message of chapters 1–55 into a nutshell (see "The One Book" in the Introduction). Yahweh is responsible for doing right by Israel, but Israel is responsible for the rightness of its own life. So what does maintaining **justice** and doing **what is right** look like? The answer would surprise the Ambassador and the Poet. It means observing the **Sabbath,** and welcoming into the community **eunuch**s and **foreigner**s who do so.

There has been one reference in previous chapters to sabbath, one to foreigners, and one to eunuchs. Sabbath observance was mentioned in order to be attacked (1:13). The attack was based on the sabbath's being observed in a religious way, as if it had an importance independently of a commitment to right living in society. We can contrast the social concern with the sabbath in Amos 8:5 and Jeremiah 17:19–27. Here the issue is different again, for the sabbath has become a mark of Jewish distinctiveness (cf., e.g., Ezek. 20; Neh. 13:15–22). It is the very mark of "holding fast to Yahweh's covenant" (vv. 4, 6).

So foreigners and eunuchs who accept this discipline are taking on the marks of Jewish distinctiveness and ought to be welcomed into the congregation. There is again a contrast with the one earlier reference to foreigners in 2:6 (NIV "pagans"), where the community is attacked for associating with them. There is also a contrast with the stance of Zerubbabel and Jeshua (Ezra 4) and later of Ezra and Nehemiah (Ezra 10; Neh. 9:2; 13:23–30) from the same period as the prophecies in Isaiah 56–66. The passage contrasts with Deuteronomy 23:1–8, too, and it perhaps pictures eunuchs and foreigners asking whether that regulation really does exclude them. They are told that Yahweh is now abrogating its requirement (Westermann, *Isaiah 40–66*, p. 313). In Deuteronomy and in Ezra and Nehemiah the stress lies on safeguarding the purity of the community, and some of these books' concerns in this connection will reappear in 57:3–13. Nevertheless the prophet affirms that a different attitude is required, and a preparedness to take a risk, when foreigners provide evidence of committing themselves to Yahweh (cf. 14:1; Zech. 2:11; 8:20–23).

56:4–5 / Eunuchs were previously mentioned only once (39:7); in this reference they are a symbol of the terrible fate of the whole Judean community. In their maimed-ness they fell short of the human wholeness that was God's ideal, and in their incapacity to beget children they could make no contribution to the future of God's people. But God welcomes them.

So eunuchs, whose name would die out, are promised that in the very house of God their name will never die out. The words take up 55:13. Perhaps their **memorial** is a literal one (cf. 2 Sam. 18:18), but perhaps the idea is that they will always be in God's mind there, which more than makes up for their memory's not being perpetuated in their children. The prophet's stance might suggest a different approach to the pain of childlessness from ones that prevail in modern societies.

56:6–7 / And foreigners have an assured place in the enthusiastic worship of that house. They indeed enable it to be what Yahweh intends, not a house where Israelites alone are welcome, but one open to all peoples. This does not mean that Yahweh is going back on the commitment to the descendants of Abraham. At its center, the community continues to be ethnically based. A confessing community has not replaced it, as Westermann suggests (*Isaiah 40–66*, p. 314). But Yahweh is also fulfilling that other implicit commitment to restore blessing to all peoples through their association with the descendants of Abraham. This welcoming of foreigners is also a response to Solomon's prayer at the original dedication of this house of God (1 Kgs. 8:41–43).

56:8 / This has implications for the community itself, for it relates to promises Yahweh made to Israel. Yahweh is fulfilling a commitment to restore the surviving Judeans (see 11:12) but is also reaffirming the commitment that goes beyond that, expressed in promises made in 2:2–5 and developed in chapters 40–55 (see also 1 Kgs. 8:41–43). There, we have noted, the promise of the coming of the nations may have been primarily designed to encourage the depressed Judean community. Here the promise focuses more on the way that this is good news for foreigners themselves. Judeans might be inclined to be offended at Yahweh's openness to such people, or inclined to wonder whether Yahweh can fulfill this commitment when the smaller commitment of bringing Judeans themselves back remains unfulfilled. If so, verse 8 reminds them that the one who speaks is the **Sovereign** Yahweh.

Additional Notes §38

56:1–8 / In the commentary we note the difference between the attitude to outsiders here and in books such as Ezra and Nehemiah. In *The Dawn of Apocalyptic,* P. D. Hanson expounds the view that the key to understanding Isa 56–66 as a whole is its background in conflicts within the Jerusalem community (rev. ed. [Philadelphia: Fortress, 1979], pp. 32–208). These chapters represent one party over against another as is seen in books such as Ezekiel, Haggai, Ezra, and Nehemiah. This involves huge amounts of guesswork as to the concrete dating, background, and reference of the material in chs. 56–66, and in general Hanson does not overcome this difficulty. In 56:1–8 in particular, the problem is that the prophet's view of temple and sabbath rather resembles that of the alleged "other side" (see B. Schramm, *The Opponents of Third Isaiah* [JSOTSup 193; Sheffield: Sheffield Academic Press, 1995], pp. 115–25; more generally G. I. Emmerson, *Isaiah 56–66* [Old Testament Guides; Sheffield: Sheffield Academic Press, 1992], pp. 81–97 and her references).

56:2, 6 / Keeping the sabbath and refraining from evil might sound like two requirements. The same is true of keeping the sabbath and holding fast to the covenant. But parallelism suggests that it is more likely that v. 2 refers to keeping the sabbath and refraining from evil (i.e., work) on the sabbath (cf. 58:13–14), and that v. 6 suggests that keeping the sabbath is a sign of holding fast to the covenant.

56:5 / **A memorial and a name** is *Yad Vashem,* the phrase that provided the name for the holocaust memorial in Jerusalem.

§39 Critique of the Community (Isa. 56:9–59:8)

While there are positive notes throughout 56:9–59:8, the dominant tone is confrontational, and even the positive notes incorporate barbed comment. The way the passages speak of *shalom,* which occurs six times (57:2, 19, 21; 59:8), sums up this point. This distinctive concentration of references finds its closest parallel in Zechariah 8, which again belongs to the same period as Isaiah 56–66. Admittedly there are no specific indications of a particular context here, and the material reminds us of Isaiah 1–12. It thus expounds something of the nature of "justice" and "right" (56:1). At the same time, the concern with *shalom* is not the only reappearance of a theme from chapters 40–55. The material takes up issues from both chapters 1–39 and chapters 40–55.

56:9–12 / The invitation in verse 9 recalls Jeremiah 12:9. It is perhaps an ironic one, as the nature of the closing statements in 57:1–2 may suggest. The point about verses 10–12 is that those who ought to act as lookouts for the community (people such as prophets and priests) are failing to do so and are therefore leaving the community vulnerable to attack. They were supposed to act like watchdogs who would warn of the approach of animals such as wolves and lions that could kill a village's sheep, but instead they are like dogs who are interested only in eating and then lying about in the sun sleeping. When robbers arrive, they wag their tails in welcome instead of barking. As lookouts, the community's leaders are **blind.** No more conclusive disqualification can be imagined. It is a strange fact that God's people regularly entrusts its destiny to a body of leaders and that these leaders consistently manifest blindness and an inclination to self-indulgence. The focus on blindness and self-indulgence also recalls Haggai 1, Malachi, and Nehemiah 5, which also originasted in Jerusalem during the Persian period.

The reference to the lookouts recalls 52:8, the only other occurrence of the word in the book (though see also 21:1–12, where the words are slightly different). In the present context, the charge of blindness recalls 42:18–19. The promise of 29:18 and 35:5 has not yet been fulfilled—certainly not with regard to the community's leaders. Their blindness includes the assumption that the indulgence of today will continue tomorrow. So the community's leaders are no more capable of living up to their job description or to the vision of passages such as 52:7–10 than the leaders who appear in chapters 1–12. The talk of lookouts and **shepherds** also recalls Ezekiel 33–34, where the prophet described his own role as lookout, and expounded Yahweh's promise of a shepherd worthy of the name. Neither aspect of Ezekiel's vision is being fulfilled in this leadership.

57:1–2 / The nature of their blindness is further expounded (vv. 1–2) and the theme of lack of understanding (56:11) is taken further (57:1). There is no word for **it** in verse 1: what **no one** takes to **heart** or **understands** is that the **righteous,** the **devout, those who walk uprightly,** are actually fortunate to **perish.** Why they perish is not explicit here, though we might have guessed the explanation from earlier passages in chapters 1–12, and 59:1–8 will soon confirm that the problems are the same as those described there.

A comment about the righteous perishing would often be part of a lament. The point here is that those who die thus escape the calamity that is to overcome the rest of the community. It is evident to anyone that death means the end of striving and pain. In death they will find **rest** and *shalom.* The living would be wise to envy them. The sentiments recall those of Ecclesiastes, though the basis here lies not in the inherent meaninglessness of human life but in the trouble that is to come on the community.

Although the opening line of 56:9 was ironic, then, it nevertheless bodes ill. The community is in terrible danger (in what way, we do not know). And no one has the insight to see.

57:3–4 / This attack on Israel's attachment to traditional religion extends to verse 13. It recalls those in chapters 1–12 and continues those that appear in Jeremiah, but is apparently quite separate from that which preceded. Presumably it indicates (as we might expect) that the worship of the period of the monarchy has continued through the sixth century B.C. into the period when some Judeans have returned from Babylon. Chapters 40–55 have suggested that the Judeans in Babylon were no more inclined to the Yahwism of the prophets than were their parents and grandparents. But the portrait here may suggest different issues from those that images in chapters 40–55 raised about worship. It may be that the prophet is attacking people who had stayed in Judah, not people who had returned from Babylon. Such people acknowledged Yahweh but did not accept the prophet's understanding of what this involved. The prophet may be trying to warn people who have returned from Babylon not to become attracted to this false form of Yahwistic religion.

Sorcery involves seeking guidance by studying the movements of the planets or other things that might be "signs" of something (the word for sorcery was translated "divination" in 2:6), and trying to do something to prevent the fulfillment of threatening signs. Children **of a sorceress** is an idiomatic way of saying "people given to divination" (cf. 1:4 and 47:12–15 for Babylon's equivalent). The phrases in parallelism indicate what is wrong with divination. Yahweh had given Israel ways of finding guidance and protection. To indulge in the traditional ways practiced by the other peoples of their land was to make themselves "people given to adultery and unfaithfulness," perhaps in two senses. They were being unfaithful to Yahweh, and they were also involved in sexual rites. They were apparently mocking the narrow stance of the group with which the prophet identifies. In turn, the prophet sees them as "people given to rebellion and falsehood" (again the references to **brood/offspring** are idiomatic expressions to suggest the people's characteristic nature). For all the talk of Yahweh's being willing to forgive rebelliousness (e.g., 44:22; 53:5, 8, 12), if the people persist in it, that willingness will get them nowhere. They are still taking refuge in gods who are a lie (cf. 28:15; 44:20).

57:5–9 / The details of their worship become more explicit in verses 5–9a. This worship involves the same elements as worship of Yahweh—**drink offerings, grain offerings, sacrifices,** the erecting of **symbols** (the same word occurs in Zech. 6:14), anointing with **olive oil** and the use of **perfumes,** and recourse to a shrine on a **high and lofty hill** surrounded by trees. But they are set in a very different context. First, the people's worship involves sexual rites of some kind (vv. 5a, 7, 8). We do not know what these rites were. They might be the ceremonial union of priest and priestess as an acted prayer for fertility in the community and in the land, or they might be the ceremonial union of priest and young girl. The worship also involved child-sacrifice in a valley outside Jerusalem, sacrifice offered to Molech and thus trafficking with Sheol itself (vv. 5b–6a, 9). Child-sacrifice was not a frequent practice, but it was undertaken at moments of great pressure as a sign of special devotion.

57:10–13 / Verses 10–13 form the closing bracket around the material beginning in verses 3–4. They do not describe the rites but evaluate them in a way that again recalls earlier evaluation in the book. These rites add a tragic irony to the note of unfaithfulness, rebellion, and falsehood. They cost great effort, and all to no avail, though people never recognized the dead end they were at (v. 10; cf. 47:13–15). The ironic closure also parallels the ironic closure of the previous paragraph in verses 1–2 but, typically, it sharpens the point. It is explicitly Yahweh who speaks in verses 3–13 (in 56:9–57:2 this was not explicit). It is thus Yahweh who wonders why they have such awe for other deities (cf. 8:11–22) and have been unfaithful to Yahweh without worrying about it, why "you have not thought about me or taken me to your heart" (v. 11; the expression parallels v. 1). Admittedly Yahweh can guess the answer, acknowledging the long silence that characterized the time of Judah's desolation and that continues despite 42:14 (cf. 62:1; 64:12). But evidently that gives no excuse for recourse to those useless alternatives, and it is unwise to assume that silence will continue for ever. Yahweh will "proclaim" their **righteousness** (to give the verb its usual meaning; NIV **expose**). That so-called righteousness consists in these same religious observances, which contrast with the righteousness of those who perish (v. 1) and will get the people nowhere (vv. 12–13a). The assessment is the same as that of the people and images of Babylon (41:16, 29).

The closing promise (v. 13b) recalls those made to the Babylonian community in 49:8 and 54:3 and to the eunuch and foreigner in 56:7. The audience has to make a decision for Yahweh if it is not to lose its share of the land, to people who might seem to have much less right to it, in the course of settling for a different **portion/lot** (v. 6).

57:14–21 / Again the language recalls the Poet's words (see 40:1–11), but these verses carry a slightly different meaning. The Poet had begun with Yahweh's uttering a repeated command to unidentified agents. **Build up, build up** corresponds to that earlier "comfort, comfort." It corresponds not merely syntactically but also in its implications for the people. And the actual verb for "build" is the one from which the word "highway" (40:3) comes. Back there an unidentified voice commissioned unidentified addressees to prepare the way for Yahweh to return to the people and/or to Jerusalem. **Remove** is the verb translated "lift up" in 40:9. Here an unidentified voice commissions unidentified addressees to prepare the way for **my people**—so the voice is actually Yahweh's own. Where does the **road** lead? Back to Jerusalem? Or back to Yahweh? Or might this be the way *to* my people (cf. the "way to Horonaim" in 15:5), which would fit with what follows?

For 56:9–57:13 has suggested that the obstacles between Yahweh and the community are now greater rather than smaller than they were in the previous chapters. In some circumstances (e.g., Exod. 32), Yahweh's response is to determine to cast them off. Here the response is rather to redouble commitment to them. Yahweh is intent on reconstructing the way for them or to them. Yahweh speaks as the **high and lofty One** of 6:1 (NIV "high and exalted"; cf. also 52:13, where the words are similar). To underline this divine transcendence the prophet adds that Yahweh **lives forever**: "lives" is the expression translated "dwells [on Mount Zion]" in passages such as 8:18. The verb eventually produces the word *shekinah*, which expresses the idea that the Dwelling of God is really known on earth even if this must be so in a way that does not imply that God has left heaven. But the prophet uses this homely expression in order to stress God's transcendence as the one who lives forever (NRSV "inhabits eternity"), **whose name is holy** (again we recall ch. 6). Yahweh's very nature is that of the awesome and transcendent one.

Yahweh's own opening words underline the solemnity of this introduction: literally "I live [the same verb] on high and holy." But then the logic somersaults: "but also with those who are crushed and humbled in spirit." The description of these people as "crushed" is the description of Yahweh's servant in 53:5, 10, and this implies a basis for the extraordinary statement that Yahweh is making. NIV's **contrite** obscures the point: the word means the people are objectively crushed, whether or not they have therefore come to feel penitent. One might have thought that Yahweh would be interested in conversation only with people who were equals, with other people of power and influence, of breadth of vision and length of experience, but this turns out not to be so. That servant passage has already affirmed Yahweh's involvement with someone who was crushed, and this promise reaffirms it. Not only does Yahweh turn the crushed person into an exalted one

(52:13; 53:5). As the exalted God, Yahweh associates with the crushed person. The "humbled" then are people who are in no danger of pretending to an exalted-ness to which they have no right. Humiliation has been the destiny of people who behaved as if they were majestic like Yahweh (e.g., 2:9, 11, 12, 17; 5:15; 10:33). It is the same word that the Poet used for the "putting down" of obstacles to the "way" of 40:3–4. If these people were ever inclined to pretend to exalted-ness, life has removed that possibility from them.

Yahweh associates with the crushed and humiliated in order not to leave them there (v. 15b). When someone has been wronged, it is easy for the awareness of that injustice to possess the whole being. Resentment then smolders on interminably. Another upside to Yahweh's having flares of temper is that Yahweh thereby gets the negative feelings out and finished with, and thus opens up the possibility of the relationship's moving forward again (v. 16a). Yahweh's wrath is like rain in Southern California, not rain in Manchester, England. It is not designed to overwhelm (v. 16b): **grow faint** is a word mainly used of people's reaction to calamity (Ps. 61:2; 77:3; 107:5; 142:3; 143:4), not least Jerusalem's fall (Lam. 2:11, 12, 19).

Here **greed** (v. 17) is the particular feature of Jerusalem's life that enraged Yahweh and led to the city's fall. It was especially a feature of the city's leadership, and it led to other wrongdoing on their part (Jer. 6:13; 8:10; 22:17; Ezek. 22:13, 27). Verse 17 is Yahweh's reflection on the preceding century. Sin led to anger and punishment, but this got no one anywhere. The people have **kept on in** their **willful ways.** Perhaps the greed of the past is mentioned here because it is the feature of their present life that most enrages Yahweh now (once again especially on the part of the powerful, see 56:11; NIV "gain"). Like the Poet, the Preacher therefore concludes that Yahweh had better try mercy rather than punishment (vv. 18–19).

The trouble is that Yahweh has tried mercy before, and verses 20–21 imply recognition of the dilemma. The fact that there are no explicit historical references in these chapters draws our attention to the fact that this is an ongoing issue, not one confined to the particular moment in the sixth or fifth century B.C. Nor does subsequent history seem to have led to any progress with this dilemma. God still wrestles with it.

Verses 14–21 are not merely a comforting moment in the context of the generally solemn section that runs from 56:9 to 59:8.

They paint in technicolor Yahweh's promise, commitment, condescension, and mercy, but they conclude with reiterated warning. None of that theology avails for people who continue to number themselves among **the wicked**. The fact that they cannot stop generating sludge means there can be no *shalom* for them. Such are the people the prophet is addressing. We have made no progress since 48:22.

58:1–9a / Chapter 58 deals with two aspects of misunderstanding of devotion, first the misunderstanding of fasting. Again the Preacher picks up the Poet's words from 40:1–11 but uses them in a new way and takes them in a new direction. Yahweh again commissions someone to **shout** (cf. 40:2, 6: NIV "proclaim/ cry out"), to **raise your voice** (cf. 40:9: NIV "lift up"), but this proclamation is to be even louder, **aloud** (literally "with your throat") and **like a trumpet** (recalling Hos. 8:1). Once again Yahweh declares **do not hold back,** but to a different end from the declaration in 54:2. There is to be another announcement **to my people.** The imperative **announce** last occurred in 48:20, where it concerned Yahweh's redemption of the servant Jacob, but this time the verb does not suggest comfort. In keeping with the present context, once again it concerns **rebellion/sin** (the words now recall Mic. 3:8).

The people have assiduously responded to the invitation of 55:6: **day after day they seek me out.** They are **eager to know my ways:** there is a marked contrast here with 42:24 and 55:8–9. So they look like **a nation that does** *tsedaqah* **and has not forsaken the** *mishpat* **of its God.** NIV takes the edge off the tragedy and the irony and lets modern readers off the hook with its repeated **seem,** which is not present in the Hebrew (contrast NRSV, though its "as if" has something of the same effect). The word "seem" suggests that the people were insincere. The prophet does not say that. They were keenly committed people. The trouble was that they were blindly so.

As happened in chapter 56 (where *tsedaqah* and *mishpat* recur, though with different meaning), the prophet thus begins with a general challenge but then particularizes it in a way that may surprise us because it focuses on an aspect of devotion. This is not what we might think of as a major ethical issue. Like the Poet, the Preacher starts from a question that the people have been pressing on Yahweh, and then reverses the direction of the challenge.

The people's question concerns **fasting.** Yahweh's response is to note that their fasting is accompanied by self-indulgence: the phrase **do as you please** (v. 3) involves that word translated as **seem eager** (v. 2). They delight to seek Yahweh, but they also delight to do what they like, even on a day when they are fasting.

When people do not eat, it can have various significances. When people are bereaved, for instance, a natural reaction is to lose interest in food. Fasting sets such an instinct in a religious setting. If we are really grieved about something that God has done, then we would expect to lose interest in food. Conversely, not eating would be a sign that we are so grieved. After Jerusalem's fall and through to the later part of the sixth century B.C., at least, people naturally thus fasted on various occasions to mark their desolation at the city's desolation (see Zech. 7:1–3; 8:18–19). But God seemed to take no notice (v. 3). The city remained unrestored.

The problem was that some of those who sought Yahweh also treated ordinary people badly, and for Yahweh the seeking and this behavior clash (vv. 3b–5). Evidently the prophet again addresses the powerful people in the community. They would be in a position (for instance) to employ people to take part in the harvest in the way described in Ruth 2. Like many employers in modern societies, both in traditional and developed countries, these powerful people assumed that their relationship with their workers gave them the right to treat them like animals. They cannot expect to do that and also expect God to hear their prayer.

Fasting is supposed to be an act of self-denial (v. 3a), so it should be a genuine one. These employers are inclined to treat people like beasts of burden, tied down and tied up. Instead, let them set these people free. When bad harvests lead to poverty, they are inclined to further victimize their own people. They use the situation to gain for themselves cheap land and cheap labor and they allow the poor to forfeit their land, their homes, and their freedom. Rather, they should **share** their resources with these people (vv. 6–7). That, not fasting, is the key to having Yahweh restore them as a city and nation (v. 8a). That is also the key to having Yahweh fulfill those promises in chapters 40–55 (v. 8b): for **righteousness** see, for example, 51:1, 5, 7; for Yahweh's **glory** appearing, see 40:5; and for Yahweh as **rear guard,** see 52:12. And that is the key to making Yahweh inclined to **answer** their prayer (v. 9a).

As well as taking up the promises of the Poet, the Preacher thus takes up the challenges of the Ambassador. Isaiah had begun by declaring that demonstrations of enthusiastic worship impressed Yahweh not at all when commitment to the needy did not accompany these demonstrations. The Preacher declares that this truth extends to demonstrations of self-humbling and self-denial.

58:9b–14 / Verses 9b–12 essentially repeat the promises of verses 8–9a but also present another concrete challenge. Yahweh challenges the powerful in the community not only to free people from bondage to debt but also to avoid practices that can get people into more bondage. Thus, they are warned against trespassing on the Sabbath (v. 13) and **malicious talk** (v. 9b), which is not merely gossip but proposals for political, legal, or social policy, or legal accusations. The destiny of the community, the restoration of blessing, and the fulfillment of promises (v. 14 re-expresses promises in Deut. 32:9, 13) depend on the community's commitment. That means the powerful must be committed to a spirituality of generosity rather than a practice of accumulation.

Sabbath, then, stands alongside fasting as a religious observance that the community needs to get clear about (v. 13). We might have suspected that sabbath observance was another practice like fasting that religious people might substitute for real commitment to Yahweh's ways (see 1:13), but here matters get turned on their heads. When the powerful fasted, Yahweh told them to forget it and to get serious about other less symbolic forms of commitment. When the powerful did not keep the sabbath, Yahweh told them to observe it, because failure to do so was a sign of not taking Yahweh seriously. When the OT elsewhere talks about humbling oneself or denying oneself (v. 3a), it refers more often to the self-denial of refraining from work than to the self-denial of refraining from food (e.g., Lev. 16:29, 31; 23:29; 27:32). As happens in a workaholic culture, in working on the sabbath people did what they pleased (the word occurs twice in v. 13) on Yahweh's holy day, as they did what they pleased in seeking Yahweh (v. 2, where the verb also occurred twice—NIV translates "seem eager"). The criterion for their spirituality was what pleased them—what worked for them, what resonated with their own experience. They were eager to know Yahweh's ways (v. 2) but they also wanted to walk in their own ways (v. 13: the word is again plural).

It is tempting to reckon that the principle behind verses 13–14 is that observing the sabbath can be a direct means of contributing to the well-being of ordinary working people (cf. Deut.

6:12–15 and the fiftieth-year rule in Lev. 25), that same well-being with which the comments on fasting have been concerned. Doing as they please then means turning the sabbath into an ordinary business day (cf. Neh. 10:31; 13:15–22). But the overt focus (as in Nehemiah) does not lie on the well-being of people. Rather, it lies on the significance the sabbath plays in developing proper attitudes to Yahweh. The sabbath is **holy** ground and the people are to keep off it. It is no time for doing business, as the temple is holy ground and is no place for doing business (cf. Mark 11:15–17—quoting 56:7).

Speaking idle words is literally "speak a word." The phrase occurs elsewhere only in Deuteronomy 18:20, where the context indicates "speak their own words." So the idea may be that people do not have the right to decide for themselves what to do on the sabbath. Specifically they have no right to indulge in the kind of talk verse 9b referred to (the expressions are very similar—"speaking evil" (NRSV; NIV reads **malicious talk**) and "speaking a word"). The sabbath is intrinsically made both for God (for the honoring of God) and for human beings (for their blessing).

59:1 / A comprehensive indictment of the community closes the critique that runs through 56:9–59:8. There will be no more critique and threat until chapters 65–66. The indictment starts once again from the fact that the people are seeking Yahweh—that is, seeking Yahweh's intervention in their life (e.g., 58:2, 9a). They are puzzled about the reason the moment never quite comes when darkness gives way to light, drought to refreshment, destruction to restoration, constraint to joy and feasting (see 59:9–14). In their prayers they asked that question and urged Yahweh to **hear** and **save**, the two characteristic petitions of the psalms. So why does everything remain promises, promises? Is the problem that Yahweh cannot hear and save, or that Yahweh does not want to?

The answer comes in two vivid images. To adapt an image from the Poet (see 50:1–2), it is a long way from Yahweh's throne in heaven to the situation on earth that requires divine intervention, but it is not the case that it is too far for Yahweh to reach. Nor (behind that, logically and chronologically) is it the case that Yahweh's ear is too heavy (literally), as if Yahweh's head therefore cannot lift so as to incline it in the direction to listen. The heavy ears sit on someone else's head: see 6:10 (Zech. 7:11 is the only other occurrence of this expression).

59:2–8 / Central to Israel's self-understanding in the Preacher's time was the notion of separation or the making of distinctions. It was a key feature of God's making the world itself as a clearly-structured place (Gen. 1) and then of God's organizing its peoples so that Israel is distinguished from other peoples (e.g., Lev. 20:24, 26; Ezra 6:21; 9–10; Neh. 9–10). This making of distinctions is the principle that underlay 56:3. It involves the distinguishing of the Levites from other families and of Aaron from the rest of the Levites (Deut 10:8; 1 Chron. 23:13), and the commission to Israel to distinguish between things that stain and things that do not (e.g., Lev. 20:25). It is a key theological idea.

The prophet makes a terrible reapplication of it. The community has effected a separation all right, but it has done so by its wrongdoing rather than by its commitment. It is a separation that has exactly the opposite effect to Yahweh's purpose in giving Israel the principle of making distinctions (v. 2). To put it another way, there is a metaphysical distinction between heaven and earth, established by the fact that Yahweh is the holy one and the people are created beings. This is a distinction Yahweh can live with. But to it the people have added a moral distinction constituted by Yahweh's **justice** (v. 4) and their **guilt** (v. 3). That is a distinction Yahweh cannot live with. Their relationship is designed to be one in which Yahweh's face is turned toward the people in love and concern that issue in action, but at present Yahweh cannot bear the sight of their wrongdoing and therefore neither does Yahweh see their need or respond to it. Yes, you are right in those accusatory prayers, Yahweh grants. I am not listening or looking and neither am I therefore acting to deliver you and fulfill my promises. But there is a reason for it. The logic is similar to that in passages such as 42:18–25 and 43:22–28.

We again recognize the diagnosis from earlier in the book (e.g., 1:15; 5:18; 6:5; 29:21; 32:7; 33:11) and from other prophets such as Jeremiah (e.g., 6:13–14). The language is also familiar from the teaching of the wise (e.g., Job 9:16; 15:31, 35; Prov. 1:16; 2:15), and the metaphors in verses 5–6 are the kind the wise used (e.g., Prov. 1:17; 6:6–8; 30:15). The conclusion (v. 8) at first seems simply to reinforce the charge of legalized wrongdoing. In the end it follows another feature of the teaching of the wise—that wrongdoing rebounds on wrongdoers. They do not commit themselves to **the way of** *shalom* and to *mishpat* in the community. They will find that they have consequently lost the way to their own *shalom*.

In Romans 3:15–17 Paul takes up the words of verses 7–8 and uses them to summarize the way in which the whole of humanity is dominated by sin. In Christian tradition, verse 2 has thus been understood to refer to a separation between humanity and God effected by human sin in general, a separation overcome by Christ's dying for us. The prophet has a different idea in mind. Here the separation is a specific one effected by the particular wrongdoing of the people the prophet addresses. It requires their facing up to this sin. The equivalent in the Christian church will then be not the general human sinfulness that is the concern of the doctrine of the atonement, but the recurrent human sinfulness that from time to time cuts the church off from God and leads to its withering. By limiting verses 2–8 to universal human sinfulness rather than to the recurrent sinfulness of God's people, the church shuts itself off from the possibility of turning away from sin and instead reinforces its separation from God. We may find ourselves paying such costs when we fail to read Scripture according to its historical meaning and confine ourselves to reading it in the light of its reapplication in the NT.

Additional Note §39

57:9 / **To Molech:** "The King" was a title for a god. The Masoretic Text often pejoratively changed *melek* ("king") to *molek* so that the title had the same vowels and thus the same shape as the word *bosheth* ("shame"). This drew attention to the shame of being associated with this god.

§40 The Prayer That Needs to Be Prayed (Isa. 59:9–15a)

59:9–15a / The section continues the theme of verses 1–8 which the opening words of chapter 56 first introduced, but the subjects are no longer "you" or "they" but **we**. The community itself speaks. Whom is it addressing? Is it simply reflecting to itself? Is this an expression of lostness like the one the Poet reports in 40:27? Not until verse 12 is there an indication that the community has raised its head from contemplating its own darkness and acknowledged that as it speaks it stands **in your sight**. It addresses Yahweh. Indeed, that is the only point where it does so. Verse 13 hastily returns to referring to Yahweh in the third person. Perhaps there is an appropriateness in this. Yahweh's eyes are too pure to behold evil (Hab. 1:13), and the community's face is too stained to look into Yahweh's.

Nevertheless, verse 12 indicates that in verses 9–15a the form changes from vision and critique to prayer. But whose prayer is it? Prophets were people who mediated the relationship between God and people, and they did so in both directions. They spoke for God to people. They also spoke for people to God. When they speak for God, they often identify with God and speak as "I." When they pray on their people's behalf, they identify with their people and pray as "we," as is the nature of intercession in Scripture.

Although they were representatives, that does not mean they spoke only when told to. Perhaps they spoke for God when God did not specifically tell them to do so (a good assistant sometimes takes initiative without waiting for the boss's word), and perhaps they spoke for the people when the people did not specifically commission them to. Our representatives in earthly government do not consult us every time they speak on our behalf, and neither do our representatives in heavenly government. When prophets such as Hosea (6:1–3) or Jeremiah (14:7–9, 19–22) intercede for their people and identify with them, this does not

necessarily mean that their words express the people's own convictions. Indeed, part of the point of having an intercessor is to
have someone to utter what you may not think to say yourself.

So here the Preacher turns from preaching to praying and
puts words on the lips of the people to God. Precisely because intercession is part of a prophet's job description, the presumption
is that the prayer is real. It is not a pretend prayer. The Preacher
represents two parties and knows that a change in both parties is
needed if the future is to be different from the past. But it is not
necessary for the prayer to be recorded in order to be effective as a
prayer. Perhaps prophets did say more words to God than they
did to human beings, but the prayers are recorded in a different
book from the one we are reading. So a prayer that appears in a
prophetic book may have further significance beyond its function
as a prayer. The implication is that the words spoken to God
should also be read by human beings. Perhaps one point is to tell
the human beings that this is the way they themselves should be
praying. Perhaps another is to reinforce the words addressed to
them. To put these two together, perhaps something distinctive
can be achieved by putting a prayer on people's lips.

Admittedly there is risk involved. The Preacher has recently
taken up some of the Ambassador's scathing words in 1:10–20,
and these included Yahweh's anger at prayers that were made
without effective action to ensure that the society was the kind of
which Yahweh approved. Suppose that the community consisted
of the sort of people we have been reading about, living in true
continuity with that presupposed by the Ambassador. Putting
prayers on their lips is then to risk making their situation worse
(as happened in connection with Hosea and Jeremiah).

On the other hand, it might have the opposite effect. They
might take the prophet's prayer on their lips, and mean it, and
change as they pray. The fact that the focus lies on their own reflection rather than on direct address to Yahweh also encourages
this idea. Telling the people the nature of a prayer is parallel to
telling them the nature of the blinding punishment that Yahweh
has declared to them (6:9–10). It is an indirect way of bringing
about change in them, so that the actual prayer becomes a possible
prayer as the declared punishment becomes an unnecessary one.

So in verse 9 the prophet develops the point made at the
end of verse 8 and acknowledges that the programmatic statement in 56:1 stands unfulfilled. Key expressions for the nature of
what the people need from Yahweh tumble over each other:

mishpat, tsedaqah, **light, brightness** (see 4:5), **deliverance.** All refer to the same event, but they characterize it from different angles. Images for the community's need tumble over each other: it is like walking in deep **darkness,** it is like trying to find your way when you have lost your sight, it is like belonging to the living **dead.** Images for the people's wrongdoing tumble over each other: it is like rebelling against authority (**offenses/rebellion**—the same word), like failing to achieve an aim **(sins),** like choosing to go the wrong way **(iniquities),** like deceiving someone about your commitment **(treachery),** like turning your back on someone. This wrongdoing involves behaving in a consistent way in relation to society. Turning one's back on other people goes hand in hand with turning one's back on God, and an encouragement of deception in human relationships and an effective outlawing of **truth** and **honesty** goes hand in hand with the attempt to deceive God. If only the people will **acknowledge** all this, as the prophet does on their behalf.

§41 A Vision of Yahweh Acting in Wrath, I (Isa. 59:15b–20)

At the center of the chiasm comprising chapters 56–66 stand three chapters that promise Jerusalem's glorious restoration, in hues even more technicolor than those of chapters 40–55. On either side of these three chapters stand shorter visions of Yahweh's coming in wrath to punish the nations, the necessary preliminary or accompaniment to Jerusalem's restoration.

59:15b / Yahweh's first such act stands in an ambiguous relationship to the prayer that preceded. It has both encouraging and worrying features. The ambiguity links with the ambiguity of those key words *mishpat* and *tsedaqah*. Yahweh is **displeased that there was no** *mishpat* (v. 15b; NIV **justice**). Does that indicate displeasure with the lack of *mishpat* in the community's own life? If so, that makes us read what follows as the inflicting of punishment on the people who have special responsibility for *mishpat* and/or who are especially involved in frustrating justice. That is good news for many ordinary people, but bad news for most of the people the prophet has been addressing over four chapters. On the other hand, Yahweh might be displeased with the fact that *mishpat* has not been implemented *for* the community, displeased that the community as a whole still lies unrestored. It is then good news that Yahweh now intends to act on that displeasure.

59:16 / Either way, Yahweh now intends to intervene personally to implement *mishpat* (v. 16). The prophet does not tell us what Yahweh was doing before noticing the absence of *mishpat*, nor who were the figures whose failure drives Yahweh to intervene, though the picture recalls 42:13–15. Here the presupposition seems to be that Yahweh has delegated activity in implementing *mishpat*.

To whom does Yahweh delegate this responsibility? Is it to world rulers, with the implication that there is no Cyrus to implement Yahweh's purpose for the community? But it was Yahweh who had raised up Cyrus, and several of his successors in turn took up his role. Is it to community leaders, with the implication that there is no Jeshua, Zerubbabel, Ezra, or Nehemiah in the community? Parallel objections apply. Is it to heavenly rulers such as those perhaps confronted in Psalm 82 and alluded to in Daniel 10–11? Is it significant that the statement that there is **no one to intervene** contrasts with the vision of one who "will intervene for the rebels" (53:12—the same verb as here)? This link draws our attention to other parallels with that vision of Yahweh's servant. Yahweh is **appalled,** as the "many" were in 52:14. Yahweh's **arm** therefore comes into play, as in 53:1, but directly rather than mediated by the servant. Yahweh's looking (with dissatisfaction) recalls the servant's looking (with satisfaction) in 53:10–11. **Righteousness** is Yahweh's sustenance as it was key to the servant's effectiveness (53:11).

59:17–19 / There are more substantial contrasts between the act of Yahweh in 52:13–53:12 and this one, which these parallels further underline. In putting on *tsedaqah* and deliverance Yahweh is putting on armor, for here there is a battle to be fought or a punishment to be inflicted (vv. 17–19), not a martyrdom to be accepted. This act of Yahweh's arm looks as much like a response to the self-exhortation in 51:9 as a fulfillment of the vision in 52:13–53:12. The commitment to deliverance has as its other side the commitment to punishment (**vengeance:** see comment on 1:24–25a), pursued with passion. We might have thought that the turn in chapters 52–53 from divine power manifest in violence to divine power manifest in martyrdom was a once-for-all turn, but here the former reappears. The relationship between these two manifestations is more dialectical and less romanticist than we might have thought. There will be an equivalent in the way in which violent punishment reappears in the NT on the other side of the cross (e.g., 2 Thes. 1:6–9).

The fact that the recipients of this punishment are **the islands** gives the audience the clearest permission to infer that Yahweh's displeasure at there being no *mishpat* denoted a concern for the community's destiny and a commitment to its deliverance, rather than a displeasure at its own life and a commitment to taking action against it. But it gives them no permission to assume that they can look forward to *mishpat* if there is no *mishpat* in their own life. The undertaking in verses 15b–19 depends on the turning of verses 9–15a.

59:20 / The point becomes explicit. **The Redeemer will come to Zion** sounds like a commitment unqualified by any conditions in terms of relationship, behavior, morality, or community. But the parallel colon goes on, **. . . to those in Jacob who repent of** (literally "turn from") **their sins.** The two verse units of poetry, which make the line as a whole deconstruct, reflect the irresolvable tension between God's grace and the need for human response. Conversely, they indicate the truth in both approaches to verses 15b–19. Yahweh is indeed committed to the community's *mishpat*. The community has to be committed to *mishpat*, too.

§42 Promises of Glory (Isa. 59:21–60:22)

In the two great central sections of chapters 56–66 (59:21–60:22 and 61:1–62:12), Yahweh addresses both the prophet and the city. In the first section, the address to the prophet comes in 59:21, while the address to the city occupies the whole of chapter 60. Admittedly Zion/Jerusalem is not named until 60:14, but the verb **arise** (60:1) repeats the exhortation to Jerusalem in 51:17 (NIV "rise up") and the verbs are feminine singular, which makes it clear enough that the prophet speaks to the city (cf. 59:20). The prophet takes up the exhortation and the promises in chapters 49–54 and once again re-expresses them in yet more glorious technicolor for people who evidently are back in Jerusalem but have not seen those promises fulfilled in their glory. They thus presuppose a similar situation to the prophecies of Haggai and Zechariah.

59:21 / Taken out of context the promise of God's spirit and God's words might address either the prophet or the community, but the fact that the voice of the Preacher has considerable prominence through this central section of chapters 56–66 (see esp. 61:1) suggests that we take verse 21 as recording Yahweh's words to the prophet. This may, however, prove to be a false antithesis insofar as the prophet stands for the people.

Yahweh's breath is **on** the prophet, and Yahweh's words are **in** the prophet's mouth. The first expression reflects the description of the promised king, the renewed community, and the ideal servant in 11:2; 32:15; 42:1 and 44:3. It thus suggests, on one hand, the promise of wisdom and the role of the servant. On the other hand, it suggests the way this clothing with Yahweh's wisdom (like the designation as servant) is indeed the destiny of the whole community. The second expression presupposes that words come from the prophet's lips, but they are not words the prophet consciously formulated. Yahweh in person speaks, using the prophet as a mouthpiece. The prophet then does not make up the words to say, nor even hear them and then repeat them, as will have happened on other occasions (see 22:14). The prophet's mouth opens, but Yahweh's words come out.

It is often suggested that prophecy "died out" in the Second Temple period. The promise in verse 21b suggests a commitment that this will not happen. On the contrary, prophecy, too, will be democratized, as Moses wanted (Num. 11:29) and Joel promised (2:28–32). Reference to the prophet's **children** and their **descendants** recalls the promise of descendants to Yahweh's servant in 53:10. All that would be implicitly good news for the community, and not just for the prophet. But Yahweh has also explicitly pointed out that a commitment of this kind to the prophet **is my covenant with them.** No prophets or other kinds of servants matter for their own sake. They matter for the sake of Yahweh and for the sake of those they serve or address.

60:1–22 / Chapter 60 is the longest unstructured stream-of-consciousness prophecy in Isaiah. A number of motifs appear and reappear in serendipity fashion. This is not to say that the poem's *thought* is unstructured. First, it contains the usual instances of words such as **for, so that,** and **although,** which suggest a chain of thinking. To appreciate its dynamic, then, we need to appreciate the underlying chain of thought to which the syntax points. Second, two themes from the tradition with which the audience was familiar underlie the chapter as a whole. One is the theme of reversal, which was prominent in the promises of chapters 40–55. The other is the theme of the nations' acknowledgment of Yahweh as the God of Jerusalem and of Jerusalem as the city of Yahweh. That is also a concern in Isaiah 40–55, but those chapters did not create that theme. In his use of this theme, the Preacher is appealing to very old traditions in Israel's faith, not least to stories of the nations' acknowledgment of Yahweh and of Jerusalem in the time of the great king Solomon.

The prophecy recalls Psalm 72 in that both combine repetition and lack of form with an underlying structure of thought in creating a portrayal of Yahweh's involvement with righteousness, prosperity, freedom, and the status and wealth of the nations. That psalm, itself dedicated to Solomon, is a prayer for (and an implicit challenge to) Judah's king. In the Preacher's time, Judah has no king, and people who prayed that psalm came to pray it as an expression of longing for the king who might one day embody its vision. The Preacher and the Poet agree that there is no space for such a king. Just as the Poet democratized the theology of kingship—making the nation rather than the king the embodiment of the vision—so here the Preacher brings about the same democratization by presenting the city as that embodiment.

How literal are the poem's promises? Their twofold background in Judah's traditions helps us to approach this question. When prophets describe the future, they do not usually do so by giving a literal portrayal of events, as if they were sharing the results of looking at a crystal ball or as if Yahweh had given them an advance video of those events. Rather, Yahweh inspires them to take past descriptions of Yahweh's acts, and past declarations of Yahweh's intentions, and to use these as the raw material for promises and warnings regarding future events. Their symbols and images are what matters. This is not to say that the details are irrelevant. Indeed, this approach makes the detail more significant. But it is significant because of the way it portrays the meaning of what will happen and the way it moves the imagination of its audience, rather than for the way it literally corresponds to actual events.

It is, then, a consistent pattern that subsequent events provide a partial fulfillment of OT prophecies, but that the promise or the warning is more splendid or more ominous than the events that do take place. The prophecy was accepted perhaps on the basis that it indeed read consistently with earlier promises and experiences of Yahweh's acts. Its partial fulfillment is then both the confirmation that it indeed came from God, and the promise that its larger vision will one day find fulfillment.

What counts as fulfillment will depend on the perspective of the audience. Jews and Christians may agree in finding such fulfillment and renewed promise in some of God's acts in relation to the Jewish people over decades and centuries since the day of the Preacher, and in looking forward to more of that. Christians also see it in what God has done in Christ and may long that there may also be more of that.

In various respects, chapter 60 takes up the Poet's vision of a great reversal of the experience of affliction. It includes the following elements:

(a) Ms Jerusalem's sons and daughters will return from their scattering all over the world (vv. 4, 9). As we have noted, the return of some Judeans from Babylon in the years after 539 B.C. constituted a partial fulfillment of that vision, but also a whetting of the appetite for a larger-scale fulfillment, and prophets such as

Zechariah reaffirm the promise. The number of people who are available to return with Ezra in the mid-fifth century (still leaving many others behind) indicates how it stands yet unfulfilled even with regard to Babylon.

(b) The disruption between the city and Yahweh is over. Wrath and attack have given way to favor and compassion (v. 10).

(c) The direction of servitude is reversed. Instead of serving the nations, the city is served by them. Instead of the city depending for its life on them, the life and death of the nations depend on their attitude to Jerusalem (v. 12). Instead of despising it, they honor it (v. 14). Instead of being milked by them, the city is nourished by them (v. 16).

(d) Instead of being forsaken and hated (presumably by her husband) and generally ignored, Ms Zion becomes an object of lasting pride and joy (v. 15).

(e) Instead of being assailed by violent attack and destruction, the city is controlled by *shalom* and *tsedaqah,* and **Salvation** and **Praise** protect it (vv. 17–18; see Additional Notes).
The Preacher also recapitulates the Poet's vision of where this will lead. The city will come to recognize Yahweh as **Savior** and **Redeemer** (v. 16). Other aspects of promises from chapters 40–55 reappear in verses 19–21.

The most dominant single motif in the chapter is the picture of the nations bringing their wealth to Jerusalem. When Solomon had first built palaces, terraces, colonnades, and the temple in Jerusalem, the nations—in the person of Tyre's king and Sheba's queen—brought cedar, pine, algum-wood, bronze, gold, spices, and precious stones. The Preacher envisions Jerusalem made wondrously splendid again, even going far beyond its original magnificence. This expansion of previous glory is often found in typology. In the same way that the Judean community's departure from Babylon was to both parallel the first exodus and exceed it in splendor, so the re-building of Jerusalem with the support of the nations is to parallel the first building and yet exceed it in splendor.

(a) It will not involve merely one king and one queen, but nations and kings, people from far shores in their **Tarshish ships** (vv. 8–9; see on 23:1), with the city's **gates** needing to be **open** 24 hours to admit them all with their wealth (v. 11).

(b) It will not involve merely one camel-train from Sheba, but whole **herds,** perhaps the entire camel population of **Sheba** (v. 6). Appropriately, they are organized by the camel-train experts, the Midianites (Gen. 37:28, 36), of whom **Ephah** is a sub-set (Gen. 25:4). Whereas Ephah was thus a grandson of Abraham and Keturah, **Nebaioth** (v. 7) and Kedar were the oldest grandchildren of Abraham and Hagar, the sons of Ishmael (Gen. 25:12–13).

(c) The events will thus involve a reunion with branches of Abraham's family that were not part of Israel.

(d) The foreign peoples will not merely provide raw materials but do the building, and monarchs will not merely wonder but **serve** (vv. 10–12).

(e) There will be **iron** where before there were **stones, silver** where there was **iron, bronze** where there was **wood, gold** where there was **bronze** (v. 17).

A further point emerges from the appearance of Tarshish ships. They provide the most concrete link with chapter 2 (2:16), which spoke of Yahweh's cutting down to size such expressions of human majesty. It transpires that, like the judgment in 1:21–31, this was a purging rather than a mere destruction. Chapter 60 as a whole suggests that the world's achievements, wealth, and power are destined not for destruction but for transformation, in keeping with the opening verses of chapter 2 (see R. J. Mouw, *When the Kings Come Marching In: Isaiah and the New Jerusalem* [Grand Rapids: Eerdmans, 1983], pp. 5–9). This is also a reminder to Christian theology that its understanding of heaven must not be too ethereal. Belief in a transformed city goes with belief in a resurrected body.

A related dominant motif of chapter 60 is the splendor of Yahweh and of Jerusalem (vv. 1–3, 5a, 19–20; for the chiastic structure of vv. 1–3, see the Introduction). What so draws the nations to pour their resources at Jerusalem's feet? This was where the chapter began. While paralleling 51:17, the opening exhortation (v. 1) also reworks it. The command is now "Get up and shine out with light" not "Wake up and get up." The Preacher has a different way of portraying what Yahweh intends, to which a different response is appropriate. The difference arises from a difference in circumstances. In Babylon in the 540s B.C. people were still under the domination of the power that had humiliated them, and they still had no alternative to living as refugees in their own country. The Poet's task was to convince them that they were about to be released and to encourage them in the light of that fact. The prophecies in chapters 56–66 presuppose people with some control over their own affairs. External oppression cannot be forgotten, but these people speak as if they were no longer as oppressed by foreign control as they once were. This is one of the indications that they belong to the period when Persia allowed the Judeans in Babylon to return, but the grand vision in chapters 40–55, namely the city's glorification, still remains for Yahweh to fulfill.

Like the prophecy in chapters 40–55, this prophecy places before the community an act that Yahweh intends to perform and urges the people to respond to that coming event. Here, however, the act is different. Yahweh is not bringing freedom but is appearing in splendor. **Your light has come** (v. 1) thus has new meaning. Light has commonly suggested well-being and happiness, while darkness has suggested oppression and despair (recently 58:8, 10; 59:9). Here light dawns because Yahweh **rises** like the sun (though v. 20b suggests an awareness of the link between darkness and sorrow, and v. 12 may have similar implications). The parallelism with **glory** also indicates that here "light" implies supernaturally dazzling brightness. The prophet pictures such a brightness dawning over Jerusalem that contrasts with the night gloom that characterizes the rest of the world. Peoples are thus instinctively drawn to this light that contrasts with the darkness around. The prophet does not tell us what will constitute this bright light except by saying it is Yahweh's presence. As in chapter 53, we are left with the picture.

Even before Herod's temple or the Dome of the Rock, the combination of the speedy Middle Eastern dawn and the white temple stone would make for a striking contrast between darkness and light in the city. Yahweh here challenges Jerusalem to believe that another, speedier and more marvelous transformation from darkness to light is happening. This one makes it possible and necessary that the city should get up, shine out with light, and stand so as to reflect Yahweh's light as it dawns (**shine** is the same Hb. word as the noun light, and **dawn** is the same word as rises). Verses 19–20 make explicit the comparison and contrast with the sun's light. The city will neither need nor experience the light of sun or moon because Yahweh will be its light. One might compare the situation during the first three days of creation when light shone in the world by God's command even before the sun and moon had been made (see Gen. 1).

What do the nations come to do? The prospect of the nations bringing all those resources to the city could only be an encouragement to the city leaders. The service of foreign kings will be expressed when their nations **rebuild** the city's **walls** (v. 10a). Actually it would be Judean bravery, skill, and sweat that would accomplish that, to strong foreign opposition (as seen in Nehemiah). This provides an illustration of the way in which the prophets' visions are not literal anticipations; Cyrus and subsequent Persian rulers made the rebuilding possible, but the believing community did the work. It also constitutes a reminder that the visions stand as embodiments of Yahweh's ultimate commitment to Jerusalem. Another example of such a vision is that of the reversal of Judah's subservience to any foreign domination (v. 12). The events of the time of Third Isaiah, Zechariah, Ezra, and Nehemiah were at least partial fulfillment of these commitments.

All this tribute and subservience might seem calculated to bring great satisfaction to the city, and the promise of it might seem ethically questionable to readers. It is then striking that there is no reference to a sense of satisfaction or enjoyment on the city's part (v. 5 suggests awe). Further, the nations do not come merely to surrender their resources to a city or to its inhabitants. They acknowledge Jerusalem because it belongs to Yahweh, the **Holy One** (v. 14). Their submission to Jerusalem is a sign of their submission to Yahweh. The herds of camels that bring gifts come **proclaiming the praise of the** LORD (v. 6). The point about their **gold and incense** is to beautify Yahweh's house and to make for fragrant worship there. In bringing Jerusalem's children back to her, far-off nations **look to me** (v. 9). The flocks from Kedar and Nebaioth will serve Jerusalem because **they will be accepted as offerings on my altar, and I will adorn my glorious temple** (v. 7). **The glory of Lebanon,** that is its fine timber, **will come to you . . . to adorn the place of my sanctuary** where I rest my **feet** (v. 13). Jerusalem's significance lies not in being the audience's city but in being the place where their God is worshiped.

Readers are still entitled to a modicum of suspicion. The fact remains that it is conveniently the audience's city that is glorified in the name of their God. In encouraging them with this promise, the prophet takes the risk that they will be more concerned for their glory than for Yahweh's. The same issues are raised as will surface again when the NT says glorious things about the church that thus turn Christian faith into a self-serving affair for Christians. We cannot know what was in the hearts of prophet or first audience in this connection. As readers, we thus need to turn our capacity for suspicion on ourselves.

Additional Notes §42

59:21 / The fact that this verse alone within 59:15b–21 has no corresponding element in 63:1–6 supports the view that 59:21 belongs with 60:1–22 rather than with 59:15b–20.

60:5a / In NIV it seems that the city is responding with joy to the return of her children. But more literally v. 5 says, "Then you will look [or see] and shine, and your heart [or mind] will dread and swell, for the wealth . . . . " NIV introduces the notion of joy into the verb elsewhere translated by a word such as "fear" (12:2; 19:16, 17; 33:14; 44:8, 11; 51:13; and KJV here), but that verb suggests that the reaction is rather one of awe at what Yahweh is doing. NIV then omits the word "for" (see Additional Notes on 1:29–30), which suggests that the reason for the reaction in v. 5a lies in v. 5b, not in v. 4.

60:18b / Most translations agree with NIV, but the expression parallels v. 17b and reads more naturally "you will call salvation your walls and praise your gates": that is, Yahweh's salvation and worship will be the city's security (cf. Zech. 2:5).

§43 Five Responses to Yahweh's Promises (Isa. 61:1–62:12)

Chapters 61 and 62 recapitulate much of chapter 60, but they do so in a new framework. They offer five responses to those promises. Whereas the prophet's word was a brisk preliminary to Yahweh's word in 59:21–60:22, in chapters 61–62 the prophet speaks a number of times in a way that has significance in its own right but also introduces recapitulations of the promises.

Accounts of a prophet's own experience or actions appear in the OT because the testimony is in some way significant for the audience, though the way in which it is relevant varies. In the classic accounts of Yahweh's commission of prophets such as Isaiah ben Amoz, Amos, or Jeremiah, the logic is, "This is why you ought to take me seriously and turn back to Yahweh" (or why you ought to have done so). In 59:21 the testimony related to Yahweh's promise that the community would always have Yahweh's word. Verse 1 of chapter 61 is a brisk introduction to the account of the prophet's message that is designed to encourage people to take its good news seriously. In 61:10 the prophet again stands for the whole community. In 62:1 the testimony encourages the community by promising it that the prophet will faithfully fulfill the calling of intercessor until Yahweh implements the already-announced purpose. In 62:6 it does the same by affirming that there is a larger company of people who will give Yahweh no rest until this happens. In 62:10 the prophet apparently speaks further, this time not in testimony but in instruction.

61:1–9 / The first of the five responses, then, is preaching. Once again the prophet takes up forms of speech as well as actual words from chapters 40–55. The first-person testimony corresponds to 48:16, 49:1–6, and 50:4–9, where it is also "the Lord Yahweh" who speaks (48:16; 50:4, 5, 7, 9). The claim that "the Lord Yahweh's spirit is on me" recalls the earlier servant passage 42:1 (and as there, capitalizing "Spirit" risks giving a misleading impression). Like the Poet in 49:1–6 and 50:4–9, this prophet reckons to be the very embodiment of that servant vision in 42:1–9. This gives us a clue to the sort of ministry the prophet exercises. To put it another way, as Second Isaiah stands in the shoes of First Isaiah, so Third Isaiah stands in the shoes of Second Isaiah.

This prophet also has a distinctive way of understanding that commission: **the LORD has anointed me.** In Christian thinking, the two expressions in verse 1a have become one and we regularly think of "anointing with the Holy Spirit," but these two were not normally associated with each other in the OT. Anointing suggests commissioning, consecrating, and authorizing. The spirit suggests endowing with supernatural power.

Anointing is a striking metaphor here. In Israel and elsewhere, people daubed priests and kings with olive oil as part of their consecration to holy office, and such daubing became a figure for Yahweh's commissioning (e.g., 1 Sam. 10:1; 2 Sam. 12:7). Prophets were not anointed (being a prophet was not an office), except in 1 Kings 19:16. Only in connection with David do the two ideas of anointing and Yahweh's spirit come closely together (see 1 Sam. 16; 2 Sam. 23). In effect, then, this prophet claims to be a David-like figure for the community, anointed (metaphorically) like David and endowed like David. The prophet is thus saying something parallel to 55:3–5. As David's task there passes from king to people, so David's commission and equipping here passes from king to prophet. The claim stands in the context of that other assumption that the prophet also stands for the people (see 59:21).

Given that the king in particular was "Yahweh's anointed" and that 45:1 has already reapplied that notion to King Cyrus, more immediately this claim takes up another expression from chapters 40–55. In both connections it forms another reworking of the idea of Yahweh's special relationship with the king. As the people and the prophet (and not merely the king) could be Yahweh's servant in chapters 40–55, so here the prophet (and not merely the king, Israelite or foreign) could be Yahweh's anointed.

Whether we think of the prophet as claiming David's mantle or Cyrus's, the task it implies is indeed the king's task. We have noted how Psalm 72 illumines chapter 60, and it now illuminates chapter 61 as well (see also 11:1–9). Psalm 72 assumes that the king's calling involves a particular commitment to the afflicted and the needy (vv. 2, 4, 12; see on 32:1–8). Here the anointed Preacher takes up that commitment. The king's task was to take action in making decisions that would favor the afflicted and needy. The Preacher's task is to make an announcement to them. Once again **preach good news** takes up from chapters 40–55 and suggests that the prophet also reckons to be the fulfillment of the commission and vision of heralds bringing good news to Jerusalem (see 40:9; 41:27; 52:7). Further, to judge from the verses that follow, the word **poor** designates the community as a whole. While chapters 56–59 presupposed divisions within the community and the leadership doing well at the expense of ordinary people, chapters 60–62 look on the community as a whole as oppressed and sorrowful, in the manner of chapters 40–55.

So despite their reconstitution in Jerusalem, the people remain poor (see on 29:19), **brokenhearted,** demoralized, crushed in mind and spirit (cf. Ps. 34:18; 51:17), **captives** in their own land (cf. Ps. 106:46), **prisoners** (cf. 49:9), people who **grieve** the continuing suffering of their city (cf. 57:17–19) and who are metaphorically smeared with the **ashes** of **mourning** (v. 3; cf. 58:5; 60:20; Lam. 3:16). They still live in a **devastated** city (v. 4), and are still shamed by the well-deserved humiliation that had come from Yahweh (v. 7).

The Preacher is sent to announce a transformation of all that and thus to **bind up** the people who are crushed in mind. That is to come about by bringing good news and announcing the coming of **freedom** (the word is otherwise used only of the freeing of slaves at the sabbath or jubilee year) and **release** for these people who are still subject to foreign control (v. 1). This is the moment of Yahweh's **favor** on one hand and **vengeance** on the other. The parallelism signals the fact that these are two sides of one idea. In taking the side of the victims and acting on their behalf, Yahweh will put down the oppressors and punish them.

So at last **comfort** will come. Once again the Preacher takes up one of the Poet's favorite expressions, in a way that brings out the two-sidedness of the notion. Comfort is both a message that makes people feel better and an act that gives them grounds for feeling better (v. 2; see Additional Notes). Their deliverance means, metaphorically, that the ashes on their heads can be replaced by a garland, that the people can receive their own anointing with **oil** that makes their faces shine and so reflect their newfound joy, and that their clothes will no longer reflect their inner brokenness and can become instead the festal garb of worship. They will stand tall and solid and secure now, displaying Yahweh's **splendor** (v. 3).

In concrete physical terms, the city will be rebuilt (v. 4). In the context it is unlikely that **they** are its inhabitants, for the passage promises what will be done *for* them. More likely the "they" are other people who are unspecified (but see 60:10). Similarly, other people will look after their **flocks** and farms (v. 5) and provide for them in abundance (v. 6b) while they are becoming "a kingdom of priests and a holy nation" (Exod. 19:6; Isa. 61:6a). This will more than make up for their material deprivation and their consequent **shame** (v. 7). The repeated word for **double** is different from that in 40:2, but the parallel is still noteworthy—especially as Yahweh goes on to promise that they will now receive their **reward** (v. 8; cf. 40:10). In the context, the **robbery and iniquity** must be that exercised against the community (cf. Deut. 28:29, 31). At last Yahweh is implementing *mishpat* on Israel's behalf and fulfilling that promise to Abraham (vv. 8b–9).

Like 40:3–5, verses 1–3 aroused particular interest among the Qumran community (who applied them to Melchizedek, understood as a member of the heavenly cabinet) as well as among other Jews (who usually assumed they were the words of the prophet himself). There would thus seem to be some arrogance about Jesus' applying the words to himself (Luke 4:14–29). There would also be good news in Jesus' declaration that their moment had come. Jesus commits himself to proclaiming the liberation of the Jewish people from foreign oppressors, though he combines this commitment with a commitment to outsiders (vv. 24–27) that corresponds to that in passages such as Isaiah 56:1–8. His audience is less pleased with this. In Luke 4 he stops short of the phrase about the "day of vengeance," but takes up such talk of "days of vengeance" in 21:22 (NIV "time of punishment"). These must come "in fulfillment of all that has been written." Jesus says that even the promise of God's day of vengeance must be fulfilled.

Paradoxically, Jesus' days of vengeance are ones exacted on his own people. More radically than was the case in Luke 4, in Luke 21 Jesus is reversing the significance of the promise. Amos did the same thing when he turned the Day of Yahweh from good news to bad news (see Amos 5:18–20). But when asked when Israel would get its freedom, Jesus answered not "Never," or "That is the wrong question," but "It is not for you to know" (Acts 1:6–7).

61:10–11 / The prophet's second response to the promises of chapter 60 is to praise. In line with the intended relationship between prophet and people, the Preacher begins now to behave in accordance with the whole people's destiny as verses 1–9 describe it. The Preacher thus models a response to which the whole people is called. They are to offer this response before the event actually happens, in accordance with the summons that chapters 40–55 often made to their audience. The symbolism of the words, with their reference to the adornment of bride or groom, suggests that the response also has the resonances of a sign, an act which expresses and effects that which it signifies.

62:1–5 / The prophet's third response is a commitment to prayer. In other contexts, refusing to keep silence out of a concern for Jerusalem-Zion's **righteousness** might suggest speaking out to her of her wrongdoing. Here it denotes speaking out to Yahweh about the fulfillment of her destiny, about her *tsedaqah*, her "vindication" (so NRSV), which means her **salvation.** We may pray for the sake of God's name, but we also pray **for Zion/Jerusalem's sake,** for the sake of the people on whose behalf we long to motivate God to act.

The context of these promises in chapters 60–62 is that Yahweh has kept promising to restore Jerusalem, indeed to make it a more splendid city than it ever was before. But the moment of that divine action seems never to come. The fact that Yahweh made a commitment to act swiftly in bringing about this vision (60:22) only makes that harder to live with. Yet it has not in the slightest reduced the prophet's conviction that this is Yahweh's intention. If we ask why this should be so, then the fundamental answer is not merely that Yahweh has announced this intention or that the prophet believes that to be so, but that it is bound up with the very relationship of Yahweh and Israel over history. To begin to think otherwise would be to question the being of God and the being of Israel.

The appropriate response when someone does not fulfill a commitment is not resignation or disillusion, but confrontation. It is to urge the person to act in accordance with the promise. That is what the prophet sets about doing. Despite 42:14, Yahweh in fact still seems to be keeping silence. The Preacher confronts Yahweh's silence with an insistence on not keeping silence. Only when Yahweh begins to shout and act in the manner of which 42:14 speaks will the Preacher quiet down. In a similar context to the present one, Zechariah notes that the world remains quiet (1:11), that nothing is happening to disturb its lazy peacefulness and bring the disruption that signifies God's act, and a divine aide responds by pressing Yahweh about how long this is to be so. The Preacher joins in such debate in the meeting of the heavenly cabinet and refuses to be similarly quiet until receiving a satisfactory response—in action and not merely in word.

As NEB recognizes, the prayer does not end at verse 1. The **till** continues its force, implicitly, through verses 2–5. There is nothing novel in the content of verses 1–5. We have heard it all before. What is new is its being turned into a prayer that Yahweh is going to have to answer in order to get any rest (cf. Luke 18:1–8). The point of the prayer is to move Yahweh. The point of relating the prayer, however, is to encourage the audience and to reassure it that the prophet is committed to fulfilling the role of a prophet as intercessor, thereby reminding it of another consideration that makes it possible to hang on in faith when nothing is happening.

Jerusalem's **new name** (v. 2) is presumably **My-delight-is-in-her** (v. 4 mg.). The idea is not that the literal name of the city is replaced by another but that the city's transformation makes it appropriate to give her an extra name (cf. the note with which Ezekiel closes, 48:35). This is so not least because she has been bearing an extra name, **Deserted,** and that needs to be replaced. The estranged couple are back together again. To mix metaphors, the estranged wife who is now a bride again will not merely wear a garland (61:3; NIV reads **crown of beauty**) but *be* one (62:3; NIV reads **crown of splendor**). The promise applies to Yahweh and Jerusalem. An image from the Middle East and Greece, in which the deity who was identified with a city might be portrayed as wearing that city with its walls like a **crown,** is here applied to Yahweh and Jerusalem. Here, however, the image is mildly demythologized: Yahweh simply holds the crown.

62:6–9 / The prophet's fourth response is to commission reminders. Out of context, one might take these as Yahweh's words. The idea of God's commissioning people to remind God of commitments that need to be kept is a paradoxical one, but no more so than the idea of someone's having the task of reminding God not to be taken in by apparent human piety (see Job 1). In this context in chapters 61–62, it is more likely that the Preacher is again the speaker, though the key point to encourage the audience is that *someone* has appointed these reminders and that they *are* going to refuse to let Yahweh forget those commitments.

The Preacher adds force to that personal commitment as an intercessor by affirming that others have the same commission

(vv. 6–7). Perhaps the claim even relates to a commissioning of supernatural figures of the kind who belonged to Yahweh's cabinet. Either way, they are like lookouts who have a special responsibility for the city's welfare (see 21:11–12). They are committed to keeping alert and active on its behalf, **day** and **night**. They are to **give** themselves **no rest**. But they also give Yahweh no rest. They are like secretaries of state whose task is to remind the king or other people in power about what needs to be done, in order to make sure that no decision fails to be implemented because someone does not quite get around to it. Like the prophet (v. 1), they **will never be silent**. They take no rest, and they give their superior no rest until the latter implements the plans.

Literally or figuratively, they take their stand on Jerusalem's walls—which are in ruins. It would be a telling point from which these lookouts would call on Yahweh to fulfill the commitment to restore the city.

62:10–12 / The prophet's fifth response is to commission workers. Again, out of context one might take these verses as Yahweh's words. But the fact that the prophet's voice has been so prominent, as well as the fact that these verses refer to Yahweh in the third person, suggests that the prophet speaks for one last time—on this occasion not in testimony but in command. The style and word choice of verses 10–12 recall chapters 40–55 in an especially systematic way. The repeated commands recall the very beginning of those chapters and the repetitions in 51:9–52:12. The command to **pass through the gates** recalls 48:20 and 52:11, though typically the meaning of the words has changed. The words that follow suggest that here the command is part of the commission to unnamed construction workers such as were commissioned earlier in 40:3–5. The purpose of the road has also changed. That was a road for Yahweh (though Yahweh would bring the people along). This is a road explicitly for **the people**. Further, in verse 10 they are brought along not by Yahweh but by **the nations**, for this summons takes 49:22 into account. Admittedly verses 11–12 return (among other passages) to 40:10–11 and depict Yahweh as the people's **Savior** bringing them home to Zion. In chapters 40–48 and 49–55 the focus was first on the freeing of the deportees and then on the city's being able to receive them: verses 11–12 sum up both aspects of Yahweh's act of restoration.

Astonishingly, once more it thus seems that nothing has changed. People were free to return, but relatively few did so directly after 539 B.C. The subsequent return of further groups such as those who came with Ezra, as well as the continuing existence of Babylonian Jewry, not as deportees or exiles but as people who were content to have settled in a foreign land, support this view. The promises of the Preacher match those of Zechariah 2, which still look for the return of the people and the restoration of the city.

Additional Notes §43

61:1–3 / On the use of this passage at Qumran and in Luke, see J. A. Sanders, "From Isaiah 61 to Luke 4," in *Christianity, Judaism and Other Greco-Roman Cults* (M. Smith Festschrift, ed. J. Neusner; Leiden: Brill, 1975), Vol. 1, pp. 75–106.

61:1–9 / Some of these words in vv. 1–9 are among ones that reappear in Jesus' blessings in Matt. 5:2–10. Jesus' blessings were evidently stimulated by such passages, especially from Isaiah and the Psalms.

61:2 / The plural in Luke 21:22 (in Gk. and NRSV) may suggest an allusion to Hos. 9:7, though it also draws attention to the two days of vengeance here in 61:2 and 63:4.

61:3 / **A crown of beauty** is *pe'er;* **ashes** is *'eper.* The reversal of syllables in the words that are otherwise the same reflects the very reversal of which the line speaks. **For the display of his splendor** is then an infinitive from the verb *pa'ar:* their splendor shows forth Yahweh's splendor. In v. 10, **adorns his head** is the same verb yet again.

62:5 / **Your sons** is *banayik* (literally, "your children"), but this makes poor sense. "Your builder" (NIV mg.; cf. NRSV) would be *bonayik:* this makes better sense in this context and fits the parallelism. The word *banayik* has occurred in 49:17, 22, 25; 51:20; 54:13 and 60:4, 9 and would thus be an easy slip.

62:6 / **Call on** comes from the verb "remember," which suggests that the task of the lookouts is to be "reminders" (NRSV thus translates "you who remind the LORD").

§44 A Vision of Yahweh Acting in Wrath, II (Isa. 63:1–6)

63:1–6 / The links with 59:15b–20 here are evident. Once again Yahweh looks and sees no one acting in relation to wrong-doing, so comes to act as a warrior clothed in battle garb and acting in wrath for the cause of vengeance, *tsedaqah*, redemption, and salvation. What is new here is the explicit connection with **Edom** and **Bozrah**. There may be several ways in which that is significant. It is the direction from which the warrior Yahweh comes to act on the people's behalf in Judges 5:4–5. It corresponds to chapter 34, which also spoke of a **day of vengeance** (v. 4). If that denoted the punishment of Edom, it is here more explicit that, if Edom is being punished it is as a representative for peoples in general (v. 6). The explicit bloodiness of the scene also compares with chapter 34. But it is the names and their suggestiveness that interest the prophet more than their literal reference. "Edom" resembles the word for "red" (see Gen. 25:25, 30), the color of blood and wine (v. 2). "Bozrah," while no doubt called that because the name links with words meaning "fortress" (e.g., 25:2, 12; 27:10; 34:13; 36:1), also links with words meaning "grape harvest" (cf. 24:13; 32:10; Lev. 26:5). So Edom and Bozrah's names suggest pools of grape juice that turn out to be pools of blood.

The conversation between lookout and warrior takes up the references to the prayer to which the Preacher and the lookouts committed themselves (62:1, 6). The return of the warrior signifies the answer to that prayer. The prophet describes the aftermath of the event rather than the event itself (cf. 52:7–10) and spares the readers from the portrayal of the actual bloody battle. This might indicate that even the prophet has mixed feelings about this understanding of God's acts. "It is almost as though the Day of Judgment is too cruel, too painful to contemplate, and the exhausted, bloodstained victor is thankful it is all over" (Sawyer, *Isaiah,* p. 196).

Yet Yahweh's explicit dissatisfaction is with having to act alone rather than with the necessity of bloodshed. Christians are sometimes unhappy with this bloody aspect to OT prophecy, but it reappears in the NT. The further reference to the day of vengeance (cf. 61:2) again invites comparison with Jesus' allusion in Luke 21:22. The imagery also contributes to the NT picture of the King of kings on a white horse, who treads the winepress of God's wrath and whose robe is dipped in blood (Rev. 19:11–18).

§45 Where Are Your Zeal and Your Might? (Isa. 63:7–64:12)

As the chiasm in chapters 56–66 treads its return path, the vision of the battling warrior (63:1–6) paired with the one in 59:15b–20. This prayer, then, pairs with the prayer in 59:9–15a. As the new vision was bloodier, the new prayer is much longer and more urgent. It has the features of a lament on the part of the community such as those that appear in the Psalms and in Lamentations, but like some of them (and like chapter 62) it unfolds as more of a stream of consciousness and closes with a question. It does suggest an alternating between confrontation (63:7–14, 17–19; 64:5–7) and plea (63:15–16; 64:1–4, 8–12), but elements of confession, questioning, prayer, appeal, and accusation interweave and repeat without forming a consistent pattern.

While the prayer's aim and many of its motifs thus parallel those of Psalms 44 and 89, it lacks their calculatedness and structure. In its pain and uncalculated form it recalls Psalm 88. Its references to the ruined state of country and temple suggest a time in the sixth century B.C. before the temple had been rebuilt, and might well thus imply a time prior to that of chapters 40–55.

63:7–9 / As is the case with 59:9–15a, it is not immediately obvious that this is actually a prayer, especially to the English reader. But **tell** is the verb that described the activity of the civil servants in 62:6 who were commissioned to remind Yahweh of outstanding commitments. The nature of intercession is to be involved in that reminding. The people were to share the prophet's involvement in such intercession. Paradoxically, however, the "telling" or "reminding" at first concerns things Yahweh has already done, so that the use of this verb also recalls 12:4 ("proclaim"). In praise we proclaim God's acts—to the world, to the people of God, to ourselves, and directly to God. We thus build up the faith of the first three audiences, but proclaiming these acts to God also has an effect on the relationship between us and God—just as something happens to a human relationship when we tell someone else how we admire or appreciate what he or she has done.

We are also familiar with the way in which compliments are often merely the introduction to a "but," and we wait for that "but." This can be a feature of praise and prayer in the Bible. While most praise is simply praise, some expresses pain as it recalls how God has acted in the past because of the contrast with the way God is (not) acting now (see, e.g., Pss. 44; 89). So it will be here.

In the past, then, Israel knew all about Yahweh's **kindnesses.** This unusual plural that begins the prayer is the same one that opens Psalm 89 (NIV "great love"). They knew all about **the deeds for which he is to be praised.** Literally, these are "the praises of Yahweh," another unusual plural that also comes at the beginning of a long recital of Yahweh's acts in Israel's life in Psalm 78. They knew all about **good** and **compassion.** As soon as the prophet's account of these acts begins, however, an irony surfaces. Yahweh's relationship with Israel began with the conviction that they would be faithful (v. 8). That was what Israel claimed in Psalm 44:18 and what Yahweh promised in Psalm 89:33, but we know already that falsehood characterizes this people (57:4; 59:3, 13). Surely Yahweh also knew that this would be so? Perhaps at some level of God's being God did know, but the Bible story portrays God living in real relationship with people and discovering things about them as these things emerge, in the same way as happens in any relationship. God thus experiences the surprise and the sadness of things not turning out in the way one hoped. God also therefore must confront the need to adapt to that and make decisions in the light of it. God then perhaps also experiences the surprise and the joy of things not turning out in the way one feared, and the need to adapt to that and make decisions in the light of it (see Jer. 18:18, and the story of God's relationship with Nineveh in Jonah).

On the other hand, the prophet does not quite say that it was *as a result of* this false expectation that Yahweh **became their Savior,** as NIV implies (**so** represents the word usually translated "and": cf. NRSV). The phrase **in all their distress he too was distressed** is very suggestive theologically, though it may not be the original text (see Additional Notes). But the prophet certainly emphasizes the reality of Yahweh's involvement with the people in their affliction in Egypt. Further, the loss of that fine phrase means the gain of the alternative reading's stress on the fact that it was Yahweh personally who was so involved ("no messenger or angel but his presence"). To "kindnesses" or acts of commitment and compassion are added **love** and **mercy** or pity, the attitude that people had missed at the fall of Jerusalem (e.g., Lam. 2:2, 17, 21). If it were not clear that Yahweh has long behaved like a father or mother in relation to the people, it certainly becomes clear in the subsequent description of the way Yahweh **lifted them up and carried them** in the past. In doing that, God was like a parent (v. 9), though also like an eagle (Exod. 19:4; Deut. 32:10–13).

63:10–11a / Here arises a "but," in a sense a double one, or even a triple one. On the people's part there was the falsehood that Yahweh was not expecting. **They rebelled.** This is the first "but." To judge from what follows, the prophet refers not to a particular moment such as those instances of rebellion in Exodus and Numbers but rather to the ongoing story of Israel's life with Yahweh. It was a story of rebellion, as Psalm 78 portrays it.

Thus far the prophet's comment is a commonplace one. Typically the parallel verb takes the statement to a new point. In rebelling they **grieved** Yahweh. Through the Poet, Yahweh had promised to call Ms Zion back into their marriage relationship when she was an abandoned wife, "grieved in spirit" (54:6; NIV "distressed in spirit"). Now the Preacher adds that it was not so difficult for Yahweh to empathize with Ms Zion in that experience because Yahweh knew what it was like to be grieved in "his holy spirit." Like Ms Zion, Yahweh has a spirit to be grieved (see Additional Notes). Grieving had been part of Yahweh's early relationship with the world as a whole. Genesis 6:6 is the first reference to God's grief. This tells of how things turned out in a way that disappointed Yahweh's hopes and expectations. Yahweh had hoped that a special relationship with Israel would be different, but things turned out the same.

When a husband or wife treats a spouse unfaithfully, the reaction of the spouse may well combine an inner hurt with a wrath that lashes out aggressively at the unfaithful one. So it was with Yahweh (v. 10). This wrath may be an explanation for the fall of Jerusalem and the deportation of its population. Herein lies the second "but" (v. 10b). At the same time, a cuckolded husband or wife will remember how things once used to be, and so does Yahweh. It is the third "but." Yahweh **recalled the days of old** (v. 11a; see Additional Notes). Elsewhere the OT emphasizes that Yahweh has more control of memory than we have, so verse 11a may suggest not only a wistful, unavoidable remembering but a deliberate one that is a sign of hope. The prophet's commemoration of Yahweh's acts (v. 7; NIV "tell") includes the fact of Yahweh's remembering (v. 11a: another form of the same verb).

63:11b–14 / If Yahweh's is a deliberate remembering, so is the prophet's. The fact that it goes on for some lines of verse marks it as deliberate, or at least self-permitted. The prophet indulges in unrestrained mulling over the question of why the recent past has been so unlike the distant past, or rather, **where** now is the one who once saved and redeemed and carried. If verses 8–9 recall especially the distress of Israel's time in Egypt, verses 11–13a focus rather on Israel's danger at the Red Sea. Then, like the act of praise after the deliverance at the Red Sea (Exod. 15), the prophet goes directly to their entrance into Yahweh's **rest** in the land, by the active presence of Yahweh's spirit (vv. 13b–14). There is some irony about the picture of God's presence at the Red Sea itself. It was "his holy spirit" that Yahweh set among them. It was Yahweh's own dynamic, supernatural inner being (v. 11b)—corresponding to the dynamic outer being expressed in the activity of Yahweh's arm (v. 12a). The irony lies in the fact that it was this inner being that they subsequently grieved, so that the prophet knows there is nothing odd about its having withdrawn, hurt and offended.

63:15–16 / Only now is Yahweh actually addressed. The plea to **look down from heaven and see** recalls another regular motif of Israel's prayers (e.g., 37:17; Ps. 80:14). The assumption is that of the child—if we can only get our father or mother's attention, then action will follow. It makes for a neat contrast with 40:26; 49:18 and 60:4. Yahweh has kept urging the community to look up and see, and the prophet at last points out that, from the people's perspective, the opposite of this is needed. The plea to look down also makes for a subtle connection with Psalm 33:13 and 102:19 and implicitly asks Yahweh to behave in the same way again. The act of remembering continues to be an important concept here.

It continues in the appeal to Yahweh's **zeal,** challenging Yahweh to do what 9:7 and 37:32 promised and what 42:13 and 59:17 claimed—to be the mighty warrior that Yahweh is supposed to be (9:6; 10:21; 42:13). The parallelism of the lines at the end of verse 15 tells us that fierce warlikeness and **tenderness and compassion** belong together, as two sides of a coin. Both the latter characteristics are words that use images taken from the human body (more literally, "the rumbling of your insides and your womb"). Again the prophet is asking that Yahweh act on the feelings claimed in 42:13–14. A mother who is stirred inside by a tenderness and compassion for her children will be capable of terrible ferocity against people who mistreat them, if that is what is needed.

To put it another way, Yahweh has claimed to be their **Father** (e.g., 1:2; 9:6 again; 43:6) and their *go'el* (e.g., 41:14; 43:14; 60:16). The prophet asks that Yahweh now behave like one. **Abraham** was the people's father (41:8; 51:2), as was Jacob-**Israel** (45:25; 58:14). They bore this family name (44:5; 48:1). But far from the Israelites' being acknowledged among the nations (61:9), even the progenitors do not acknowledge this people. Abraham and Israel do not treat this people as their descendants and therefore pass on to them the privileges of being their children. Their earthly fathers have cut them off. That makes it the more pressing that Yahweh indeed treat them as father. It is perhaps this consideration that makes the prophet abandon for a moment the usual OT restraint over calling Yahweh "Father."

63:17–19 / The prophet can perhaps imagine the response this appeal deserves. How can people who have acknowledged their failure as children and acknowledged the way they deliberately frustrated their father's hopes and expectations (vv. 8–10) summon up the affrontery now to tell Yahweh how to behave as father? And yet admittedly, that is what children are always in a position to do. As we have noted, and as Hosea 11 puts it, parenthood is something that parents can never get away from. You cannot divorce your children and end parenthood as you can divorce your spouse and end a marriage. A mother cannot stop being a mother. Verse 15 has presupposed that the rumblings of her insides and her womb do not depend on whether her offspring deserve them (see commentary). Indeed, the prophet plays double or nothing with the question about affrontery. Parents—and children too—are sometimes inclined to assume that it is the fault of the parents if their children go wrong. So the prophet asks, **Why, O Lord, do you make us wander from your ways and harden our hearts so that we do not revere you?** (v. 17a).

"Wander" *(ta'ah)* was originally a verb to describe wandering about in the desert, when you do not know where to go (Gen. 21:14; 37:15) or have lost the path (Ps. 107:4). It is something that sheep are especially inclined to do (Ps. 119:176). "Wander" is then a verb that can describe someone's moral life after leaving the right path—something some children do as soon as they are born (Ps. 58:3). People can sometimes make themselves wander (Jer. 42:20; cf. Hos. 4:12), but the fault usually lies with bad leaders (Isa. 3:12; 9:16), people like Manasseh (2 Kgs. 21:9) or Israel's Baal prophets (Jer. 23:13) or Judah's own prophets (Mic. 3:5; Jer. 23:14). These people behave like incompetent or negligent shepherds who fail to look after their sheep (Jer. 50:6). In 53:6 the people accepted responsibility for this wandering. Now the prophet pushes the responsibility back on Yahweh and in a way puts Yahweh in the same category as Manasseh and the false prophets. As if the point were not clear enough, the second question "Why do you harden our hearts?" implies that Yahweh has treated Israel and Pharaoh in the same way and that Yahweh lies behind the recalcitrance that Israel begins to show even at Sinai. And all that is not just a matter of the distant past, but of the present as well.

They are, of course, outrageous questions, but one of the points about prayer in Israel was to ask outrageous questions and make outrageous statements. Moses' prayers at the time of that recalcitrance at Sinai (Exod. 32–33) illustrate this, though they are not the first instance (see, e.g., Gen. 18:22–33). Job's prayers (Job 3–31) are the extreme example of theological adventurousness in speaking with God. Admittedly his example and Jeremiah's (see 14:1–15:21) show how risky prayer is, for Yahweh may answer. But that fact means that prayer does not have to be theologically correct. It is a conversation.

There are two positive implications in the prophet's extraordinary charge. The first is that more hope lies in Yahweh's responsibility than in human responsibility. If we wander from Yahweh's ways simply because we are inclined to wander, then trying to stay in Yahweh's ways involves trying to pull ourselves up by our own bootstraps. However, if our being the way we are is in some sense the result of Yahweh's action, or even of Yahweh's inaction (the verb might be rendered "let us wander"), then prayer can appeal to a potentiality outside us. The second positive implication is related to the first. It is the nature of a lament to assume that Yahweh is sovereign and to attempt to get Yahweh to act in light of this. There is no point in prayer if we believe that everything depends on us. The challenge of prayer is to get Yahweh to act with the drive and authority that we know

Yahweh has, and outrageous statements in laments constitute attempts to do so.

In a sense, the affrontery continues with the bidding **return for the sake of your servants** (v. 17b). It was a prophet's job to use the verb "return" in the imperative. The Poet did it in 44:22. But that is a bidding *to* the people by the prophet speaking on Yahweh's part. It is in a lament that the bidding is addressed *by* people *to* Yahweh (e.g., Ps. 6:4; 80:14). Indeed, getting Yahweh to "turn" is a basic concern of a lament, related to the notion of gaining Yahweh's attention (see v. 15). The two possible uses of this imperative illustrate the uncomfortable place where a prophet lived—between God and people, called to confront both.

The outrageousness continues in verses 18–19. Only **for a little while** did the people possess Yahweh's **holy place** (well, four hundred years). All that the prophet's generation has experienced is Yahweh's declining to be sovereign in their life and declining to treat them as a personal possession (contrast Deut. 28:10). The charge is similar to that in 40:27. And this has been so **from of old.** We do not know how long a time separates Jerusalem's fall in 587 B.C. from this prayer. It might be a matter of decades. It might be more than a century. But it clearly feels longer than the period during which the temple stood in its glory, because it occupies the whole of the community's own experience.

64:1–4 / Again there is an irony about the prophet's **Oh, that . . . ,** for the word again echoes Yahweh's, in 48:18 ("If only"). As was the case there, here past tense verbs follow, literally "If only you had rent . . ." Any hopefulness regarding Yahweh's doing that again is only implicit. Literally, verse 1 continues the plaint that Yahweh has not been intervening in world affairs in the way Psalm 18 and Habakkuk 3 describe, and in the way Psalm 144 urges. In fact, the picture of Yahweh tearing the sky-curtain apart in verses 1–4 is even more forceful than ones that appear in these other places. There is thus a poignancy about verse 4: only Yahweh has ever done that, but Yahweh has not done it for a long time.

64:5–7 / A second claim about responsibility (the first was 63:17–19) now follows. Again this challenge invites protestation, which will come in due course (65:1), but in the meantime the prophet seeks to forestall it. There is an obvious reason that Yahweh declines to be involved in the people's life. Yahweh "comes to help" or "meets" (NRSV) people in the context of a two-way commitment. They will be people who do more than remember the past and hope to get Yahweh to remember them. These people will also **remember your ways.** The phrase again makes clear that remembering is like knowledge—a matter of deliberateness and action, and an activity that we can control. The community has not been controlling and implementing its memory (v. 5a).

There was a time when this was not so, a time of doing **righteous acts** (v. 6), but that has passed, and the righteous acts of the past are not worth anything when we turn to another way (see Ezek. 33:12–13). The unrighteous acts of the present pollute any past righteous acts and the people who did them, so that they are as unacceptable as someone who is stained through contact with a corpse or a cloth stained with blood (perhaps menstrual blood). Alternatively, verse 6 may refer to "righteous acts" in the context of unorthodox worship that are stained by their context (cf. 59:12; 64:4–5). Verse 6a has been used as a "proof text" for universal sinfulness. Either way, like 59:7–8 it is actually a contextual comment on the sinfulness of the people of God, by which we as the people of God today need to measure ourselves.

To put it another way, sin shrivels us and then carries us off like the wind (v. 6b). **No one calls on your name or strives to lay hold of you** (v. 7a). But what lies behind all that? The fact that **you have hidden your face from us.** It is impossible to talk to someone or to try to embrace someone who has turned the other way. It is Yahweh who has caused the shriveling (v. 7b). The charge is the same as the one in 63:17: we are what we are because of what you have made us. Your turning away came first. If you turned back to us, things would be different.

64:8–12 / A number of the themes of the prayer occur again in this final plea. Once more there is an appeal to a **Father,** this time accompanied by the recognition that Yahweh is also the **potter** (v. 8). Like the father image, we have seen this potter image earlier in the book, and the prayer reworks both of them. In acknowledging that God is God and that in the end human beings have to trust themselves to God's insight and purposefulness (29:16; 45:9), the prayer appeals to the helplessness of the clay (see also Jer. 18). As the potter, Yahweh is the one who formed Israel (43:1; 44:2; the same word), and as **the work of your hand** they are a people to whom Yahweh has made promises (60:21). And this is true of all of us (NIV **we all**), as sinfulness is true of all of us (v. 6; and cf. 53:6 "we all"/"us all").

Once more there is an appeal to memory, but this time it is **do not remember our sins forever** (v. 9). Memory is both a security and an insecurity, both a determinative aspect of being a person and one that most imperils relationships. The prayer again urges that Yahweh be sovereign in remembering. It is the other side of not being **angry** (cf. v. 5) **beyond measure.**

Once again there is an appeal to **look upon us** (as 63:15), to stop being someone who is resolutely turned the other way (cf. v. 7b). Once again there is an appeal to the fact of being **your people** (cf. "my people," 63:8; "his people," 63:11; "your people," 63:14, 18), "all of us" again. Once again there the prayer grieves over the destruction and desolation of land and city (v. 10; cf. 63:18–19). Once again there is reference to holiness and splendor. Here the state of **our holy and glorious temple** (v. 11) contrasts with Yahweh's "holy and glorious throne" (and temple) in heaven (63:15). Once again the prayer asks, Will you still **hold yourself back?** (cf. 63:15; NIV "are withheld"). Will Yahweh still **keep silent?** (cf. 57:11).

Additional Notes §45

63:8b–9a / The Masoretic Text combines two understandings of these verses, in the "written" text and the "read" text. The former is what the consonants of the text actually say. NRSV follows it and renders "he became their savior in their distress. It was no messenger or angel but his presence that saved them." That involves changing one of MT's vowels. The read text is the version that people were expected to read out in the synagogue. NIV follows that and renders "and so he became their Savior. In all their distress he too was distressed, and the angel of his presence saved them." That involves changing one of MT's consonants. "It was no messenger" is *lo' sar.* "He too was distressed" is *lo sir.* The "written" text works better as poetry as it generates a sequence of regular lines through vv. 8–9. Further, "the angel of his presence" in the "read" text is an odd expression.

63:10 / The phrase "holy spirit" comes in the OT only here and in Ps. 51:10–12. There "holy spirit" is in a parallel position with "steadfast spirit" and "willing spirit." Each phrase suggests the impact of God's spirit (which is steadfast, holy, and generous, among other things) on the human spirit. Here the link with 54:6 again suggests a comparison with the human spirit. Yahweh's holy (i.e., supernatural, divine) spirit is grieved just as Ms Zion's human spirit was grieved. While the Holy Spirit's activity includes this holy spirit, the Holy Spirit's activity also includes many other aspects of God's activity, such as the acts of God's hands. The capitalization causes us to narrow our view of the Holy Spirit's activity in OT times—as if the Holy Spirit was present only where a phrase such as "holy spirit" occurs.

63:11 / KJV/RSV "Then he remembered the days of old . . . " correctly represents MT. NIV's translation perhaps reflects the conviction that Yahweh cannot be speaking from v. 11b onward, but its addition of the first **his people** is gratuitous and its marginal rendering is difficult to justify. It is simpler to see v. 11a as the continuation of v. 10 and to see v. 11b as beginning the prophet's questioning that will become an explicit address to God in v. 14b.

63:16 / The word translated **but** and **though** most commonly means "for," and this latter meaning makes good sense each time here (so JB).

63:17 / The verb "harden" (*qashakh*) occurs only here and, in a different sense, in Job 39:16. It resembles one of the verbs used to mean harden in Exodus (*khazaq*) and another verb used in Exodus for stiffening one's neck (*qashah*). It therefore recalls both Yahweh's hardening of the Pharaoh's heart (the stiffening of his resolve) and Israel's resistance to Yahweh, and invites the inference that Yahweh was behind the second in the same way as the first.

63:19 / There are no word for **yours** or **but** or **like** in the Hb. (see mg.). A more literal translation is thus "We have been from of old people whom you have not ruled, people who have not been called by your name."

64:1 / In MT this is the second half of the previous verse, 63:19b (heightening the impression that it refers to the past); in printed Hebrew Bibles 64:2 is thus 64:1 and so on through chapter 64.

64:5b / RSV translates more literally "Thou wast angry, and we sinned; in our sins we have been a long time, and shall we be saved?" The Hb. of the second half is obscure but the first half is clear enough and fits with the context in attributing the people's sin to Yahweh's attitude to them.

§46 Yahweh's Closing Critique and Vision (Isa. 65:1–66:17)

In these last two chapters of the book, once more we cannot discern an order or structure. The succession of phrases that look like introductions to prophecies (65:8, 13, 25; 66:1, 5, 12, 22) and the movement between verse and prose suggest that here it is not because a prophet let a stream of consciousness have its way. It is, rather, because a number of separate prophecies have been accumulated at the end of the book. These different prophecies have overlapping themes, and this has presumably contributed to the arrangement. The prophecies also have a number of points of contact with 56:1–59:8, and this may have contributed to their placement here in the chiasm that comprises chapters 56–66 as a whole. Further, the way they rework images such as heavens and earth and the servants of Yahweh may have contributed to their location at the close of the book. The chapters form a conclusion to the book as a whole. The themes and actual language of chapter 1, the book's introduction, are repeated in this conclusion. Thus, we find references to the people forsaking Yahweh, to their rebelliousness, to their acts that displease Yahweh, to their religious observances in gardens, to their destiny to be shamed, and to the unquenchable fire.

65:1–7 / It is hardly a coincidence that Yahweh's words take a form appropriate for a retort to a bold prayer. The fact that Yahweh declares the solemn intent **I will not keep silent** (v. 6) confirms this. As happens in the story of Job, Yahweh is at last goaded into a response, but the response might make the person regret ever having prayed. How dare anyone claim to have been seeking a Yahweh who had hidden (and making that an excuse for sin)? Yahweh has been standing there before the people (as once before Abraham in Gen. 18:22 mg.) waiting for a prayer to be prayed (vv. 1–2). The context again makes clear that when the OT talks about seeking Yahweh, it refers not to seeking a religious experience but to asking God to do something—here, asking for the restoration of city and community. Given the comment above concerning the possible date of 63:7–64:12, historically it may be that quite an interval has passed since the prayer, enough time for the promises in chapters 40–55 to have been delivered. Yahweh's response then implies, "OK, I have done what you asked, and met with no response" (so Westermann, *Isaiah 40–66*, p. 400). Yahweh's own claim recalls 55:6 and, behind that, 30:1; 31:1; 45:11, 19; 51:1. How dare anyone claim that Yahweh has not been keeping promises? Yahweh can quote promises and ask why they have not been claiming them.

It is not that people are not praying. They are praying, and that makes it worse. At the same time, verses 3–7 either cause us to assume that the people critiqued here are not the people praying in 63:7–64:12, or send us back to re-read the prayer in 63:7–64:12. Like the audience in 1:29; 8:19–20 and 57:3–13 (cf. v. 7a), this people is involved in the traditional religion that has always co-existed in Israel with orthodox Yahwistic faith (**both your sins and the sins of your** ancestors)—as it usually does in Christian cultures. That they **sit among the graves** (v. 4a) presumably involves attempts to consult the dead. They were concerned to observe rules about cleanliness and pollution (v. 5a), but do not keep the requirements of the Torah (v. 4b). The people may think that in the context of faith in Yahweh they can offer a mixed worship just as legitimately as a worship approved by prophets such as Isaiah, but the Preacher does not view it that way.

65:8–16 / The division presupposed here suggests another reading of 63:7–64:12 as Yahweh makes a threat and offers a choice. The community comprises two types of people—those who are **my servants** and those who indeed **did not answer** when **I called,** because they were too busy worshiping the gods **Fortune** and **Destiny.** For the first time, the terms **my servants** and **my chosen** describe a group within the community, in effect a "faithful remnant." It is a fateful moment as the prophet gives up on the notion of the whole community as chosen servant. For all Yahweh's efforts to make this ideal work, in the end it has to be abandoned. Jacob's "seed" will indeed **possess my mountains** and **inherit them,** and they will enjoy the benefit of the land on either side from the Mediterranean **(Sharon)** to the Jordan **(the Valley of Achor,** near Jericho). But these promises now apply only to this faithful group, not to Israel as a whole.

Of course it had always been the case that many Israelites belonged to the chosen people in name only and had sacrificed their place within this company, but the conceptualization here is new and sad. To put it another way, when earlier prophets had declared that calamity would fall on the people, there was little talk of exemption from calamity for people who were faithful to Yahweh (such as the prophets and those who identified with them). The text implied that such people shared in that calamity. Jeremiah was taken off to Egypt, Ezekiel to Babylon. The expectation here that Yahweh will bring about a discriminating judgment affirms that Yahweh will be faithful to those who are themselves faithful. Jesus takes up both the notion that judgment falls on the city as a whole (e.g., Luke 19:41–44) and the notion of a discriminating judgment (e.g., Matt. 25:31–46), but he implies that the former is a this-worldly reality, the latter a feature of the End.

The opening **therefore** in verse 13 indicates that the phrase that follows does not begin a different prophecy. It is, rather, the classic transition from indictment to declaration of the sentence that underlines the nature of Yahweh's threat. It is a chilling description of the fate of people who turn their backs on Yahweh. But Yahweh's threats are always designed to be self-frustrating, and no doubt Yahweh wishes their result to be that everyone join the company of "my chosen servants" to fulfill the old vision.

The promise of **another name** (v. 15; cf. 62:2) is accompanied (or explained) by the provision of a new name for Yahweh, God of Amen or God of Truly (v. 16). The significance is clear enough even if the form is puzzling. Those who choose to be the faithful remnant will prove that faithfulness of Yahweh which they might feel has been at issue through these chapters. The joy of restoration **(eat . . . drink . . . rejoice . . . sing)** will mean that the grimness of the past **will be forgotten.** The reference to forgetting the past recalls the exhortation in 43:18–19 (as does v. 17 as a whole) though, characteristically for the book called Isaiah, its meaning has been reworked.

65:17–25 / But what right has Yahweh to declare that past troubles will be hidden "from my eyes" (v. 16)? Only the right that comes from the wonder of that restoration. Once again the passage begins with a "for" that NIV omits (cf. NRSV; see on 1:29–30) but that indicates a connection with the preceding passage. Further, Yahweh literally says "I am creating" (also in v. 18; see NRSV).

The people may not be able to see anything, but Yahweh is already in the midst of this new sovereign act.

Out of context, Yahweh's description of a **new heavens and a new earth** (v. 17) would sound like an abandonment of this cosmos for the creation of a new one, but verses 18–25 make clear that the language refers to a radical transformation of this cosmos, specifically of the city in which the people live. "Creating a new . . . " suggests "re-creating."

What does the creation of a new heavens then denote? Earlier parts of this book have made it clear enough that problems in the heavens and on earth are two sides of a single coin. The heavens are the garrison of supernatural forces whose battling lies behind battles on earth (13:5), the heavens mirror the actions of Yahweh on earth (13:10), and the heavens are shaken as the earth is when Yahweh acts in wrath (13:13). The armies on high as well as the powers on earth must be put in their place (24:21). The destruction of evil in heaven (34:4–5) must accompany the destruction of evil and opposition on earth. The darkness of heaven both mirrors and brings gloom on earth (50:3). The heavens are as transient as the earth (51:6).

This talk moves between referring to the heavens as part of the physical cosmos and as part of the metaphysical cosmos. Again these are two sides of one coin (cf. 24:23). The idea of the heavens constitutes the Israelite vision of the crowded heavens of Middle Eastern stories about the gods, except that here there is no doubt that Yahweh has ultimate power over all other supernatural forces, whereas in those other stories power moves to and fro. We may find it difficult to work with the mythical language of such pictures, but it is equally difficult to find another way of picturing the reality to which it refers. That reality is the fact that the conflicts, violence, and power struggles of earth cannot be explained in purely earthly terms. There is also "war in heaven" (Rev. 12:7).

If there is to be radical renewal on earth, then, there needs to be radical renewal in heaven. Only then can the vision of verses 18–25 be fulfilled. Only then can Yahweh **rejoice** (v. 19). Yahweh's rejoicing (it is rare for this verb to have God as subject) goes along with Yahweh's forgetting (v. 17).

If a battle must be won in heaven before there can be fulfillment of Yahweh's vision on earth, this may provide a theological clue as to why the promises in chapters 40–66 never came about for some centuries. They could come about only in connection with the great victory in the heavenly battle (Rev. 12:9–10). On the other hand, that only relocates the problem, for they remain unfulfilled. In another sense the battle is not yet over (Rev. 12:12–17). The martyrs and the rest of the church thus continue to ask "How long?" along with those who prayed the prayer in 63:7–64:12.

When their prayer is granted, then they will see the fulfillment of God's original creation vision, of a full human community life with God in which joy replaces grief (v. 19), long life replaces earthly death (v. 20), fulfillment in work replaces frustration (vv. 21–23). There will be an end to the argument between them and God about who is calling and who is not answering (v. 24). This is a significant promise for a world like our own characterized by grief, premature death, frustration in work, and broken relationship between humanity and God.

Verse 25 identifies this vision with that in 11:6–9. It also adds the somber line based on Genesis 3:14, **but dust will be the serpent's food.** This surprising comment implies that, for all the vision of new creation, the factors that led to the original human act of uncreation have not been removed. It seems odd that there was present in God's good creation a creature who encouraged humanity to do other than God said. In parallel, it seems odd that this creature should also be present in the renewed Jerusalem. Perhaps the implication is that such life is no more designed to be challenge-free than life in Eden was. But here, more clearly than in Genesis 3:14–15, the description concludes with a promise that the serpent's action will not spoil things (v. 25b). When we set the passage in a broader biblical context, that reference to the serpent also draws our attention to the fact that long, full, ordinary earthly life is designed to be continued as, or succeeded by, or transformed into, eternal life.

66:1–6 / The first major section of chapters 56–66 included a comment on the kind of people to whom Israel's high and majestic God pays attention, who contrast with people who have recourse to the practices of traditional religion (57:3–13 and 14–21, see especially v. 15). The comment recurs here, in reworked form, in an equivalent position in the last major section. Like prophecies such as those of Haggai, Zechariah, and Malachi, these chapters generally have rather a high view of the temple and its significance (see, e.g., 60:13), but lest it should be overestimated it is here put in its place. The chapters thus achieve the same balance as Solomon's prayer in 1 Kings 8. That prayer enthuses over the

temple's significance, but does so in the context of an acknowledgment that Yahweh, who dwells in thick darkness, cannot be
contained by the building that Solomon has constructed. That acknowledgment undermines any inclination to take everything that
comes in between as the whole truth. **Heaven** is like the **throne** on
which Yahweh actually sits. **The earth** is like the **footstool** on
which the divine feet then rest. That fact makes a laughing-stock
of the notion that people will then build a **house** where this God
can relax.

One might be tempted to retire in confusion and disillusion.
How can we know this God? We can know this God by paying attention again to what we have been told. "Look down from
heaven and see," the prayer in 63:15 pleaded. Yahweh picks up
the plea. I do look down, says Yahweh, and I have told you who
are "the ones I look down to" (v. 2b; NIV **esteem**). They are the
humble (*'ani*), the people who do not count. They are people who
are lame or disabled in spirit (*nekeh;* the adjective is otherwise
used only of Mephibosheth in 2 Sam. 4:4; 9:3), beaten down or
smitten (this adjective comes from the verb *nakah,* used in 57:17;
58:4; 60:10—and 1:5; 53:4). **Contrite** gives the wrong impression.
The word denotes not an attitude of sorrow but an emotional
brokenness. They are people who **tremble at my word,** who have
seen some of the things God has done to the people and are afraid
that God may do it again. As in the link passage 57:14–21, the experience of being put down by God creates a division between
two types of people—those who recognize it, and those who do
not. People who enthuse about the temple (v. 1a) and offer all the
right sacrifices can be no different in God's eyes from people involved in all sorts of worship abominations. Verse 4b then takes
up 65:12b when it says **for when I called, no one answered** and
implies that the reason for this is that they are indeed involved in
traditional religion as well as temple worship, and this is probably
also the point about verse 3.

Verse 5 is the clearest indication within these chapters of a
conscious division in their community. There are people who
tremble at Yahweh's **word,** people who are still consumed by an
awareness of the calamity Yahweh has brought and/or the calamity Yahweh might bring and whom their own people **hate** and **exclude.** The latter apparently scorn the possibility of some act of
community renewal, and they are presumably the kind of people
who are involved in traditional religion. They are open-minded
about forms of religious observance and intolerant of the purism

of the people with whom the prophet identifies. We do not know enough about the actual life of the Second Temple community to know how to relate this division in the community to other divisions of which we know in the period, though here the stance of the prophecies fits more with the stance of Ezra and Nehemiah. Yahweh declares that the place of their "orthodox" worship (combined as it is with their abominations) will be the place of their punishment (v. 6).

66:7–17 / "When, when?" is a question behind much of chapters 56–66. "Now, now," Yahweh finally responds, or perhaps "instantly, instantly." When it comes, transformation will come in a moment, like a woman giving **birth** as soon as her waters break instead of going through four or ten or twenty-four hours of **labor** (vv. 7–8). Verses 9–13 then take the metaphor of a woman in labor further. The problem might be that Jerusalem knows all about being in labor but still struggles and tires for what seems an eternity (and in due course dies of exhaustion without giving birth). "Would I let that happen to Jerusalem?" Yahweh asks. The answer is a resounding No! (v. 9). She will give birth, and if the members of the audience, who are her children, rejoice in anticipation of that now, they will **drink** at her **breasts** (vv. 10–11: the **for** in v. 11 is more literally "so that").

Once again the promise goes on to link with 57:14–21, which spoke of those to whom *shalom* was promised and those who would never experience it. Here the prophet promises the *shalom* **like a river** of 48:18, fullness of life (v. 12). Whereas 30:28 compared the scorching breath of Yahweh to **a flooding stream** ("a rushing torrent"), now that comparison becomes a positive image for the way the fullness of the nations will come to glorify the city. The often promised **comfort** will at last be here (v. 13).

Verses 14–17 again assume that good news for Jerusalem has to be seen in the context of trouble for wrongdoers. Once again Yahweh's **servants** are a group within the community rather than the community as a whole.

Additional Notes §46

65:1–66:17 / See, e.g., M. A. Sweeney, *Writing and Reading the Scroll of Isaiah: Studies of an Interpretive Tradition* (2 vols.; VTSup 70; eds. C. C. Broyles and C. A. Evans; Leiden: Brill, 1997), vol. 2, pp. 455–74.

65:1 / To bring out the links, we might render "I was ready to be sought [cf. 31:1; 55:6] by people who did not ask [cf. 30:2; 45:11]; I was ready to be found [cf. 55:6] by people who did not seek me [not the same verb as the first one; cf. 45:19; 51:1]." Paul applies the words to Gentiles in Rom. 10:20–21.

66:3 / The Hb. more literally says "one who sacrifices a bull one who kills a human being one who offers a lamb one who breaks a dog's neck . . . . " NIV infers a comparison between two sorts of people. JB infers that the community simply included both sorts of people. Most likely the point is that the same people were involved in both sets of activities, as in Ezek. 8 (Motyer, *The Prophecy of Isaiah*, p. 534). Either way, the verse reads more coherently if all the abominations are worship practices.

66:16–17 / Out of context, the reference to **judgment upon all** people would sound like a final judgment of the whole world, but the verses on either side refer to the more local affairs of Jerusalem. This makes it more likely that the reference is to a judgment of everyone in the city, a judgment that will vindicate Yahweh's servants and bring the death of people involved in traditional religion. The picture of the latter in v. 17 with the reference to eating rats seems exaggerated in order to emphasize the prophet's distaste for the traditional practices.

§47 A Final Vision for the Nations (Isa. 66:18–24)

The closing concerns of the book raise the eyes to a broader horizon and correspond in their openness with the initial concerns in 56:1–8. Once again the prophecy incorporates a final retrospective on a familiar theme, this time that of the drawing of the nations to recognize Yahweh. But, once again, this is no mere repetition but incorporates a revolutionary new idea in the last reel of the film. For the first time Yahweh declares that the surviving remnant of Israel is to go out to far off nations **that have not heard of my fame or seen my glory** (v. 19). Verse 20 then interweaves this vision with the expectation that these far off nations will bring the rest of the scattered people back to Jerusalem. Verse 21 then exceeds the significance of even this vision with the revolutionary notion that Yahweh will **select some of them also to be priests and Levites.** They will be admitted to the privileges of leading in worship and teaching to which most who were born Israelite could not aspire.

The book actually closes (v. 24) with an imaginary picture of the contrast between the worship of the temple mount and the nearby burning in the Valley of Hinnom (see on 30:33; 50:11). While this burning may go on continually, it is hardly equivalent to the medieval notion of people suffering the pain of burning in hell forever. Nevertheless, it may seem strange that the book should ultimately close with this picture. In synagogue worship verse 23 is repeated after verse 24, while in Christian worship the problem is "solved" by not reading the passage at all. Verse 24 closes the book called Isaiah as it began in 1:2, with a chilling challenge designed to make people turn from the way of rebellion. While the book comes to a close with this distasteful picture, the aim is that the lives of readers may not close there but be driven back to the restoration of verses 19–23. Whereas most prophetic books close with a promise of restoration, Isaiah thus parallels

Hosea 14:9, which sets before people the choice between the way of righteousness and the way of rebellion. It parallels Malachi 4:6b with its warning of a curse upon people who do not turn. And it parallels Jonah 4:11 as it leaves the audience a question to answer. Jesus's utilization of v. 24 in Mark 9:48 corresponds to these prophetic challenges.

For Further Reading

There is substantial bibliography in Broyles and Evans, *Writing and Reading the Scroll of Isaiah*, pp. 717–71. I completed this commentary in the first half of 1998 but have included reference here to one or two important works that have appeared since.

Ackroyd, P. R. *Studies in the Religious Tradition of the Old Testament.* London: SCM, 1987.

Barton, J. *Isaiah 1–39.* Old Testament Guides. Sheffield: Sheffield Academic Press, 1995.

Bellinger, W. H., and W. R. Farmer, eds. *Jesus and the Suffering Servant.* Harrisburg, Pa.: Trinity, 1998.

Blenkinsopp, J. *Isaiah 1–39.* Anchor Bible 19. Garden City, N.Y.: Doubleday, 2000.

Broyles, C. C., and C. A. Evans. *Writing and Reading the Scroll of Isaiah.* 2 vols. VTSup 70. Leiden: Brill, 1997.

Brueggemann, W. "At the mercy of Babylon." *JBL* 110 (1991), pp. 3–22. Repr. pages 111–33 in *A Social Reading of the Old Testament.* Minneapolis: Fortress, 1994.

———. *Isaiah.* 2 vols. Louisville: Westminster John Knox, 1997.

———. "Unity and Dynamic in the Isaiah Tradition." *JSOT* 29 (1984), pp. 89–107. Repr. pages 252–69 in *Old Testament Theology.* Minneapolis: Fortress, 1992.

———. *Using God's Resources Wisely: Isaiah and Urban Possibility.* Louisville: Westminster John Knox, 1993.

Calvin, J. *Commentary on the Book of the Prophet Isaiah.* 4 vols. Edinburgh: Clark, 1850–1854.

Carr, D. "Reaching for Unity in Isaiah." *JSOT* 57 (1993), pp. 61–80. Repr. pages 164–83 in *The Prophets.* Edited by P. R. Davies. Sheffield: Sheffield Academic Press, 1996.

———. "Reading Isaiah from Beginning (Isaiah 1) to End (Isaiah 65–66)." Pages 188–218 in *New Visions of Isaiah.* Edited by R. F. Melugin and M. A. Sweeney. JSOTSup 214. Sheffield: Sheffield Academic Press, 1996.

Childs, B. S. *Isaiah*. Old Testament Library. Louisville: Westminster John Knox, 2001.

Clements, R. E. *Isaiah 1–39*. New Century Bible Commentary. London: Marshall/Grand Rapids: Eerdmans, 1980.

―――. *Old Testament Prophecy*. Louisville: Westminster John Knox, 1996.

Clifford, R. J. *Fair Spoken and Persuading: An Interpretation of Second Isaiah*. Ramsey, N.J.: Paulist, 1984.

Conrad, E. W. *Reading Isaiah*. Minneapolis: Fortress, 1991.

Darr, K. P. *Isaiah's Vision and the Family of God*. Louisville: Westminster John Knox, 1994.

Ellul, J. *The Politics of God and the Politics of Man*. Grand Rapids: Eerdmans, 1972.

Emmerson, G. I. *Isaiah 56–66*. Old Testament Guides. Sheffield: Sheffield Academic Press, 1992.

Hanson, P. D. *The Dawn of Apocalyptic: The Historical and Sociological Roots of Jewish Apocalyptic Eschatology*. Philadelphia: Fortress, 1979.

Hayes, J. H., and S. A. Irvine. *Isaiah, the Eighth-Century Prophet*. Nashville: Abingdon, 1987.

Holladay, W. L. *Isaiah*. Grand Rapids: Eerdmans, 1978.

Irvine, S. A. *Isaiah, Ahaz, and the Syro-Ephraimitic Crisis*. Society of Biblical Literature Dissertation Series 123. Atlanta: Scholars Press, 1990.

Johnson, D. G. *From Chaos to Restoration: An Integrative Reading of Isaiah 24–27*. JSOTSup 61. Sheffield: Sheffield Academic Press, 1988.

Jones, D. R. "Isaiah—II and III." Pages 516–36 in *Peake's Commentary on the Bible*. Edited by M. Black and H. H. Rowley. London/New York: Nelson, 1962.

Kaiser, O. *Isaiah 1–12: A Commentary*. Old Testament Library. Translated by J. Bowden. 2d ed. London: SCM/Philadelphia: Westminster, 1983.

―――. *Isaiah 13–39: A Commentary*. Old Testament Library. Translated by R. A. Wilson. London: SCM/Philadelphia: Westminster, 1974.

Lowth, R. *Isaiah*. London: Dodsley, 1779.

Melugin, R. F. *The Formation of Isaiah 40–55*. Beiheft zur *Zeitschrift für die alttestamentliche Wissenschaft* 141. Berlin/New York: de Gruyter, 1976.

―――. and M. A. Sweeney, eds. *New Visions of Isaiah*. JSOTSup 214. Sheffield: Sheffield Academic Press, 1996.

Mettinger, T. D. *A Farewell to the Servant Songs.* Lund: Gleerup, 1983.

Miscall, P. D. *Isaiah.* Sheffield: Sheffield Academic Press, 1993.

Motyer, J. A. *Isaiah: An Introduction and Commentary.* Tyndale Old Testament Commentaries 18. Edited by D. J. Wiseman. Leicester/Downers Grove, Ill.: InterVarsity, 1999.

———. *The Prophecy of Isaiah: An Introduction and Commentary.* Downers Grove, Ill.: InterVarsity, 1993.

Mouw, R. *When the Kings Come Marching In: Isaiah and the New Jerusalem.* Grand Rapids: Eerdmans, 1983.

Muilenburg, J. "The Book of Isaiah Chapters 40–66: Introduction and Exegesis." Pages 381–773 in vol. 5 of *The Interpreter's Bible.* Edited by G. A. Buttrick and others. Nashville: Abingdon, 1956.

Oswalt, J. N. *The Book of Isaiah.* 2 vols. Grand Rapids: Eerdmans, 1986 and 1998.

Rendtorff, R. *Canon and Theology.* Minneapolis: Fortress, 1993.

Sawyer, J. *Isaiah.* 2 vols. The Daily Study Bible Series. Edinburgh: St. Andrew's/Philadelphia: Westminster, 1984.

Schramm, B. *The Opponents of Third Isaiah.* JSOTSup 193. Sheffield: Sheffield Academic Press, 1995.

Seitz, C. R. *Zion's Final Destiny: The Development of the Book of Isaiah: A Reassessment of Isaiah 36–39.* Minneapolis: Fortress, 1991.

———, ed. *Reading and Preaching the Book of Isaiah.* Philadelphia: Fortress, 1988.

Skinner, J. *The Book of the Prophet Isaiah.* 2 vols. Rev. ed. Cambridge: Cambridge University Press, 1915 and 1917.

Smith, P. A. *Rhetoric and Redaction in Trito-Isaiah: The Structure, Growth, and Authorship of Isaiah 56–66.* VTSup 62. Leiden: Brill, 1995.

Sommer, B. D. "The Scroll of Isaiah as Jewish Scripture, or, Why Jews Don't Read Books." Pages 225–42 in *Society of Biblical Literature 1996 Seminar Papers.* Atlanta: Scholars, 1996.

Stone, B. W. "Second Isaiah: Prophet to Patriarchy." *JSOT* 56 (1992), pp. 85–99. Repr. pages 219–32 in *The Prophets.* Edited by P. R. Davies. Sheffield: Sheffield Academic Press, 1996.

Sweeney, M. A. "The Book of Isaiah in Recent Research." *Currents in Research: Biblical Studies* 1 (1993), pp. 141–62.

———. *Isaiah 1–39.* Grand Rapids/Cambridge, U.K.: Eerdmans, 1996.

Tomasino, A. J. "Isaiah 1.1–2.4 and 63–66, and the Composition of the Isaianic Corpus." *JSOT* 57 (1993), pp. 81–98. Repr. pages

147–63 in *The Prophets.* Edited by P. R. Davies. Sheffield: Sheffield Academic Press, 1996.

Vermeylen, J., ed. *The Book of Isaiah.* Leuven: Leuven University Press, 1989.

Watts, J. D. *Isaiah.* 2 vols. Waco, Tex.: Word, 1985 and 1987.

Westermann, C. *Isaiah 40–66.* Old Testament Library. London: SCM/Philadelphia: Westminster, 1969.

Whedbee, J. W. *Isaiah and Wisdom.* Nashville: Abingdon, 1971.

Whybray, R. N. *Isaiah 40–66.* London: Oliphants, 1975. Repr. Grand Rapids: Eerdmans, 1981.

———. *The Second Isaiah.* Old Testament Guides. Sheffield: JSOT Press, 1983.

Wildberger, H. *Isaiah 1–12.* English Translation. Minneapolis: Fortress, 1991.

———. *Isaiah 13–27.* English Translation. Minneapolis: Fortress, 1997.

Williamson, H. G. M. *The Book Called Isaiah: Deutero-Isaiah's Role in Composition and Redaction.* Oxford: Clarendon Press; Oxford/New York: Oxford University Press, 1994.

———. *Variations on a Theme: King, Messiah, and Servant in the Book of Isaiah.* Carlisle: Paternoster/Grand Rapids: Eerdmans, 1998.

Subject Index

Scripture Index

23, 192, 241; **33:8–10**, 233; **33:10–12**, 189; **33:11**, 329; **33:12**, 214; **33:13–16**, 189–90; **33:14**, 344; **33:16**, 46, 130; **33:17**, 190; **33:17–19**, 190; **33:20**, 18, 212; **33:20–24**, 190–91; **33:23**, 187; **34**, 126, 196, 197, 199, 353; **34–35**, 6, 184, 193, 200, 201; **34–39**, 8, 13, 201, 315; **34–66**, 34; **34:1–3**, 193–94; **34:1–8**, 214; **34:1–35:10**, 193–200; **34:2**, 41, 210; **34:4**, 41; **34:4–5**, 194, 368; **34:5**, 200, 210; **34:5–8**, 194–95; **34:8**, 197; **34:9–17**, 195–96; **34:13**, 353; **35**, 14, 199, 224, 295; **35:1–2**, 196, 197; **35:3–4**, 196–97; **35:4**, 180, 208; **35:5**, 14, 320; **35:5–6**, 197; **35:6–7**, 197; **35:8–10**, 197–99; **35:9–10**, 200; **35:10**, 295; **36**, 225; **36–37**, 10, 122, 127, 130, 160, 165, 190, 202, 216, 220; **36–39**, 3, 29, 151, 176, 179, 193, 208, 218; **36:1**, 208, 353; **36:1–3**, 203–4; **36:1–37:7**, 201–8; **36:1–37:38**, 56; **36:1–39:8**, 34; **36:3**, 129; **36:4**, 2, 10, 208; **36:4–10**, 204–6; **36:6**, 209; **36:9**, 176; **36:10**, 19; **36:11**, 129; **36:11–17**, 206; **36:13**, 2; **36:14**, 10; **36:16**, 10; **36:18–20**, 19, 209; **36:18–22**, 206–7, 209; **36:18–37:7**, 209; **36:21**, 207, 211; **36:22**, 129; **37**, 232; **37–39**, 77; **37:1–4**, 207, 210; **37:2**, 3; **37:3**, 129; **37:5–7**, 208, 211; **37:6**, 10, 218; **37:7**, 209; **37:8–13**, 209–10; **37:8–35**, 209; **37:8–38**, 209–15; **37:10–13**, 79; **37:11**, 193; **37:14–20**, 210–11; **37:15–20**, 218; **37:16–20**, 11; **37:17**, 358; **37:20**, 23; **37:21**, 10; **37:21–29**, 211–12; **37:22**, 67; **37:23**, 8; **37:24**, 2, 176; **37:25**, 23; **37:30–32**, 212–14; **37:31**, 51; **37:31–32**, 50, 51; **37:32**, 358; **37:33**, 10; **37:35**, 178, 232, 238; **37:36**, 19, 80, 83, 221; **37:36–38**, 214, 216; **37:38**, 19, 215; **38**, 216, 217; **38–39**, 216, 217, 220; **38:1**, 3; **38:1–3**, 221; **38:1–8**, 220–21; **38:1–39:8**, 216–21; **38:3**, 110; **38:6**, 178, 216; **38:8**, 221; **38:9–20**, 11, 218–19; **38:10–14**, 221; **38:15–16**, 221; **38:18**, 110; **38:19**, 110, 221; **38:21–22**, 219–20; **39**, 96, 216, 217, 219, 220, 222; **39–52**, 101; **39:1**, 216; **39:1–8**, 45, 244; **39:2**, 4; **39:5–8**, 201; **39:7**, 262, 316; **39:8**, 110, 221; **40**, 30, 201, 216, 225, 230, 244, 259, 274; **40–42**, 239, 244; **40–48**, 20, 230, 255, 270, 280, 281, 282, 285, 312, 351; **40–49**,

285; **40–53**, 24; **40–55**, 5, 6, 8, 9, 12, 13, 15, 16, 90, 124, 198, 199, 222, 223, 229, 231, 238, 248, 249, 257, 261, 287, 289, 296, 313, 314, 315, 317, 319, 320, 321, 326, 334, 338, 345, 346, 347, 349, 351, 355, 366; **40–66**, 193, 368; **40:1**, 59, 89, 90, 296; **40:1–2**, 222, 223–24; **40:1–6**, 289; **40:1–11**, 6, 14, 222, 229, 313, 322, 325; **40:1–16**, 299; **40:1–31**, 222–29; **40:1–43:13**, 261; **40:2**, 325, 348; **40:3**, 23, 86, 228–29, 323; **40:3–4**, 222, 324; **40:3–5**, 224, 234, 348, 351; **40:4**, 265; **40:5**, 177, 222, 326; **40:6**, 4, 23, 114, 177, 229, 280, 296, 325; **40:6–7**, 287; **40:6–8**, 222, 224–25, 281, 282, 314; **40:7**, 50, 240; **40:9**, 229, 323, 325, 347; **40:9–11**, 222, 225, 270; **40:10**, 282, 348; **40:10–11**, 351; **40:12–17**, 225–27; **40:12–24**, 19; **40:12–31**, 11, 222, 276; **40:13**, 55, 240; **40:13–14**, 16; **40:14**, 240; **40:18**, 226; **40:18–20**, 227, 255; **40:19–20**, 226; **40:21–22**, 226; **40:21–24**, 227; **40:23–24**, 226; **40:25**, 226; **40:25–26**, 227–28; **40:26**, 41, 141, 226, 358; **40:27**, 12, 232, 240, 252, 282, 285, 292, 331, 361; **40:27–31**, 226, 228; **40:28**, 283; **40:28–31**, 252, 290; **40:31**, 293; **40:48**, 351; **41**, 30, 247, 259, 260, 267, 301; **41–42**, 302; **41–47**, 276, 279; **41–48**, 281; **41:1**, 236, 240; **41:1–4**, 193; **41:1–7**, 11, 230–32, 293, 294; **41:1–20**, 230–35, 243, 244; **41:1–42:14**, 14; **41:1–42:17**, 239, 257; **41:2**, 101, 234–35, 265, 269; **41:2–4**, 236; **41:3–16**, 237; **41:5**, 283; **41:5–7**, 240; **41:8**, 238, 239, 276, 359; **41:8–9**, 281; **41:8–10**, 239; **41:8–13**, 10, 246; **41:8–16**, 12, 230, 232–34, 239, 241, 246, 291, 292, 294; **41:8–20**, 284; **41:8–45:4**, 281; **41:9**, 238, 239; **41:10**, 239; **41:14**, 8, 11, 17, 198, 359; **41:14–16**, 246; **41:16**, 8, 240, 322; **41:17–20**, 11, 230, 234; **41:20**, 8, 262; **41:21–27**, 236–37; **41:21–29**, 11, 236, 239, 241; **41:21–42:17**, 24, 236–43, 244; **41:22**, 243; **41:25**, 101, 239, 243; **41:27**, 24, 243, 347; **41:29**, 240, 322; **42**, 301; **42:1**, 24, 237–39, 243, 287, 301, 337, 345; **42:1–4**, 232, 239–40, 247, 281, 293; **42:1–9**, 6, 10; **42:1–9**, 18, 236, 237, 239, 346; **42:3**, 110; **42:4**, 293; **42:5–9**, 241–42; **42:6**, 138, 243, 283, 284; **42:6–7**, 271; **42:7**, 14, 197; **42:10**,